C000217349

20

2022

2 6

2023

Voices In Flight: RAF Escapers and Evaders in WWII

Voices In Flight: RAF Escapers and Evaders in WWII

Martin W. Bowman

Pen & Sword
AVIATION

4

First Published in Great Britain in 2014 by
Pen & Sword Aviation
an imprint of
Pen & Sword Books Ltd
47 Church Street, Barnsley, South Yorkshire S70 2AS

Copyright © Martin W Bowman, 2014
ISBN 9781783831753

Typeset in 10/12pt Palatino
by GMS Enterprises

Printed and bound in England by
CPI Group (UK) Ltd, Croydon, CR0 4YY

Pen & Sword Books Ltd incorporates the Imprints of Pen & Sword
Aviation, Pen & Sword Family History, Pen & Sword Maritime, Pen & Sword
Military, Pen & Sword Discovery, Wharncliffe Local History, Wharncliffe
True Crime, Wharncliffe Transport, Pen & Sword Select, Pen & Sword
Military Classics, Leo Cooper, The Praetorian Press, Remember When,
Seaforth Publishing and Frontline Publishing.

For a complete list of Pen & Sword titles please contact
PEN & SWORD BOOKS LIMITED

47 Church Street, Barnsley, South Yorkshire, S70 2AS, England
E-mail: enquiries@pen-and-sword.co.uk
Website: www.pen-and-sword.co.uk

Contents

Acknowledgements

I am indebted to all the contributors for their words and photographs, especially Len Manning. Thanks also go to my fellow author, friend and colleague, Graham Simons, for getting the book to press ready standard and for his detailed work on the photographs; to Pen & Sword in particular, Charles Hewitt and Laura Hirst; and to Jon Wilkinson, for his unique jacket design once again.

Prologue

Truth Is Stranger Than Fiction

David Masters/BBC

'I hope you will forgive me this evening if I bring in a personal note. For I'm going to introduce to you an old friend of mine. Actually we were learning to fly together in 1913 before the last war. We trained together at the civil schools at Hendon on some of the curious and primitive machines of those early days - the comic box kites and the funny little monoplanes which if they got off the ground at all staggered along painfully at about 50 mph - rather different from the Wellingtons and the Hurricanes of today. But all the same, as you will hear later, it seems to have been quite a useful sort of training. Well, this friend of mine served all through the last war as a pilot in the RFC and the RAF and in 1918 ended up as a Wing Commander with the DSO, the MC and the DFC for his distinguished services. Although he left the RAF after the war he kept up flying and from then onwards took an active and prominent part in civil aviation. Then, at the beginning of the present war, although now fifty years of age, he felt that he was still capable of doing a useful job of work in the air as an active pilot, so he joined up again in the RAF - but this time as a pilot officer, the equivalent of a second lieutenant. How far he was justified in doing this you will be able to judge for yourselves from an account he is going to give you of an exciting incident in France in which he took part the other day and for which he was awarded a bar to the DFC he had won twenty-two years ago.'

BBC Broadcast, July 1940

In April 1940 after he had given convincing proof that he could fly, Louis Arbon Strange DSO MC DFC was granted his commission as a Pilot Officer. He must have given some of the officials a headache, for he was rather a problem. The rules and regulations laid down that he could not fly and rules and regulations must be obeyed. Then some genius discovered that the regulations applied only to government aircraft and not to those hired or requisitioned from commercial firms for government use and Pilot Officer Strange was therefore able to fly on operations instead of sitting in an office chair. As the young pilot who first tested him suggested, it really was rather funny; but it has its serious side to those who realize that only by utilizing all the ability of outstanding men in the proper manner will this nation and civilization survive.

No man in the whole service was happier than Colonel Strange when he donned the uniform of the Royal Air Force again as Pilot Officer Strange. The nightmare of the past six months, of trying to get money out of the Treasury to pay wages, of coping with difficulties day after day, was over. He was back in the service he loved, helping the country. His responsibilities had fallen away from him. The wing commander of the last war was glad to be the pilot officer of this. Within weeks of his rejoining the Royal Air Force the Germans vanquished Holland and Belgium and began to roll back the French. Under the German pressure the bases of the British squadrons operating in France were continually being shifted. Pilots flew until they were nearly overcome with fatigue; aircraft - men toiled all the time to make adjustments and service the aircraft in order to keep the fighting pilots in the air. It was impossible to take either pilots or aircraft men off their operational duties to flyaway or repair the aircraft collected in the aerodromes further back. The British army, moving rapidly and fighting night and day, called for rations; the tanks and anti-tank guns kept up an insatiable demand for ammunition. Such were the conditions pertaining in the latter half of May which led to one more remarkable exploit on the part of Colonel Strange. As supplies were being demanded and several damaged aircraft were grounded at Merville aerodrome, it was decided on 23 May to send Colonel Strange over to Merville with a fleet of civil aircraft to deliver supplies and a party of mechanics to effect temporary repairs to any aircraft in order to get them home.

It was a fine morning when they took off from an aerodrome somewhere in England and headed for the Channel across which Colonel Strange had flown so often in the old days of war and peace. His pilot, Bill Ledlie, who was famous in civil aviation, knew his way about the air lanes of the continent as surely as a London bus driver knows his way from Oxford Circus to Marble Arch. The tragic panorama of war unfolded as Colonel Strange looked down on the roads of France. Refugees on foot and in cars were streaming along, the cars looking ridiculously like sheep owing to the fact that they mostly had mattresses rolled up and fastened to the top of them. Flying over the woods in the direction of Ste-Omer he noticed a lot of popping noises and concluded that they were passing over machine-gun and rifle ranges where the French soldiers were practising. The glow of tracer bullets soon made him realize that they were being attacked from the ground. A short distance ahead were a dozen German tanks drawn up under some trees on the outskirts of a village, with the black swastika painted in a white circle on their brown and green camouflaged tops. The pilot dived down at them just over the tree tops, while the German crews began frantically to cover the tanks with camouflage nets. Transport vehicles were parked all around and at the sight of the British aeroplane the German soldiers bolted for the cover of the ditches and opened fire on the aircraft.

'We flew lower still and hurried on,' he said afterwards. 'When we arrived at Merville the great fleet of civil air transport quickly unloaded their food and ammunition and left for England to obtain more. There were some losses, but it was worthwhile. The rest of us quickly got busy servicing the Hurricanes we had come to rescue. The first was soon away, a good many bullet holes in it, the variable pitch airs crew control tied into fine pitch with a bit of copper wire and a piece of telephone cable back to the cockpit to enable the pilot to change pitch by breaking the copper wire with a good tug and other simple devices to make good broken controls and shot-away instruments.'

The pilot who flew this Hurricane away was reported to his base as having been shot down near Merville and his commanding officer was rather surprised when he landed at his home station in another Hurricane. Meanwhile Colonel Strange was busy trying to get another Hurricane patched up sufficiently to enable it to fly. Bombs dropped from time to time, sniping took place along the road. Bursts of gunfire broke out and died away, but Colonel Strange and his mechanics toiled away at the Hurricane to make it work.

Just before midday a proper dog fight broke out high in the sky near the aerodrome. The deadly stutter of the machine-guns made Colonel Strange pause in his task and look up, just as a white parachute billowed out near a burning Hurricane which dived away to crash nearby. The fighter pilot landed right on the aerodrome.

'Would you like another aircraft?' Colonel Strange asked him.

The fighter pilot was delighted. It was true that the Hurricane offered to him was a little the worse for wear. There were various bits missing and odd lengths of telephone cable and copper wire attached to it here and there as well as a plentiful supply of bullet holes. But the engine worked all right and it flew, so that was good enough for him. Thanking the tanned pilot officer with the greying hair the young fighter pilot got into the cockpit and flew off to England, where he landed safely at his base.

Amid all the stress of work in those desperate days his commanding officer recalled that he was the second pilot who had been shot down that morning at Merville and had flown back in another Hurricane. 'I'd like to see that officer at Merville. Just send out and drop a message asking him to fly the next Hurricane back here himself,' he said.

The message was duly sent.

'Later in the afternoon, about the time we got the third Hurricane working properly, I was surprised to see one of our own aircraft leave a busy little dog fight and streak down to drop one of the familiar little red and blue message bags telling me to bring the next serviceable Hurricane back to England before nightfall' explained Colonel Strange. 'It was a strange sight in a sky - with a Tiger Moth and an Autogyro, bringing back sharp memories of peacetime flying, now floating around absolutely unconcerned on their message-carrying jobs. You might have thought they were helping the police to handle the traffic on Derby Day.'

The order to fly the Hurricane home delighted him, because it gave him the chance of testing his theory that once a man has been taught to fly by the RAF he can fly anything, no matter what type, providing he remembers to turn all the taps and push and pull all the knobs of a modern aircraft in their proper sequence and has the good sense to inquire about the aircraft's peculiar habits from someone who knows her ways,' as he once remarked. But there was no one at Merville who could explain to him and although he had never flown a Hurricane before and had no guns with which to defend himself he calmly climbed into the patched-up aircraft and flew it off as though it were a Tiger Moth or one of his old Henri Farmans of the last war. Far from being worried, he was as happy as an undergraduate going on holiday. The undercarriage came up at his touch and the Merlin engine ran like silk.

Then his troubles began. Tracer began to come up at him from the hillsides as the Germans attacked him. Being anxious to save the Hurricane which he had gone to such pains to repair, he decided to climb. Pulling back the stick, he sailed up to 8,000 feet. Like magic the sky ahead became filled with the bursting of anti-aircraft shells as the Germans put up a fierce barrage. In the eyes of an old campaigner, the position was decidedly unhealthy, so he side-slipped down to avoid disaster.

But the leader of six Messerschmitts looking for stragglers noticed him and dived down to shoot him to bits. Colonel Strange, seeing the tracer and feeling the bullets ripping into one wing, side-slipped the other way to meet with similar treatment from an attacker on that side. If he could have pressed the button on his control column and set his guns blazing he would have been quite happy to take on the Messerschmitts, but he had nothing with which to hit back. His only defence was his skill as a pilot. He was compelled to match his mature experience against armed might and youth. There followed the maddest chase he has ever taken part in, one which called out all the old evasive tactics to defeat the enemy, while the German guns stuttered and Colonel Strange hedge-hopped over the tops of trees, skimming the roofs of cottages and showing those Germans that his hand had lost none of its cunning even if he was turning grey. He roared between the dwellings in a village street, turned on one wing and shot between the trees in the drive of a chateau. When it seemed that he must surely crash into the front door, he pulled back the stick and leapt over the roof and dived down the other side, giving the enemy such a run as they had never had before.

Superb judgment and brilliant flying kept his pursuers at bay as he hugged the ground down a wooded valley and down a chateau drive and once almost through the chateau front door, until suddenly, twisting downstream in a wooded valley, he slipped out clear over some sand dunes and out to sea, where the fleet off Boulogne opened up on the pack at his heels. Directly the naval gunners saw the hard-pressed Hurricane they sent such a hail of fire at the Messerschmitts that the Germans turned and fled. One salvo was enough for them and breathing freely once more, Colonel Strange pulled back the stick and leisurely and thankfully and perhaps a little regretfully to look back at the smoke of battle round Calais and Boulogne, a weird picture in the misty red light of the setting sun like a Turneresque picture and on the other side the quiet peaceful countryside of Thanet. He had safely run the gauntlet.

Then, home to roost, as he had done so many times twenty-five years before, thinking of my son and his regiment somewhere inland from Dunkirk and wondering what kind of miracle could save them all and if the people at home had any real picture in their mind's eye of the scene so close to them on the other side. The refugees, the burning villages, the noise and smoke of battle and how they would stand up to the onslaught if and when it came and would they remember the defeat in Flanders with no less honour than the victories which will follow in the last rounds of their fight for freedom.

And that was how the man who was supposed to be too old to fly saved a modern aircraft he had never flown before and won the Bar to his DFC [on 11 June].

During the bad weather in January 1941 I was forced by snowbound roads to take refuge in a wayside inn somewhere in England, where I got into conversation with a Canadian airman who touched on the unbelievable happenings of those days. 'Yes and there was a pilot officer who managed to bring out a Hurricane. When he got home he refused to give it up. He said he'd saved it, so it was his and he was darn well going to fly it.'

I smiled. When he had gone to see the state of the roads I said to my companion, an officer in the Royal Air Force: 'That was Strange!'

Truth is stranger than fiction.[1]

Endnote

1   Exceptional work demands an exceptional man, which perhaps explains why Squadron Leader L. A. Strange DSO MC DFC and Bar who formed No. I School of Aerial Gunnery and won such high honours in the last war is now devoting all his energy and knowledge and outstanding organizing ability to some of the most important work of all, the training of British parachute troops.

On 21 June 1940 Squadron Leader Strange was appointed CO of the newly created Central Landing School (CLS) at RAF Ringway near Manchester. This unit (which later was redesignated No.1 Parachute Training School RAF (PTS) was charged with the initiation, development and organisation of the UK's sole parachute training facility and which later pioneered the parachute training curriculum of the Allied airborne forces. Using the techniques developed under Strange, the PTS trained over 60,000 Allied personnel and paratroopers at Ringway 1940-1946.

On 5 May 1941 the Merchant Ship Fighter Unit (MSFU) was established at RAF Speke near Liverpool and Strange was appointed as CO. The MSFU developed the 'CAM Ship' for the catapult-launching of Hurricanes for convoy defence. A catapult for training volunteer pilots was erected at the airfield. With insufficient aircraft carriers available, there was the so-called 'Air Gap' within which merchant shipping was out of reach of land-based aircraft on both sides of the Atlantic. Fighters launched by catapult from merchant ships were felt to be a potentially effective against Focke Wulf Condors. About 50 Hurricane Is were modified by General Aircraft for catapult launch and 35 merchantmen were configured to carry catapults, with the first Atlantic crossings in April 1941. The Catapult Aircraft Merchantmen (CAM) and their 'Hurricats' claimed seven Focke Wulf Condors destroyed 1941-43, while the deterrent effect was even more important. In September 1941 he was posted as CO, RAF Valley, although illness prevented him from fulfilling the post. From August 1942 until the end of the year he served with Group HQ at Uxbridge. Three months as CO, RAF Hawkinge followed before a transfer to 12 Group HQ as a supplementary Squadron Leader.

In December 1943 Strange was then posted to 46 Group as Wing Commander, Operations. There he assisted in the planning for Operation Overlord, landing in Normandy himself on 15 June. He had six airstrips under his control in the expanding beachhead as this time. He was also responsible for the control and administration of a series of Temporary Staging Posts (TSP) supporting the Allied campaign. During the advance that followed the break-out from Normandy, Strange personally 'liberated' Château Lillois, 24 years after he had been the first to announce the departure of the Germans from there in 1918. In October 1944 Strange served with the HQ, 1st Allied Airborne Army. He was also at SHAEF Forward Headquarters in Reims on 6-7 May 1945 to witness negotiations to the German surrender on all fronts. He eventually reached the level of Wing Commander and retiring from the service in June 1945. For his wartime contribution Strange was awarded the OBE and the American Bronze Star. He bought an Auster Taylorcraft Plus D light aircraft and flew it in the 1950 Daily Express Challenge Air Trophy at the age of 59, being the oldest of the 76 competitors. He continued to fly regularly. Strange died in 1966 aged 75.

Chapter 1

Escape In Two Wars

A. J. Evans MC and bar

A. J. Evans joined Innes Court OTC on 5 August 1914. He transferred to the Intelligence Corps, crossed to France August 1914 as Temporary 2nd Lieutenant and took part in the Retreat. He joined the Royal Flying Corps in February 1915, observer in 3 Squadron till September 1915; awarded MC for continuing to observe while attacked by German aeroplane at Loos. Pilot in 3 Squadron in spring 1916, taken prisoner on 16 July 1916 after forced landing behind German lines. Escaped from Clausthal camp, recaptured on Dutch frontier. Escaped successfully into Switzerland after eighteen nights' walking. In command of 142 Squadron in Palestine in February 1918. Captured by the Turks and returned to Egypt at the Armistice, he was awarded a bar to the MC for numerous attempts to escape.

Those who have reached a certain age can now look back on the conditions in which British prisoners of war existed in Germany in the two wars and make some rough comparison of the difficulties and problems which faced those who attempted to escape. It may be said at once that although a far higher percentage of the prisoners of World War II tried and kept on trying to regain their liberty, yet the numbers who succeeded in escaping from Germany were considerably less than in World War I. The cause of this is not far to seek and is certainly not due to lack of skill or enterprise among the prisoners. It was due firstly to the vigorous control by the Gestapo in World War II and secondly to the fact that escaping had 'grown up.' In this war both the prisoners and their guards had far greater knowledge than in World War I and much of the knowledge was gained from the numerous escaping books which were published between the two wars. Some of these books were translated into German and Italian and even became compulsory reading for the camp commandants and prison guards in those countries. If anyone, fearing a future war, is doubtful of the wisdom of publishing such a book as this, he may be assured there is no escaping knowledge to be found here which is not already common property. In the books on escaping written after the Great War, little was left untold so that the prison guards were, from the start, fully aware of nearly every trick that had been used in former days. The prisoners also read the books, for frequently copies of some of these old escaping stories found their way under various guises into the camps. It is probably true, however, that the guards gained more from these books than the prisoners, for the possible tricks which a prisoner can play, the disguises which he can adopt and the bluffs which can be attempted, are strictly limited by the conditions in which he lives; these conditions are controlled to a large extent by his guards.

Given time and the necessary knowledge, the Germans are capable of working out schemes for dealing with most eventualities. They judged, quite rightly, that the barracks, forts, disused factories or other large buildings employed as prisoner-of-war camps in the Great War, were by no means the best type of prison from a security point of view. They offered too many opportunities for ingenuity and depended for their efficacy too much on locks, keys and stone walls. All these obstacles had been shown by long experience to be relatively ineffective as preventatives to a determined escaper. Furthermore each new type of camp presented a fresh problem for the guards and new opportunities for the prisoners. In the Great War it was a fact, well-known to prisoners, that to get out of a newly-formed camp was relatively easy. The prisoners themselves, studying the problem from the inside, were by far the best discoverers of weak spots in the defences and it was not until the prisoners had exploited these weaknesses that the Germans were able to block the easiest exits one by one. But the process took time; the prisoners became more skilful and escaping knowledge accumulated, so that escaping never ceased; in fact, it increased very much towards the end of the Great War. From the German's point of view, the obvious answer was to simplify the problem and as far as possible to confine all prisoners to one type of camp, so that the lessons and experiences learnt in each camp could be made common property.

It is hard to imagine a type of camp more suitable for the purpose than the one they selected for standard use. The prisoners were housed in long wooden barracks of a type very similar to those used by the military authorities in England. These barracks were surrounded by a double fence of barbed wire, the fences being from nine to twelve feet high. In between the fences (which were about six or seven feet apart) quantities of roly-poly barbed wire presented a most formidable obstacle. No prisoner could contemplate with equanimity the possibility of being hitched up on this barbed wire and thus presenting a legitimate target for any bloody-minded German sentry. At night the wire perimeter of such a camp was brilliantly flood-lit from pylons outside and at intervals along the fence fourteen-foot-high towers were erected. On each tower was a machine gun and a small searchlight. Thus it was fairly easy to ensure that there were no blind spots. Such a system of defence, though extremely good, was not absolutely impregnable. On at least two occasions prisoners escaped over the wires by making use of the floor of the tower to obscure the sentry's view; an almost incredible performance, taking into consideration the disheartening noise a wire fence makes if you try to climb it. On another occasion one of the most successful escapes of the whole war was made by first short-circuiting the electric system and then storming the wire in the dark with scaling ladders.

With rare exceptions then, prisoners discarded the idea of escaping over or through the double wire of the main defences and resorted to tunnelling, bluff and change of identity. To take the last of these three first. It sometimes happened that officers of all services and still more frequently sergeants of the RAF were able to get into touch with the large camps for 'other ranks' of the Army. From these big camps working parties were sent out daily into the fields or factories. Many an escape started by an officer or sergeant changing his identity with a private soldier. But even working parties were well guarded (far better than they were in the last war) and often months of preparation and waiting were necessary before an opportunity arose. Nor was it easy to obtain the information and equipment needed, such as papers, food and civilian clothes, in a men's camp. At first the Germans allowed the RAF sergeants to work in the fields outside their camps. The sergeants volunteered to work, but did so little and were such an unmitigated nuisance that the Germans, at a very early date, vetoed these working parties and guarded RAF sergeants nearly as closely as they guarded the officers. Tunnelling has always seemed to me to be a poor way of getting out of a camp. The few tunnels that succeeded (such as the Holzminden tunnel in WWI) have become famous and rightly so for the difficulties are enormous. The disposal of earth is a terrible problem all on its own and was particularly difficult to solve in the new standard camps in Germany. In Luft I the prisoners of war overcame it at first by making holes in their trouser-pockets, filling the pockets with earth and walking round the compound gently shaking themselves. In due course a thin deposit of fresh earth was noticed by observant Germans and all sentries were instructed to walk about with their heads down, looking for further indications of tunnels. But tunnels are vulnerable in so many ways. To make a long tunnel requires an elaborate organisation, many workers and months of work. The opening and closing of the mouth of a tunnel is a perpetual anxiety and, as the tunnel lengthens, the problem of supplying the worker at the face with fresh air is a civil engineering problem of great difficulty. Most tunnels are betrayed, sometimes by traitors, but more often by indiscretion among the workers; for not everyone is capable of unceasing caution for months on end. The amount of labour devoted to tunnels in this war is really astounding, but relatively few have been successful. It must not be thought, however, that even unsuccessful tunnels are waste of time. On the contrary, the planning and organisation of a tunnel from a prison camp is an occupation so absorbing that no prisoner taking part in such an effort will suffer from that type of melancholia known to prisoners as 'barbed wire disease.'

If prisoners are to retain their sanity, it is necessary for them to have an outlet for their mental and physical energies and, if to this is added an element of danger and a large prize for success, so much the better. Attempting to escape, especially by tunnelling, fulfils all these conditions and is the most effective occupation for assuring the health of prisoners of war.

When all is said and done, pure bluff in this war, as in the last, has paid by far the best 'escaping' dividends. The Germans have not changed their mentality - if anything, I believe they are more stupid and easier to bluff than they were twenty-five years ago. Perhaps the Hitler regime with its rigid discipline and discouragement of individuality accounts for this and explains why, in spite of their increased experience in guarding prisoners, the same old types of bluff have been reproduced with monotonous success. Those prisoners who have been in the hands both of the Italians and the Germans report that the former were far more difficult to bluff. This one would expect, for the Italians are the more quick-witted.

One of the best instances of bluff in this war is, I think, that of two soldiers in an 'other ranks' camp. By chance these two found a pot of white paint and two brushes. There was only one exit from the camp and that was through the main double gates. From the Commandant's office inside the wire, a road led directly to the main gate. Starting from the office, the two soldiers, as though on fatigue duty proceeded to paint a white line down the centre of the road. They took their time about it and the guards got used to seeing them on this work. At last they reached the gate and seeming in no hurry, stood there chatting and smoking until someone opened the gates for them and told them to get on with the job. The same thing happened at the outer double gate. Outside the camp they continued to paint a line down the centre of the road till, seizing the opportunity of a convenient corner, they unobtrusively disappeared.

It will be noticed that the fullest use was made of the sentry's psychological defects. The timing was excellent. Any hasty action makes a sentry think and this must be avoided at all costs. But to prolong operations as these escapers did, doing everything in slow time required very considerable nerve. To some extent the Germans recognised their own natural stupidity and compensated for it by appointing especially intelligent men as 'security officers.' These officers were completely responsible for the defence of the camps and it was their duty to reduce the opportunities of bluff to a minimum and on the whole they succeeded.

There is, therefore, no doubt in my mind that the first step to freedom the escape from the actual camp was generally more difficult in this war than it was in 1914-18. The next step, the journey through Germany and the final return home, was much more difficult for a variety of reasons, particularly during the last two years of the war. First and foremost there was the close and cruel grip of the Gestapo on the whole country. The Gestapo wove its way into everyone's life and regulated everybody's movements. It was extraordinarily efficient. Not only were there large numbers of prisoners of war on whom watch had to be maintained, but there were also many millions of foreign workers who, if not kept under control, would have been a serious menace to Germany. This resulted not only in there being intensive searches round the camps when any considerable number of prisoners of war escaped, but also there were at all times numerous searches and 'checkups' in progress throughout Germany. An escaping prisoner of war was quite liable, having successfully avoided his own man-hunt, to run into someone else's. The effect of this, unless your papers were perfect, was the same; arrest and examination, which usually terminated the adventure. The amount of passes and papers a man had to have in order to justify his existence outside the limited area where he was permitted to live was fantastic. Of course one might be lucky, as many escapers were and miss all the searches and controls; in which case travelling by train was no more difficult than it was during the Great War, perhaps even easier, because the Hitler Germans were more inclined to keep themselves to themselves. Sergeant Nabarro, for instance, made a truly wonderful trip through Germany by train, although he knew but few words of German. He changed trains several times and bought tickets without apparent difficulty. His method was to give the name of the station in a bold manner and plank down sufficient money. The most dangerous moment occurred when he was sitting peacefully in the corner seat of a carriage full mainly of German civilians. To his consternation a nice old woman opposite him leant forward, touched him on the knee and said something to him in German which he found quite unintelligible. When he failed to react, she repeated her remark more clearly and the rest of the occupants of the carriage began to take an interest. On the rack behind him, Nabarro had a very

Nazi-looking peaked cap. He stood put on his cap, looked as fierce as possible and said one of the few German words he knew; Scheitz (an obscene German word). The whole carriage gasped with horror. Nabarro stalked to the door and there turned round and glared at the cringing occupants. Schweinhünde! he said (this means 'pig-dog' and in German is a very insulting and foul expression). Then he went out and stood in the corridor. No German felt in the least inclined to approach or question such an unpleasant man. They left him severely alone.

Considering the number of foreign workers in Germany one would have expected that walking through the country would have presented few difficulties. Sometimes this was the case and several escapers tramped long distances without hindrance, but usually an escaper ran into a control post and was picked up. I am inclined to think that prisoners made too little use of bicycles as a means of progress. On a bicycle a man could travel very nearly as rapidly as on the halting German railway system; also it is more difficult to stop and question a man on a bicycle unless preparation has been made to do so, such as a barrier across the road.

One sergeant in the RAF stole a bicycle from a village in the centre of Germany and rode many hundreds of miles to the Baltic without once being stopped. Not only did he succeed in doing this, but he changed his bicycle for a better one several times en route and as he pedalled through Germany, he often stopped and talked to British prisoners working near the road. Either he was unusually lucky or he had a natural gift for this sort of thing. He finally stowed away on a ship and reached Sweden. From his description the whole trip sounded ridiculously simple, but then the story of a first-class escaper who has luck on his side usually does sound almost too simple to be interesting.

The ease with which this sergeant bicycled to safety calls to mind another RAF pilot, Flying Officer T. Milroy Gay, who, on 14 September 1941, after bombing Brest, bailed out of his Hudson over that peninsular and landed a mile or two from the coast in the northwest. This was always reputed to be a most dangerous spot. Milroy Gay, however, in full flying kit and in broad daylight, walked along the high road seeking help. A few German lorries passed, but no one took any notice of him. At last he saw a one-armed man working in a cottage garden, so he went up to the gate and hailed him. The man proved to be an old soldier who had been wounded in the last war. He asked Milroy Gay to come in and have a drink. After a few brandies Milroy Gay asked him when and from where the next train left for Paris. He was told that a train departed at 5.30 pm for Le Mans. So he borrowed a suit of civilian clothes, bought a first-class ticket and caught the train. At Le Mans he changed trains at night; always a dangerous operation for an escaper and arrived at Paris without incident. If there had been a taxi at the Gard du Nord I am sure he would have taken it for the journey across Paris; as it was, he caught the first available train down to Tours. At Tours he left the station, where there was usually a control post at night, without being questioned and wandered about the town during curfew hours without being arrested, till an early-opening cafe provided him with breakfast. He was pondering over the best method of crossing the line of demarcation when a young man sat down at his table. 'You are an RAF pilot, yes?' Milroy Gay agreed with him.

'Well,' went on the youth, 'I am a member of the Resistance and am going south. Would you like to come too?

'I don't mind if I do,' answered Milroy Gay. He crossed the Pyrénées with the minimum of trouble, but was arrested in Spain and spent three unpleasant weeks in jail before returning home. Somehow I feel rather glad that his luck or his skill (I am not sure which) failed him at the latter end; otherwise it seemed really too easy. [2]

But to return to Germany and the difficulties of escaping from that country. It is only in Northern Holland that the western frontiers of Germany are not protected by the Rhine and the Maas; always serious obstacles to escapers. In 1914 Holland was neutral and though the border between Germany and Holland was by no means easy for a tired man, nevertheless, once over, an escaper was welcomed by the Dutch and sent back to England.

In the 1940-45 war the boundary between Germany and Holland was feebly guarded by towers or log huts about one kilometre apart and usually connected by a not very formidable wire fence. From time to time the ground between the towers was patrolled. Few escapers seem to have had any serious difficulty in overcoming this obstacle. The best way was to approach the frontier at night in open country, for in wooded country the Germans had a nasty habit of posting stationary sentries behind bushes. After the patrol had passed it was fairly easy to cross the wire and even if a considerable noise was made in doing so, sufficient time always elapsed to make a safe 'getaway' before the Germans arrived to investigate. Once in Holland, however, trouble was very far from being over. Proximity, trade relations, intermarriage and the similarity of language made it inevitable that the successes of Hitler and the lure of his doctrines should hold many attractions for youth. A certain number, therefore, of young Dutchmen were drafted into the Nazi police which controlled Holland. These Dutch Nazis were extremely dangerous to escaping prisoners, for they knew the difference between a Dutchman and an Englishmen, which the normal German sentry did not. Also Holland is cut up by canals and the bridges are easy to guard. Swimming canals is not a task to be undertaken lightly by an escaper, desperately tired and half starved as he usually is.

One man who swam a canal in winter only avoided freezing to death by getting into a pigsty and cuddling an old sow. 'She stank a bit,' he told me, 'but she was wonderful.'

The following story of an RAF pilot who bailed out over Holland illustrates the sort of difficulties encountered. His aircraft was shot down and he landed in the first light of dawn not far from his burning machine, on an island a few miles long by about half a mile wide, formed by canals. He found himself in a field with a herd of cows. For a while he lay recovering from his rather heavy fall. When he felt better he started to walk towards the gate, but noticed that, owing to the heavy dew, he left a distinct trail of footmarks in the grass as he walked. With the burning machine so near he knew that a German search for him might begin at any moment, so he rounded up the cattle and drove them with him, thus obliterating his traces. Near a house he hid in a hedge and eventually attracted the attention of a labourer. The Dutch farmer was too frightened to take him into the house, but gave him food and some civilian clothes. Thus equipped, he reconnoitred one or two of the bridges, but found them all guarded, so he approached a house and knocked at the back door. His reception there was at first very chilly but finally the inmates seemed to thaw and advised him to attempt to cross by a certain bridge at the north end of the island. He left the house feeling a bit uncertain in his mind whether these Dutch had given him this advice to assist him or betray him. But half an hour later, when he observed several lorry loads of German troops moving rapidly towards the indicated bridge, he realised his doubts were justified.

Before anyone blames the father of a family for such a betrayal, it is well to remember that the penalty for assisting a escaper was death for himself and probably deportation for his family and that the dangers in Holland were far greater than in France or Belgium. Such a Dutchman under favourable circumstances might have been prepared to help an evader, but in this case he probably considered escape to be hopeless and assistance fatal to himself and his family.

It was obvious to this airman that the northern bridges would soon be impassable, so with the utmost caution he made his way in the opposite direction. Many of the smaller bridges over canals in Holland may be lifted at one end to allow barges, to pass under them. At one of these bridges he saw about a dozen civilians, together with a few German soldiers, waiting on his side of the canal for the bridge to be lowered. On the far side was a control post and a couple of German sentries. As it was still early in the morning he thought that there was a fair chance that all sentries had not yet been warned to look out for an English airman and in any case the longer he stayed on the island the more certain he was to be captured. So he joined the crowd. No one took any notice of him except a pretty girl with a baby and a pram. She glanced at him and then turned away and then looked at him again. He was sure she had guessed who he was. He moved quietly up to the pram and for a few minutes, whilst waiting for the bridge to be lowered, played with the baby. No word was spoken. When the time came to cross he took the handles of the pram and she put her arm through his and helped by a bright smile from the girl to the sentry, they crossed over together in perfect safety. I am glad to be able to record that this particular airman reached home, as he well deserved to do, though the long journey through France and Spain was far from sure and easy.

Another way out of Germany was through Switzerland, but Switzerland was entirely surrounded by our open enemies or by an unfriendly Vichy France. The Swiss frontier itself was probably as easy to cross in this war as it was in the last, but the approaches were even more difficult because the Germans near the frontier were constantly on the lookout for escaping prisoners. The Baltic outlet to Sweden was, for some unexplained reason, exploited more successfully in 1940-45 than in 1914-18. It may be that the actual difficulties in both wars were roughly the same and that the greater success in this war is a measure of the increased skill of the escapers.

It is at any rate certain that in World War II the neutral skippers trading between German ports in the Baltic and Sweden had a very lively fear of the Gestapo. Only on rare occasions have they been known to accept willingly an escaper on board their ships. This is not surprising, considering that each ship before it left port was subjected to a close search in which stink or tear bombs were sometimes used by the Gestapo to smoke out anyone fleeing from Germany.

Not only had an escaper who had reached a Baltic port to find means of boarding the right ship from a heavily-guarded quay, but he also had to find a place in it where he could stow away until the ship was at sea. It was advisable also for the would-be stowaway to select a ship which was about to sail and to have with him ample food and water. If he hid in an empty coal bunker he was liable to spend the next few days avoiding avalanches of coal being poured down on top of him. The Blue Peter, a flag flown twenty-four hours before a ship leaves port, was a great help, but in war-time ships do not always leave at the appointed hour.

Even outside the three-mile limit it was not always advisable for an escaper to declare his identity. There is a story of one man who, when half dead from hunger and thirst, got a very poor reception indeed when he presented himself to the captain. The captain was both angry and terrified and actually turned the boat round towards Germany again. It was only the exceptional powers of persuasion possessed by this ex-prisoner which induced the captain to change his mind. With all these difficulties to overcome, it is marvellous to me that so many men succeeded in getting away by this northern exit.

One of the outstanding features of this war is the number of airmen who, having bailed out over Holland, Belgium and France, succeeded in getting home without ever having been in the hands of the Germans - that is to say by evading capture rather than by escaping. No doubt they were greatly helped by the heroic assistance often given them by the Resistance movements in these occupied countries, but usually they owed their avoidance of immediate capture to two facts. The first is the initiative, determination and skill of these young men. With rare exceptions, every member of a crew that bailed out ran, hid and bluffed like a first-class criminal with the police on his heels from the moment he touched ground. The second is the outstanding courage shown by the ordinary peasant farmers and their families. Every civilian in the occupied countries was fully aware of the risks involved, for the Germans had no hesitation in shooting anyone who assisted an evader. Nevertheless, it was usual for every evader, in spite of these desperate risks and often in spite of a close German search of the district, to be hidden, clothed and fed and finally guided into safe hands. The children of these countries played a very large part, for they treated these fortuitous descents from the sky and the subsequent evasions as a new and exciting game. Indeed, most children of twelve would hardly have a memory of a time when there were no hated invaders for them to cheat and deceive. They played their part marvellously and many an evader, with the Germans all around him, has followed a small child to a safe hiding place. For those of us in England who have only known danger from bombs, it is hard to imagine a daily life in which at any moment a parachutist might arrive in our back garden and we might be asked on the instant to take a desperate risk, not only for ourselves, but also for our loved ones. This is a terrifying thought, yet most French families accepted it as part of their patriotic duty as a liberation from frustration and as a means of reburnishing the honour of France dimmed by the surrender.

The story of Flight Lieutenant Barclay will illustrate some of these points. He was a fighter pilot and was shot down over France. Being too low to bail out, he was forced to land in a ploughed field. There was a village about half a mile away;

near him in a corner of the field was a copse. His opponent in a Me 109 had no intention of allowing Barclay to evade into the quiet countryside, so he swooped repeatedly and prepared to fire if Barclay showed any signs of issuing from his machine. Barclay realised this and also knew that he had but little time to spare before the Germans encircled him. In order to convince his opponent that there was no need to hang about, Barclay lay back in his seat with his face turned to the sky, his mouth open and his eyes shut, pretending to be dead. This had the desired effect and the Messerschmitt flew off. Barclay immediately jumped from his aeroplane and after an attempt, which failed, to set it on fire, ran at full speed for the copse. He had hardly got into the undergrowth before he heard lorries and motor bicycles coming towards him. Something had to be done quickly, for the copse was clearly the first place the Germans would search. He turned his tunic inside out. It had white silk linings to the sleeves. He threw away his flying helmet, ruffled his hair and pulled his trousers down over his flying boots and then rolled himself in mud and leaves. It was not a very good disguise, but it was the best he could do in the time at his disposal. Collecting a big bundle of sticks, he cautiously approached the edge of the copse and peered through a thick hedge on to the road. Although he could hear cars and motor-bicycles in the near neighbourhood, the road at that moment was clear. With some difficulty he pushed his way through the hedge, still carrying the bundle of sticks, but as he did so a lorry-load of German troops came round the corner. Leaning on one stick, with the bundle of firewood over his back, he stood still at the side of the road and watched them go by. They took no notice of him. A moment later Barclay seized the opportunity to cross the road and thus broke through the ring of encircling Germans.

A few days later he found a warm welcome in a peasant's house. They were delighted to see him and to shelter him; so proud of him were they that he was treated as a sort of pet. Nothing was too good for him. They deprived themselves that he might eat of the best, they invited their friends to visit him and they took him to the village pub, where all the world drank to his health. It was really amazing how little regard some of these peasants paid to security. They must have realised the dangers they were incurring, though probably those who ran risks had had no practical experience of the Gestapo. Barclay, however, had no delusions. He thanked them kindly, but after a day or two moved off on his lonely walk southwards His next hiding-place was very different. He was equally well treated and made equally welcome, but for fourteen days he had to remain in a back room, only issuing for a few minutes each night for brief exercise in the garden. One day a small girl arrived with a civilian suit for him and instructions that he should catch a certain train for Paris. He was given his ticket. There appeared to be little risk, for he spoke French moderately well and everyone except the Germans were on his side. The biggest danger for Barclay lay in his appearance. He was a tall, fine-looking fellow and even in French clothes could hardly avoid being conspicuous, for there were few healthy young men left in France in those days. As he stood on the platform waiting for his train a German officer with his batman came and stood a few yards away. This at first did not disturb Barclay in the least, but soon he noticed, out of the corner of his eye, the German looking at him repeatedly and suspiciously. Barclay did his best to appear unconcerned, but when suddenly the German turned to his batman and, indicating Barclay, whispered something, it was obvious that action had to be taken and taken quickly, but what? He turned slowly and glanced round him. At that moment a group of old market women with baskets on their arms clattered noisily on to the platform. Without a moment's hesitation Barclay gave a cry of joy and rushed towards them. He threw his arms round the first old woman and whispered as he kissed her, Aidez moi, je suis aviateur Anglais. In a flash she not only grasped the situation, accepting the terrible risk, but acted as though she had been in the Comedie frangaise all her life. She went off into a spout of French: they all shook him by the hand and they all kissed him; they welcomed him home. The German recalled his batman (who had by then moved round behind Barclay) and got into his reserved carriage. Barclay got into a carriage with the old women and was safe. I know of no better example than this of spontaneous skill on the part of an evader and of courage and quickness of brain (which is the heritage of the French) on the part of those peasants. Barclay was an outstandingly good escaper; cautious, bold and intelligent. Having successfully passed this crisis, he returned home with little difficulty. But I have to record with real sorrow that this remarkable and charming young man was later killed in action.

Every evader or escaper has, with few exceptions, at least one moment of acute anxiety when his fate hangs in the balance. We hear of those ruses which were successful, but we seldom hear of those which failed. In general, however, it may be said that those who relied implicitly on bluff and on the stupidity of the German sentries got their reward. But when dealing with German officers and still more with the Gestapo, a nimble tongue and an unusually quick wit were needed, though it sometimes happened that a common British soldier succeeded in disguising his identity even when faced by an intelligent German officer backed by interpreters.

I always enjoy the story of the three privates of the 51st Division who, following the fall of Calais, changed into civilian clothes and after a short spell of working on the land as peasants marched the whole length of France to the Pyrénées, which they finally crossed on their own after three attempts. The crisis in their escape came early during this remarkable trek.

In appearance they were typical Scottish gillies; broad, strong, thick-necked and taciturn. They bore no resemblance to the French peasants; they knew nothing of the country and its customs and they spoke not one word of French. How they got through to Spain is a mystery which the few words they spoke to me on their adventure leaves unexplained. At one place they were stopped by a German officer who, naturally suspicious, asked them who they were and whence they came. According to their prearranged plan they refused to understand and answered in Gaelic, their native language. They continued to talk in Gaelic among themselves. The officer then sought the assistance of various interpreters who tried the Highlanders in every known language, but without result; they went on talking Gaelic. Finally, in despair, the German produced a map of the world and laid it on the table. He indicated by signs that they should point to their country. After careful study, one of the Scots slowly and deliberately placed his finger in the middle of the largest bit of land on the map; the middle of Russia.

'Oh, you are Russians, are you? We never thought of that!' And as there happened to be a treaty between Russia and Germany at that time the men were liberated once more to continue their march south. Whether these Highlanders knew of the treaty and chose to indicate that they were Russians for that reason I never found out: they did not impart unnecessary information to anyone!

Very few men have evaded from Germany. The conditions for evasion were exceptionally unfavourable. The man who bailed out and came down in Germany found instead of friendly farmers, a hostile population. Every German who caught sight of an evader would surely report his presence to the Gestapo and it was even probable that if several aircraft had been shot down, a parachutist might actually descend into the midst of a man-hunt.

Later on in the war, when the Allies first entered Germany, there were several indications that the German farmers, once the fear of the Gestapo was removed, were prepared to ensure themselves against the future by assisting an evader. Far the greatest number of evaders from France were members of the American Air Force. This is to be expected for the bombing of French targets in 1943-4 was carried out largely by the Americans. Each Flying Fortress had a crew of ten, as opposed to seven in a Lancaster and the bombing was nearly always done in daylight.

For some reason, possibly because the escape hatches on their machines were larger or more conveniently placed than in most of the RAF planes, the Americans were exceptionally good at getting out of an aircraft when it was fatally hit. I believe it is true that once at least a whole crew of ten which had bailed out successfully also succeeded in returning home. When the American armadas of several hundred machines roared overhead with German fighters swarming round them, it can be well understood that the inhabitants of the country, both German and French, took a very lively interest in the proceedings. The Germans stood by to send out search parties, the French peasants to give assistance to parachutists when they could do so without too much danger to themselves.

Most people imagine that the whole of France was swarming with Germans. But this was not the case. The chance of a man who had bailed out arriving on a spot far removed from any German was really very good. The great majority of those who bailed out and reached the ground unhurt in daylight had time to dispose of their heavy kit and their parachutes (or more often to find a peasant who would do it for them) and to reach a good hiding place before the Germans arrived. Intelligent tricks were often played to put the searcher off the track. One man laid out a trail of his flying kit: goggles, helmet, gloves, boots, etc., in one direction and then ran in the other, with great success. A leafy tree in a forest was often found to be most useful, for it is impossible to search each tree. Usually, however, the peasants or villagers knew just where to hide an evader and the children took the most active part as guides. There is every reason to believe that the Germans were aware of the constant stream of successful evaders who crossed the Pyrénées and returned through Spain to England. The Gestapo in France were gingered up by some high authority, control posts were placed at stations exits and the most brutal measures taken against those who assisted evaders. But still the evasions went on with only temporary checks, for the cleverness and courage of those who helped evaders more than matched the increased energy and brutality of the Gestapo.

Gradually as time passed, a network of underground resistance (whose raison d'etre was the rescue of evaders) was built up in the territories occupied by the Germans. This resistance movement was particularly strong in Belgium and France. It existed under greater difficulties and dangers in Holland; and in the latter part of the war, the Danes showed themselves both courageous and ingenious at the same perilous work. The earliest indication that some such movement would develop was the appearance of a young Belgian girl in the office of the British representative at Bilbao. She said that there were two British soldiers outside in a cafe and asked for permission to bring them in. Having done so, she asked the Consul for 10,000 francs. When asked how she could justify a demand for such a large sum, she answered that she had brought these two men by herself all the way from Belgium and intended to go back for others. For three years this heroic girl, helped only by another girl of her own age (about twenty) conducted small parties of evaders from Belgium and Northern France, across the Pyrénées and handed them over to the British authorities in Spain. Eventually her activities became too well known to the Gestapo for her to remain in the north. She moved her sphere of operations first to the neighbourhood and then to Bordeaux, always with the Gestapo close on her tracks. In 1944 it became clear that if she remained in France and continued her work she must soon be taken by the Gestapo. Although she had opportunity to save herself, as she had saved so many others, she refused to leave France and was eventually arrested by the Germans. She disappeared and her fate is unknown.

At the end of July, 1944, Madame X and her old mother lived in a tiny cottage in a remote village in the Rouen district. During the previous years she had harboured many evaders and at the time of the great German retreat, five airmen were living in her cottage or in the buildings around, waiting for the arrival of the armies of the Allies. Those weeks when the weary, spiteful and demoralised German troops passed through the country were particularly dangerous, both for evaders and more especially for those patriots who were hiding them.

However quiet and remote a village might be, there was always the chance that hundreds or even thousands of retreating Germans might suddenly appear and billet themselves in every nook and corner; descending like a swarm of locusts, they ransacked the villages, eating up every scrap of food they could find. These men were too tired to maintain discipline, they had seen too much of death to have any respect for human life. At one moment they were near to tears; in fact, many wept bitterly and poured out their sorrows to Madame X in self pity at their sufferings; at another moment they were ready to shoot to kill in savage spite if any incident displeased them.

For twenty-four hours twelve of these Germans slept and fed in Madame X's kitchen whilst the five British airmen hid as well as they could in the other two rooms in the cottage. She and her mother would have been shot immediately had these evaders been discovered. Every minute of those twenty-four hours was one of intense danger and strain. She practically gave up hope that they would win through, but her courage never failed. Then the Germans departed and she left the cottage to make arrangements for a safer hiding place in the woods.

But though the days of the German retreat were often desperate and fearful days for the inhabitants, I sometimes feel inclined to pity the German soldiers, who with blazing hatred round them, struggled out of the land they had dominated for so long.

The Mayor of E. told me the story of the battle which took place when his village was liberated. 'The British were in the wood over there,' he said, 'and the Germans occupied those orchards and held the line of trenches and fox-holes that you can see. It was a splendid battle and I directed it.'

'Really!' I said in some surprise. 'How did you do that?'

'From my Mairie,' he answered with mounting enthusiasm. 'I got on to the village of X where the British were. You see, the Germans as they retreated, forgot to cut the telephone lines. There were Germans in my Mairie; it was their headquarters, but I had my office to myself. I got on to my friend at X and told him to fetch the Commander of the British Artillery. Then I sent out my runners. I learnt where the Germans had placed their batteries and where their infantry was concentrating. And the British commander took my orders and I directed the battle. Ah! but the British guns shot marvellously. In that battle only five British soldiers were lost. It rained shell on the Boche and they retreated.'

'Marvellous!' I said, 'and after the battle...?' 'Ah, then I went out with my gun and watched for stragglers.'

'Any luck?' I asked.

'Yes, I got four. Then the liberation came.'

Now, a sense of duty is usually one of the reasons why a prisoner of war refuses to 'stay put,' but to the true escaper it never has been and never will be the major reason. The true escaper tries to get away because his natural attitude is 'agin the government,' and he strongly objects to his liberties being restricted by a lot of bastards whom he despises. He also enjoys the adventure for its own sake and the fact that considerable risks are attached puts escaping into the same class of amusement as big-game hunting under severe conditions. The rewards of success are very great and the penalties of failure are not excessive.

The Geneva Convention of 1929 was thoughtful enough to lay it down that no prisoner of war might be punished by more than thirty days' solitary confinement for a simple escape. To a young man lately arrived in a prison camp from a pleasant and civilised mess thirty days' solitary often seemed sufficiently severe, but to the hardened prisoner of some years standing it appeared insignificant and was sometimes even looked upon as a welcome relief from overcrowded quarters. Sometimes solitary confinement entailed desperately short rations and no smokes, but in most well-organised British prison camps adequate arrangements were usually devised by which food, literature and tobacco could be conveyed surreptitiously to the inmates of the prison cells. In the Great War very heavy sentences were sometimes imposed on recaptured prisoners, especially if they made a habit of attempting to escape, but in this war, with some notable exceptions, the Germans have obeyed the Geneva rules and on the whole have imposed lighter sentences than we in England imposed on Germans. A normal sentence on a recaptured English prisoner was five to fifteen days' solitary confinement, whilst our sentences on Germans were more frequently over twenty days.

For all other crimes, apart from escaping, a prisoner of war is tried and punished under the military laws of the detaining power. Thus if he bashes a sentry on his escape he will be tried by court-martial for assault, or if he kills a sentry or anyone else during an escape he will be tried and certainly condemned for murder. If he steals a German uniform in which to escape he will be tried for theft. If he tunnels through the walls of his prison or cuts the bars, he will be up on a charge of wilful damage to government property. A simple escape is, therefore, not quite so easy to accomplish as some may think, but the Germans, in spite of their passion for courts-martial, acted in general with considerable leniency towards offences committed during escapes and entered, as far as the German make-up will allow, into the spirit of the thing. They recognised that our prisoners of war considered it their duty to escape and though the commandants and guards must have had great difficulty in restraining themselves from reprisals on recaptured prisoners, nevertheless they obeyed, with all the humour they could summon, the orders from above. Befehl ist Befehl (orders are orders) as the Germans say and they accepted the maxim both for the prisoners and for themselves. Courts-martial are, however, what the Germans really enjoy—they seem particularly suited to their temperament. The strict rules of procedure, the formalities, the dignities due to rank, the endless forms to fill up and sign, are all part of a well-regulated way of life which they understand and in which they have existed since their earliest days. The courts-martial are usually conducted by quite an unnecessary number of high-ranking officers; in fact they use their courts-martial as a means of giving employment and pay to otherwise useless and inefficient dug-outs. At a German court-martial on a prisoner the proceedings are usually conducted with admirable precision. The evidence is fully sifted. The prisoner is allowed a competent officer to speak in his defence. But the result is invariably the same. The prisoner is found guilty and sentenced to a maximum penalty. In cases where a death penalty may be imposed an observer from a neutral country is usually present and shorthand notes of the trial are forwarded to the prisoner's homeland. As a death sentence may not be carried out for three months after judgment, it has, I believe, been often possible for our Foreign Office to put in a special plea through the neutral power, but I do not know whether this has ever been effective.

The love of rule and order is the basic cause of unfitness of most Germans for the very individualistic efforts necessary for a successful escape. It may be thought that an escape from England is so difficult in war-time as to be hardly worth trying. But I am not convinced even of this, for between England and Ireland boats were continually passing. With properly-forged papers and good English, such as any prisoner of war could learn in a year, such an escape should have been possible and would have been accomplished, I feel sure, if our best escapers had been presented with such a problem.

156 RAF men successfully escaped from German PoW camps in Western Europe.

1,975 men evaded capture after having been shot down in Western Europe.

Endnotes
2   Milroy Gay left Gibraltar on 27 January 1942 on board corvette HMS *Pelican,* arriving in Liverpool on 6 February. He received a MiD on 11 June 1942.

Chapter 2

Escape of
Captain A. D. Taylor

During the weeks which followed the evacuation from Dunkirk the escapers began to reach home by boat across the Channel. In those days before the Germans had taken full control of the coast, it was not very difficult to find a boat; it was largely a question of luck and the fishermen were sometimes able to give active assistance. One of the first escapers to reach England in this way was an Irishman - Lieutenant Doherty. After failing to catch the last boat from the Dunkirk beaches he managed to acquire some civilian clothes and wandered westwards, keeping near the coast. As he talked excellent French and knew French customs he was in very little danger of being picked up by the Germans in the confused conditions which existed at that time in Northern France. To the Germans he was indistinguishable from a bombed-out refugee. One day he went into a farm in the hopes of finding food and perhaps lodging for the night, but it was deserted. The farmer and his family had fled, leaving behind all the animals untended - the pigs starving in their sties and the cows moaning to be milked. This was more than Doherty, who was himself a farmer, could stand. He decided to stay there and look after the animals; he took the place over in fact and soon had everything in order. When the Germans arrived a few days later he sold them butter and eggs at a good profit.

As always in those early days, the German invaders behaved very correctly, for it was part of their policy to encourage the French farmers. When a fortnight or so later the owner of the farm rather shamefacedly returned, Lieutenant Doherty handed over the farm to him in excellent condition.

Meantime, Doherty had employed his time and opportunities to other purposes as well as farming. He negotiated with a fisherman for a boat and having, with many regrets said good-bye to his farm, sailed away one dark night back to England. Lt Doherty made escaping sound very easy.

Captain A. D. Taylor was also among the first escapers to arrive in England after a far more adventurous trip. Here was a natural escaper, the genuine article, who looked upon his escape as a magnificent adventure, which it was and told his story with real humour. He seemed to know instinctively when it was worth taking a chance and when he bluffed he went to the limit. He was so good an escaper that I am sure only rank bad luck could have prevented him from getting home. On the whole I think the Germans got rid of him cheaply, for he would have been a perpetual nuisance in a prison camp.

On 18 May 1940 his tank became involved in a tank battle near the village of Donge on the Brussels canal. From his description this battle did not in the least resemble the tank battle of my imagination. It was a scattered, unregulated affair, spread out over a wide district. He was chasing one tank down a country lane and strongly suspected that he was being chased by another, when the disaster occurred. His tank took a corner too fast, skidded violently and landed in the ditch at the side of the road—and that was that.

Though a bit shaken, no one was hurt. When the crew at length succeeded in extricating themselves there was not a soul in sight, the countryside was deserted and the battle had passed on. Without help nothing could be done to unditch the tank. Now that the excitement was over, Taylor, having had little or no sleep for the last four days and nights, realised that he was extremely tired. It was a beautiful day, with a hot sun and cloudless sky, so, picking a shady spot, he lay down and soon fell asleep. He was woken by a German soldier prodding him gently in the stomach with a bayonet. After being marched to a nearby village he was locked up in the church with a mixed batch of French and British prisoners. The search and interrogation which prisoners of war underwent in those days was mild compared to what it became later. At that time Germany had more prisoners than she could cope with; she was winning the war and was therefore not greatly interested in the plans of her opponents - she was doing all the planning.

Two days later Taylor took part in a parade of prisoners through the streets of Brussels and as was the common lot of British prisoners, was ill-treated, starved and insulted by his guards. Finally he was lodged in the Grenadier Barracks at Brussels, where some decent German officers took pity on the condition of the British and bought food for them in the town. There he remained till May 23rd when, in a straggling column of prisoners, he marched once more eastwards. The days were very hot and there was a terrible lack of water which was even more serious than the lack of food. Often the inhabitants of a village through which they were passing would bring out pails of water and the guards, though allowing the French to drink, refused to allow the British; it seemed to be the Germans' policy to exhaust and humiliate the British in every way they could. When some of the prisoners, who were too weak to go on, fell out of the column, they were forced back with rifle butts and many were brutally killed.

From the beginning Captain Taylor had determined to escape. At length his chance came. Some exceptional straggling and bunching, not entirely fortuitous, drew the attention of the guards and Taylor dived through the hedge. The column passed on and no one had seen him go. Only a few hours of daylight remained, so he lay still in the shelter of the hedge until it was dark, when he heard someone calling him from a house about thirty yards away. They had seen his escape and, though frightened, were willing and anxious to help. An hour later he set off again, much refreshed after a good meal, dressed in civilian clothes and in good heart.

His first astonishing objective was his tank, from which he hoped to rescue his shaving kit and some other personal property. In this first march he walked mostly at night and across country, obtaining food without much difficulty from outlying farm-houses. There were not many Germans in the locality and the inhabitants, though always rather frightened, were friendly and helpful. By this time he had grown a beard and the blue serge suit was so dirty that he could pass easily as a tramp or a refugee. Somewhere en route through Malines he picked up a map of France out of a school atlas and arrived at his tank after a week's march. Apparently his tank had not been touched and there was no one about. He was just preparing to enter it when a German soldier appeared from behind a tree. Nein, das ist streng verboten, he said and moved Taylor on. This irritated Taylor a good deal; he felt it was his tank. The loss of the shaving kit and personal belongings was a great disappointment, but the encounter gave him confidence; he had met a German and had not been arrested. He apologised in French and went on his way, but henceforth travelled mostly in the daytime and on the roads, thus greatly improving his rate of progress.

During the next fortnight he was stopped many times by German sentries and asked for his papers. After an encounter or two of this sort Taylor developed a confidant technique and no longer cared a hoot for German sentries. His usual plan, when asked for his papers, was to fumble in his pockets and curse, exactly as a man does when he has lost his railway ticket; then, when the sentry became impatient, he would point to a house in the distance (where clearly he had left his pass) and taking the sentry by the arm, attempt to drag him in that direction. This ruse, with variations, carried Taylor through many villages full of German soldiers. Eventually he reached Ellezilles on the Brussels-Lille road, where he was stopped by a German of a more intelligent type. Taylor tried the old trick, saying that he was a native of Flobecq. (He always kept the name of a local village in his mind for this very purpose.) But this time, to his dismay, he was asked to describe the village square and give names of the streets. Having a nimble imagination, he supplied this information with little hesitation, but by sheer bad luck a French farmer happened to pass at that moment. The German beckoned to him and asked if he knew the village of Flobecq. ' Certainly,' said the farmer and when asked proceeded to describe the main square and name the streets, giving answers which did not in the least tally with those given by Taylor. Once more Taylor was put under lock and key and two days later again found himself marching eastwards in a weary, straggling column of prisoners. But he was by no means discouraged. With his previous experience to back him, he was confident of escaping.

Even in those early days some sort of normal life was creeping back into the villages of France. Men and women were carrying on with their daily tasks and many of the cafes were open. It was whilst passing one of these cafes where the seats straggle on to the pavement, that Taylor saw his chance and took it. When no guard was looking he sat down quickly and called for the waiter. The column of miserable humanity moved on and left him sitting. He now determined to make for his old billet at Touffleur, where, during the ' phoney war,' he had made many friends whom he wished to meet again, not only with the idea of getting help and advice but from pure curiosity to find out how they had fared.

Henceforth he walked with somewhat greater caution, but nevertheless passed right through a German HQ, which was then established at Pacq. In addition to his disguise of a thick beard and his now extremely disreputable blue suit, he made a habit of carrying an agricultural implement and found that, with this over his shoulder, he was seldom stopped; he became, in fact, part of the countryside and no doubt looked like a villager pursuing his lawful occasions. After a long journey through La Basse, Bethune, St. Pol and St. Risquiers he reached the village where he had been billeted, only to find it full of German troops. This did not deter him in the least from calling at the house where his old mess had been. To his great disappointment he found it deserted. He went into the house and locked the door. Going into the dining-room, he was horrified to find dirty plates on the table still unwashed from their last meal three weeks before and the whole place in disorder as they had left it in their hurried departure.

Taylor, having an exceptionally tidy mind, felt strongly that this was not the condition in which a respectable officers' mess should leave a good billet so he set to work and washed the crockery and tidied the place up. It is almost unbelievable. Then he went upstairs to tidy the bedrooms. Whilst there he heard knocking on the door and putting his head out of the window saw two Germans trying to get in. Occupe! he shouted and waved them away.

Danke! said the Germans and departed.

It is a little difficult to understand why these Germans, if they were seeking billets, allowed themselves to be turned away by a man who spoke French. It is possible that they were intending to enter an apparently empty house in an unofficial capacity and for unauthorised purposes. Unregulated looting was streng verboten in the German army and on the whole the German behaviour in France was surprisingly correct. The word 'correct' was how the French described it at first; later they realised that there were more ways of killing a cat than by skinning it alive.

He looked up many of his old friends in the village and though they were too nervous to give him much help, they were able to give him much needed information about the course of the war. They told him that the remnants of the British Army were in the neighbourhood of Boulogne and Dunkirk and Taylor decided to go in that direction. In actual fact the evacuation from the beaches had now ended and no organised British army remained on the Continent.

During the next fortnight he wandered northwards, making for Calais. As he approached that area the dangers and difficulties increased. It is the story of bluff, ingenuity and 'timing'; a story of numerous small incidents when his own excellent judgment of whether boldness would pay, or whether extreme caution was necessary, enabled him to avoid capture. Near Calais he found the situation hopeless and turned south-west along the coast towards Abbeville, hoping desperately to find a boat. All this time he had kept careful notes in writing on matters of military interest that he saw, oblivious to the fact that, since he was in civilian clothes, he would most certainly have been shot as a spy had he been caught with these notes on him. On the Grand Pont bridge at Abbeville he was stopped and questioned by a German sergeant. Being quite used to this by now, it did not alarm him and he poured out his usual piteous story of how he had been bombed out, lost all his papers and now, as a miserable refugee, was hunting for his wife and family, a story so perfect by now that he almost believed it himself. The sergeant, however, proved particularly tough and though not appearing to doubt the truth of the story, locked Taylor up in a cellar for the night to be on the safe side. Also in the cellar was a French sergeant. A man full of gloom; a defeatist pure and simple. He and Taylor talked through most of the night. 'The French are beaten,' the sergeant told him, 'the army is rotten; the politicians are rotten there is no hope of recovery. England must soon be invaded and the war is lost.' He advised Taylor to surrender. There was no sense in continuing and there was no hope of escape, urged this miserable man.

Taylor at this time must have been profoundly depressed and unusually tired, for he allowed himself to be over-persuaded and next morning confessed to the astonished German that he was a British officer and wished to give himself up. He had some difficulty in establishing his identity and for a long time the German sergeant flatly refused to believe him. Finally he was put in charge of a sentry and marched to the German commandant in the next town. On the way an incident occurred which might well have had very serious results. Taylor had written his observations on German military matters on odd bits of paper torn from his note-book. He had done this for safety, so that they could be hidden easily. As he was being marched along it suddenly dawned upon him that, should these notes be found, he stood an excellent chance of being shot as a spy. He decided that he must destroy the notes at once, but with the sentry behind him this was a tricky business. As, however, he would surely be searched at the Commanture, this was his last chance and the notes were not even hidden; he could feel them in his pocket, two bits of paper, one covered with notes and the other yet a blank. Choosing his moment, he pulled out one piece of paper, but was 'spotted' by the sentry, who covered him with his rifle and ordered him to pass over the paper. With intense relief, Taylor saw that it was the blank sheet and on they marched.

At the Commandant's office he was given a seat in the garden and, with a sentry on guard, was told to wait. He waited for an hour or two and during that time destroyed the notes and revised his views on the situation. He now regretted bitterly having surrendered, cursed the Frenchman and determined to escape again on the first opportunity. With his experience he had little doubt he could manage this and was consequently more cheerful than might have been expected. At long last the Commandant sent down word that he was too busy to bother with Taylor and gave instructions that he was to be included in any column of prisoners that happened to be passing. So again Taylor found himself a member of a long column of prisoners, but this time mainly consisting of civilians sent off to work in Germany. As they approached Risquiers he found an opportunity to escape again. Again he passed through the countryside in his usual manner, his confidence now fully restored and this time he made his way to Le Touquet. Here he called on Grant, the golf professional, whom he had known well in the days of peace. Grant was at home and quite undisturbed. For a week Taylor stayed at his house. The first evening, after a shave and a good clean up, Taylor and Grant celebrated their meeting by dining at the Balmoral Hotel in one of the biggest restaurants in Le Touquet.

'But weren't there a lot of Germans about?' I asked, astonished.

'Oh, yes,' said Taylor 'swarms of them, but we were quite safe. No one took any notice of us, for who would expect to find an escaping British officer in such a place?''

The final escape to England is almost too fantastic and too simple to believe. The first necessity was a boat. Exactly the right article was discovered in the Le Touquet Sailing Club, but unfortunately it was without a mast. With the help of the local blacksmith, however, they rigged one up and a few days later Taylor, choosing his weather and his time, not only sailed out of Le Touquet, but was picked up by one of our patrol boats just outside the Estuary.

Chapter 3

The Three Musketeers

Battle weary and bloodstained, twenty-three year old Private (later Captain) Gordon Instone, a gunner in the ranks of the 2nd Searchlight battery of the 1st Searchlight Regiment, Royal Artillery stood on the beach at Calais and stared towards England, just twenty-one miles distant. It was 21 May 1940. The Channel stretched before him like a great lake, terminated by the cliffs of Dover which on that perfect, cloudless day he could see quite clearly in the distance. There was safety, tantalizingly close but hopelessly out of reach and there also was his fiancée Elizabeth. Instone had been in France for three months, one of the quarter of a million volunteers and Territorials making up the British Expeditionary Force (BEF) dispatched by a confident government in London to bolster the French army but the Wehrmacht had outflanked them and tanks had bypassed the static defences of the Maginot Line before bursting through Luxembourg and Belgium. The BEF fell back until it reached the coast of northern France and a desperate evacuation began at Dunkirk as a valiant perimeter defence tried to hold off the German armour, buying the time needed by the Royal Navy and the hastily assembled armada of small ships to take many hundreds of thousands of stranded soldiers off the Dunkirk beaches. Every hour counted in which they could deny the main coastal road to the German tanks but now Calais's harbour and gare maritime were in flames and it was now 'every man for himself'.

Instone's duty had been to assist in maintaining the weapons and equipment, including telephones, of about twenty searchlight detachments. He was therefore a skilled fitter and electrician. On 21 May his unit, by means of a portable receiving set, took in the astounding news, issued by the BBC, that Boulogne had been entered and captured by enemy tanks. No one at first believed it; it seemed impossible. If true, however, it meant that all the troops in the neighbourhood of Calais were surrounded and were likely in the near future to be attacked by German tanks from the south. Soon after the receipt of this disastrous news, survivors from Boulogne began to trickle in and the accuracy of the BBC could no longer be doubted. That night it was decided to withdraw all units into the outer perimeter of Calais whilst one brigade of infantry attempted to hold up the German advance in the Boulogne road. As night came on heavy mortar and gunfire could be heard approaching ever nearer from that direction. The roads between the searchlight battery and Calais being already controlled by the Germans, the transport vehicles and heavy equipment of the units were immobilised and destroyed and the men in small parties made their way cautiously over the fields, dykes and canals, past the German patrols and joined up with the garrison at Calais just before dawn.

Calais itself had no defences against an attack from the land side. There were two coastal batteries, but as their guns pointed only out to sea, they never came into action. In all and including about 800 French troops who fought well, the total garrison in Calais amounted to hardly 3,000 men, consisting mainly of a battalion from the 60th Rifles, one battalion of the Queen Victoria's Rifles and one from the Rifle Brigade. In addition there was a battalion of the Royal Tank Regiment and an Anti-Tank battery besides fragments of many other units, including military police, clerks, cooks and dispatch riders. Their heavy equipment consisted of six light tanks and the same number of anti-tank guns. Opposed to this force and travelling rapidly up the road from Wissant, were nearly 200 German tanks, supported by 30,000 infantry from two Panzer divisions and several batteries of artillery. The Luftwaffe was also there in strength to give ample support to the ground forces. Beyond Calais were the beaches of Dunkirk, where 300,000 men of the BEF, now nearly defenceless, were awaiting evacuation. The warding off of a disaster, greater by far than British arms had ever suffered, depended almost entirely on the defence of Calais where this handful of men held up the enemy advance for a few fateful days. Besides the lack of men and equipment, the garrison were short of food and a further tragedy must have seemed like a final disaster. On the afternoon of 23 May two motor ships docked in Calais, having on board munitions and equipment for the infantry. The difficulties of unloading were much increased by swarms of refugees and various small units who, seeking the nearest port crowded towards the docks with vehicles of every description and jammed the roads about the harbour. Nearby the docks were two hospital trains which had reached Calais after vainly attempting to embark their 600 wounded at Dunkirk and Boulogne. One ship was emptied and partially filled with wounded. The second ship was still partly full of most valuable and needed stores when, either owing to a misunderstanding or possibly to a false order passed by a German agent, the second ship as well as the first, moved slowly away from the docks and to the dismay of all, set sail for England.

For three days the garrison were bombed and shelled and mortared; Stukas in relays roared down on them with screaming sirens; they were sniped at from all sides by Fifth Columnists and by Germans who made their way in disguise into the town which was still full of French civilians. It was impossible to deal effectively with snipers who could turn themselves into civilian non-combatants at a moment's notice. A tank barrier was formed by placing about 200 motor transports engine to tail-board in front of the trenches. This proved most effective when covered by heroic men with antitank guns. The rain of shells and mortar bombs never ceased, though from time to time it rose to even greater intensity. There was neither rest nor shelter for any man of the little garrison.

The casualties mounted rapidly and intolerable weariness all but incapacitated the remainder, but still the Germans failed to make good the road to Dunkirk. Two German batteries firing from the woods at Guines were especially offensive and it was a great moment when two destroyers, HMS *Verity* and HMS *Windsor* appeared a mile off the coast and concentrating their fire on the battery they could see, put every gun but one out of action.

Over Calais hung a heavy pall of smoke rising from a fire in the oil storage tanks on the west of the town. This smoke had some advantages for the garrison, for it made it more difficult for the Stukas to operate. All this time the military police kept order in the town and sternly refused to allow the war to interfere with discipline. One despatch rider, carrying an urgent message, was stopped by them in a burning street and his name and number taken for being improperly dressed; he was not carrying his gas-mask! It is also true that when water was practically unobtainable, it was still possible to find bottled beer in the shops and pay for it.

At one time during the siege two more ships entered the harbour and preparations were made to evacuate at any rate some of the garrison by sea. Instone was among those who were marched from the trenches to the harbour and his contingent waited in the comparatively peaceful dock area, hoping and praying that they would be in England in a few hours. The suspense, with that hell behind them and the hope of safety before them, was desperate. Then came a counter order and with indescribable feelings of frustration and disappointment they were marched back into the battle with instructions to fight to the last man and the last round. By then little ammunition was left to fight with; the anti-tank guns were nearly all out of action and the perimeter was no longer defensible. 'We started to walk along the beach' recalled Instone 'but each time a shell whined overhead we threw ourselves flat until our battle-dresses were covered with sand. Steadily our numbers diminished as the insatiable mortars took their toll. One after another men staggered and fell, their painful moans and cries for help following us pitifully along the beach. Gunner Williams was hit in both legs. He was conscious and smiled as I knelt beside him, but I could do nothing for him. I threw down my rifle and trudged on as best I could but the pace grew slower and the heat more intense. This was my third day without sleep and I was numbed with fatigue.'

At dawn on Sunday 26 May the few hundred men who remained retreated to the beaches, carrying what wounded they could with them. Even then, though repeatedly called upon to surrender, they refused and many stood waist deep in the sea as their only cover against the German fire. As our men stood in the water, the Germans opened up on them with artillery, with mortars and finally with machine guns from the dunes. At 9 am the German artillery were reinforced by the Luftwaffe and from 10 am onwards there were continuous low level attacks from three squadrons of Stukas. The weather was very hot, the sky cloudless and the sea like a lake. The English coast could be seen clearly. Two hundred only of the garrison now remained and these had had neither food nor sleep for three days. With their armament reduced to one Bren gun and one magazine, the defence of Calais was over. The last order, 'every man for himself' was given. Many men attempted to reach the British lines near Gravelines. 'About a hundred of us were left' recalled Instone 'and were halfway to Dunkirk when a German tank blocked our way. Its turret turned towards us and one of the crew jumped out with a revolver. We raised our hands, prisoners of the Third Reich.'

Instone and the rest of the survivors were rounded up on the beaches about five miles from Calais by German tank personnel. He had come through the battle miraculously unscathed, though his battle dress had been holed several times by splinters. On one occasion a shell had burst above a group of seven or eight men and he alone had been unwounded, but probably most of the survivors could tell of similar experiences. No one could have remained alive and unwounded through the siege of Calais without quite unusual luck and it will be seen in this story that Instone's luck, aided by his skill, held to the end of his adventures. Instone and those around him, on his suggestion, made a pile of their private papers and set fire to them. In due course they were formed up and marched back through Calais and finally imprisoned in the football stadium at Desvres, which had been converted into a collecting camp for prisoners of war. There were five to six thousand prisoners in the grounds, most of whom had been captured at Calais; of these about 1,000 were British. There were about twenty or thirty guards, half a dozen being trained bullies who did all in their power to make life as unpleasant as possible for the prisoners. Most of the men in the camp were utterly worn out and had had no food for five or six days, but all the food they got there was a cupful per day of very thin bean soup with half a cubic inch of horseflesh in it.

About 10 am on the morning of 27 May, the day the Belgians surrendered, Wing Commander Basil E. Embry DSO AFC[3] commanding 107 Squadron, was brought into the camp. Embry was born in Gloucestershire in 1902 and as a young boy at Bromsgrove School he developed an avid interest in aviation. In 1921 he joined the Royal Air Force with a short service commission as an Acting Pilot Officer. In 1922 he was sent into Iraq, serving under future Air Marshals Arthur Harris and Robert Saundby. By 1926 Embry's enthusiasm, professional application, boundless energy and flair for the unconventional had put him on the fast track for promotion within the RAF and he was rewarded with the Air Force Cross in that year's New Year Honours and appointment to a permanent commission. Promoted to Flight Lieutenant, Embry returned to Britain in 1927 as an instructor at the Central Flying School, Uxbridge. In 1934 he was posted to India to serve in the Indian Wing on the North West Frontier. He was promoted Squadron Leader in 1935 and served in the Second Mohmand Campaign of 1935. He was awarded his first DSO for operations in Waziristan in 1938. He was further promoted in 1938 to Wing Commander. After five years service he returned to Britain in 1939.

The energetic Embry led 107 Squadron from the front and he saw extensive action during the campaigns in Norway and France, often in the face of heavy losses and overwhelming opposition. On 25 September 1939 Embry led a 3-plane formation on a reconnaissance sortie into Germany. Intercepted by German fighters, Embry's aircraft suffered serious damage to wings and fuselage and he carried out a one-wheel force-landing landing on returning to RAF Wattisham. Throughout the remainder of 1939 and into early 1940 the unit made numerous attacks by day and night on a variety of targets, including U-Boats.

Embry had been leading twelve Blenheims when they flew into the expected curtain of flak en route to bomb German troop concentrations near St Omer. Embry was on his last sortie as CO of 107 Squadron before handing over to Wing Commander L. R. Stokes. Embry's Blenheim (L9391) was severely damaged and Corporal G. E. Lang DFM, his WOp/AG was killed. Embry was described by aircrew as a 'little ball of fire'. AC1 D. M. Merrett, an armourer in 107 Squadron at the time, wrote that 'For us the 'Phoney War' never existed; due in large part to Embry's terrific drive. He realised right from the start that the war would have to be pursued relentlessly and within his powers as a squadron commander he ensured that this was done. Embry expected everyone to match his own fierce energy and enthusiasm: a tall order. He commanded the greatest respect and admiration but not in my view at least, affection. 'Battle Orders' were issued almost daily and the squadron was constantly on operations, although this did not invariably result in bombs being dropped because targets were not always reached or located. This increased the armourers work, for aircraft returning with bombs had to be de-bombed and there was considerable changing of bomb loads as different targets were selected by 2 Group.'

Embry led twelve Blenheims on 27 March 1940 when he sighted a German cruiser and four destroyers about seventy miles NNW of the Hrons Reef in the Heligoland Bight. The formation followed the ships and four minutes later sighted most of the German Fleet on its way to support the invasion of Norway. An attack was made out of the sun, engaging the *Scharnhorst* and *Gneisenau* and a message was sent giving the position and course of the Fleet. Because of poor communications, this information only reached the authorities when the aircraft landed back at Wattisham some hours later.

On 12 May twelve Blenheims on 107 Squadron led by Wing Commander Embry took off from Wattisham at 0810 hours and headed for bridges on the road from Maastricht to Tongres, which would be bombed from 6,000 feet, a height that Embry considered would be the most effective. Fifteen miles before the target the Blenheims too were fired at by anti-aircraft fire, which continued all the way to the target. However, despite this they flew on and dropped their bombs. One of the bridges was damaged but one Blenheim was shot down and every other aircraft was damaged during the run-in. Then the Bf 109s attacked, shooting down three of the remaining Blenheims; the eight survivors, though severely damaged, managed to make it back to Wattisham. On 22 May 59 Blenheims attacked the German columns advancing to the French coast Three aircraft were lost. Wing Commander Embry led 107 Squadron in an afternoon attack on troops closing in on Boulogne, hitting vehicles in the fields. The Squadron mounted a second attack that day in the same area and Embry led a third with 110 Squadron, making a dual attack on a German HQ at Ribeaucourt. With darkness and fog at Wattisham, landings were made at Manston in Kent.

On 27 May Embry bailed out of his Blenheim from about 4,000 feet and descended into an orchard near St. Omer. He was unhurt except for a piece of shell which had lodged in the fleshy part of his leg. Pilot Officer T. A. Whiting DFC, his observer, bailed out also and was captured. At first Embry's wound gave him little trouble. Many Germans were in and around the orchard, so there was no chance of evasion and he was soon in their hands. Once they learned his rank he was treated with becoming dignity and in due course was transported in General Guderian's own staff car to the German HQ. Here he was put in charge of a young staff officer who spoke excellent English and was responsible for Embry's safe retention. It was also this officer's job to extract as much military information from his guest as could be obtained by tactful means. That evening they had dinner together and over a bottle of wine swapped lies till midnight. Embry at any rate drew freely on an extensive imagination and doubtless the German did the same. The rather tough examination of prisoners which was usual in the latter part of the war was not then part of the German system. Embry had a particularly nimble brain, so it is more than probable that he deceived the Germans on many points and gave nothing away.

Next day, after an uncomfortable night in a stable, Embry was removed from headquarters in a staff car, decanted from this into a lorry and finally arrived at a dirty prisoner-of-war cage walking on his flat feet in the pouring rain. Conditions in all German concentration camps were much the same, for it is probable that the Germans never anticipated capturing so many prisoners, particularly French prisoners, who were invariably treated far better than the British.

Embry and Flight Lieutenant Wilfred Patrick Francis 'Treacle' Treacy decided that they would escape together at the first available opportunity. Treacy, one of fourteen Irishmen who were RAF pilots in WWII, had joined 74 Squadron with Pilot Officer Bryan Vincent `Paddy` Byrne and Sailor Malan and was B Flight commander at the beginning of the war. In spring 1940 Treacy flew a Spitfire and saw combat on 24 May with an Hs 126 and a Ju 88. He was reported as bailing out of K6992 South of Dunkirk the next day but he returned by boat. Two days' later, on 27 May, his fighter patrol was patrolling over Dunkirk and Boulogne when off Calais they sighted three Dornier 17s, two of which were shot down, whilst the third made an attempt to escape inland followed by Treacy. About 40 miles inside the coast, Treacy opened fire again and last saw the Dornier with its port engine on fire, circling slowly to earth. At the same time he noticed a strong smell of glycol coming from his Spitfire and so turned instantly for home. His best chance was to attempt to reach British troops in Dunkirk. At first he mistook Calais for Dunkirk and it was not until he was some ten miles from Calais, flying very low, with an engine seizing badly, that he realised his mistake. He turned immediately eastwards, but, as he presented a very easy target for low flak, he was hit repeatedly and forced to twist and turn. This operation finally removed any chance he might have had of reaching the lines to the north and he had no option but to make a 'wheels up' landing half a mile south of Gravelines. He was unhurt, but was immediately surrounded by German flak gunners who were very pleased with themselves for a success for which they took the full credit. A sergeant said something to him in German and when Treacy shrugged his shoulders and looked blank, the sergeant walked round behind him and kicked him and continued to kick him until his officer, who had been watching with an amused smile on his face, told him to desist. Treacy was not the type of man to let little incidents of this sort fade from his memory. Shortly afterwards, a car with a German captain and a doctor arrived. The captain produced a slab of Cadbury's chocolate and breaking it into about twenty small pieces, gave one to each of the gunners as a reward.

Treacy was questioned by an interpreter on the lawn of a big house at Oye-Plage (Pas-de-Calais) south of Dunkirk which had been taken over by the Luftwaffe headquarters staff, but he refused to give more than his name, rank and number. The Germans, said the interpreter, would be in England in a month. It would not be necessary to force a crossing of the Channel as air attack would be sufficient to compel surrender. When France had been beaten and Paris entered, the Italians would enter the war. Only the north of France would be occupied by German troops; the south of France would remain free, for Germany had no serious quarrel with France and would only take from her Alsace and Lorraine. Why, he asked Treacy, were the British bombers dropping bombs and incendiaries on the Ruhr, where there were no military targets? Why did the British wireless continue to broadcast nothing but lies? Treacy felt it politic to make no reply. With two French officers, for whom the interpreter expressed open contempt, Treacy was removed in a car to Desvres 45 kilometres south of Oye. During the drive a sentry with a sub-machine gun stood with his back to the windscreen, but as it was after 8.30 pm when they left the Luftwaffe headquarters, Treacy had high hopes of not reaching their destination before dark and so of finding an opportunity to escape. This would almost certainly have happened but when they lost their way, the French officers, to Treacy's intense disgust, asked obligingly for directions from the natives. The French morale at that time and more particularly among the officers was deplorable.

At Desvres their driver had the greatest difficulty in finding anyone who would accept his prisoners. They visited infantry, tank and even Luftwaffe units, but all refused to guard them for the night. Finally they were put in an attic with a tiny window at the top of a three-storied house, where they passed a comfortable night. Next day they were taken to the football stadium. The British officers occupied the grandstand and there Treacy found Flying Officer P. Casenove on 92 Squadron, who had force-landed his Spitfire I at Calais after combat with German fighters on 24 May. Whilst they were talking a German sentry came up and, telling Treacy by signs that he was to sit down, addressed him at considerable length. The substance of his remarks, kindly translated by a British officer, was: 'You English flying pig; you will be made to walk to Berlin and lick the boots of Field Marshal Hermann Goering.'

That evening the column of prisoners, nearly a mile long and which included Embry, Treacy and Instone left in the direction of Hucqueliers, which they reached about seven in the evening. There a priest interceded with the Germans and permission was given to the inhabitants to feed the prisoners. Some good hot soup and boiled potatoes made a great difference to their morale and to their strength. That night Embry and Treacy discussed the possibility of escape and decided to attempt it next day. All the prisoners were locked into the church. So crowded were they that there was hardly room to lie on the floor; it had also been pouring with rain and everyone was wet through, so that the unusual sight of a completely nude man asleep on the high altar was easily explained.

The column left Huequeliers about 5 am and at midday Embry asked Treacy whether he was ready to go. Treacy answered 'Yes,' so with nerves all taut for the coming attempt which at the best was highly dangerous and at the worst certain death they marched on, Treacy a pace or two ahead of Embry. This column of prisoners was particularly well guarded; very little straggling was permitted and when the column passed through woods or villages there was always a marked increase in the activity and vigilance of the guards. It seemed as though deliberate efforts were being made to break the spirit of the men. The marches were dragged out interminably and for the first five days, little or no food was given to the British. If any man fell out, he was encouraged to continue with the butt end of a rifle; if water was offered by the villagers, who frequently stood by the roadside with buckets in their hands; it was dashed to the ground by the guards. Often there were tears in the eyes of the French women as they watched this pathetic column of exhausted men stagger by. The British brought up the rear and on the few occasions when soup was available during halts, it was given first to the French and little, if any, reached the British end of the column. Gordon Instone was twice struck with a rifle butt and was only saved by his helmet from serious injury. Most of the men had already been fighting for several days with practically no food or sleep before the march started in the sweltering heat and it was only natural that morale should have become exceedingly low as a result. Even so, they were greatly cheered when an RAF fighter appeared overhead chasing a German bomber which it shot down very neatly into a wood half a mile away. When three cheers broke out at this heartening sight, the Germans were furious and threatened to shoot.

At the head of the column there was a lorry on which was mounted a machine gun and crew, followed at about a 150 yard interval by other lorries, also with machine guns and so on, down the column - the tail being brought along and stragglers rounded up by a few troops with rifles and Tommy guns. A sidecar combination on which a machine gun was mounted was attached to the column. This man's operational method was to come past the prisoners from behind and then to take up a convenient position from where he could watch the prisoners pass. He would then repeat the manoeuvre. The impression that this made upon a prisoner was of a succession of motor-cyclists passing the column at frequent intervals, though in reality it was always the same man. Embry and Treacy soon came to the conclusion that the best time to make an attempt to escape was when the column was marching on a long, straight road, for that was the only time when the attention of the guards relaxed. The two men were being marched along one of the poplar-lined roads, keyed up to take the first chance that offered, when Embry saw at the side of the road a signpost on which was written his own name; marvellous to relate, there was a village called Embry. He instantly decided that this was his cue and without hesitation dived out of the column and lay still in the ditch at the side of the road. Cover was of the poorest and he was exposed to view, but no one had seen him go. Dead men at the side of the road were not an uncommon sight, so the column moved on and left him lying there unnoticed. Treacy recalled that Embry dived from the column like a shot out of a gun and left him 'all standing.' About a hundred yards further on Treacy threw himself into a ditch at the side of the road and lay under a bush unseen while the column moved by. Whilst the column was still in sight the double escape was discovered by the Germans. Treacy saw the column halt. There was much shouting and running up and down and reforming the lines; but the guards dared not leave the column in order to make a search, so the column at last moved on again and out of sight. When it was dark Treacy went back to look for Embry, but failed to find him, so, using the stars as a guide, he set off southwards. He chose a southerly direction because he thought it would be easier to cross the enemy lines on the Somme rather than through the besieging forces around Dunkirk. He was dressed in uniform, flying boots, but had no hat.

Meanwhile, Embry lay in an uncomfortable and exposed position by the main road on which there was a considerable amount of German traffic. The only cover he could see was a wood 300 yards away across a field. He determined to make an attempt to reach the wood. In the field was an old woman milking a cow and it now appeared that she alone had seen his escape from the column, for she looked towards him as he started to crawl and then signalled to him with her hand when he should move forward and when he should lie still. Thus, by slow degrees and largely owing to the courageous help of this old woman, he edged himself across the field till at last he reached the cover of the wood.

The next ten days were pretty grim. That part of the country where he found himself was infested with Germans; they seemed to be in every farm-house and almost in every wood and the peasants and small farmers were usually too frightened to give help. He found great difficulty in getting food and reasonable civilian clothes, without which it was impossible to move about in the day-time. At last he acquired a pair of blue trousers from a farmer and took an old coat off a scarecrow and, thus equipped, made better progress. During these ten days Embry seldom entered a house. The weather was often wet and to add to his troubles he was in great pain from the wound in his leg. As there was no chance of any proper medical assistance, he was compelled to operate on his leg with a penknife; a most unpleasant and painful experience which exhausted him so much that he lay up for two days in a wet wood, trying to recover his strength and almost unable to move. There is no doubt that Embry must have been exceptionally tough to have survived those ten days. Starving, wet through continually, with a painful wound, alone in a country crawling with Germans, his position was pretty desperate. Whatever were his thoughts during those desperate days, about a fortnight after his escape from the column he was walking south along the roads of France, clad in blue trousers and scarecrow coat and apparently completely recovered. Embry's normal appearance was not such as would mark him as particularly

British. On the contrary, in non-British clothes he would pass easily as a native in almost any part of the continent of Europe. He was about 5 feet 8 inches in height, with a well-knit frame and square, powerful shoulders. He was very dark, with thick black hair and a complexion to match. A notable feature were his eyes which were blue and singularly bright and he had the habit of fixing anyone to whom he spoke with a penetrating and, until you were used to it, an almost embarrassing gaze. In the nondescript clothing such as he wore on his walk through France, he would pass naturally as a bombed-out refugee (of which numbers were wandering about), without arousing the least suspicion and this was the role he adopted.

From time to time he was stopped by German controls and asked for his papers, but for the most part these incidents presented no serious difficulties to an unusually intelligent man whose appearance was in his favour. When questioned he would throw up his arms and in passable French, give a harrowing if incoherent description of the destruction of his village by German bombs. 'No, he had no papers; they had all been blown up together with his wife and family and now he was hunting for his old mother who had last been heard of in this district.'

His story passed muster without much difficulty. There were so many refugees that it was impossible for the normal German to distinguish the false from the true. One day he was passing through a village in his usual inconspicuous way when he heard behind him the ringing footsteps of three men marching in step. He stood aside to let them pass. To his dismay, he realised instantly that the men were British Tommies, dressed; it is true, in civilian clothes, but marching straight to captivity. He took the great risk of stopping them and giving them some sane advice, but unfortunately they had already drawn suspicion upon themselves. A few minutes later, Embry and the three soldiers were arrested and separated from each other. Embry was brought before a German officer to whom he explained as usual, that he was a Belgian refugee. To his horror the German, who turned out to be an interpreter, addressed him in fluent and seemingly perfect French without, as yet showing any signs of disbelief. Embry felt that this could not continue and in order to cover his own poor French, quickly explained that his native tongue was Flemish. The interpreter instantly addressed him in Flemish, of which language Embry knew not one single word. The situation was desperate. 'Hush,' said Embry, taking the interpreter aside, 'I must confess I have not been telling the truth. I am a Gael.'

'A Gael? What's that? I've never heard of one,' answered the astonished interpreter. 'Where do they come from?'

'From Southern Ireland,' said Embry, inventing rapidly.

'Well, that's interesting. But what are you doing here? '

'Hush, I'm running away from the London Police. I have been in England, blowing up pillar boxes and the police are on my track.'

'Grand fellow,' said the interpreter patting him on the back enthusiastically. 'Good luck to your great work. You talk Gaelic, of course?' he added, as a slight suspicion entered his mind.

'Naturally,' said Embry, 'it is my native tongue.'

'Well, say something in Gaelic then,' the interpreter told him.

Without hesitation Embry proceeded to let off the few sentences in Urdu which he knew by heart as the result of a sojourn in the East.

'Good,' said the interpreter, 'that's Gaelic. I speak a little myself.' To his great surprise, Embry found himself once more free to continue his journey towards Paris.

Embry seems to have passed through a country infested with Germans with little difficulty and it was an ill chance that landed him once more in the hands of the enemy. He had just swum the Somme and was crossing a field when, in the dark, he ran straight into a number of German soldiers. He was instantly collared and beaten up and finally, after a most unpleasant and painful experience was taken before a German officer to whom he told his usual and now familiar, tale. The German made the following answer.

'I don't believe a word of what you say. I think you are a British officer trying to escape. You are in civilian clothes so that, if you are what I think you are, you will be shot as a spy tomorrow.'

After these discouraging remarks, Embry was led away to a large farm-house which proved to be a German HQ. The building formed three sides of a square and the fourth side consisted of a wall in which was the main gate. In the middle of the court-yard was an enormous manure heap on which ducks, chickens and pigs roamed at will. About mid-day, Embry was deposited in a small room, normally used for storage purposes. A sentry was placed over the door and a second sentry stood in the courtyard outside the only exit. After carefully considering his position, Embry came to the conclusion that his chances of being shot the following morning were distinctly promising; for the possibility of passing successfully through an interrogation made by a competent man who spoke French well, was almost nil. His story would be exposed as a lie and with the German suspicions aroused, he could think of no other story likely to hold water. He could talk no other language but English sufficiently well to pass as a native. He had been caught in the German lines dressed in civilian clothes, so he could see no good reason why he should not be shot as a spy. He asked his sentry for a glass of water and when he returned with it, hit him as hard as he could on the point of the jaw, killing him. Just outside the exit into the court-yard was a second sentry with his back towards him. As Embry came out, the man turned and at that moment Embry hit him with his full force on the side of the head with the butt of the rifle. His head caved in and Embry rushed along the side of the building towards the gate, clutching the rifle. There was no one about in the court-yard. Just as he came to a passage between the two buildings, a German soldier came round the corner carrying two buckets of water and stood for a second, a look of intense astonishment on his face. Embry hit him, too, in the same manner and with the same result and then dived into the manure heap and dug a passage for himself through the straw and well into the muck. It was not long before the hue and cry started, but no one thought of the manure heap. Many hours later, during the night, he crawled out of the manure and got out of the court-yard without being observed. Once more he was on the roads of France, making his way toward Paris in close company with the German army, also marching in the same direction. One cannot help imagining that he smelt strongly of manure.

A few days later he found an old bicycle shop full of odds and ends and bits of bicycles. After two days hard work, he constructed a bicycle out of odd pieces and on it made much more rapid progress until the bicycle was commandeered from him by a German soldier. At this time his wounded leg began to swell up and give him great pain. Nevertheless he finished the journey to Paris on foot. Paris was full of German troops, but Embry passed inconspicuously, a dirty, ragged, limping figure, through the streets. For some reason he had great difficulty in finding the American Embassy. When at last he succeeded in finding it, he put on a slight American accent and attempted to pass himself off as a citizen of the USA who had been bombed-out and overwhelmed by the advancing German armies. He was interviewed by a sharp young American girl who mistrusted either his accent or his story and accused him without hesitation of being a British officer in disguise. When he confessed the truth, he was told that it was not in the power of the Embassy to give him much help. He was lent a few hundred francs with the advice to apply to the Salvation Army HQ. His subsequent adventures in Paris are complicated and obscure. For several days he was locked up in a barred cage under stinking conditions, with all the riff-raff of the criminal underworld. For many days he walked the streets disclosing his identity to prosperous-looking Frenchmen and borrowing money from them. He also entered shops and asked them to lend him money. Money was a necessity, either for purposes of bribery or to enable him to obtain a bicycle.

At last, after a terrible time in Paris he, by some means, got hold of a bicycle and in one day rode to the neighbourhood of Tours, a distance of 145 miles. This was a truly remarkable performance because his leg, now swollen to double its normal size, was giving him great pain. At Limoges he was given help by some French officers, but by now his leg was so bad he could hardly walk. He went into hospital for a few days, but dared not stay, because the Germans might arrive in the town at any time, so with French help he went on, in spite of his condition, to Toulouse and thence to Marseilles. With a special pass obtained from French friends he journeyed to a small port on the coast near Perpignan, where he and two other escapers attempted to steal a boat with the object of reaching Barcelona. They were arrested by the French police and spent the night with the Foreign Legion. By this time his physical condition was really desperate and he began to wonder whether, even if he succeeded in escaping, he would not lose his leg, or possibly his life. When he had reached the very limit of his endurance and was no longer capable of physical exertion, help arrived and he reached England with unusual speed where, owing to his magnificent constitution, he recovered rapidly.[4]

In spite of his exhaustion and in spite of what he had already been through, Gordon Instone somehow retained sufficient strength and courage to make two attempts to escape. In the first he was discovered crawling through a hedge during a temporary halt. He was thrown roughly back into the column and warned that he would be shot if he attempted to escape again. The second and successful escape took place in broad daylight while they were passing through a village near St. Pol. There was a stream running by the side of the road and Instone, seizing a favourable moment, plunged into it and hid in the rushes. For an hour he remained up to his neck in water, his face plastered with mud, whilst an intensive search was carried out in the barns and hedges in the neighbourhood. At last the Germans gave it up and the column moved on. Emerging very cautiously from his muddy bath, Instone made his way across a couple of fields to a barn a few hundred yards distant.

There, after narrowly avoiding two German soldiers, he was discovered by a farmer, but, there being a German headquarters in the village, he was too frightened to help either with food or clothes and was only anxious that Instone should depart quickly. Instone at that time was in a pitiable state. He was still in battle dress but so dirty as to be almost unrecognisable as a British soldier. From lack of food and from the long marches, he had almost reached the limit of his strength. He had made no plans and found it difficult to solve the problem of where to go next. Holland and Belgium had been invaded; to reach Switzerland he must pass through most of the Wehrmacht; Spain was nearly 500 miles away. After much thought he decided to head for the north of France in the hopes of getting a boat or even of making a raft on the chance he might be picked up by the Royal Navy. His decision made, he lay down on a heap of straw and went to sleep. At midnight he roused himself and although still unbelievably weary, started on his long and lonely trek towards the coast. The days which followed differed little one from the other except in degrees of hunger, cold and exhaustion. He had no map, so he steered by the stars or used his watch and the sun as a compass. He fed on raw vegetables and slept in the woods during the day; at night he pushed on across the fields, realising that he could not go on much longer because his last strength was ebbing fast. After crossing a river near Hesdin, he came upon a friendly farmer. For the first time for many days he had a good meal and a long sleep in safety and warmth.

Next day, dressed now in blue workman's overalls instead of his battle dress blouse, he continued his march, feeling marvellously refreshed and encouraged. He even felt cheerful enough to undertake offensive action against the enemy when opportunity offered. Finding a German telephone cable, he disconnected the aluminium sockets, removed the terminals and re-assembled the line, thus concealing the break. He passed a German sentry without arousing suspicion by pretending he had a wooden leg. But, though temporarily cheered by these minor successes, soon a desperate weariness came upon him again. Finally he developed a high fever from prolonged exposure and exhaustion and was taken into a home for the aged and imbeciles where he was given food, medical attention and put to bed in an attic. By 4 June, having been in bed a week, he had recovered sufficiently to walk about in the grounds. On that particular day some German medical officers were visiting the home seeking additional accommodation for their wounded. Instone mingled with the inmates and shammed insanity with such success that one of the German medical officers expressed sorrow that one so young should be thus demented! The superintendent of the hospital was very friendly and he informed Instone that a RAF officer was being hidden at a farm near the village of Buire-le-Sec (Pas-de-Calais). Instone at that time was feeling desperately lonely; he yearned for English companionship. So, borrowing a bicycle, he rode to Buire-le-Sec and started to look for the farm where the RAF pilot was supposed to be in hiding. He saw, standing in the doorway of a farm-house a 'farm boy' well over six feet tall, wearing clothes which fitted him so badly that the sleeves were nearly up to the elbows and the trousers little below the knees. Instone guessed at once that this must be the Englishman. In this however he was quite wrong for Flight Lieutenant 'Treacle' Treacy was an Irishman if ever there was one.

'You're British?' said Instone and the two shook each other warmly by the hand. For the first time for many weeks Instone and Treacy were happy. Retiring to the little garden behind the farm, they exchanged the stories of their adventures.

After his escape, Treacy's had gone about two miles across country and was about to cross a sunken road when, right underneath him, he saw about twenty or thirty motor vehicles drawn up. 'I skirted round these and continued my way south. Then I came to some houses. When crossing a field near the houses a terrific clamour suddenly broke out. This was caused by three Germans not more than about ten yards away from me. Two were fighting and shouting, punching each other and the third was trying to keep them quiet by shouting ' Hush ' at the top of his voice. They never saw me at all and shortly went back to their billets. I continued on south. Soon the sky had begun to cloud over and I could not use the stars. When dawn came and the sun rose I found I had walked in a circle.

'I decided to hide myself in the hay in a barn. The first barn entered was full of Germans, but they did not see me. Eventually I found an empty barn and went to sleep under the hay. I had a couple of biscuits and about ten lumps of sugar. That day a German entered the barn with a dog and the dog sniffed the hay about me, but the German called him off. That night I came out and went to the farmhouse which was only a few yards away from the barn. I asked for a glass of water. They gave me milk, chocolate, a loaf of bread and a tin of sardines. I continued south the next night. After about midnight the sky clouded over and again at dawn I found I had walked in a circle. I made my way to another farm and hid myself in a cartload of straw. The farmer found me there and gave me a suit of civilian clothes. This farm was halfway between Campagne-les-Hesdin and Buire-le-Sec (Pas-de-Calais).

'I lay there all day while German artillery passed, going south towards the Somme. Next night I set off again, going south and had the same weather; fine to midnight, when it clouded over so that I made very little progress. I made my way to a farm and lay there in some loose hay and next afternoon was found by the farmer's wife. She asked me who I was and I told her. That night she brought me into the house and gave me food. They kept me there, though the place was entirely surrounded by Germans. I lay there in the loose hay for three days and every day the Germans came in and took handfuls of it away and every night the farmer and his wife came and put some more back again. Then I moved up into a loft, where I stayed for another three days. At this time the Germans left this village to go south. It would then be about June 3rd or

4th.'

Treacy and Instone planned to escape together and they decided to make for Camiers on the coast and to meet again in a week's time after they had collected the necessary kit. But the Germans were intent on moving all French males of military age to Germany, so that it was thought advisable for Instone to move to a more secluded farm belonging to the Duvier family at Campagne-lès-Hesdin where he bedded down behind bales of straw in the hayloft. He became fully occupied, not only on the farm and with housework of every description; from feeding the pigs to making the bread, but also fell in love with Yvonne the Duvier's 19-year old daughter, a love which was fully reciprocated. Convent educated, Yvonne was a tall, long-legged girl of about 19 with a fresh complexion sprinkled with freckles, large grey eyes and a mass of honey-coloured hair. Where her cotton dress opened at the neck, her throat showed strong and sun-tanned. He on the other hand had a gingerish beard, long matted hair, filthy clothes and a rank smell. She thought he was an old man until he cleaned himself up and put on a new shirt. Then she told him, 'Tu es jeune et vraiment beau (You are young and really handsome').

Instone found the parting from Yvonne and her parents by no means easy, when on the morning of 10 June he and Treacy, now well equipped for the adventure, set out fort Camiers. After an arduous march, they reached the village only to find it full of German troops and the coast heavily guarded. The chance of getting hold of a boat seemed hopeless. However, they walked on into the village fearing that, if they turned back suddenly, it might arouse suspicion. Passing a German HQ and several sentries they were at last stopped by a German soldier. Instone, who now spoke French extremely well; persuaded the man that they were refugees, but the German warned them to leave the next day. They then called on the mayor and disclosed their identity but he, having several Germans billeted on him, could give no help. Eventually they slept in a garage and only escaped from the town with much difficulty the following day. By this time Instone had developed a special technique for dealing with German sentries. He would walk up to them and speak to them sympathetically in French. This apparently so flattered them that he was invariably allowed to pass without being asked for his papers.

On the outskirts of the village, Instone and Treacy found a boat, but they saw a patrol approaching and realised that the only thing to be done was to retrace their steps twenty-five miles back to the farm whence they had started. Next day they arrived there, worn out and disheartened to find that a RAF bomber had been shot down in the neighbourhood. One of the crew was supposed by the Germans to be hiding in a farm nearby and a search was in progress. The Germans had arrested twenty boys; one from each of the farmhouses and threatened to shoot them if the missing pilot was not handed over within twelve hours. When Instone and Treacy heard of this, they offered to surrender, but the villagers indignantly refused to allow them to do so. Next day the boys were lined up for execution, in the village square, but after a tense and dramatic scene, during which two of the boys fainted, the execution was called off by the Germans. Perhaps it was never intended to be more than a threat. Owing to this incident, the whole district was highly dangerous for escapers. Instone, however, could not easily move. He had hardly recovered from his illness, his legs were swollen and his feet blistered as a result of the fifty mile march to Camiers and back; furthermore, owing to the excellence of his French, he was in much less danger than Treacy. With the greatest regret he and Treacy decided to part. Treacy once more headed southwards.

Instone headed back to the Duviers' farm. Yvonne was delighted to see him but the Germans were at that time collecting all Frenchmen and were threatening to shoot them if the crew of RAF aircraft that had crashed in the district were not handed over so Treacy decided to leave the Duvier family before it was too late. On 13 June he set off alone, Instone deciding to stay as he thought he was in less danger. After three nights Treacy reached Crècy where he decided to make for the coast again. Returning to Buire-le-Sec, Treacy met three soldiers of the Black Watch and on 3 July the four men headed for the Baie d'Authie near Berck-sur-Mer. Next day they explored the coast in broad daylight and actually found a boat. Then, since the Bay seemed deserted, they lay on the beach, resting and smoking, discussing how to make oars or get material for a sail. Unfortunately, but not unexpectedly, they were seen by a German patrol through binoculars and in due course four German soldiers arrived on bicycles. Treacy told them in a mixture of French and sign language that they were bombed-out natives of Tournai (a town which he knew had been sufficiently destroyed) and added that they had left at the last moment and had neither papers nor possessions. The Germans apparently believed this, but 'you may be saboteurs,' they said and searched them. All three men of the Black Watch had their pay books on them, which not unnaturally raised suspicion. On being searched again at Groffliers one of them was found to have a photograph of himself in uniform and a kilt, with 'Aldershot' stamped on the back. Even then the Germans were not sure, till one of the Tommies gave the show away by shaking his head in answer to the question, 'Are you an English soldier?'

Treacy remained on the doubtful list until an interpreter was found who spoke sufficiently good French to make further bluff impossible.

A few days later Treacy found himself once more in a concentration camp; this time in the Exhibition grounds at Lille with a number of British troops from Camiers. Treacy found a corrugated iron shed which had a hole in the wall backing on to the street. He managed to squeeze through the hole, so that within an hour or so of entering the camp he was free once more for the second time. Outside were a number of French people looking for relatives among the many French prisoners of war in the camp. He revealed his identity to one woman, telling her he had just left the camp and she found him a refuge in a private house where he stayed for five days. When he left he was given a bicycle, an identity card, some money, food and a map, as well as an address to go to in Fauquesberques. Once more he made his way to the Baie d'Authie, through a country in which every village was full of Germans. This time he made his reconnaissance of the bay under cover of darkness and after many nights of search he found a boat in the back of a farmyard on the River Authie. It was three feet wide, six feet long and blunt at both ends. He bought it for forty francs. In three days of hard work he made some oars and then with a compass and enough water to last for five days, with the help of the farmer, launched the boat during the night of 13/14 July and paddled off towards the open sea. There were sentries posted on two of the bridges under which he would have to pass, so he got the farmer to cover the boat with hay and thus, disguised as a haycock, floated down the river. The River Authie flows into the sea through numerous small channels which, when the tide is out, are shallow and very muddy. Treacy missed the main channel in the dark and had a long and exhausting struggle, lugging and sometimes carrying his heavy boat through the mud, so that it was not till half an hour after sunrise, instead of two hours before dawn that he reached the sea. It was impossible to wait till night because there was no shelter anywhere, so he decided to start immediately.

He was about a mile out from Berck-sur-Mer when he heard machine-gun fire. Splashes all around him indicated clearly enough that he was the target and though two machine-gun batteries in the dunes below Berck fired at him for almost half an hour, he was slowly creeping out of range and they failed to hit him. The gunners realised this and soon the one-sided contest neared its end as four heavier guns opened up. By now two miles or so off shore the Germans fired single shots at him for another half an hour, all falling fifty to 100 yards short, until eventually a splinter holed the boat above the water line. The German gunners, expecting Treacy to turn around and row back towards the shore, ceased firing for five minutes, but when he did not do so they opened up a more rapid fire for a further ten minutes. Then a mist descended. At around midday, however, now about ten miles west of le Touquet, Treacy was spotted by two German aircraft flying low over the water, obviously looking for him. One of them found him and turned towards him in a shallow dive. Thinking that he was about to open fire, Treacy dived overboard. When he came up the aircraft was flying low overhead. He saw the rear gunner wave at him, clearly indicating that he should get back into his boat, which was now about fifteen yards away. Treacy boarded his boat again with great difficulty and then, as the aircraft passed over him again, saw the observer pointing to the shore. Treacy perforce turned his boat and pretended to row landwards. But for every feeble stroke he made in that direction he gave a couple of back thrusts towards England, choosing each time a moment when the position of the aircraft made observation difficult. From time to time, as the aircraft passed over him, the rear gunner fired into the water behind him. This went on for half an hour, very little progress being made in either direction. Suddenly the aircraft flew off. Either they had run out of petrol or had perhaps decided that these operations were futile. Treacy, much relieved though extremely tired, turned the boat and rowed as hard as he could towards England, praying that the mist would come down again. It was not long before he was seen by a German seaplane. It landed beside him, picked him off and took him, once more, back to a German prison. The crew of the seaplane were very sore with the RAF because, they said, they had shot down some of their ambulance planes. To this accusation Treacy replied that we had still more reason to be angry because their submarines had sunk our hospital ships. This, of course, they refused to admit, but informed him that the war would be over in three months and that he would be home by Christmas.

The naval authorities at Boulogne were, according to Treacy, 'a sarcastic lot of gentlemen.' They told him they knew he had been given a book to read on escaping, but unfortunately, as he, Treacy, no doubt now realised, these rules for escaping did not work. When Treacy protested, quite correctly, that he had been given no instructions on escaping, they told him that if he tried any more silly tricks he would be shot without hesitation. Eventually he was taken to Le Touquet where he was interrogated by the Luftwaffe, who particularly wanted to know what he was doing in France and how he had got there. Oblivious or perhaps regardless of the fact that he stood an excellent chance of being shot out of hand as a spy, Treacy spun them a yarn which did not include the fact that he had already been taken prisoner twice before. His interrogators clearly did not believe this story and said so, but they were very pleased with themselves at capturing him and considered that he had 'put up a good show.' These pleasantries came to rather an abrupt end when a nasty-looking German, who up to that moment had not spoken, asked Treacy if he could identify himself. Treacy protested that he had no means of doing so. 'Then you will be treated as a spy,' was the answer.

That night he spent in Le Touquet gaol with two German airmen who had two days' confined to barracks for sleeping while on duty. Next day, 15 July, Treacy was again interrogated for several hours by the Luftwaffe. He persuaded them without much difficulty that he knew something about flying and gave his name, rank and number (the latter inadvertently wrong), but refused to give an account of his movements or to say how long he had been in France. They said they would check up on him by wireless to London.

Considering Treacy's very unconciliatory way of answering questions, it must be owned that the Germans, having decided that he was an English airman, behaved in a fairly reasonable manner. I cannot help wondering whether our authorities would have tolerated so much impudence from a German airman. However, instead of shooting him, they tried to break his morale. He was flung into a cell in which there was practically no light or air. There was no bedstead in the cell and no bedding of any kind. It was completely bare. In one corner there had been a lavatory, but all the lavatory fittings had been removed. In spite of this fact the French prisoners had continued to use it as a lavatory. Further details may be left to the imagination, but it suffices to say that the cell was indescribably filthy and stank abominably. For six days Treacy shared this foul cell with an infantryman from the KOYLI and a private of the Grenadier Guards. On 20 or 21 July all three were removed to Tournai. There they were forced to scrub the floors of the barracks. In spite of this hard treatment, Treacy's morale remained intact; he only loathed the Germans more and eagerly seized any opportunity for getting his own back. For instance, one day, when Treacy was scrubbing a floor in the barracks, a German electrician on a high ladder was mending a wire in the ceiling. The floor was wet and it only took a very light touch by Treacy to bring the electrician and the ladder crashing to the floor. Next day he saw the electrician with his arm in a sling. Treacy avoided any blame for this misadventure.

From Tournai they were taken to Renaix, where they spent the night in very dirty cells and the next morning joined forces with about 300 British soldiers from hospital who were going to Lokeran. On arrival there Treacy and three others were put into a small cell in the cloth factory which had been turned into a prison camp. Here they remained three days till they got a chance of complaining to the Red Cross and by their intervention were allowed out into the main camp. The Germans, however, took away their civilian clothes and forced them to wear Belgian uniforms. Fortunately they neglected to look into the two bags which Treacy was carrying, one of which contained a second suit of civilian clothes. I regret that I have never 'cleared up' this extraordinary incident, told me by Treacy himself. How could he, in the circumstances in which he had been living, have acquired two bags (one packed with civilian clothes) and having miraculously obtained them, how could he have passed them through a whole series of interrogations and cells unsearched? It is an unsolved mystery.

Amongst the British officers in the camp were two doctors, who, when they heard of Treacy's past adventures, produced from their kits a compass and a map of Belgium, which they generously gave him.

For a fortnight or more before coming to this camp Treacy had been kept on very short rations and in the camp the food was nothing like sufficient. One loaf of bread between four men, some ersatz coffee and a small cup of rice or peas was all they had. Treacy, though desperately hungry, was not yet seriously weak from lack of food. As some prisoners of war had previously escaped from Lokeran, the guards had lately been doubled, but instead of doubling the number of posts they had doubled the guard at each one with the result that the sentries, having friends to talk to, were even less dangerous to an escapee than they had been before.

Treacy's plan of escape was bold but simple. One of the rooms had a domed glass roof with iron girders beneath it. When the German sergeant in charge of the camp called for 'lights out,' two or three of the British officers, on the pretence of going out to the lavatory, got into this room and hoisted Treacy up so that he could grip the girders. He pulled himself up and then, by smashing one of the panes, got on to the roof of the building. It was a dark night, but nevertheless on the roof he was terribly exposed. He made his way with infinite caution to the edge of the flat roof and finally dropped to the ground without being heard or seen. From there he climbed a wall and found himself in the garden of a convent.

All this had not only required great skill, but also more than a fair share of luck. The sentries were mostly older men who had been prisoners in England during the last war. Rather unexpectedly they showed little enthusiasm for their work. In the convent garden Treacy changed into civilian clothes and leaving there without much difficulty, crossed the Escaut at 5 am by means of a ferry (the bridge having been blown up). He kept going southwards for the next two days and nights and eventually, worn out by hunger and fatigue, he was taken in and cared for by a Belgian in the district of Cysoing. Here he lay up for a week, gradually recovering his strength.

During the following eight weeks he stayed with a French family in the neighbourhood of Bouveries. He felt the hopelessness of trying to reach the north coast again and as yet he knew too little of the conditions in southern France. Where he was - working as a peasant on the land - he seemed fairly safe from capture. At that time some very curious rumours were whispered through France, based, as far as I know, on no foundation at all. Nearly all escapers in France were told by the peasants that in a few days, aeroplanes from England would land and rescue them. Very often the 'rendezvous' with the aeroplane was given in great detail, but usually the information was vague. Many escapers waited anxiously for days and were then told that the coming of the planes had been postponed. Again and again this happened. There is no question that those who passed on the rumours fully believed them to be correct. But who started the rumours and with what object, no one has yet found out. Treacy was warned many times to be ready to leave by plane and his decision to remain on the farm was partly due to the feeling that if a miraculous method of escaping by aeroplane had been 'laid on' he would be a fool to leave the district.

Instone, meanwhile, had been picked up in a café by a German officer. Instone was fully aware of this danger and had a well rehearsed story for such an eventuality. When interrogated he posed successfully as a Belgian refugee, but nevertheless, to his great disgust, he was pushed into a lorry with two German sentries and told that he was now on his way to a labour camp in Germany. After a journey of fifteen to twenty miles along country roads, Instone saw his chance and took it with a courage it is impossible to praise too highly. After all he had been through, he was prepared to take any risk to avoid the life of a slave labourer in Germany; the thought was quite intolerable. For a time he pretended to sleep, until he saw through his half-closed eyes, that one of the sentries was also dozing and the other, with his helmet on the floor and his rifle between his knees, was peacefully eating his rations. Picking up a portion of a wheel jack which lay behind him, Instone suddenly leapt up and with two blows killed both his guards. Fortunately, neither had time to cry out and the rattling of the lorry drowned the noise of these operations. The lorry continued at high speed. Instone then climbed on to the tailboard and as the vehicle slowed for a corner from there jumped on to the road. The fall dislocated his shoulder and lacerated his knees and elbows, but he reached the cover of some woods without being seen.

After half an hour's rest, he made off in the direction of Hesdin, back to his friendly farm. An elderly French couple took pity on him, sheltered him, clicked the shoulder bone back into place, let him rest and then sent him on his way. He set out thankful that his luck had held again. On arrival at Hesdin he learnt that a French lieutenant, Roger Creplet, had lately arrived and was also being hidden. A week later Instone and Creplet decided to make the journey to Paris together. During the 'Phoney War' Creplet had been one of the garrisons of the Maginot Line and only a few weeks before he met Instone had returned to Paris on short leave and there married a young wife. Naturally Paris, in spite of its occupation by the Germans, drew him as a magnet. It is also probable that, for a Frenchman, Paris was the safest place to hide and if it was safe for a Frenchman, why not for Instone, who by now talked French well enough to pass as a Frenchman with any German who was not a skilled interpreter? So the two set off for Paris together. On the whole it was a pleasant journey of nearly 200 kilometres and it took them about a fortnight. They travelled mostly by day, sleeping in barns and feeding on fresh fruit and raw vegetables, though sometimes they obtained food and lodging in the villages. They crossed the Seine in a dinghy in the company of three German soldiers on leave (paying two francs for the trip) and that night reached the small town of St. Germain and lodged in a cafe.

Getting into Paris presented some difficulties because all the roads were closely barricaded. They succeeded finally by approaching the driver of one of the fifty police vans which were running a shuttle service, bringing refugees out of Paris and setting them on the road twenty miles to the north. Instone and Creplet told the driver that they were two escaped French soldiers. He then agreed to 'arrest' and take them into the city. The Germans searched the van at the barriers, but merely thought they were two convicts. For the next two months, July and August, Instone worked in Paris. For most of the time he lived with Roger Creplet and his wife, passing off in the neighbourhood as a cousin. In the daytime he worked as a fitter in a garage where German ambulances were repaired. How he was able to work or buy food or even exist in moderate safety without correct papers, it is difficult to understand. At night, after his labours for the Germans, he frequently salved his conscience by doing skilful damage to the telephone system. Being an electrician he was therefore also a capable saboteur. He also acted as a maid of all work in the Creplet ménage, washing up, cooking the dinner and last but not least, standing in the endless food queues in the Paris market. He joined heartily in the standard Paris amusement of misdirecting Germans and spent some of his spare time in the museums and the art galleries where endless parties of German soldiers on leave were conducted round by French guides; in fact he faded into the normal Parisian life of those days and appears to have aroused no one's suspicions. There is no escaper that I know of, who had quite Instone's flair for camouflage. From the first, he never had the least difficulty in passing German sentries and nor did his quick wit and sound judgment ever fail him. At the same time he was prepared, if the occasion required it, to take drastic and decisive action almost regardless of the risk involved. Each desperate deed was accompanied by cunning and judgment of a high order.

His two escapes, one from the column and the other from the lorry, were admirable instances of his ability to combine daring with skill. In Paris he quickly learnt to talk French well and also made the fullest use of his abilities as a mechanic and electrician. One day, when talking to some French soldiers, he learnt that the Germans had set up a demobilisation bureau for French soldiers in the Place de la Concorde so He visited the HQ and by questioning those who had been through this 'sausage machine' got minute details of the discharge papers, ration card and a travel permit required and the questions which were asked. These papers were so numerous and the questions asked so pertinent, that the hope of passing successfully would be small but all the information required was condensed on to one relatively small piece of paper, which Instone, with great labour and the help of his host's typewriter, proceeded to forge. He then filled in suitable answers in indisputably French handwriting. Finally, with the help of a raw potato, he fixed the necessary stamp and filled in the colonel's signature in blue ink, on the basis that the more different coloured inks there are, the more authentic a form will appear. With this document (in which he had incidentally promoted himself to sergeant) he presented himself at the second stage of the demobilisation 'machine,' having skipped the first. In a small office at the local police station, before a German corporal and a French policeman, he was officially demobilised and given 200 francs. Later he was given a further 800 francs together with a ration card, permet de travail and permet de domicile. His position was now practically impregnable, for his papers were in order; they were not even forgeries. He now felt himself adequately equipped to leave Paris and to try to reach Marseilles.

On 8 September he set out alone and after a tedious and rather miserable march reached Châlons-sur-Saone on the 21st of that month. Hunger, cold, wet clothes and blistered feet never worried him seriously, but the lack of company depressed his spirit and lowered his morale. Knowing little about the line of demarcation, he decided that it would be easier and safer to cross in the daytime. Perhaps he thought there might be fewer sentries, or that if stopped he could, with his perfect French and perfect papers, bluff it out with ease. Actually the line of demarcation was never difficult to cross if the available facilities were employed. On each side of the line in nearly every village guides could be found who for a fee, which varied from a few francs to a few thousand francs, would conduct individuals or even small parties over the line at very small risk. The basis on which the fees were computed was a rough means test, but escaping combatants either paid half the price or were taken over for love.

Advancing with great caution, Instone reached what he believed to be unoccupied France where his papers passed their first scrutiny by a German NCO and a French policeman but they were not valid once he was beyond the demarcation line. The unoccupied part of France, though administered from Vichy, had very little real independence. German soldiers patrolled both sides of the border - as Gordon Instone quickly discovered. It was a mistake for British evaders to assume every French man or woman they met would be their ally And they could never be sure whose side the officials and police of the Vichy-run French government were on. Two German soldiers stopped Instone and ordered him back into the occupied zone. In spite of all his protests and indignation, Instone was led across some fields and along railway sidings into the waiting-room of Châlons-sur-Marne railway station. Here he was questioned by a German officer. Instone produced his papers and told a piteous story of his wife and child, who he said, were dying in Lyons hospital. He got no sympathy. He was told that, as he was of military age and had broken German demobilisation orders in crossing the line without special permission, he would be sent as a labourer to Germany. Once again he was under lock and key with two sentries outside the door. For a time he waited miserably for the morning train to Paris but he was determined to make one more effort for freedom. Although he had been searched, his satchel, which contained a reserve of civilian clothes, maps, compass, shaving kit and tinned food was left on the floor of the waiting room unnoticed.

That evening he kicked on the door until an officer appeared and speaking in French begged to be allowed to buy food at the station buffet. After some hesitation the officer gave consent. Instone sauntered out of the door and down the platform as casually as he could, trying not to draw attention to himself. The buffet was crowded with French civilians and German soldiers who had apparently just come off guard duty. One of Instone's sentries waited outside the door and the other came in with him. Seizing an opportunity when the inside sentry was engaged in conversation, he slipped out of the door back on to the platform. By great good luck the sentry outside, though only two feet away, had his back turned and was momentarily engaged in trying to keep the entrance to the buffet clear. Quickly and silently Instone slipped along the platform till he came to a door with a notice in German written on it. There was no time to hesitate. He opened the door and went in, shutting it quietly behind him. It was apparently a German mess, for six officers were sitting at a table drinking beer. They looked up in surprise. Though seriously shaken, not for a second did Instone hesitate; it was essential that he should look as if he had a right to be there. He was an electrician, he told himself and he had come to mend the light. In his blue workman's overall and carrying his satchel, he was well dressed to play the part. He walked up to the electric light on the far wall, took out the bulb and cleaned the shade. He then fiddled with the switch for a moment or two in a professional manner and finally reassembled the light. After demonstrating that the light now worked perfectly, he bowed to the officers and walked out again on to the platform. To his intense relief his two sentries were three platforms away on the other side of the station but almost immediately they spotted him. One blew a whistle. Luckily, a goods train was then pulling in and prevented them from crossing the line. They dived down the subway between the platforms. The few minutes' respite was what Instone needed. He ran for his life and as he did so he could hear the sentries shouting and the echoing of their boots as they clattered down the subway in his direction. Instone raced down the platform to where a number of country women were removing some cases from a railway wagon. Instone rushed headlong towards them and pushed his way in among them, panting out urgently: 'Evade anglais! Aidez-moi, s'il vous plait.' The women heard the shouts and running feet of the German guards and, taking in the situation, they all closed in around him in a second. He bent down low, concealed by their long skirts, ample figures and their large market baskets held high above him and they all passed down the platform together and out of the station in a little convoy with Instone in the middle, through a small gate and out onto the road beyond. Once outside, he mingled with civilians and made his way rapidly to the outskirts of the town. Passing half a dozen sentries with all his old cunning, Instone reached the demarcation line for the second time in twelve hours. Here he fell in with two French labourers and, for a fee of a hundred francs, was conducted across the line without serious difficulty. To make sure he was really over it, he asked a boy the time, there being an hour's difference between German summertime and the time in unoccupied France. From the boy's answer he knew he was safe. But he was far from free.

As the German army advanced through Europe they pushed before them a mass of refugees of many nationalities who converged on Marseilles in the hope of escaping by sea. Towards the end of 1940 escape by boat was nearly impossible and escape via Spain was both difficult and expensive. Though money could buy most things in Marseilles, successful escape was by no means assured even by the most lavish expenditure. To get out of France legitimately, through Spain and Portugal, exit visas had to be procured from all three governments and though much could be done by bribery, the credentials of very few refugees could bear close inspection. In order to escape illegally over the mountains one had to trust oneself to the smugglers, most of whom blood-sucking blackmailers; who alone knew the mountain paths. Besides refugees, numerous escapers and evaders from the northern battles had crossed into Vichy France, only to be imprisoned by the French in conditions which gradually increased in severity. To these refugees and escapers must be added an astonishing mixture of spies, agents, deserters and criminals of every description. Marseilles, always notorious as a city of intrigue and wickedness, was now more than worthy of its reputation.

Though the Vichy government broke off diplomatic relations with Britain as a result of the attack on French shipping at Oran, the attitude of its officials in Marseilles remained ambiguous. In theory the British servicemen were now in a neutral country and should be interned for the duration of the war. Indeed, new laws demanded every effort to stop them getting home. A key clause in the armistice agreement the Vichy government made with Berlin stated that 'the French government will prevent members of the armed forces leaving the country to England or to any other foreign country whatsoever'. Accordingly, on 14 July 1940 the Vichy government issued an order for all British servicemen at large to be interned in Fort St Jean, a medieval prison-like barracks in Marseilles harbour, where they shared their barracks with the French Foreign Legion. The internees received three meals a day and a generous ration of red wine receiving and they were allowed out into Marseilles in the evenings provided that they gave their parole and promised not to escape. The French cared very little if the prisoners made use of these opportunities to prepare escapes. Later, after a German mission had inspected the camp, conditions became more rigid.

Among those at Fort St. Jean was 'Treacle' Treacy, who on 16 October, bronzed and well from working on the land, had crossed the line of demarcation between Ste. Julien and Martin le Riviere to unoccupied France, where there were fewer Germans and where he might reasonably expect help from the inhabitants. He crossed without difficulty and to his surprise he found the French in Free France most unfriendly, but, after many complicated adventures, made his way via Limoges to Marseilles, where he was arrested and interned in Fort St. Jean. One day in November 1940 Treacy was talking with a group of fellow officers at Fort St. Jean when a voice said: 'Hello Pat'. Turning round, he saw that it was Gordon Instone, whom he had last seen in June in northern France. Instone had reached Marseille on 8 November. As with others before, he was advised to go to the Seamen's Mission and it was there one morning that a French gendarme told the assembled company that he was instructed by the Vichy Government on behalf of the German and

Italian Armistice Commissions, who objected to their presence in Marseille, to escort them to the Fort. Owing to his now fluent French, Instone was given the job of interpreter in the French commandant's office and was appointed as assistant to another senior British officer at Fort St Jean, Captain L.A. Wilkins, 2/5th West Yorkshire Regiment.

One escape attempt at this time involved three army officers who had pooled their resources and had, incredibly, bought a schooner for 100,000 francs and secretly provisioned with bread and water sufficient for about a hundred British soldiers for two or three days at sea in the Mediterranean where it was hoped that they would be picked up by a passing ship of the Royal Navy. It was surely the most ambitious escaping plan ever conceived. Elaborate arrangements had had to be made for the actual escape from the Fort of so large a number of men. The escapers were divided into parties of ten, each under an NCO; an interval of ten minutes being allowed between the departure of each party. On the night the escapers made their way through Marseilles and the docks to the agreed meeting-place a strong Mistral blew which made the scheme quite impracticable. After spending many hours cramped in a boathouse longing for the wind to drop, the escape was finally abandoned and all returned to the fort disappointed and depressed.

Pat Treacy told Instone that he had acquired a passport[5] and did he have any plans for escaping. Instone's reply was that a scheme was being hatched to get himself and three army sergeants to Spain over the Pyrenees, but they were short of money. Treacy promised to get two thousand francs to help Instone if he would agree to take two RAF sergeants with him as well and he agreed. Towards the end of December, however, Instone heard that Fort St Jean was to be closed at the beginning of January 1941 and all the British internees were to be transferred to the French military concentration camp at St. Hippolyte, near Nimes. Treacy and Instone decided to join up with others and attempt the dangerous and difficult winter crossing of the Pyrénées into Spain. On 25 December Instone handed in his parole to the French commandant, saying that he intended to escape and therefore no longer wished for special privileges. The commandant expressed considerable surprise, remarking that he could not understand the mentality of the British who attached so much importance to the letter of a contract and went to the trouble of handing in a small piece of paper before escaping. The plan was to take the train to Perpignan 25 miles from the frontier and cross the relatively low foothills at the eastern end of the Pyrénées and reach the British Consulate at Barcelona without being arrested by the Spanish police. After two false starts, caused by a heavy fall of snow (it was the worst winter for forty years) and by a hitch in getting the necessary money, Captain Fitch and Corporal W. West, Highland Light Infantry, escaped on 24 December. Two days later Company Quartermaster Sergeants David Lepper, 2nd/5th West Yorkshire Regiment and M. J. McLear, 2nd South Wales Borderers; Sergeant S. T. Jackson RASC of the 57th Division; Sergeant-observer R. W. Lonsdale on 107 Squadron RAF; Sergeant J. H. Wyatt on 49 Squadron RAF; and Gunner Instone followed. Bribing the guards on duty, these six men simply walked out of the fort. They caught a train to Perpignan where they hired a taxi for 300 francs to make the journey to within a mile or two of the frontier to Cerbère practically on the Spanish border, before crossing into Spain with a French guide to whom they had paid a not-inconsiderable sum. The guide was a deserter from the French army and being wanted by the police was as keen as any of the others to escape successfully from France. As a further inducement he was promised a thousand francs when the party reached Barcelona.

They proceeded on foot up the mountain, walking through the vineyards in Indian file. After five or six hours of arduous climbing they reached the summit, 3,000 feet above the sea. It was a fine clear day, but so bitterly cold that to find water they had to break several inches of ice on the mountain streams. On their left they could now look down on the village of Port Bou and the blue Mediterranean beyond. By 8 pm that evening, having evaded the French and Spanish patrols, they began the descent into Spain. Here they lost their way, for the guide knew the mountain paths no better than they did. It was too cold to wait for daylight and food was running short, so, after a council of war, they decided, although desperately tired, to make directly for Figueras in the hopes of getting a train from there to Barcelona. With tempers somewhat frayed they struggled on, each man finding his own path as best he could. Soon afterwards David Lepper's leg, which had been injured some months previously by a kick from a German sentry, gave out and he fell exhausted. Instone, who seems to have been the strongest of the party, supported him down the mountainside. At the first village they came to Instone asked the way from a Spanish priest, who, most fortunately, taking them for Frenchmen, did not report them to the Spanish police. Later they exchanged a packet of cigarettes for a bottle of wine and slept that night in a haystack.

At dawn next day they set off again. In Caret, a small village five miles north of Figueras, a motor-bus passed them and stopped two hundred yards ahead. Four Spanish Guardia Civil armed with rifles sprang out. All were arrested except for the guide, who fled into the long grass at the side of the road the moment he saw what was afoot. The others were marched back to the village through which they had just passed. Here they were searched; their knives confiscated and told they would be taken to Figueras that afternoon. They stated immediately that they were British escaped prisoners of war and claimed the right to repatriation from a neutral country according to international law. No notice whatever was taken of these pleas. They were marched to Figueras under heavy guard, where, twice more, they were searched; particulars, rank, name and number being taken and were finally thrown into a cell about twelve feet square. In this cell there were already about twenty prisoners, including ten soldiers who had previously escaped from Fort St. Jean. There was insufficient room in the cell even to lie down on the floor. Here they spent ten wearisome days under appalling conditions.

The food consisted of two hundred grammes of bread a day (two small rolls) and a plate of beans for breakfast, boiled potatoes for lunch and wet boiled rice for supper. Cigarettes could be bought from the guard for a shilling each. Guards, none of whom were more than sixteen or seventeen years old, wore gym shoes, a blanket over their shoulders for a coat and carried Belgian rifles and Russian steel helmets. The only window in the cell was bricked up leaving a six-inch aperture and as it was midwinter long hours were spent in total darkness, though occasionally they were able to buy a candle from their guards. For all natural functions a pail was placed in the middle of the cell and removed only once in twenty-four hours. This made the atmosphere of the cell so foul that many of the prisoners were violently sick. At night they huddled together for warmth on the damp stone floor without straw or blankets; such was the treatment meted out by the Spaniards to escaping prisoners of war. Eventually they got in touch with the British Vice-Consul at Gerona who made vain attempts to see the prisoners. He sent in stores to them, but these were stolen by the guards. In spite of such conditions, depressing beyond belief, the cheerfulness and morale of the prisoners remained marvellously good and from the example set by the British, prisoners of other nationalities took courage.

On the eleventh day Instone's party were marched out of the fort with a hundred Spanish political prisoners. To the amazement of the guards, who thought the treatment during the past week was severe enough to demoralise anyone, the British marched two miles to Figueras station singing at the top of their voices. There they were crowded into cattle trucks and arrived at Barcelona at midnight; they were then separated from the political prisoners and marched through the town to another station, where they were entrained for Cervera and eventually locked up in Cervera gaol. Here the conditions were, if anything, worse than at Figueras. The cell was six feet by eight and the only means of sanitation was the usual bucket. Two verminous and filthy blankets were given to each prisoner and the food rations were much reduced. The only hope of maintaining strength or even life was to pool all valuables and to purchase at exorbitant prices extra food from the guards. In this way Instone sold his gold watch for thirty pesetas, for which he got one packet of cigarettes and four small rolls of bread. In the cell everyone grew beards and suffered their first experience of lice. Nothing is more demoralising than the realisation that one is lousy and that nothing but a modern delousing machine can rid one of these obscene pests.

For a fortnight Instone and his party lived in these dreadful conditions, being allowed out of the cell for exercise each day for a quarter of an hour only. Eventually they were moved in cattle trucks to Saragossa gaol, where once more they were stripped and searched. Through all these searches Instone managed to smuggle the remains of his money and certain important photographs which he had taken at Marseilles, hiding them sometimes in his socks or, as he did at Saragossa, in a faked bandage on his arm. On entering Saragossa gaol all prisoners were forced to cry 'Viva Franco' and give the Fascist salute. One British soldier who refused to comply with these orders was knocked down by the sentries and lay with blood pouring from his mouth and nose. The Saragossa prison, as was usual with prisons in Spain, was desperately overcrowded and it was hard to find room to lie down. Next day, chained by the wrist in pairs, the British prisoners were pushed into lorries and taken down to the station and in due course reached Campo de Concentration de Prisioneros de Miranda de Ebro (Miranda de Ebro concentration camp) about fifty miles south of Bilbao, in the Miranda mountains, 2,000 feet above sea level. When Instone and his party first arrived it contained fifty Polish officers and 250 Polish NCOs and men; sixty Belgians, thirty-five Frenchmen; fifty British soldiers and various others, including twenty German deserters. There were in this camp, representatives of nearly every European nation. Altogether, including 500 Spanish political prisoners, there were about a thousand miserable inmates. The conditions in this foul and overcrowded camp were as bad as any prison in Spain. The food was utterly insufficient to maintain strength and the prisoners sold all their possessions, including their clothes, for extra food. Every man there was covered with lice and nearly everyone had dysentery and scabies. Each morning and evening a long column of prisoners were marched to the parade ground, where they were compelled to shout in unison Una, Grande, Libre, Arrita Espana, Viva Espana and were flogged if they refused. In view of the lousy condition of the prisoners, their heads were shaved. The British Embassy at Madrid did their best to alleviate the condition of the British in this dreadful camp, but during the first two years of the war, whilst Franco was still confident that the Germans would win, there was little that the Embassy could do, for their hands were tied by the weakness of the British position. Instone and his companions remained at Miranda for nearly four months, suffering from disease and gradually wasting away. During these months his weight fell from eleven and a half stone to eight stone. He became like all others who had long been in the camp; a living skeleton.

It was not until 9 March 1941 that a group of two dozen or so soldiers and airmen, including Wyatt, Lonsdale and Instone, was released. Instone celebrated by eating fourteen sausages and six eggs with infinite relish before retiring to bed. After this astonishing effort he felt he could die happy, though, strangely enough, he suffered no ill effects. They were transported to the British Embassy at Madrid and they reached Gibraltar on 12 March. Back in Marseilles 'Treacle' Treacy assumed the responsibility of officer in charge of escapes with Lieutenant Colonel Jimmy Langley as his deputy.

Langley first met Treacy in November 1940 in Fort Jean. 'His name was not unknown to me, since while in hospital at Lille we had heard through the medium of one of our padres that Treacy had been shot by the Germans in the prison at Loos. Since the padre had declared he had actually seen the execution, I was naturally somewhat surprised to see Treacy. He informed me that the misunderstanding had come about in this way. While in the prison he had been allowed some exercise on a small yard and the padre had arrived to visit him at a time when he was lounging at one end of the yard while a number of German soldiers were being drilled at the other end. The padre, not understanding a word of German, immediately assumed that he was witnessing an execution and not wishing to see Treacy actually shot he retired and reported the fact to the inmates of the hospital.

At this time, in view of my wounds, I obtained permission from the French authorities to live in a hotel. This was most satisfactory from the point of view of escaping and Treacy decided that he would absent himself from the camp and join me at this hotel. For some days everything went well, Treacy and I sharing a large double bed at night and passing the day planning escapes.

Unfortunately, however, the proprietor of the hotel got wind of what was happening and used to visit my room at various intervals during the night to ensure himself that I was alone. During these visits Treacy used to hide himself under the bed, but as this was extremely low and Treacy a very large man, the noise he made getting there soon betrayed our plans and he was forced to remove himself to a small room on the top floor of a hotel in the Vieille Port.

I am not quite certain how he managed to arrange to have a room, but I believe he persuaded the proprietor that he was a refugee Irish priest from the Occupied Zone who had lost all his papers. During the months of November and December we worked together on numerous schemes. The first and perhaps the most amusing was one to obtain Yugoslavian passports, with a view to crossing into Spain as Yugoslavian commercial travellers. We both considered it unlikely that anyone on the Spanish frontier would speak any of the language of Yugoslavia, but in order to make absolutely certain we spent several days learning, I think it was, Serbian phrases.

The passports were to be made out on the name of Tracovitch and Langovitch and were guaranteed to be genuine. This scheme finally broke down, due to the ever-increasing price demanded by our contact at Vichy. Originally we had agreed to pay 2,000 French francs on delivery of the passports and another 1,000 francs to a Spaniard at Barcelona. However, the price rose steadily and the passports were not produced, so that we were forced to abandon what appeared to be a very good plan.

Our next effort was an attempt to get away by sea in conjunction with a number of somewhat doubtful Frenchmen and a Spaniard who claimed to have commanded the International Brigade at the famous battle outside Madrid, where an entire Italian armoured division was wiped out. Failure here was due mostly to the immense difficulties in obtaining petrol for the boat in question. Both Treacy and I inspected the yacht and I am certain had we succeeded in obtaining the petrol we should have had little or no difficulty in getting clear of the harbour under cover of darkness and in reaching a Spanish port.

Our third and last joint scheme was to be smuggled on board one of the ships going to Beirut from where we considered the chance of reaching Palestine to be good. The originator of this scheme was a Frenchman who stated he was working for the British and who would come with us, provide the necessary money, arrange the hiding-place on the boat, etc., on condition that we guaranteed his immediate return to England on contacting the British authorities in Palestine. Neither Treacy nor myself believed there was a word of truth in this, since at least half of the population of Marseilles claimed that they were working for the Allies. However, the hiding-place chosen was the ship's refrigerator, since it was never searched and it was the only place where it was believed we should be protected from the tear gas which the Germans and Italians were popularly believed to use in order to root out stowaways in the more inaccessible parts of the ships proceeding to North Africa, Syria, etc.

It was considered an even chance as to whether we should be able to survive the intense cold in the refrigerator, but by now we were both so bored that we were prepared to take the risk. Everything had been arranged and we went to a final rendezvous at a small cafe when the Frenchmen told us he was no longer able to come with us, having received orders to proceed immediately to Paris, to contact other people working for the British. However, in order not to let us down he had informed his contacts of the boat, etc., that we should still be coming and handed each of us a packet which contained 10,000 francs, a revolver and ammunition. Both of us were convinced that this was a 'plant' and that we should be arrested the moment we boarded the ship and be condemned for a long period of imprisonment for having carried arms while internees in a neutral country. The Frenchman spent the best part of the night trying to persuade us that the whole affair was genuine, but without success and we left, congratulating ourselves on having escaped from the trap.

(Four years later, in London, I was accosted by the Frenchman in question and to my intense surprise learned that every word he had spoken was the truth. I asked him why he had given us revolvers and he stated that he felt that without arms we should have had little or no chance of making our way from Beirut to Palestine.)

After this Treacy decided to push ahead with his individual scheme of obtaining an Irish passport and by this means travelling to Spain. He intended to pose in front of both French and Spanish authorities as a student from Dunkirk who had had to leave due to the war and now wished to return to Ireland. In order to pass what he felt would be a searching cross-examination on Dunkirk and his life there he enlisted the aid of a French merchant seaman who had spent a large period in this port and he spent hours learning the names of cafes and streets, etc. In addition to this he procured a book giving the names of the schools in Dunkirk, together with those of the masters. At the end of a fortnight there was very little he did not know about Dunkirk and if required he was even able to produce a few racy stories about some of its inhabitants. It was as well that he had taken all these precautions because he was interrogated at the Marseilles Town Hall by a Frenchman who had lived in the town for twenty-five years and who claimed to be a personal friend of the headmaster of the school on which Treacy had picked. He, Treacy, had considerable difficulty in clearing this fence as the Frenchman pressed him for details of the headmaster's life. However, he got away with it by stating that as a mere pupil he was not intimate with the headmaster!'

One of Langley's last memories of Marseilles was of Treacle' Treacy on 22 January 1941, who, having obtained an Irish passport and a legitimate French exit visa for Spain and Portugal, was standing on the platform of the station waving good-bye. 'He was dressed in a black overcoat with a large moth-eaten astrakhan collar, holding in his right hand an equally moth-eaten umbrella. He had won this coat in a raffle and was very proud of it. He told me later that he travelled the whole way back to England in it and that it caused no little comment on his arrival at a London station. I would always regard him as one of the greatest characters I ever met and his adventures while escaping are some of the greatest of the war.'

Treacy travelled to Vichy with the passport, saw the necessary authorities, got an exit visa and finally travelled de luxe to Lisbon via Narbonne, Barcelona and Madrid. He left Lisbon by air and reached Barnstaple on 30 January.

Squadron Leader Treacy DSO became Squadron Leader of 242 Squadron, seeing combat on the 1st and 5th of April 1941. The Hurricanes of 242 Squadron flew from Martlesham Heath to the Stapleford Tawney airfield on 9 April. On the squadron's first operation out of Stapleford on 20 April, three Hurricanes collided in cloud over the Channel after finding themselves suddenly under attack from German fighters. The pilots drowned when their Hurricanes crashed into the sea, one of whom was Squadron Leader Treacy.[6]

Langley, who had been passed unfit for further military duties, departed with 25 other repatriation candidates on 24 February, reaching Gourock on 17 March 1941.

On 4 April when Instone and the rest of the party left Gibraltar aboard HMT *Empire Trooper* for Liverpool they had not gone far before the ship developed engine trouble (caused, so rumour had it, by sand having been put into the turbines by the German crew before capture) and was obliged to return to Gibraltar. They transferred to the aircraft carrier HMS *Furious* and completed the voyage to Belfast, Northern Ireland on 11 April. In England Gordon Instone's mother was waiting for him. His mother had never believed the official telegram saying he had been killed in Calais and all his civilian clothes were cleaned, pressed and hanging neatly in his cupboard waiting for him. She showed him the pile of letters of commiseration that had arrived following his 'death'. He glanced at the local newspaper and there was a photograph of his fiancée Elizabeth all in white with an army lieutenant on her arm. Instone had been away, presumed dead for a year and she had married someone else!

Endnotes

3   Later, ACM Sir Basil Embry GCB KBE DSO and three bars, DFC AFC.

4   The 'little ball of fire' three times captured but never made a PoW, landed at Plymouth on 2 October after this epic journey and he subsequently became involved in night fighting before making a tour of command posts in Operation Crusader in the Western Desert and in Fighter Command in England. On 27 May 1944 Air Vice Marshal Basil Embry replaced Air Vice Marshal J. H. d'Albiac at 2 Group HQ, Bylaugh Hall, five days before its transfer to 2nd Tactical Air Force. Embry's task was to prepare 2 Group for low level day and night operations to support Operation Overlord - the invasion of France - planned for mid 1944. On 1 June 2 Group was transferred first to Fighter Command then, when this divided to form Air Defence of Great Britain (ADGB), into 2nd Tactical Air Force. After two months sick leave Embry was posted to 6 Group as Senior Air Staff Officer in the rank of Group Captain. After only three weeks he was offered command of a night-fighter wing in RAF Fighter Command, which was accepted, although he reverted to the rank of Wing Commander. The wing disbanded in December 1940 and Embry became AOC RAF Wittering, returning to the rank of Group Captain in March 1941 Embry often flew radar equipped night-fighters on 25 Squadron. In July 1941 he was given the ceremonial title of an Air Aide-de-Camp to the King and was Mentioned in Despatches in September. In October 1941 he was seconded to the Desert Air Force as an adviser and saw action in the Desert War. Embry returned to Britain in March 1942 and served as AOC Wittering again and as AOC 10 Group, Fighter Command. In June he was again Mentioned in Despatches but he was passed over as the prime candidate for leading RAF Bomber Command's newly formed Pathfinder Force in July 1942 before being given command of 2 Group Bomber Command, which was about to join the 2nd Tactical Air Force, in June 1943. Although he was now an Air Vice Marshal, Embry continued to fly on operations where possible, piloting each type of light bomber in his command to ascertain the strengths and weaknesses of the tools available to his aircrews. He usually flew as a 'wingman' in a formation, flying under the name of 'Wing Commander Smith'. He pushed fervently for 2 Group's re-equipment with the Mosquito FB VI, which became the highly potent workhorse of

the Group by 1944. By October 1943 Embry's efforts had made 2 Group a highly effective weapon, with bombing accuracy and serviceability among the best in the Allied Air Forces. The group's contribution to the war effort, such as the bombing of V-l launch sites in France and the anti-transportation offensive prior to D-Day was arguably decisive. In December 1944 he was appointed a Companion of the Order of the Bath. Embry's Mosquitoes also undertook specialist precision bombing operations such as the attack on Amiens jail and in 1945 (21 March) on Gestapo headquarters in Copenhagen and Odense (17 April). On 31 October 1944 Embry took part in a successful low-level attack undertaken by Mosquitoes of Nos. 21, 464 and 487 Squadrons on the Aarhus University, Denmark, which housed the Gestapo HQ for the whole of Jutland. For '...(pressing) home his attacks with a skill and gallantry in keeping with his outstanding reputation..' in the latter three operations he was awarded the DFC. He was also honoured after the war by the Danish Government for his part in these operations, being awarded the Order of Dannebrog, Commander 1st Class. On 20 July 1945 he was awarded a third bar to his DSO. Other honours included the Netherlands Order of Orange Nassau, Grand Officer; French Croix de Guerre and Legion d'honneur and Croix de Commandeur). After the war the gifted Richardson would write 'Wingless Victory', the story of Basil Embry, his CO when at Wattisham earlier in the war. Shortly after the end of the war Embry was knighted, with his appointment as a Knight Commander of the Order of the British Empire (KBE). He was later to receive further knighthoods with higher precedence, in 1952 he was promoted to Knight Commander of the Order of the Bath (KCB) and in 1956 Knight Grand Cross of the Order of the Bath (GCB). He was Commander-in-Chief Fighter Command from 1949 to 1953. Embry was appointed Commander-in-Chief of Allied Air Forces Central Europe. His outspoken criticism of the NATO chain of command and organisation framework ensured however that he was retired early from the Royal Air Force in 1956. In 1956 Embry briefly relocated to New Zealand where he wrote his autobiography, titled 'Mission Completed'. In March 1956 accompanied by his wife Hope, he emigrated to Western Australia and began a new life as a sheep farmer, purchasing a 1,400-acre property at Chowerup. He also acquired land at Cape Riche, east of Albany and moved here in the late 1960s. Embry became active in the politics of agriculture through the Farmers' Union of Western Australia. He was elected General President in 1971 and held office for two years. In 1972 he led a delegation through South East Asia and instigated the establishment of the Rural Traders Co-operative (W.A.) Ltd. He was the president of the RAF Escaping Society and worked himself at a punishing pace until he became ill in 1975. Basil Embry died in Boyup Brook, Western Australia in 1977. On 19 April 2007 Spink & Son auctioned the remarkable and unique medal group of Air Chief Marshal Sir Basil Embry, selling for £155,350.

5   It had occurred to Treacy that he was an Irishman, a native of Eire and therefore neutral. He was clearly a poor student of Dublin University (where in fact he had studied) who had been caught up in the maelstrom of a European war and stranded without papers on the beaches of Marseilles. Here he had been frequently arrested by the French under the suspicion that he had taken part in the war. His situation was desperate. With roughly these thoughts in his mind, he wrote a piteous letter to the Eire consul at Vichy and was delighted when in return he received an Irish passport. This was almost too good to be true.

6   He was lost flying Hurricane Z2887 with Flying Officer Hugh Ian Lang in Z2634 and F/O Norman Douglas Edmond on Z2632 in a three way collision in dense cloud. Squadron Leader Alastair Grant Lang, Ian's brother on 156 (Pathfinder) Squadron on Lancaster's who himself was shot down on May 4 1943 over Dortmund, wrote: 'My brother, Hugh and another pilot and W.P.F. Treacy DSO found themselves suddenly under attack from German fighters; all collided together, when their Hurricanes crashed into the sea and drowned. A search of the area proved fruitless. I had only spoken to him on the telephone the previous evening; poor boy such a terrible waste.' Flying Officer Norman Douglas Edmond was a Canadian who served on 615 Squadron during 1940. The Station Intelligence Officer stated that in trying to avoid enemy aircraft, it was Treacy who collided with his wingman (Edmond) with the momentum of the collision carrying them into the Hurricane being flown by Hugh Lang. See also, *RAF Fighter Command Losses of the Second World War Vol. 1 1939-1941* by Norman L. R. Franks (Midland 1997). He had 5 (2+3) 'kills' (official 3.33) and 27th May (Me 109E & Do 17).

Squadron Leader Louis Arbon Strange, DSO DFC* leaving Buckingham Palace in September 1940 with Miss Susan Strange, after being presented by the King with a Bar to the DFC which he was awarded in the Great War. Squadron Leader Strange, who helped to create the Royal Air Force, retired as a Wing Commander, but joined up in World War II as a Pilot Officer and after an adventurous escape from France in a Hurricane took over the secret training of the British parachute troops.

ir Chief Marshal Sir Basil Embry GCB KBE
SO and three bars, DFC AFC.

Flight Lieutenant Hedley Fowler.

Fowler had joined the RAAF in January 1937, went to Britain with a short-service commission and then to France with 615 (County of Surrey) Squadron, as part of the Air Component of the BAFF (British Air Forces in France). Fowler was then twenty-three. He shot down two Me 109s and a Dornier 17 in the short period between 10 May and 15 May, the day he himself was brought down in a fight with a Dornier 17. A troublesome PoW, the Germans finally sent him to the notorious Colditz Castle, where other unsuccessful escapers were kept.

Back in England Fowler volunteered to test the Typhoon as a fighter bomber. He was killed on 26 March 1944 while engaged on dive-bombing trials at Crichel Down, Dorset with two 500lb bombs. In both dives the bombs got cleanly away, but on climbing up to the second dive the Typhoon broke up in the air. Spectators on the ground saw Fowler thrown clear from the cockpit, but his parachute only partially opened and he was killed instantly.

Hauptman Franz Xaver Graf von Werra with his pet lion *Simba*, which he kept at his aerodrome as the JG3 unit mascot.

Hauptman Franz von Werra's downed Bf 109E-4 (Werke No. 1480) on 5 September 1940 after he was shot down over Kent.

A member of Hauptman von Werra's ground crew showing the tail of his pilot's Bf 109 and his victory Abschüsse (kills).

Pilot Officer Gerald 'Stapme' Stapleton on 603 Squadron who was originally credited solely with shooting Von Werra down.

A contemporary news cutting showing Leutnant Alfred Plank von Bachselten (third from left) and his crew passing through London on their way to prison camp. Von Bachselten is trying to conceal his Iron Cross from the cameraman.

The Luftwaffe crew who stayed for breakfast, at Ostern in 1941. (Left to Right) Gefreiter Blasius Regnant, observer/bomb aimer; Gefreiter Bruno Kauhardt, Bordfunker (radio operator); Leutnant Alfred Plank Bachselten, pilot; Unteroffizier Walter Richter, Bordmechaniker (flight engineer).

View from a Heinkel
111 en route to
England.

An injured and smiling
Luftwaffe officer being
marched off into
captivity flanked by
two MPs on the
platform of a London
railway station.

A Luftwaffe NCO about to board a train and into captivity.

A thoroughly dejected Luftwaffe airman with his few belongings on the platform of a London railway terminus ready to be taken to a prison camp in the north of England. Some Luftwaffe aircrew who were shot down early in the war believed that their incarceration would only be temporary as they were convinced that a German invasion would free them for flying duties once again.

A Heinkel 111 similar to the one flown by Leutnant Alfred Plank Bachselten.

Squadron Leader Derrick D. W. Nabarro.

Reinhard Kollak a Bf 110C fighter pilot of 1./NJG4 (left) during a medal awards ceremony with Major Walter Ehle on the right and General Kammhuber, centre. On the night of 24/25 August 1942 Kollak shot down 'Douggie' Baker, captain of Stirling W7572 OJ-R on the raid on Frankfurt for his tenth Abschüsse (victory). Kollak was born at Frogenau in East Prussia on 28 March 1915 and began his military career by joining the Reichswehr. In 1935 he was transferred to the Luftwaffe where he trained as a fighter pilot. Upon completion of his training in the spring of 1940 Kollak was posted to the I./ZG1 and participated in the Campaigns in France and the Battle of Britain. In October 1940 Kollak was posted to the newly formed 1./NJG1. He claimed his first night victory while flying as a Feldwebel with I./NJG1 when he destroyed a Whitley in the early hours of 17 June 1941. Kollak was destined to become the highest scoring non commissioned Nachtjagd pilot who, together with his Bordfunker Hans Herman, was credited with 49 victories in over 250 sorties, all at night.

'Florentino' Goïcoechea of Ciboure, a tall, sturdy Basque smuggler, who knew the routes to Spain like the back of his hand. Immensely strong and agile, he would carry some of the weaker or wounded airmen on his shoulders across the often swollen, fast-running Bidassoa River which formed the frontier.

One of the first courier volunteers, Andrée Dumont, known as 'Nadine' was just 18 when her country capitulated to the Germans.

'Nadine' Dumont and her sister Lily

'Nadine' Dumont recovering at home after the war following her incarceration in Ravensbrück and Matthausen Concentration Camps. Micheline Dumont (aka 'Michou') replaced her 19-year old younger sister Andrée, known as 'Nadine' in the Comète Escape Line after she was caught in August 1942 and sent to Ravensbrück. Micheline, who later married Pierre Ugeux, a major in the Special Operations Executive in France, and Andrée, who survived the horrors of Ravensbrück were awarded the George Medal, the highest decoration that can be awarded to a foreign civilian for bravery. Andrée was made an OBE and was awarded the King's Medal for Courage.

Monsieur Dumont who was arrested by the Gestapo and incarcerated in a concentration camp where he was murdered by being buried alive in a cellar full of quick lime on 9 February 1945.

German soldiers inspecting papers at a checkpoint.

'Florentino' Goïcoechea (right) reunited in 1977 with Group Captain Bill Randle, one of more than 300 evaders 'Florentino' and his wife Katalin (centre) escorted across the Pyrénées for the Comète Line. (Sergeant W. S. O. Randle was shot down over Belgium on 16/17 September 1942 piloting a 150 Squadron Wellington on the raid on Essen). 'Florentino' received the George Medal, together with the King's Medal for Courage. He was severely wounded in the leg in July 1944 but survived the war. He died in July 1980 and is buried at the foot of his great love, the Pyrénées.

French Maquis arming themselves for a raid against their German oppressors.

Andrée de Jongh ('Dédée') a slight young woman who appeared to know no fear never asked or expected anyone to do anything she could not undertake herself and she made the double crossing of the Pyrénées 24 times, leading escaping airmen over the perilous mountain section into Spain. She was betrayed and arrested on 15 January 1943. Twenty-three members in the Comète Line were shot.

They included Dédée's father Frédéric 'Paul'/'Kiki', a headmaster (top right), who was arrested on 7 June 1943 and was executed on 28 March 1944 at Mont-Valerien, Paris by firing squad. Some 130 members of the Escape Line did not return from German concentration camps.

Andrée de Jongh recovered to return to nursing and devoted herself to caring for lepers in the Congo, Cameroon, Ethiopia and Senegal. Among her many awards was the George Medal, which she received from King George VI in 1946.

The border post on the
road from Cerbère to
Spain.

St Jean de Luz and the
Pyrenees.

The road from Lux-
St-Sauveur to
Gavarnie in the
Pyrénées.

The famous Rock of Gibraltar.

'Patrick O'Leary' alias Capitaine Albert-Marie Guérisse of the Belgian Army, pictured by a street photographer in Marseille while travelling incognito. The O'Leary Escape line was used by hundreds of evaders to reach Spain and finally Gibraltar and freedom. O'Leary was betrayed in 1943 but survived the war.

21-year old Warrant Officer Herbert John 'Dizzy' Spiller DFM navigator on 103 Squadron at Elsham Wolds.

Crew picture at RAF Binbrook in 1941 showing 'Dizzy' Spiller second from left, back row.

Squadron Leader Sidney Horace Fox DFM.

Oberleutnant Reinhold Eckardt of 7./NJG3 who shot down Halifax W7653 DY-A on 102 Squadron on 27/28 April 1942. Eckardt, who had 22 night and 3 day victories in ZG76, NJG1 and NJG3 and was awarded the Ritterkreuz was KIA on 29/30 July 1942 after combat with a 102 Squadron Halifax at Kampenhout, 9 kilometres North of Melsbroek, near Brussels after his third Viermot victory of the night. He had to bail out and became entangled in the tailplane. His bordfunker, Feldwebel Frank, bailed safely. Three Day victories as a destroyer pilot plus 17 aircraft destroyed on the ground.

Chapter 4

Escape to death!

'It's all over now and we're out of it until the end of the war.'
Letter from Stalag Luft I, Barth in Pomerania sent home by 23-year-old Flight Lieutenant Hedley Fowler in May 1940.

Born in London on 8 June 1916 Hedley Nevile 'Bill' Fowler was educated at Rugby School. His father was a Paymaster-Commander in the Royal Navy and he was great-grandson of Sir Henry Ayers, a Premier of South Australia for whom Ayers Rock was named. Fowler's family moved to Adelaide in South Australia in 1920 before returning to the England in 1924 so that Fowler could attend Rugby School. He returned to Australia in 1933 before enlisting in the RAAF in 1936 and then transferring to the RAF. Fowler was granted a short-service commission as a Pilot Officer on 19 February 1937. He was trained at No 6 Flying Training School at Netheravon before being posted to 3 Squadron on 22 May. He then served as a fighter pilot on 615 (County of Surrey) Squadron commanded by Squadron Leader Joseph Kayll, flying Gladiators. He joined the Squadron in October 1939 before converting to Hurricanes in May 1940. Fowler and 615 Squadron had arrived in France in November 1939 as part of the Air Component for the BEF. When the German invasion of the west commenced on 10 May 1940, the Squadron was still converting onto Hurricanes, although they were in action from the very start. Fowler's recollection of those few days is of long, sleepless periods and of enemy aircraft which came over in clouds. Mostly they were dive bombers and Heinkels, usually escorted by Messerschmitts. They flew in perfect formation. It was summer and the days were fourteen or fifteen hours long.

Fowler shot down two Me 109s and a Dornier 17 in the short period between 10 and 15 May, the day he himself was brought down in a fight with a Dornier 17. That morning his friend Flying Officer Leslie Redford Clisby was seen going down in flames near Rheims. Clisby was a south Australian mechanic who had enlisted in 1935 as a cadet in the RAAF at Point Cook near Sydney and had gone to Britain on a short-service RAF commission in 1937. Born in McLaren Vale, South Australia on 26 June 1914, Leslie Clisby lived in Walkerville, Adelaide, until joining the RAAF as a cadet at the age of 21. Despite having to bail out of a Gypsy Moth trainer on one occasion, he passed out from Point Cook on 29 June 1937, obtaining a Permanent Commission. The following month he departed with other graduates for the England to take up a short service commission in the RAF, Australia having no modern air force at this time.[7] He was 25 years old when he was sent to France with No.1 Fighter Squadron AASF, as one of the crack peace-time pilots who held off the Luftwaffe during the tragic period in which France and the Low Countries tried to keep back the German tide. He was stationed near the Maginot Line, not far from where 'Cobber' Kain, the New Zealand ace on 73 Squadron was operating. The citation to his DFC, announced a few weeks after the crash at Rheims, gives a glimpse of his vivid career: 'One day in April 1940 this officer was the pilot of one of the three Hurricanes which attacked nine Messerschmitt 109s, one of which he shot down. On the following day he destroyed another Messerschmitt 109. In May 1940 this officer was engaged in six combats against the enemy, in which he shot down eight enemy aircraft...'[8]

Three days before Clisby crashed his Hurricane's rudder was shot away in a rear attack by a Messerschmitt after he had shot down three other Messerschmitts at Maastricht. On 13 May he claimed a Bf 110 12 miles SSW of Vouziers and a Heinkel He 111 at Coulommiers, 18 miles south-eats of Vouziers. Hurricane and Heinkel landed close together, the occupants of both aircraft unhurt. Clisby emerged from his damaged Hurricane, drew his revolver and pursued the German crew over the rough fields, firing as he gained on them. The Germans pulled up, their hands raised and Clisby marched them away to a nearby village, handed them over to the French and made his way unconcernedly back to his squadron.

Throughout his career in France, Leslie Clisby clung to his tattered RAAF blue uniform. 'It will see me through,' he told a war correspondent who was among his closest friends. He was still wearing it that last day at Rheims. In 1938 Clisby had attended a gunnery school at Sutton Bridge and there he and Flight Lieutenant Fowler were known to all as 'The Diggers.' Both then wore the RAAF blue, which regulations permitted them to wear until their uniforms wore out, when they were replaced by the lighter blue of the RAF.

Fowler and five others took off into a cloudless sky on 15 May. They reached Vitry half an hour later, refuelled and waited for orders, yarning with two French officers who were seated on an absurdly tiny tank which had been sent there for airfield defence work. When the orders came, they were familiar ones. The bridges over the Meuse were to be bombed again and Fowler and his five companions, with six fighters from 607 Squadron, were to provide high escort. Fowler had the rear position, a tricky one in which one eye had to be kept on the movements of the formation and the other eye on possible attackers.

Twenty-thousand feet over Dinant, flying along the Meuse, Fowler suddenly saw a pair of enemy aircraft coming out of the sun. Fowler gave the warning on the radio telephone and was so busy watching and warning that he did not look over the other side of his aircraft. He first knew that trouble was near at hand when a hail of bullets and fiery tracer showered his Hurricane. Some hit and Fowler turned his craft so swiftly that he almost lost consciousness. When he recovered he saw a Messerschmitt 109 flashing past on his left. Fowler went into a dive, got behind the Bf 109 and began pumping bullets into it. The '109 turned over nose first and went straight down. But the German's companion had seen what had happened and he came in on Fowler's port quarter - the side unprotected by armour plate. Suddenly the instruments in Fowler's Hurricane began falling out of a shattered panel and the windshield was hit. A mass of flame came up. Fowler's boots were burning. He pulled up out of the dive, untied his strap, tipped the Hurricane over on its side and let himself fall out. He pulled the ripcord and floated down into a silence and peace that was startling after the roar of combat. Below, under a bright sun, lay the silvery winding Meuse and the green of the Forest of Ardennes.

He heard a rushing noise, getting louder as he floated down. Then from the ground came a sheet of flame. What he had heard was the sound of a crashing aircraft; the flame came when it crashed. It was either his Hurricane or the enemy's Messerschmitt; Fowler never knew which. He landed in the Ardennes Forest, just missed a tree, came to rest in a bush and cut himself clear of his parachute. There was a little clear stream nearby. Fowler used it as a mirror to examine and bind up his head. He buried his pay book in the river and began walking. He walked almost all that day, listening to the sounds of artillery and other fire which seemed all round him. One or two aircraft passed over. He heard explosions from the direction of the Meuse.

Later in the day the trudging airman encountered a patrol of French engineers, who pointed their revolvers at him. He convinced them with his identity card and accompanied them along the road. The party had been left behind to blow up some of the Meuse bridges and find their own way back as best they could. Hours later the little party met the remains of a platoon of French infantry with an officer in charge who said they were trying to get back to their company. Fowler decided to join them. They marched all that afternoon, being dive bombed at intervals by Stukas and Henschels and slept that night in a wood. The party had been joined also by a number of civilian refugees and numbered then about thirty.

It was a comparatively quiet night in the wood, except for the sound of distant explosions. Fowler's feet were blistered and when they set off next day he 'borrowed' an old cart horse which had been left in a field harnessed to a plough. Several others in the party had already 'found' bicycles for themselves.

The noise of firing, which had been going on all day, suddenly began to sound from ahead instead of behind. The party conferred and decided to split into two groups and go round the village ahead, instead of through it. Fowler had picked up a rifle from among the many abandoned along the road, together with five rounds of ammunition. The section to which Fowler attached himself moved around the village in a. series of short hops from cover to cover. They were moving from one clump of bushes to another when a machine gun began firing from the direction of the village. Fowler saw some of the men in the middle of the field drop in their tracks. The rest waited and then the French officers and an infantryman started off for the copse next to the one they were occupying. They had gone twenty yards when the machine gun fired again. Both fell into a ditch. Whether they were hit or escaped, Fowler did not know. Ten minutes later there was a distant rumble, seconds later a clatter close at hand. Then a detachment of German tanks rounded the clump of bushes, a manhole cover was raised and an officer with a Tommy gun covered the party. It was over. For Fowler it meant the beginning of two years and a half as a prisoner of war in Germany.[9]

No one at home was fooled by Fowler's apparent acceptance of his fate. His father, a retired naval commander, knew that meek submission was not in his son's nature: that the sentence in the letter had been put in deliberately to convey to his captors the impression that he had no I intention of making a bid for freedom. In subsequent letters Fowler continued to lull the enemy into a false sense of security. He asked for a sextant to be despatched from England. He asked for reference books and assured his parents that he was going to make the best use of this 'heaven-sent' opportunity of concentrated study. To the Germans it seemed that here was an officer well content to spend the rest of the war in captivity. The ruse worked. His act of appearing to co-operate with the German Commandant and his staff was so excellent that after a time he became a trusted person and was allowed to go along to the stores where the Red Cross parcels were kept. In time he was able to secrete sufficient odds and ends of material to make a rough-and-ready German-type uniform, smuggling anything he felt he could use into odd corners awaiting the right moment for a break-out.

When Fowler first arrived at Stalag Luft I at Barth on 5 July 1940 he had discovered that comprehensive tunnelling schemes were already in operation, but he did not feel inclined to join them. The Germans had rigged up instruments to locate any tunnelling and such escape bids were fraught with danger. The prisoners were able to fox the Germans to some extent by cunning systems of their own: by fixing up a dripping tap they were able to imitate exactly the sound of underground digging, which nearly drove the Germans mad in their efforts to locate. At this time, indeed, the Germans were often forced to dig tunnels of their own, rigging them out as underground listening posts so that they could keep check on the activities of their captives. The prisoners, not to be outdone, poured boiling water into any German holes they came across thus depriving the Kommandant of some of his keenest 'ferrets' for considerable hospitalisation periods.

Fowler considered that he had a better scheme. On 5 November 1941, as his parents were reading his latest 'I am quite happy and content here' letter, Fowler entered the parcels room, leaving a guard standing outside and quickly changed into his home-made German uniform. Then, putting his carefully saved rations into an old mail bag which he had brought along for the parcels, he walked boldly out of another door into the compound reserved for German troops. He had already estimated that he had only thirty seconds to make his getaway and so, selecting a moment when no other German was looking in his direction, he scaled the perimeter wires (only a simple fence, very different from the one surrounding the RAF compound) and made quickly for a wood on the outskirts, where he changed into the civilian clothes he was wearing under his Nazi uniform. His daring deserved a better fate. He managed to reach Sassnitz and attempted to stow away on a Swedish ship; but whilst at the docks he was arrested by a German policeman and in the local police station he was stripped and revealed as an escaping prisoner of war by the RAF identity disc around his neck. He was returned to Stalag Luft I and sentenced to fourteen days solitary confinement and then sent to the supposedly 'escape proof' camp Oflag IVC at Colditz Castle, arriving on 1 December 1941.

At Colditz, Fowler found Wing Commander Douglas Bader in charge of 'special operations' against the Germans. Fowler's plan was an exceedingly hazardous daylight departure - through the main gate. A tunnel was, however, necessary in order to accomplish the preliminaries of the plot. The scheme needed clothes for Fowler and his five accomplices to change into, before they could pass themselves off as four Polish orderlies accompanied by two German guards. To obtain these clothes, Fowler and his comrades started a tunnel into the guards' clothing store and as their starting point they chose an entirely novel spot - the office of the Stabsfeldwebel. By picking the lock of his door and then making a suitable key for subsequent use, they were able to gain entry into the office at odd times and carry out their tunnelling where it was least likely to be suspected by the Germans. To get to the clothing store they had to tunnel under the Stabsfeldwebel's office and the sick bay beyond it, but this procedure took many months.

It was not until 9 September 1942 that Fowler and British Army Captain Lulu Lawton, Lieutenant Geoff Wardle RNVR and three Dutch lieutenants: Beitz, Donkers and Damiaen Joan van Doorninck of the Royal Dutch Navy, were ready to make their attempt. All went well as the six escapers and two assistants entered the office during the previous evening and opened up the tunnel. However at around midnight there was an alarm and the Germans searched the castle. Fortunately, the office door had been relocked and this satisfied the searchers that nobody had entered the office. After entering the clothing store the tunnel was sealed up to allow later use (it was discovered the following day during the search for the missing officers). At 0730 the escape party left the store, timed to be shortly after the change of the German sentries; the idea being that the new sentries would be unaware of who had already entered the store.

The party, led by van Doorninck (dressed as the German NCO)

proceeded past several sentries and using a forged pass, marched out boldly with their escort. All seemed to be well as far as the final gate when it was discovered that none of their skeleton keys would fit the lock. They were just about to give up their original plan and make a mad dash to freedom by scaling the gate when they were halted by one of the sentries rushing up to the party. Very humbly the sentry apologised for delaying the party, produced a key to the gate, saluted smartly and ushered the six from the main gate to freedom!

They had decided to split into pairs as soon as they were outside the camp, but in a very short time two of the pairs had been spotted and were recaptured, leaving only Fowler and van Doorninck, still wearing the uniform of a 'German officer.' Their task was now even more difficult as the Germans had been alerted to the escape and the prisoners needed to watch out for danger. They walked as quickly as their tired legs would carry them and by nightfall on the first day they had put a considerable distance between themselves and the camp. Their garb was certainly mixed, but it appeared to cause no comment in an area where many foreign workers were clothed in a combination of old uniforms and civilian gear scrounged from friendly villagers. The Dutchman, by some miracle, had been able to retain his passport through all the scrutinies at the camp and had forged a Swiss visa; Fowler had only a home-made German identity card.

They travelled on foot to Penig (about 31 kilometres) and from there by train to Plauen via Zwickau. They caught the train to Stuttgart where they stayed overnight in a small hotel. The next day they caught a train to Tuttlingen and walked to the Swiss border. En route they were stopped by an SS policeman, but their forged papers were sufficient to pass inspection. They crossed into Switzerland at 0130 on 13 September and were taken to the British legation at Berne. Fowler received a great welcome from the British Consular staff. The other four escapers were recaptured close to Colditz.

Fowler left Switzerland on 25 January 1943 with Major Ronald Bolton Littledale. Born summer 1902 in Northwich, Cheshire, the only son of Captain John Bolton Littledale and his wife, Clara Stevenson, he was educated at St. Aubyn's, Rotttingdean and then Eton College. Littledale was then trained at the Royal Military College and was commissioned as a Second Lieutenant on 1 February 1923. He served with the King's Royal Rifle Corps (KRRC) in the British Army of the Rhine, and India, Palestine and Northern Ireland, rising through the ranks during the 1920s and 1930s. Littledale took part in the defence of Calais serving as a Major. On 26 May 1940 he was captured by a German patrol near the Fort at the harbour mouth. With other captured officers he was marched across northern France for about ten days and then taken by train from near Luxembourg to Trier, Mainz and onward to Oflag VII-C Laufen in mid June 1940. In March 1941 he was transferred to Stalag XXI-D, Poznań in Poland. As a prisoner of war he made several escape attempts.

In May 1941, with two other British officers; Lieutenant Mike Sinclair and Gris Davies-Scourfield, he escaped by hiding in a modified handcart carrying rubbish to a pit outside the camp. They made contact with the Polish underground movement in Warsaw but, after parting company, Davies-Scourfield was recaptured in March 1942. Littledale and Sinclair were recaptured in Bulgaria after eight months of freedom and handed back to the Germans. The three were all sent to Oflag IV-C at Colditz Castle, Littledale arriving there on 15 July 1942. On 15 October 1942, together with Captain Pat Reid, Lieutenant Commander William E. Stephens RNVR and Flight Lieutenant Howard D. Wardle, he escaped from Colditz, and travelling with Stephens arrived in neutral Switzerland on 20 October 1942.

Fowler and Littledale travelled across unoccupied France into Spain on 30 January 1943. They were arrested by the Spanish authorities later the same day and taken to a military prison at Figueras where they were held in filthy and cramped conditions until 22 February 1943. They were then taken to the British Consul in Barcelona from where they travelled to Gibraltar, arriving on 25 March 1943.

Fowler and Littledale returned to England shortly afterwards. For his successful escape, Fowler was awarded the Military Cross, which was gazetted on 14 December 1943. For his escape and actions whilst in captivity Major Littledale was awarded the Distinguished Service Order on 4 May 1943. He was killed in action on 1 September 1944, commanding the 2nd Battalion of the King's Royal Rifle Corps and is buried at Airaines Cemetery in France.

After resting in luxury, Bill Fowler returned to England by a roundabout route without further incident and for his daring part in this escape was awarded the Military Cross. Later he was to pass on the benefit of his experiences in escape methods at lectures for other aircrews. But soon Fowler tired of bragging about his escape. It was not enough that he had successfully thwarted the Germans. He must get back into the air again. The authorities told him plainly that he would not be allowed to fly over Europe with the risk of recapture by the Nazis, but he pressed for an early return to fighter aircraft and to do a useful job. After being promoted to Squadron Leader he found the job he was looking for. It was in March 1944 when top secret plans were being completed for Operation Overlord, the invasion and liberation of Europe.

One major snag remained before the Royal Air Force could play its allotted role; what was required was a super dive-bomber to reduce to impotence the mobility of the Panzer Groups. The RAF's powerful successor to the Hurricane, from the same stable, was the Typhoon. But, although it had already proved itself more than a match for the Luftwaffe when serviceable, it was in the throes of a series of teething troubles. Fowler volunteered to test the Typhoon as a fighter bomber and was attached from Fighter Command to the Aeroplane and Armament Experimental Establishment at Boscombe Down. On 26 March he was engaged on dive-bombing trials at Crichel Down, Dorset with two 500lb bombs. In both dives the bombs got cleanly away, but on climbing up to the second dive the Typhoon broke up in the air. Spectators on the ground saw Fowler thrown clear from the cockpit, but his parachute only partially opened and he was killed instantly.

Fowler had escaped from the Germans only to die in England. But his death had in some measure paved the way for the great victory which was to follow. Let no one imagine that Hedley Neville Fowler, whose body now lies in a peaceful grave at Durrington, Wiltshire, would have wanted it any other way.[10]

Endnotes

7   *Aces High* by Christopher Shores and Clive Williams (Grub Street, London, 1994).

8   It was estimated that Clisby's score amounted to 16 and 1 shared destroyed and 1 unconfirmed destroyed but other researchers, notably Lex McAuley in Australia, put Clisby's total, including his pre-May claims, to 9 and 3 shared destroyed. *Aces High* by Christopher Shores and Clive Williams (Grub Street, London, 1994).

9   *RAAF Over Europe*, edited by Frank Johnson (Eyre & Spottiswoode, London, 1946). Of the two Point Cook 'originals' Fowler met in prison, one was Flight Lieutenant Guy E. Grey-Smith, a bomber pilot who fell into enemy hands on 12 May, a day or so before Fowler was captured. Flight Lieutenant Guy E. Grey-Smith was shot down flying a Blenheim IV on 139 Squadron on the infamous Maastricht bridges raid. His two crew were killed The other was Flight Lieutenant A. R. Mulligan, who was taken into captivity on 13 August 1940, soon after a successful low-flying attack in a Hampden from 150 feet on the Dortmund-Ems Canal which earned him the DFC.

10   *Escape – to death!* By Leslie Hunt, writing in *RAF Flying Review,* December 1957.

Chapter 5

Escape of
Hauptmann von Werra

*Von Werra...must be classed among the great escapers of this war - he had the
authentic touch.*
A.J. Evans, *Escape and Liberation 1940-45.* [11]

Franz Graf von Werra was born on 13 July 1914, to impoverished Swiss
parents in Leuk, a town in the Swiss canton of Valais. The title Baron came
from his biological father Baron Leo von Werra, who, after bankruptcy,
faced deep economic hardship. Because relatives were legally obliged to
look after the Baron's wife and his six children cousin Rosalie von Werra
persuaded her childless friend Louise Carl-von Haber to permit the Baron's
two youngest, Franz and his sister, the benefits of wealth and education.
The Carl-von Habers did not tell the children their true origin. In 1936, von
Werra joined the Luftwaffe. Commissioned as a Leutnant in 1938, at the
beginning of the war, he was serving with Jagdgeschwader 3 in the French
campaign. An able officer, he became Adjutant of II Gruppe, JG 3. He was
described as engaging in boisterous 'playboy' behaviour. He was once
pictured in the German press with his pet lion *Simba*, which he kept at the
aerodrome as the unit mascot.

Von Werra scored his first four victories during the Battle of France in
May 1940. After downing a Hawker Hurricane on 20 May 1940, on 22 May
he claimed two Breguet 690 bombers and a Potez 63 near Cambrai. In one
sortie during the Battle of Britain on 25 August he claimed a Spitfire west
of Rochester and three Hurricanes shot down as air victories, also including
five on the ground for a total of nine RAF planes destroyed. Four airborne
victories were credited by the Germans. The particulars of the actions are
uncertain as no matching incident has been found in British records. On 5
September 1940 von Werra's Bf 109E-4 (Werke No. 1480) was shot down
over Kent. It is unclear which of his adversaries was responsible for this
victory. It was originally credited entirely to Pilot Officer Gerald 'Stapme'
Stapleton on 603 Squadron. However, the Australian ace Flight Lieutenant
Pat Hughes on 234 Squadron was posthumously awarded half of the credit,
in the Citation (*London Gazette*, 22 October 1940), awarding him a Bar to his
DFC). Some sources suggest that Pilot Officer George Bennions of 41
Squadron may have initially damaged von Werra's fighter before Hughes
and/or Stapleton also scored hits on it. [12] Other sources suggest Flight
Lieutenant John Terence Webster on 41 Squadron as the victor.

Von Werra crash-landed in a field and was captured. Initially, he was
held in Maidstone barracks by the Queen's Own Royal West Kent

Regiment, from which von Werra attempted his first escape. He had been put to work digging and was guarded by Military Police Private Denis Rickwood, who had to face von Werra down with a small truncheon, while von Werra was armed with a pick axe.[13] He was interrogated for eighteen days at Trent Park, a mansion in Hertfordshire which before the war had been the seat of Sir Philip Sassoon.[14] Eventually von Werra was sent to the London District Prisoner of War 'cage' and then on to PoW Camp No.1 at Grizedale Hall in the Furness Fells area of Lancashire, between Windermere and Coniston Water. On 7 October he tried to escape for the second time, during a daytime walk outside the camp. At a regular stop, while a fruit cart provided a lucky diversion and other German prisoners covered for him, von Werra slipped over a dry-stone wall into a field. The guards alerted the local farmers and the Home Guard. On the evening of 10 October, two Home Guard soldiers found him sheltering from the rain in a hoggarth (a small stone hut used for storing sheep fodder, that are common in the area), but he quickly escaped and disappeared into the night. On 12 October he was spotted climbing a fell. The area was surrounded and von Werra was eventually found, almost totally immersed in a muddy depression in the ground. Werra was sentenced to 21 days of solitary confinement and was subsequently transferred on 3 November to Camp No.10 in Swanwick, Derbyshire. In Camp No.13, also known as the Hayes camp, von Werra joined a group calling themselves Swanwick Tiejbau AG (Swanwick Excavations, Inc.) who were digging an escape tunnel. On 17 December 1940, after a month's digging, it was complete.

The camp forgers equipped the group with money and fake identity papers. On 20 December, von Werra and four others slipped out of the tunnel under the cover of anti-aircraft fire and the singing of the camp choir. The others were recaptured quickly, leaving von Werra to go it alone. He had taken along his flying suit and decided to masquerade as Captain van Lott, a Dutch Royal Netherlands Air Force pilot. He claimed to a friendly locomotive driver that he was a downed bomber pilot trying to reach his unit and asked to be taken to the nearest RAF base. Codnor Park Station, a local clerk became suspicious, but eventually agreed to arrange his transportation to the RAF aerodrome at Hucknall, near Nottingham. The police also questioned him, but von Werra convinced them he was harmless. At Hucknall, a Squadron Leader Boniface asked for his credentials and von Werra claimed to be based at Dyce near Aberdeen. While Boniface went to check this, von Werra excused himself and ran to the nearest hangar, trying to tell a mechanic that he was cleared for a test flight Boniface arrived in time to arrest him at gunpoint, as he sat in the cockpit, trying to learn the controls. Von Werra was sent back to Hayes under armed guard.

In January 1941 von Werra was sent with many other German prisoners to Canada. His group was to be taken to a camp on the north shore of Lake Superior, Ontario, so von Werra began to plan his escape to the United States, which was still neutral at the time. On 21 January, while on a prison train that had departed Montreal, he jumped out of a window, again with the help of other prisoners and ended up near Smiths Falls, Ontario, 30 miles from the St. Lawrence River. Seven other prisoners tried to escape from the same train, but were soon recaptured. Von Werra's absence was not noticed until the next afternoon. After an agonizing crossing of the frozen St. Lawrence River, von Werra made his way over the border to Ogdensburg, New York and turned himself over to the police. The immigration authorities charge him with entering the country illegally, so von Werra contacted the local German consul, who paid his bail. Thus, he came to the attention of the press and told them an embellished version of his story. While the US and Canadian authorities were negotiating his extradition, the German vice-consul helped him over the border to Mexico. Von Werra proceeded in stages to Rio de Janeiro, Brazil, Barcelona and Rome. He finally arrived back in Germany on 18 April 1941.

Franz von Werra became a hero. Adolf Hitler granted him the *Ritterkreuz des Eisernen Kreuzes* (Knights Cross of the Iron Cross). Von Werra was tasked to improve German interrogation techniques for captured pilots based on his own experience with the British system. He reported to the German High Command on his treatment as a PoW and this improved the treatment of PoWs in Germany and he wrote a book based on his experiences entitled *'Meine Flucht aus England' (My Escape from England)* although the manuscript remained unpublished. Von Werra then returned to the Luftwaffe.

Gerald Stapleton was born in Durban, South Africa in 1920. In January 1939 he took up a short service commission in the RAF and eventually joined 603 'City of Edinburgh' Squadron in December 1939, prior to becoming one of the outstanding fighter pilots of the Battle of Britain, accounting for nearly twenty enemy aircraft destroyed, probably destroyed or damaged. Indeed all his scores were achieved on Spitfires during this Battle and he was revered as one of Richard Hillary's contemporaries in whose book *The Last Enemy,* he features. Gerald was awarded the DFC on 15 November 1940. Nicknamed 'Stapme' after a phrase used in his favourite cartoon 'Just Jake', in February 1942 he became flight commander of 257 Squadron, then joined 2 ADF at Colerne the following year before becoming a gunnery instructor at RAF Kenley and Central Gunnery School, Catfoss. He returned to ops in August 1944 to command 247 Squadron on Typhoons. He received the Dutch Flying Cross for his part in the Arnhem operations. Forced to land inside German lines in December 1944, he spent the rest of the war in Stalag Luft I on the Baltic coast. Post-war he joined BOAC, then returned to South Africa but retired to England where he was a very popular figure at numerous air shows during the year.

'603 Squadron lost 13 pilots during the summer of 1940 with many more seriously injured, most of whom were good friends of mine. Throughout the war I lost many more friends and colleagues yet I survived to tell my tale. 603 Squadron arrived at Hornchurch from Scotland on 27 August and were embroiled in the action the very next day, losing three pilots killed. Pilot Officer Don Macdonald and Flight Lieutenant Laurie Cunningham died when we were bounced by 109s whilst still trying to gain a height advantage. Macdonald was on his first patrol and had only 15 hours on Spitfires while Laurie Cunningham was experienced with over 160 hours. On our last patrol of the day we were bounced again and Pilot Officer Noel Benson was shot down. 'Broody' had over 160 hours on type - but experience didn't count for much when you were bounced unseen.

'In an attempt to avoid this happening again, our CO, Squadron Leader 'Uncle' George Denholm, climbed us on a reciprocal heading to that given by the controllers after take-off. Only when he believed we had gained sufficient altitude did we turn towards the enemy.

'The loss of Flying Officer Robin Waterston in combat on the 31st was a blow to the whole Squadron. He was my closest friend and the brightest character in the Squadron. During that day while we were airborne, our ground crew had a bad time of it when Hornchurch was bombed. Four of them were killed adding to the toll. With no time to grieve we just got on with our job. We had to - we were fighting for our lives, our freedom and our country. Despite the casualties, I recall we also had great fun. It was an exciting time and we lived life to the full - each day was treated as if it were our last.

'On 5 September, we lost a good friend and an excellent Flight Commander, Flight Lieutenant Fred Rushmer. 'Rusty' had refused Uncle George's orders to rest and exhaustion was probably a contributing factor when he was shot down and killed in combat with 109s. We had taken off from our forward base at Rochford when, at about 29,000 feet, we spotted a number of Dorniers below us escorted by 109s. I dived to attack the bombers but was engaged by a pair of Messerschmitts. I certainly hit one as I saw glycol streaming from the radiator but in my attempt to finish him off I was fired on by another German so I broke off my attack and continued my dive.

'In the heat of the battle I didn't see anything of Rusty but Bill 'Tannoy' Read later said he saw Rusty's Spitfire dive straight down vertically from altitude, through the bomber formation. He had obviously been hit.[15]

'A short while later I managed to shoot down a Messerschmitt 109 which, unlike my first attack, was possible to confirm. During my dive from altitude I spotted a Spitfire at about 6,000 feet diving vertically towards the ground, its tail shot away. I then spotted a lone 109 in the same airspace as an RAF pilot descending by parachute. I latched onto the German and pursued him at low-level over the Kent countryside. As I fired short bursts he attempted to shake me off but I could see my tracer striking his aircraft and I closed in. I remember at one stage being concerned that there was a village in my line of fire. He had nowhere to go but down and eventually force-landed in a field. I flew low over the site. The German was soon apprehended, initially by the unarmed cook from the local searchlight battery!

'It was a short time after the war when I learned that the pilot was Oberleutnant Franz von Werra, his exploits made famous in the book and film *The One That Got Away*.[16] By all accounts he was an arrogant little man who was willing to die to enhance his reputation. Well, he didn't get away from me!'[17]

Hauptmann von Werra spoke English fluently with a strong foreign accent and from the first was full of bounce and impudence. He had hardly climbed out of his crashed Me 109 and been captured by the Home Guard, before he started betting bottles of champagne with anyone who would take him that he would escape from England. He passed in the usual way, still extremely cheeky, to a normal prisoner-of-war camp in England where he must have been a very bad influence from our point of view. In due course, he escaped, but was recaptured after a short, sharp chase. After doing his spell of 'solitary' he was returned to camp and a month or so later he escaped again.

Early one morning, soon after he had gained his liberty, he was walking along a solitary road in the neighbourhood of Hucknall aerodrome, when the opportunity came to him to put into operation his carefully thought out scheme. Running beside the road was the local railway line and von Werra entered a small station at about 6 am and knocked on the station-master's door. He was dressed in a whitish boiler suit, under which he wore his full uniform with his iron cross and all his decorations. He was without a hat. In his fluent but curious English, he told the station-master a remarkable yarn. He was a Dutchman, he said, attached to the Royal Air Force and the pilot of a Wellington bomber. They had just returned from bombing Denmark and had force landed over the hills yonder. No, none of them was hurt but as he had secret instruments on board he had left his crew to guard the machine and had come away himself to fetch help. Would the station-master kindly ring up the nearest aerodrome and ask them to send out a transport to fetch him. The matter was urgent. This was a remarkable story and might well have deceived anybody, but the station-master was a canny old Scot and instead of ringing the aerodrome he rang the police. In due course the police arrived but found von Werra, or van Lott, as he now called himself, not the least dismayed. He told them the same story with a few embellishments, gave them a graphic description of his passage across the North Sea on one engine and wound up with a moving peroration on his joy and thankfulness on reaching England once more. The police listened with bated breath to this heroic story and then, I regret to state, swallowed the bait, hook, line, sinker and all. They did ask for his '1250' (identity card), but van Lott glibly explained that, being a Dutchman with a family in Holland, he was not allowed to carry the 1250 for fear of reprisals on his family. This satisfied the police and they rang up Hucknall aerodrome and asked for transport to be sent and at the same time more or less guaranteed van Lott's authenticity.

In due course, transport arrived and van Lott departed for Hucknall aerodrome in a RAF van. His build-up as a genuine Dutch pilot was already quite impressive. On arriving at the RAF station, von Werra had the infernal cheek to ask to see the Commanding Officer. It was then about 7 am and the CO being in bed was, quite rightly, not prepared at that hour in the morning to 'interview any damned Dutch pilot who happened to have made a forced landing in the neighbourhood.' For the time being Von

Werra was put in charge of the station duty officer. On the whole, I consider that this officer comes rather well out of the affair. From the first he was suspicious of von Werra. Von Werra's method was to keep up a continuous flow of conversation. He recounted, in greatest detail, his doings of the previous night. They took off, he said, from a northern aerodrome at 1800 hours, crossed the North Sea and reached their target exactly as briefed - it was a well-known Danish aerodrome. 'But we are not bombing Denmark' interposed the duty officer. 'Yes, we have just started' answered von Werra and swept away any objections with a detailed description of the attack. The flak had been heavy, he said and the mist made the target difficult to see. They had made a couple of bombing runs, the second one at a very low altitude and had dropped their bombs on to a line of sheds or hangars according to instructions. No, he had not got a direct hit, but one near miss must have done considerable damage. Then his port engine had been hit by light flak and they had had the devil of a job crossing the sea, always losing height, etc. It was a thrilling story, crammed with fictitious detail but everyone seems to have neglected or forgotten his imaginary crew waiting anxiously for help near their imaginary crashed Wellington. 'What is that kit you are wearing?' asked the duty officer, when he could get a word edgeways into von Werra's stream of talk, 'that's not a RAF issue, is it?' he continued looking with some gleam of suspicion at von Werra's boiler suit.

'Oh, no,' answered von Werra, not for a moment at a loss. 'Before the war I was a KLM pilot on the line between Antwerp and Cologne. This is the kit we used to wear in those civilian days and I find it far more comfortable. It is very hot in a Wellington, you know, unless you have to fly high - Too hot for the heavy kit they issue' and he led the conversation to less dangerous topics.

From time to time during this tête-á-tête, which lasted for nearly three-quarters of an hour, the duty officer's suspicions were aroused only to be allayed once more by glib answers. Von Werra was really a marvellous talker. At last it occurred to the duty officer that no one had yet been rung up nor had the crash been reported. 'Don't you think you ought to get on to your station?' he said 'and report that you are safe?' Von Werra agreed.

'Where is your station?'

Von Werra gave the name of a station, far north, on the east coast of Scotland and a call was put through. From that moment von Werra began to show signs of an uneasiness. I suppose he thought a call, exposing him, might come through at any minute. He did not know our telephone system. By this time it was well after 8 am; the station was coming to life and a few 'phone calls were coming through to the duty officer'.

'Can I use your lavatory?' asked von Werra.

'Certainly.'

'Where is it?'

'Wait a minute, I'll come with you,' said the duty officer, feeling suddenly most unwilling to let von Werra out of his sight. At that moment the 'phone rang and a message of some importance occupied the duty officer's attention. Von Werra, fearing the call might be from the station in Scotland, made clear signs that he wished to visit the lavatory without delay.

'Turn to the left at the bottom of the passage,' said the duty officer trying to cut his 'phone call short.

Von Werra departed, but in a few seconds put his head round the door.

'Did you say, turn to the left or the right?' he asked.

'The left' and the duty officer went on with his work. 'He would never have come back like that,' he said to himself, 'if he had been trying to bolt.'

When, however, five minutes or so had elapsed and Von Werra had not returned, he began to get slightly anxious. He went down to the latrines. No one there. Then he saw that the door of one of the 'cabinets' was shut and the 'engaged' sign was on the bolt. For a minute or two he waited, then, hearing none of the usual noises, he went up to the door and saw that it was not fully shut though the bolt had been pulled across to make it appear as though it was. There was no one inside. He instantly grasped the fact that Von Werra was a 'wrong 'un' and took the swiftest and sanest action within his power. He tore back to his room and put through a few urgent calls to salient points in the camp - the guardroom, the gate, flying control, etc, giving a brief description of von Werra and issuing orders that he should be grabbed and held if seen. Then he rushed on to the aerodrome. On the far side from the RAF station at Hucknall aerodrome, is the Rolls-Royce testing works. No one, not even an RAF pilot is allowed to enter the precincts. In those days it was out-of-bounds to all ranks. At the moment there was no aerial activity on the station, but the duty officer could see that movement was going on around a Hurricane on the tarmac on the far side. He commandeered a car and racing around the perimeter reached the Rolls-Royce works just in time.

Von Werra was sitting in the Hurricane and one mechanic was standing on the wing explaining to him all the taps and plugs and the drill for taking off and landing. A second mechanic was preparing to start up the engine.

'Come out of it!' roared the duty officer.

'Oh, it's you, is it?' answered von Werra, smiling gaily- 'What a pity. I have never flown one of these before. I have always wanted to, so much. Just let me have one little flight - just around once, not more, please.'

'Come on,' said the duty officer, climbing on to the wing and grabbing him by the arm.

'If you insist' and he climbed out, shrugging his shoulders in disgust. On the way back to the aerodrome, von Werra, once more in the best of humours, owned up to being a German officer prisoner of war. He treated the whole episode as a tremendous joke, apologised for the trouble he had given and was soon after removed to his prison camp and, no doubt, to a week or two of solitary confinement.

The escapologist can hardly avoid regrets that von Werra failed in this bold attempt. It was truly a magnificent effort of bluff against great odds and if it had not been for the sensible and rapid action of the duty officer it would certainly have succeeded. No one, as far as I know, has ever explained how he persuaded the Rolls-Royce mechanics to allow him even to sit in a Hurricane. To have persuaded anyone, under these circumstances, that he, who did not know even the drill, was justified in flying it must have required a story, invented on the spur of the moment, of quite exceptional plausibility even for von Werra.

'As far as I know, only one man has stolen an aeroplane from the enemy in this war and escaped in it and in the last war, I believe, no one accomplished the feat. Early in 1940, during the invasion of Norway, a Norwegian pilot managed to tow a German seaplane round a small headland and then started it up at leisure and took off. He arrived safely at a port in Scotland. Much against the Norwegian's wishes his CO insisted on flying the machine and on his first flight crashed into the sea so that it was no more seen. The CO survived.

'I know of one other man, an American pilot, Lieutenant Kelly of the USAAF, who had a good try at stealing an FW 190. He had been shot down over France and was making his way, dressed in civilian clothes, in the general direction of Spain, when he passed a German aerodrome. He was extremely tired of walking and with a 300 or 400 mile walk still ahead of him the idea of a glamorous and quick return to England appealed immensely. He had no difficulty in entering the precincts of the aerodrome - in fact, he told me, it was no better guarded than one of our own. He wandered about for a bit, looking into several hangars and finally favoured one in which was a perfectly good FW 190, with its nose pointed to wide open doors. There were no Germans in the hangar so he climbed into the cockpit. Those who have seen the instrument board of a modern aircraft will not be surprised at Kelly's dismay when he saw the immense array of strange taps and plugs and dials without which the modern pilot is apparently unable to fly. As Kelly understood no German the labels and instructions, which the Germans scatter around their instrument board more generously than we do, were of no value. He turned a lot of taps and he pressed a lot of knobs hopefully, but without any result and after half an hour had regretfully to climb out and continue his journey on foot. When Kelly eventually reached England, after many adventures, the first thing he wanted to learn was how to start a FW 190. It is probable that if Kelly could have started the German fighter, no one would have been able to prevent him from taking off and if there had been enough petrol he would have reached England. Whether he would have succeeded in landing there without being shot down is very doubtful. Probably his best chance would have been a very low approach over the Channel and a crash-landing in the first convenient field. It is probable that, in spite of the wide dispersal of aircraft which makes efficient guarding of a modern aerodrome extremely difficult, it was easier and safer to steal an aircraft in the last war than in this. But I can't help feeling that if anyone really deserved the honour of doing so it was von Werra.

A month or two after von Werra's recapture the 'Powers That Be', in their wisdom, decided to send him to Canada. Of course, a chit was sent with him to warn those who were to guard him in Canada that he was a persistent escaper and a particularly 'naughty boy.' Somehow, the chit got lost or mislaid on the way over and he arrived without a black mark to his name.

Just how von Werra escaped from Canada to the USA I have never been able to find out. Rumour has it that he crossed the St. Lawrence on ice floes, but however he did it, it was a wonderful feat accomplished by very few.

America was then neutral and von Werra had made a perfectly legitimate escape to a neutral country. He had by the rules of war a right to return to Germany and fight again. Nevertheless, the Americans stretched their consciences and popped him into prison. But the damage had already been done. As soon as von Werra reached New York he had visited the German Consul and from there sent by wire a long and detailed report, of all he knew, to the Fatherland. After a week in prison, on the untenable charge of crossing the Canadian border without proper papers, Von Werra was bailed out by the German Consul for 10,000 dollars and spent a most enjoyable few weeks in New York (he was a great man with the ladies) whilst preparing his onward journey. Finally, he jumped his bail, travelled down to Chile and thence made his way home to Germany.

Very deservedly he received the *Orde pour le Merite*; for not only was his escape a brilliant feat but the information he carried with him was of the greatest value to his side. The last heard of Von Werra was a rumour, believed to be true, that he had been killed fighting on the Russian front.

Von Werra had been deployed initially to the Russian Front as Gruppenkommandeur of I./JG 53 and he raised his tally by 13, to 21 aerial victories during July 1941. In early August 1941 I./JG 53 withdrew to Germany to re-equip with the new Bf 109F-4 and relocated to Katwijk in the Netherlands. On 25 October 1941 von Werra took off in Bf 109F-4 (Werke Nr. 7285) on a practice flight. He suffered engine failure and crashed into the sea north of Vlissingen and was killed. His body was never found.

Endnotes

11 Hodder & Stoughton Ltd, London 1945.

12 Flight Lieutenant Paterson Clarence (Pat) Hughes DFC (19 September 1917-7 September 1940) was the top-scoring Australian flying ace of the Battle of Britain and one of 24 Australians who lost their lives during the battle. He joined the RAAF as a cadet in August 1936, transferring to the RAF under the Short Service Commission scheme, sailing for England on 9 January 1937. By June 1940 he was flying Supermarine Spitfires on 234 Squadron at RAF St Eval in Cornwall. He was credited with the first confirmed kill for the squadron with the shooting down of a Ju 88 near Lands End on 8 July and a kill shared with another pilot on 28 July. In August 234 Squadron transferred to RAF Middle Wallop in Hampshire. Hughes claimed two Me 110s on 15 August and he achieved further double victories on 18 and 26 August, making him a fighter ace and resulting in the award of a DFC. Hughes claimed further double victories on 4, 5 and 6 September, bringing his official tally to 12 and two shared victories. In early evening of 7 September, 234 Squadron ran into a force of 60 German aircraft consisting of Dornier Do 17s and escorting Bf 109s. Hughes was leading his Section in Spitfire X4009 and dived to attack the bombers. After attacking a Do 17 from close range, a large section of the bomber broke away and appeared to hit Hughes' Spitfire. There is anecdotal evidence that he deliberately rammed the bomber. Hughes bailed out of the Spitfire, but his parachute failed to open and his body was found in the garden of a house in the nearby village

of Sundridge, Kent. Hughes died around 18.30 hours. His Spitfire crashed soon afterwards at Darks Farm, near Bessels Green, Kent. During the same action, Hughes' CO, Squadron Leader Joseph 'Spike' O'Brien, was also killed. Hughes' was officially credited with 14 victories. He received a Bar of his DFC on 22 October 1940 and he was posthumously credited with a half-share in the shooting down of Oberleutnant Franz von Werra. *Aces High* by Christopher Shores and Clive Williams (Grub Street).

13   There is no mention of this escape attempt in the book *The One that Got Away*.

14   After the war it became Trent Park teachers' training college.

15   Rusty's grave in the churchyard at All Saints, Staplehurst, Kent, was only officially confirmed as being his in 1998 (marked 'Unknown' until then). That day I was reunited with a number of my former ground crew at the rededication ceremony. Rusty made the national news 58 years after his death.

16   The book by Kendall Burt and James Leasor was published in 1956. The film of the same name which starred Hardy Kruger as von Werra appeared in 1957.

17   It later transpired that the parachutist was fellow 603 pilot; Pilot Officer Robin Rafter, flying his first patrol with us. Having suffered severe head injuries after being flung from his disabled Spitfire, he subsequently spent time in hospital recovering. Sadly, he was killed during his very next patrol after rejoining the Squadron, when his Spitfire dived out of formation while we were still climbing to intercept the enemy. Luck finally ran out for me on 23 December 1944. As part of a force of 16 Typhoons from 247 and 137 Squadrons at Eindhoven we were ordered to seek out 15+ German tanks forcing their way into the American sector. The weather was awful and we were lucky to avoid collisions. Unable to locate the tanks we were ordered to split into our individual squadrons and continue the armed reconnaissance. I spotted a train and led the attack. One of my rockets must have entered the firebox as there was a terrific explosion and my radiator was punctured as I flew through the debris. I tried to nurse my aircraft back at low level but simply ran out of height. I force-landed about 2 miles inside the German lines and was taken prisoner. I was initially taken to a rear echelon platoon HQ and from there, ironically by train, to the interrogation centre at Oberursel, near Frankfurt. I was then taken to Stalag Luft I, Barth, on the Baltic Coast where I remained until May 1945 when I was repatriated as part of Operation 'Exodus'.

Chapter 6

The Day The Luftwaffe Stayed For Breakfast

One of the main Luftwaffe targets in May 1941 was Liverpool, which was bombed by 43 Heinkel He 111s and Ju 88s on the night of 1/2 May and by another 79 German bombers on the night of 2/3 May. Beaufighters accounted for two of the raiders along the south coast on the night of 1/2 May. The night following, a Beaufighter If on 604 Squadron shot a Ju 88 down over Hampshire. Flight Lieutenant Edmiston on 151 Squadron was credited with a Ju 88-A5 of 1./KG30. Edmiston fired and put both of Feldwebel Erwin Geiger's engines out and the German pilot crash-landed in shallow water near the beach at Weybourne, Norfolk. The crew was captured and the Junkers was recovered intact. At the end of August 1940 151 Squadron had been withdrawn to the Midlands for rest and to begin retraining for night fighting. Based at RAF Wittering with Hurricane Ic and Boulton Paul Defiant I turret-gun fighters, 151 Squadron also detached aircraft to RAF Coltishall, Norfolk, on night standbys. Like most every other RAF squadron in France in 1940, 151 Squadron was severely mauled, but its Hurricane Is scored a number of victories based for a short time at Abbeville and Vitry-en-Artois. Now, in May 1941 the Stukageschwader of Jagdfliegerführer 2 and Heinkel 111Hs of Kampfgeschwader 53 in Fliegerkorps I respectively were using these very same French airfields in the nightly bombing assault on Britain. KG53, the famous Legion Kondor, comprised five units, with Stab./KG53, E./KG53 and I./KG53 at Lille-Nord, II./KG53 at Vendeville and III./KG53 at Vitry-en-Artois. One of the Heinkel 111H-4 pilots at Vitry was 22-year old Leutnant Alfred Plank von Bachselten, an Austrian by birth. His German crew comprised Gefreiter Blasis Regnat, a 22-year old observer/navigator, 20-year old Gefreiter Bruno Kauhardt, the radio operator/air gunner and Unteroffizier Walter Richter, the 21-year old flight engineer.

On the night of 3/4 May von Bachselten's crew was one of many engaged in bombing operations over the United Kingdom. In all, 298 Luftwaffe bombers set out for Merseyside, twenty to Hartlepool, 24 to Portsmouth and 99 others bombed various targets. For the luckless citizens of Liverpool this was the third night in succession that their city had been selected as the target by German bombers. Ranged against the Luftwaffe raiders were RAF Fighter Command squadrons equipped mainly with Havoc Is, Beaufighter Ifs, Spitfires Is and IIAs, Hurricane Is and IIs and Defiant Is. Despite its shortcomings as a day fighter, the Defiant, with its electrically operated Boulton Paul 'A' Mk.IID turret containing four .303

Browning machine-guns, each with 600 rounds per gun, was a potent weapon at night. (Flight Sergeant Edward Thorn and his gunner, Sergeant James Barker, of 264 Squadron, claimed over thirteen victories on Defiant night fighters).

In 12 Group in the West Midlands, Sergeant Henry Bodien and his WOp/AG Sergeant Wrampling, a 151 Squadron Defiant I crew, was on standby at Wittering. Bodien, born in Hackney, East London in 1916, had joined the RAF in September 1933 as an Aircraft Apprentice at Halton and trained as a fitter. He was later accepted for pilot training and on 28 October 1940 arrived at 6 OTU from 48 (Coastal) Squadron for fighter training as a sergeant. Bodien and Wrampling were something of old hands on 151 Squadron, having shot down a Dornier Do 17Z of 3./KG2 near Corby on the night of 4/5 February. Then, on the night of 9/10 April they shot down a He 111P of II./KG27 flown by Unteroffizier Rudolf Müller, over Birmingham. Müller and one other of his crew bailed out before the Heinkel hit a balloon cable and crashed on houses in Hale's Lane, Smethwick, killing seven civilians as well as the two remaining crew. One of the airmen who bailed out fell on a roof and was badly beaten by local people before he was taken away by the military authorities.

Bodien and Wrampling took off from Wittering at 2328 hours on a 'Freelance patrol'. 151 Squadron shared Wittering with the Beaufighter I night fighters on 25 Squadron, who earlier, at 2228 hours, had sent off on patrol, Sergeant M. M. Hill and his gunner, Sergeant B. J. Hollis. They were unable to intercept the enemy bombers raiding Liverpool but elsewhere Fighter Command had some success. Havocs on 85 Squadron patrolling over East Anglia claimed a He 111 damaged near Dunwich. Near Halesworth, Suffolk another Havoc intercepted a pair of Heinkels and claimed one damaged while the other raider carried out violent evasion action and escaped into the night. On the south coast two He 111s were shot down by 219 and 604 Squadrons and a Ju 88 of II./KG77 was shot down into the English Channel by a 29 Squadron Beaufighter If. Wing Commander Tom Pike on 219 Squadron was credited with the destruction of a He 111, which crashed at Arundel, while Flight Lieutenant Woodward on 600 Squadron downed a Ju 88 over Dorset.

Aboard Heinkel 111H-4 werk no. 3235 A1+LK though, everything was going according to plan. Leutnant Alfred Plank von Bachselten had reached Liverpool without incident. (The German bombers flew individually under cover of darkness and on various tracks to converge at a pre-arranged time in their target area). Liverpool was near the limit of the Heinkel 111H-4/5's range and beyond the limit of German fighter cover. Von Bachselten crossed over the burning dock area and added their bombs to the conflagration before turning for home, hoping that they could evade the fighters and defences. Anti-aircraft batteries claimed three enemy bombers destroyed this night, a 'probable' and another 'damaged'. One of the German losses came from von Bachselten's Gruppe. Leutnant Karl Baller and his crew of a He 111H-5 of 2./KG53 were lost when they crashed into the River Mersey after striking a balloon cable. Patrolling south of Liverpool Flight Lieutenant Deanesly of 256 Squadron destroyed a Do 17 over North Wales and a Ju 88 over Cheshire. On the return journey a number of Luftwaffe aircraft took a direct course which brought them along the North Norfolk coastline. There they could obtain a navigational fix from the Cromer lighthouse high above the town, which remained on throughout the war and was an acknowledged navigational aid to the Luftwaffe prior to crossing the North Sea. Nearby were the tall masts of the West Beckham CH (Chain Home) radar station.

The early night was clear and fine but in the very early hours of the Sunday 4 May moonlight silhouetted the inland intrusion of the waters of The Wash over which the Heinkel flew. Defiant Is and Beaufighter Ifs from Wittering were directed by GCI (Ground Controlled Interception) and AI (Airborne Intercept) radar units onto the string of German bombers returning that night. Among the defending fighters in patrol action this night was the 25 Squadron Beaufighter If crewed by Sergeant M. M. Hill and his gunner, Sergeant B. J. Hollis and the 151 Squadron Defiant I flown by Sergeant Henry Bodien with Sergeant Wrampling uncomfortably manning the gun turret. Over Norfolk during the early hours of 4 May these two crews attacked an enemy bomber and both laid claim to it.

Landing back at Wittering Hill and Hollis were debriefed by the Intelligence Officer and submitted their claim for 'a He 111 destroyed at 0025 hrs near Breedon-on-the-Hill'. Similarly, Henry Bodien and Sergeant Wrampling gave their report and claimed a He 111 destroyed. While both crews laid claim to the enemy bomber, there is no doubt that the victim was Heinkel He 111H-4, Werk Nr. 3235 A1+LK piloted by Leutnant Alfred Plank von Bachselten. The Austrian pilot dived his Heinkel through 10,000 feet in an attempt to evade his attacker, levelling out over the North Norfolk coastline before turning the stricken bomber through a right-hand turn. With landing and navigational lights switched on, he knew he had to crash land in the first available field. On his final approach he sought to maintain sufficient air speed to 'lift' the Heinkel over some hedges which appeared in front of him, rather than to slide through it. Von Bachselten crash-landed the doomed Heinkel at Sharrington, near Holt, five miles inland from the Norfolk coast, at 0204 hours DBST (Double British Summer Time). Al+LK made its final approach heading in a SW direction on a course approximately 220 degrees magnetic. After coming to rest three of the crew clambered out and prepared to destroy their aircraft, which, thanks to the skill of the pilot, had survived a 'wheels up' crash landing mostly intact other than the propeller blades, which were bent around the engine nacelles and damage to the long glass nose sustained when it slid through twin hedgerows each side of a farm service lane. Gefreiter Bruno Kauhardt was found to be dead, so the crew carefully removed the body of the Bordfunker from the aircraft and placed him in a hollow close to the gateway to the field where he would be easily found and some distance from the aircraft, which they now intended to destroy by using a self-destruct device. When this failed to ignite they pumped aviation fuel up from the main tank and ignited the aircraft by soaking their flight maps in fuel. Equipment such as cameras and film of the night raid together with maps and documents were destroyed. The crew intended to masquerade as 'Dutch' airmen and so they emptied their pockets of German coins and other items in a hedge near the crash site.

Shortly after, Roy Lovell, an Army despatch rider from Brinton Road army camp, who lived in Sharrington, having heard the noise of the approaching aircraft, journeyed up the farm lane on his motorcycle to investigate. By the time Lovell arrived the aircraft was on fire and the crew beside the aircraft. He quickly withdrew from the scene to get assistance. Soon, all that would remain of the

Heinkel would be a burnt out black shell with the vertical tail-plane, which still carried the swastika insignia and a yellow 'L' on the upper wing tip. The RAF later recovered seven light (7.92mm) MG 15 machine guns and the wreckage of large external bomb racks.

Police Constable R. Massingham was on duty at Holt police station He recalls: 'The clocks were put forward one hour on this date and it was questioned whether the crash was at 1 am old time or 2 am new time. I received the call, which stated that, an aircraft bad come down in a field at Sharrington, It was not known whether it was British or German. It was on fire. Having reported that fact I was instructed to go to the scene. On my arrival I found that the plane, which was a Heinkel 111, had pancaked through a lane into a field on the Holt side of Sharrington 'Swan' Public House. PC Bunnett of Binham was already there. The plane was on fire. We found the dead gunner in a ditch nearby. He had been shot through the heart. We pulled him out and he was searched. It was ascertained that a dispatch rider had come along, presumably saw some of the crew near the plane and gone far help. We thought there were four in the aircraft so a search of the area was made to locate the other three.'

Unbeknown to PC Massingham, the crew, having set fire to the aircraft, had left the field and had made their way towards the main Fakenham to Holt road. The night was now still and quiet and the crew chatted quietly between themselves. Mrs Allison, who still lives in the cottages at the end of the lane, was alone with her two little girls as her husband had been called away to the war. They watched from their bedroom window as the glow in the adjacent fields got larger and then heard the crew talking between themselves as they arrived at the main road. Having no contact with local inhabitants the crew elected to walk in the direction of Holt, the nearby market town and walked unchallenged through the village of Letheringsett and into Holt. In the early hours of Sunday morning Holt was deserted. Fatigued by the night's events, the crew sought shelter inside a pillbox, which at that time had been constructed on the small square adjacent to the main Holt Post Office. Suitably rested and having failed to find any police officers or military authorities to whom they might give themselves up, the crew walked through Holt and off along the Kelling road via Kelling woods over the heath towards the coast. The crew of Heinkel Al+LK finally reached the coast at Bard Hill, Salthouse Heath, at dawn. There the crew lit a small fire to warm themselves and this brought them to the attention of two servicemen manning a small caravan radio beacon installation.

PC Charles Barnard, a local Kelling police officer, was going about his duty when he cycled over the heath at 6.10 am on Sunday morning, when he came upon the German aircrew. Barnard did not hesitate and he apprehended the airmen. However, when he took the crew home to his wife and two young children at the Kelling police house where they lived, the 'capture' evolved more into a social event. Mrs Vera Barnard gave them tea and breakfast and the crew signed their names and addresses in her husband's 1941 diary pocket book, which she still has. The crew was introduced to the Barnard's two little girls, who still vividly recall the time their father brought the German airmen home for breakfast! They recall the crew's appreciation of the English flowers on her kitchen table and thanking her for her care: saying she had acted to them as a true mother would.

Meanwhile, acting Sergeant George Chapman, a policeman 6 feet 3 inches tall, had been unsuccessful in his hunt for the German airmen, who were now known to be wandering around Norfolk. Chapman, who because of his height rode a specially constructed police cycle with two crossbars, one below the other (now preserved in a local museum) decided to extend his search by calling on PC Barnard at Kelling Police House. When Chapman arrived he was amazed to see the constable and his family having tea with the Germans and exchanging names and addresses for after the war!

PC Massingham continues. 'I received a message that the three had been picked up at Bard Hill (Salthouse Heath) and taken to Kelling Police House. I escorted them to Holt Police Station and they were later handed over to the Military at Gresham's School, Holt. I spoke to the pilot, who informed me in broken English that he had been to Liverpool that night and had made plenty of fires. He said he was very shy of our Spitfires. He also informed me that he had taken all minor roads after setting light to his plane, also burning the film they bed taken during the raid on Liverpool. This crash happened on the Sunday morning and at 2 pm I was instructed to guard the aircraft until 9.30 pm. A collection was made for the Red Cross and several pounds were collected from people visiting the area that day.'

When the 'captured' crew were finally presented late in the day to the main police station in Holt the senior officer on duty, no doubt in response to the apparent casual 'surrender' by the German crew, was heard to say, 'I suppose you Germans think you are going to win this bloody war'?

Later that day the crew was duly handed over to the military authorities at the Gresham School Hall, which was then used by the army as the school had been evacuated to Newquay, Cornwall. The crew was transported initially to Newmarket where they were sheltered for the night in a stable; this time under armed guard. During the night they were joined by Leutnant Joachim Wreschnik, pilot of a Ju 88A-5 of 3./KG77, which he had crash-landed at Welney Wash after his starboard engine failed on the return flight from Liverpool. After struggling on for some distance the port engine failed and caught fire. Baling his crew out over March, Cambridgeshire, Wreschnik belly-landed in a field after skimming over the top of a wood. He suffered head and facial injuries but jumped to safety. Not satisfied with the progress the engine fire was making towards destroying his aircraft, he proceeded to empty his pistol into the engine nacelle in an attempt to make the fire spread. Unfortunately for him, the Home Guard disarmed him and extinguished the fire before the Ju 88 was too badly damaged - not that it contained any new features or equipment of any consequence.

After a night in the stables the Germans were taken to London by train. Still with thoughts towards an escape route Alfred Bachselten sought a corner seat, only to find that on that journey to London all stations were called 'BOVRIL'. They were marched under armed guard from the platform at Liverpool Street railway station and later transferred to a prisoner of war camp. Gefreiter Bruno Kauhardt, initially, was buried in the churchyard at Brinton, nearby, but at the end of the war he was re-interred at the German Military Cemetery at Cannock Chase, Staffordshire, 30 miles north of Birmingham in the centre of England.

Although a moonlight night the Heinkel crew had been unable to identify the attacking aircraft. The intelligence report describes how .303 bullet strikes were found in a section of the starboard wing, entering from below and ahead. Further .303 hits were found in the starboard fuselage and the bomb doors so unless Sergeant Hill carried out an extraordinarily aerobatic head-on night attack with machine guns only, one has to find favour with the Defiant crew of Bodien and Wrampling. The Beaufighter combat report states, 'Saw enemy aircraft on port wing, applied full flaps to slow aircraft to attack from astern - No return fire was experienced.' Alfred Bachselten would recall his evasive flight pattern. It would require a very good recovery to fit the crash landing pattern whereby the aircraft approached flat to slide across two fields and a double hedge to come to rest in another field. The P RO crash report mentions '.303 strikes in the starboard fuselage and wing entering from below and ahead',which is the hallmark of a Defiant attack and consistent with the heavily armed top turret normally used attack patterns.[18]

Even now crops do not grow well at the site of the crash, which in May 1991, Alfred von Bachselten and his wife Dolly, visited, with ex-Cromer resident and historian, Russell Reeve and the late Helmut Rix, a former Luftwaffe fighter pilot and PoW who lived in England after the war. Russell recalls: 'Alfred Bachselten having read in my report of the distress experienced by Mrs Allison and her family at the time of the crash, felt he would wish to meet her and a new friendship was established with photographs and offers of tea after the delay of a mere 50 years! Alfred Bachselten engaged the present owner of the ex police house in conversation and photographs were taken. By chance a Norfolk Constabulary police car passed slowly on the roadway, no doubt wondering what all the fuss was about. 'Even after the passage of years I find difficulty in adequately expressing my feelings of admiration for the conduct and bravery of the late PC Charles Barnard. At the end of a rather extraordinary day we were to return to Cromer for tea. The assembled company mused on the futility of war and the significance of lasting friendship. We were pleased to walk up Happy Valley and round the lighthouse, which previously had been viewed only from the air. We gazed across the bleak North Sea enshrouded that day in mist. Alfred Bachselten had obtained his Luftwaffe logbook and other material. The entry 4 May 1941 merely recorded 'Did not return'. - I am glad they did.'

Endnotes

18 Henry Bodien was promoted to Pilot Officer and was awarded the DFC in March 1942, subsequently being promoted to flight lieutenant on 1 May 1943 and finally squadron leader. He was posted to 21 Squadron on 13 February 1944 and flew Mosquito fighter-bombers on Day Rangers over Europe. He finished the war with five confirmed victories, two of them while flying Mosquito II night fighters of 151 Squadron with Sergeant G. B. Brooker as his navigator/radio operator, in 1942-43. In September 1944 he was awarded the DSO. During the Korean War Bodien was attached to the USAAF, 1950-51 and he flew B-26 bombers on night interdiction missions, being awarded the US Air Medal. From May 1951 to January 1952 he commanded 29 Squadron and he left the RAF in April 1953 to take up a position in the RCAF.

Chapter 7

Window To Freedom

Sitting in his room at the Royal Air Force College at Cranwell, Squadron Leader D. D. W. Nabarro, Education Officer and instructor to the cadets, looked out of his window and remembered another window through which he scrambled to safety after kicking a German guard senseless. But that was only one of many incredible escapes which led Sergeant Pilot Derrick Nabarro to freedom and earned for him the first Distinguished Conduct Medal to be awarded to the Royal Air Force.

Born on 4 July 1921, Derrick Nabarro had not long left Preston Grammar School when, as a 19-year-old second pilot on Whitley V Z6561 on 10 Squadron at Leeming, he released 3,500lb of bombs on Bremen on 27/28 June 1941 with the cool judgment of a veteran airman. A few minutes later, caught in the searchlights, his Whitley received a direct hit on the port engine. The aircraft staggered under this mortal blow. Nabarro, his nose broken and scalp badly torn, watched the falling pressure gauge for the starboard motor. Then he heard Sergeant N. J. Gregory the skipper yell out: 'I'm ditching!' They were over Kiel Bay. Pilot Officer Alexander Knox Watson the rear-gunner, alas, had already bailed out over the sea and was never seen again. But the pilot and the wireless operator, Pilot Officer G. M. Frame, navigator and Pilot Officer J. D. Margrie and Nabarro clambered into the dinghy and bailed out furiously with empty Very Light cartridge cases. They had not long to wait for help, for a German Air/Sea Rescue launch was quickly on the scene. Aboard the German craft they were searched, given coffee and dry clothing while their own uniforms were drying and then taken to the nearest Luftwaffe airfield for interrogation. For Derrick and his pals it seemed the war was over.

But this was not the sort of future which Derrick Nabarro could accept without question. Separated from the rest of the crew for transfer to a permanent PoW camp, his mind soon turned to the possibilities of escape and on the train journey to the camp at Bad Suiza (nicknamed 'Hell's Kitchen' by the prisoners), he took advantage of his guards' preoccupation to unscrew the maps of the district which were displayed on the walls of the compartment. Such documents were invaluable to a man who was bent on escape. He stuffed them carefully inside his clothing. At Bad Suiza he found that many of his fellow prisoners were wounded and dispirited; some had been there since Dunkirk, a year before and had lost their enthusiasm for escape. There were of course several of the usual tunnel schemes in operation, but he did not join in these. 'Tunnels take too long,' he whispered to Bill, another prisoner who hoped to find an easier way out' and every day means another chance of discovery. We want to make a quick getaway. Just wait for the right moment and then.'

They were standing in the compound, idling watching the German guards in their tower at one corner of the barbed-wire perimeter. Bill raised his eyes and inspected the structure. 'The goons have a good view of the whole area up there,' he said 'but there's a blind spot. If anyone made a break immediately under the tower, they couldn't be seen.'

'But how could you get under the tower without them spotting you?' asked Nabarro.

'That's a matter of luck, of course. But if the guards' attention could be distracted at the crucial moment. . . .'

The preparations had to be carefully made and took some weeks. Saving precious rations from his Red Cross parcels, Nabarro bartered them for a compass and some German money; then he copied a new map of France which he borrowed from one of the French prisoners. Meanwhile he enlisted the aid of some of the other prisoners in making a point of sunbathing and playing cards at the foot of the tower, so that the guards would become accustomed to seeing them there. Less than two months after being shot down, Nabarro was ready to leave for home!

It had been decided that the best way to distract the attention of the guards was to organise an open-air boxing tournament. On the crucial day, the scene was set carefully. Flight Sergeant J. A. McCairns took charge of the boxing programme and a crowd of prisoners lounged on the ground round the ring. Among them, immediately under the tower and sitting on a blanket which hid their escape haversacks, were Bill and Derrick. The second round had been planned as a particularly thrilling spectacle which would divert the guards...

The bell rang and the boxers lunged into each other. The audience stood up and roared their approval.

'Now!' said Derrick, between gritted teeth.

The two men stood up, collected their haversacks and quickly scaled the wire under the guards' tower. At this precise moment McCairns shook the blanket on which they had been seated, to create still more confusion.

They were clear of the wire. Now they only had to run some twenty yards along a river bank to the shelter of bushes. The roar of the crowd continued manfully, five...only ten yards now...seven...five.

'Rat-tat-tat-tat-tat!' The machine gun from the tower barked out and guttural voices shouted a warning. Within a few steps from safety, the escaping pair had been spotted and the ping of the bullets was the death knell of their escape. There was nothing they could do except hold up their hands in subjection.

This was the ignominious end of Escape No. 1. Solitary confinement was the inevitable punishment, but it served to steel Nabarro 's resolve to make another attempt as soon as possible, after his 'solitary' was over he quickly recruited a new accomplice, a German speaking Belgian prisoner named Godfrey. By resuming his bartering Derrick Nabarro gradually acquired a new stock of Reichmarks and a civilian suit. Bill unselfishly donated his precious compass which German searchers failed to unearth.

This time the plan was different. On the fateful morning in December 1941, armed with brushes and bucket. Derrick crossed into the Belgian compound and Godfrey informed the guard that they were detailed to clean the Commandant's office. Once in the building, they tore off their greatcoats and hid them where their helpers would retrieve them later, picked up the previously-deposited kit and, with felt covering their hands and boots, quietly scaled the wire into the Commandant's orchard and crossed the river by the bridge. The details of this part of the plan had been worked out carefully in advance. They realised that the Germans, when the escape had been spotted, would be bound to check all West-bound routes towards Belgium, so they deliberately went in the opposite direction, further into the heart of Germany. Arriving at a station two-and-a-half miles away. Godfrey boldly booked tickets on the Berlin-bound train. Their plan was to get off at Naumburg and then take a train in the opposite direction, through the area they had just left and straight to the Belgian frontier.

They sat in different parts of the train all the way and at Naumberg Godfrey bought two tickets for Gerolstein, about 50 miles from the Belgian border. Their return journey began. . . .

'Bad Suiza.' The German porter called out the name of the station as the train pulled up at the platform. Nabarro sat hunched up in his seat, praying that the halt would not be a long one, praying that the Germans would not decide to search the train. Suddenly, as he gazed fearfully out of the carriage window, he came face to face with another British prisoner on the platform outside! This man was evidently a member of a working party which had been sent from the camp to unload Red Cross parcels. Turning his face hurriedly away, Nabarro was sickened by the thought that perhaps one of his own compatriots might involuntarily give him away in that moment of startled recognition. But all was well. If the Englishman had seen him, he gave no sign of having recognised the fleeing prisoner. Soon the train was on its way again and Bad Suiza was left behind. The following 24 hours was a nightmare which Derrick Nabarro will never forget - train journeys, bombing raids and long waits at dismal stations, fraught with the danger of recognition and exposure.

Kassel was being heavily attacked by the RAF and this and the subsequent delay, made them miss their connection. Twelve hours to wait for the first train in the morning! They arrived at Koblenz next evening and found themselves faced with another ten hours' wait. They washed and shaved in the station lavatory and then went into the restaurant for a meal. It was nearly their undoing. At another table a German boy in the uniform of the Hitler Youth began eyeing them inquisitively. 'Watch that youngster!'

hissed Godfrey. 'He suspects something.' The boy was staring at them with brazen curiosity. Soon he rose from his table and went out, obviously with the intention of reporting his suspicions to someone in authority.

'It's getting too hot here,' said Nabarro. 'Can't we lay up somewhere until it's time for our train? '

There was only one place where they could be sure of privacy and Derrick and Godfrey went to it. For the next few hours they occupied adjacent cubicles until, early the next morning, they deemed it safe to come out again and board their train for Gerolstein.

But here, within fifty miles of the Belgian border, the calendar caught them out. It was now Sunday and all the travellers (except Derrick and Godfrey) were in their 'Sunday best.' Their unorthodox clothes made them the immediate target of the elderly policeman at Gerolstein. He called after them. Deciding it was useless to run, the two men walked on, pretending not to realise they were the subject of his call. But it was no use. The policeman insisted on checking their documents and promptly marched them to his house at the end of the village and placed them in a cellar which apparently served as the village 'lock-up.'

'You stay in there for the night,' said the policeman as he locked the door behind them. 'In the morning we'll send you to a proper prison.'

Nabarro's eyes pierced the gloom in the cell. There were already three other men in the small cellar and Godfrey, speaking to them in French, discovered that they were two Frenchmen and a Belgian who were waiting transport to the prison at Treves to serve their sentence.

'I expect they will send you there with us,' said one of the Frenchmen, whose name was Pierre.

Nabarro surveyed the situation in which they now found themselves. If they once got back to a proper prison, the chances of making a break would be greatly reduced. They would have to try and get away from this place before the transport came in the morning. He communicated this thought to Godfrey, who put it to the others. They all agreed to join in. The cellar was hopeless; but in the corridor outside? Nabarro called the policeman and asked to go to the toilet. Escorted to the small, bare room; he saw what he was looking for: a small window over the stone wash basin. It was barely large enough to allow a grown man to squeeze through, but it would have to do. 'You can't get out of there, don't worry,' said the policeman, as if reading his thoughts. 'Don't waste your time thinking about it.'

'Escape?' laughed Nabarro quickly. 'Oh, not for me. I've tried it too many times already. All I want is to get back to my PoW camp and wait for the end of the war.'

Well satisfied, the policeman escorted him back to the cell. In the small hours of the morning Nabarro explained his plan to the others. It was still dark when the policeman awoke them in the morning. 'The transport will be here in half an hour,' he said. 'You'd better get yourselves ready to move.' The men raised a feeble cheer. 'It'll be nice to get back to a proper prison again,' said one. 'Anything rather than this cold hole.'

'Hadn't we better have a wash first?' asked Godfrey innocently. 'We don't want to go back to a proper prison looking like this. People might think you hadn't looked after us very well.'

The policeman hesitated. 'All right,' he said at last, 'I'll go and get a lamp.' He turned away from the cellar door, leaving it ajar, as Nabarro had anticipated. Without waiting another second, the five of them rushed out of the cellar - Godfrey first, followed by Pierre, Nabarro and the other two - into the corridor, along to the toilet, with the startled policeman hot on their heels. Godfrey was up on the washbasin, struggling with the window. In a moment he had flung it open, had squeezed through it and jumped out on the other side. Pierre followed next. The other Frenchman and the Belgian held the door back as the policeman tried to batter his way in. Now it was Nabarro 's turn. His head and shoulders were through the window opening when the door suddenly burst in and the policeman rushed at him. Nabarro felt his legs grasped from behind: he lunged backwards with all his strength and kicked the policeman to the floor. He didn't have time to feel sorry for the old man. Three pairs of fists were battering the policeman into insensibility and then they were away, up upon the basin and out through the window. In a copse they paused, gulping for breath, waiting to determine their next move. Angry cries were coming from the village and they heard the yelping of dogs and the frantic ringing of church bells. The hunt was on! Scattering pepper (which Nabarro had thoughtfully included in his kit) over their trail, they were off again into the woods. After a mile or two they stopped again. They could hear no more of their pursuers. It was a clean getaway! By nightfall they had reached the Siegfried Line. Once over the frontier, Nabarro and Godfrey decided to separate from Pierre and the other two. 'If you get to Paris,' said Pierre as they said goodbye. 'Go to this address. I will try to contact you there.'

In the Ardennes they went to Godfrey's own village and Godfrey remained there to work with the Belgian Underground, so Nabarro pressed on into France alone. By the end of the month he had met up with Pierre again in Paris. 'The best thing to do now is to get into Vichy France,' Pierre told him. 'There are no Germans there. Then give yourself up to the French police. There is an Underground escape route for British prisoners, through Marseilles. They'll put you in the right way.' But not all the French police were anxious to help an escaping British airman, as Nabarro found to his cost. After giving himself up, as directed, he found himself taken, not to Marseilles, but to an internment camp at Ste-Hippolyte near Nimes. Nabarro found an escape method after weeks of thought and it bore out his contention that the best escapes are always the simplest. This one entailed merely the removal of obstructing bars on a floor grating and escaping through the sewer. In a matter of hours, after ploughing through gallons of filth and slime, Nabarro was free again. He walked into Monte Carlo where he was fortunate enough to contact the local Underground.

One memorable night five weeks later a total of 120 men and women hid under tarpaulins on the deck of a cargo ship leaving Marseilles. With enemy aircraft flying overhead to intercept illegal shipping, they spent seven nerve-wracking days and nights in the slow and dangerous journey through the Mediterranean to Gibraltar and freedom. Nabarro and his companions, without any of the 'gadgets' later available for aircrews, had escaped from the very heart of Germany.

After his arrival in Scotland and the subsequent award of the DCM. Sergeant Derrick Nabarro was commissioned and spent the rest of the war giving lectures which helped many others to evade capture. At the end of hostilities he left the Service, went to Manchester University where he took his Arts degree and returned to the RAF in 1950 as an Education Officer. And every now and then, in the course of his duties, he would take a Busman's holiday - interrogating cadets and others who are 'captured' during Escape and Evasion exercises in England![19]

Endnotes
19 Adapted from an article written by Leslie Hunt in *RAF Flying Review,* March 1959.

Chapter 8

Aachen Adventure

On the night of 9/10 July 1941 Pilot Officer Basil John Allan Rennie, the South African pilot of Hampden I AD924 on 144 Squadron, was one of about 80 bombers returning to Hemswell from a bombing raid on Aachen. On this night 39 Hampdens, 27 Whitleys and sixteen Wellingtons were dispatched in what was the first large raid on the town. It was heavily bombed with many bombs exploding in the central areas where the cathedral , the town hall, two hospitals and 1,698 houses and apartment blocks were destroyed or seriously damaged. About sixty people were killed, 106 were injured and 3,450 people were bombed out. [20] One Whitley was shot down. A few kilometres short of the target AD924 was caught in a cone of ten searchlights at 15,000 feet and was far behind the rest of the bombers and losing height when a Bf 109 night fighter shot away their controls and set a petrol tank on fire. Rennie bailed out after Sergeant G. F. Bottomley the observer and the wireless operator Sergeant Thomas Henry Marquiss but Sergeant Edward Roy Berkey, the Canadian rear gunner was already dead. The Hampden crashed near Dilsen in Belgium. Rennie saw the other two members of his crew coming down, held in the beams of the searchlights but Marquiss, possibly hit by debris from the Hampden did not survive. Bottomley was taken prisoner.

As he descended from 5,000 feet Rennie lost his left boot. He fell on to the telegraph wires in a small village a few miles north of Hasselt and had some difficulty in extricating himself from a complicated entanglement of wires, ropes and harness, but after a struggle he succeeded and slid down a telegraph pole into the village street, leaving his parachute up on the wires. Incidentally the parachute had his name on it - a thought which, afterwards troubled him a good deal and might have led to very serious consequences had he been captured in the later stages of his escape. The village appeared to be deserted as he limped along with only one boot on. He had had enough excitement for that night and did not care who captured him. The natural instinct is to sit down and enjoy a cigarette. Rennie walked slowly through the village without any conscious intention of escaping. More than anything else he felt at that moment a great desire for peace and sympathy. Going round a corner, he came upon a dozen Belgian civilians, who were watching the display of searchlights and anti-aircraft fire, which was still in progress. The moment they caught sight of him they recognised who he was. Two of them seized him by the arms and rushed him into a house and down into the cellar where he lay, still somewhat dazed but slowly recovering. Whilst he was there, Germans entered the village and with great banging of doors and much shouting, started to make a methodical house-to-house search. One of the Belgians came down to the cellar and leading Rennie out by the back door, watched him crawl carefully into a wheat-field behind the house. A wheat-field is an excellent hiding place, providing you leave no trail of broken stalks to mark your entry. Rennie lay quietly among the wheat, listening till the sounds of the search died away. Resting there, he gradually began to recover his morale. It came to him very forcibly that a number of simple peasants had already taken big risks to save him from capture and he felt that it was about time that he did something for himself. The neighbourhood of the village was obviously dangerous for him; with his parachute still hanging up on the telegraph wires, the place was sure to be searched again intensively in the morning. It was past midnight and although it was a clear moonlight night, the moon was yet low and progress along the dark side of the hedgerow was possible. He crawled out of the wheat and made his way carefully along the side of the road for half an hour without seeing anybody.

At last he came upon a solitary man, leaning against a tree, watching the sky where searchlight fingers wandered and coned from time to time. The man was very big and was dressed in civilian clothes. Rennie approached without being seen or heard till he was within a few paces when the man sprang round and stared at him in astonishment. In moderate French Rennie explained who he was and what he wanted - shoes, clothes, a little food and drink and a cigarette - or perhaps the man would hide him? The Belgian took Rennie by the arm in a powerful grip and led him along a path through a field. A feeling of increasing uneasiness crept over Rennie as he walked beside the Belgian; he did not like the man's silence, or perhaps it was the firm grip on his arm. His whole being became alert and all his instincts of self preservation were aroused.

Suddenly, not fifty yards ahead of them, the beam of a searchlight sprang into the air - the Belgian was clearly leading him straight to a searchlight battery. Non! hissed Rennie, pulling back and trying to disengage his arm, Voila les Boches!

Allons, answered the man, tightening his grip on him with both hands.

The Belgian was a big, powerful fellow and Rennie, though powerful for his height, saw from the first that the man over-matched him in strength. Without hesitation he kicked the Belgian so effectively that he fell noiselessly in a heap and lay unconscious. Rennie then moved quietly back to the main road and continued along the hedge until he reached the outskirts of the village. Here he came upon a small group of peasants, who were terrified when they recognised him as an RAF pilot; they were Flamands and he had some difficulty in making himself understood. They were unwilling to help - they were too poor, they said, to give him clothes and were obviously too frightened to hide him, But they showed friendship by giving him cigarettes and pointing him on his way. It was 3am of a very bright moonlight night when he found himself walking southward along the towpath of a canal (of which there were many in that part of the country). All around the countryside was flat and there was no good cover for hiding; there was nothing to be done but to go on. He felt hunted and alone in the world and horribly conspicuous in the moonlight as he hobbled along with only one boot.

After walking for half an hour he saw someone coming towards him along the towpath. He needed help urgently, for it was nearly daybreak, but at first he was unable to distinguish whether it was a friend or foe. When they were about fifty yards apart Rennie realised suddenly that it was a German soldier with a rifle slung over his shoulder. There was no cover. If he ran for it he might be shot and even rouse the neighbourhood. When hardly a dozen yards apart the German realised that Rennie was in a strange uniform. As they came close together the German stared, then shouted in his face. Then, suddenly looking up, Rennie pointed with his left hand over the German's shoulder and cried out Achtung! The German turned his head quickly and as he did so Rennie kicked him violently with his only boot and all his strength. The German fell with a terrible cry and the rifle slipped from his shoulder. Rennie snatched it almost before it had reached the ground and with the butt hit him on the side of the head. Then he chucked the rifle into the canal and dragged the corpse off the towpath. He stamped the body well into the mud at the side of the canal. Then, gathering some reeds, he laid them over the grave to hide it. There was a pool of blood on the towpath which he obliterated with a few handfuls of gravel. With his hands now covered with blood, he continued his walk along the path.

It was now after 4am and Rennie owned that he felt very tired. Finding a patch of grass near the towpath, he lay down and went to sleep. It was not good cover, but he was exhausted by all he had been through. About 7am he woke in bright sunlight and saw a man walking towards him. Rennie waited until he was quite near and then almost in a whisper said, *Bon Belge*? for he had learnt during that night that there were two sorts of Belgians, *Bon Belge* and *Boche Belge* - those who are loyal and those who helped the Germans either openly or in secret. When Rennie whispered *Bon Belge*? the man understood him immediately. The man, who was dressed in miner's clothes, first looked about to make sure there was no one in sight and then answered, *Qui*!

Rennie was a nasty sight; there was blood on his uniform and on his face and hands. He washed quickly in the canal and then he and the miner made their way across the meadows and reached a house at Eisden, fifteen kilometres north of Maastricht without apparently being seen by anyone. Here he hid in the garden and an amazing thing happened. Parcels of civilian clothes were thrown over the wall to him and before long he had sufficient to clothe at least five men. He had certainly been seen by friends and probably his presence in the district had been reported to the Germans. He changed into civilian clothes and then, borrowing a suitcase, packed into it his dirty bloodstained uniform. This case he carried with him during the whole of the rest of his adventures as far as the Pyrénées - an act of inconceivable folly, which without doubt would have cost him his life had he been caught. Rennie's danger was even greater than would at first appear, for he not only kept the tell-tale uniform and his identification discs, but he had also left his parachute with his name on it among the telephone wires, making the train of circumstantial evidence complete.

He had not been in the garden very long when word was received that the Germans were coming. Unfortunately the Burgomeister's secretary was a Boche Belge. Once more he went out at the back and hid in a wheat-field and when the Germans searched the house and garden, steps had already been taken to ensure that they would find nothing suspicious. At last the search died down and Rennie, now in passable civilian clothes, well provided with food and carrying his suitcase, made his way southwards, to Hasselt, for some days without having any adventure worth recording. Later he was passing through a small village in the early morning when he heard the faint sound of a voice which was somehow familiar. The words were quite inaudible, but the intonation struck a chord in his memory. Could it be from another member of his crew? He put his ear against the closed shutters. Suddenly he realised it was Alvar Liddel's voice giving out the 7am news on the BBC. Obviously the house contained friends, for the penalties for listening to the BBC were extremely severe. He crept round to the back of the house and threw open the door suddenly. Two girls who were sitting in a corner close to a wireless set uttered screams of surprise.They were obviously frightened and switched off the wireless quickly - they had been caught red-handed.

Rennie shut the door and in quite passable French, explained who he was and was given a joyous welcome. He stayed one night at the cottage, but next day, at midday on 12 July, transferred his lodging to the cellar of a hotel. The proprietor, whilst billeting Germans, was at the same time an ardent patriot whose son desired above all else to get to England to join the Belgian army. He and Rennie decided to join forces. With plenty of money and all the necessary forged papers they left by train for Liège and on 15 July crossed the border into France. Paying a man 500 francs to row them across the St Quentin canal, they reached Paris on 17 July and stayed there with friends for two days before taking the train to Tours and travelling on foot south-east to the Demarcation Line between Occupied and Unoccupied France near Givry (Saône-et-Loire). Very foolishly they did not trouble to get a guide and so spent two nights and a day being chased round and round in the woods with sentries on all sides of them. Rennie and his companion eventually ran into a stray German sentry off duty when they were almost through the lines. He asked them where they were going. 'To Tours,' they answered. 'Well, you are not allowed to pass through here,' he said and sent them on into Unoccupied France, which was exactly what they wanted. It was an excellent ruse and was used on many occasions by many escapers in similar circumstances.

After a night in a wood near la Charmée they were caught by two gendarmes, but were released on payment of 200 francs. Walking to Tournus they caught a bus to Lyon, a train to Marseilles, where they stayed briefly in a hotel, before continuing on 24 July by train to Perpignan. After five days they moved out of the town and lay up for another five days in a vineyard. Returning to Perpignan they moved out of the town and hid for another five days in a stable near a friendly farm. Returning to Perpignan they found two guides and left with them across the Pyrénées at 9pm on 9 August, spending the night in the mountains. On 10 August they reached Vilajuiga, 15 kilometres from the French border and stayed with the father of one of the guides who took a message from them to the British consulate in Barcelona. Vice-consul Dorchy picked them up that night in his car and subsequently arranged for their journey to Madrid. Rennie and two other escapers were flown from Gibraltar to Oban in Scotland on 4/5 September 1941.[21]

Endnotes

20 *The Bomber Command War Diaries: An operational reference book 1939-1945* by Martin Middlebrook and Chris Everitt.

21 Flight Lieutenant Rennie MC died on 19 October 1942 at 14 OTU. *Escape and Liberation 1940-1945* by A. J. Evans (Hodder & Stoughton Ltd 1945)/*RAF Evaders: The Comprehensive Story of Thousands of Escapers and Their Escape Lines. Western Europe 1940-1945* by Oliver Clutton-Brock (Grub Street, 2009).

Chapter 9

Flaming June

The sky over Hamburg in January 1942 was apt to be a lively place. On the night of the 15/16th of that month when 96 aircraft were dispatched to bomb Hamburg in difficult visibility the crew of Stirling W7461 OJ-N on 149 Squadron at Mildenhall in 3 Group met with a very hot reception from the powerful ground defences. Flying Officer William George Barnes' crew dropped their bomb load as squarely on the target as the bomb aimer and the pilot could contrive. Then the big aircraft shuddered as a direct hit carried away the starboard inner propeller. Shortly afterwards the behavior of the gauges showed that more than one of the fuel tanks had been holed, so that petrol was pouring out fast. As the aircraft turned on its homeward course heavy cloud stretched as far as could be seen ahead. Every man on board - all sergeants - wondered how far they would get before the inevitable happened. Would it be a case of jumping before they got clear of enemy-occupied territory, or would they have to ditch the Stirling in the winter wastes of the North Sea? The night was freezing cold; there was no telling whether the cloud mass reached right down to the earth's surface; so that neither prospect was inviting.

As the long trip dragged on everybody realized that Barnes was doing a nice job. Although he had only three good engines, he nursed the aircraft along carefully, using the fuel from the leaking tanks first and running his remaining engines at the best economical settings. At the same time he shrewdly allowed the big machine a small but constant loss of height in order to get every last yard out of the power available. At last they knew they had crossed the continental coast and were over the North Sea. To the crew of any aircraft suffering 'trouble' this part of the journey home always seemed an eternity. The men were all grimly tensed bundles of nerves. They said little. They listened to the engines' beat, tried to think of other things and went on waiting for the faltering note that would mean that the worst had happened. Through a small break in the cloud, they saw that they had passed over the English coast, some miles off course, but still going fairly strong. With nervous tension relaxed, a wave of cheerfulness seemed to pass down the machine. The crew eased themselves in their positions and there was talk and some laughter.

'Do you reckon we can make it?' asked the co-pilot, Sergeant Douglas 'Douggie' A. Baker.

Barnes shrugged. 'See that everyone's got a pack on and get them forward' he said. 'However far we manage to geo, we dare not try and scrape down through ten-tenths cloud. You heard the engineer? We're nearly dry and the engines may cut at any moment.'

As he spoke he was turning the aircraft on the correct course for base, although Baker knew he could never reach it. During the next five minutes, which Baker admitted felt nearer five years; the crew - Cyril William Dellow, observer; Townsend, Heron, Cook and Richard Thomas Patrick Gallagher, rear gunner - got ready and lined up. Then the first engine cut. Almost immediately the remaining two ceased running and the propeller blades became visible, spun for a short time and then jerkily came to a standstill. Briefly the skipper gave the order to bail out, his voice sounding unnaturally clear in the sudden silence. This became even more noticeable by reason of the whispering whine of the air outside as he put the big aircraft into a controlled dive. Baker, as was his duty, stood by and watched the five members of the crew drop away through the escape hatch and instantly disappear in the clear moonlight above the vast carpet of cloud. Then he climbed back up beside the skipper and made his report. 'Everybody away' he said. 'Are you all right? Shall I go now?'

Barnes nodded briefly. 'Hoppit' he said 'and don't waste time.'

Douggie Baker therefore obediently jumped down between the two pilots' seats to get clear as soon as possible in order to give his captain every chance. But as he did so the rip-cord of his parachute caught on some projection. What it was he never knew, but the immediate result was that his parachute pack opened and in the fierce draught from the escape hatch the silken folds of the canopy bellied out behind him and blew inside the aircraft. Baker admitted that he was more terrified at that moment than he had ever been in the whole of his Air Force career. He knew in that moment that the parachute was probably tearing and ripping itself against the mass of awkward angles, handles and objects with which the interior of any aircraft fuselage is crowded. His hopes of using it as a support in the air, even if he managed to get it clear, could be counted as practically nil. Yet his duty was plain and he acted promptly. Grabbing the shroud lines in his hands, he wrenched himself up between the seats again and shouted out what had happened. 'Don't wait until I've got the damned thing clear' he yelled. 'You can get past these lines. Come on, get away!'

The skipper's reply however, was typical. 'Don't be a bloody fool' Barnes said. 'Get down and get that thing untangled. Shove it out of the escape hatch. You've still got a chance. If you can't go, I can't...'

Baker scrambled down again. What sort of time was left he couldn't tell. When the engines had first cut and the crew had gone away he had marked the altimeter height at 6,000 feet. How long had passed since then he did not know but he realized that the aircraft had been rapidly losing height. Meanwhile, the problem before him was complicated. If he dived straight out of the escape hatch the chances were about a million to one that his parachute would not follow him. If it did, it would merely be a few wisps of ripped and torn silk which would be less support on his journey towards the earth than a girlfriend's sunshade. On the other hand, if he sat on the hatch laboriously gathering up the billowing folds of the canopy from inside the machine and pushed them out, it was a thousand to one that they would merely entangle themselves around the tail of the aircraft. Nevertheless, the second alternative was obviously the better. Baker therefore scrambled down to the hatch, sat on the edge with his legs dangling over and gathered his rigging lines hand over hand, as quickly as he dared, wondering how many tears had developed.

As he worked he could feel the whole fabric of the parachute thrashing on the bottom of the fuselage in the incoming draught. Then, as he paid out bunches of the fabric, the force of the wind outside made it jerk violently in its grasp. Soon he found he could hardly hold against this wrenching pull. The part of the parachute outside the aircraft was pulling itself out of his hands, with part still inside the aircraft. He wondered wildly what he could do. The question was answered before he had time to work it out. The answer came in the form of a thudding crack over the head dealt him by the edge of the escape hatch. The outside part of the parachute had completely 'taken charge' and dragged him bodily out of the machine. He was three parts dazed, but when his senses cleared he realized that he was floating in cloud with the parachute somewhere up above his head in the blackness. Perhaps it was natural that Baker's first instinct was a surge of thankfulness that he was still alive. From the comforting feel of his weight in the web harness, he knew that he was not falling freely. The parachute was sufficiently intact to be giving him support although he had no means of knowing just how much. His second thoughts were for the aircraft he had left and for his skipper. But although he listened carefully he could hear nothing, which was not surprising since the aircraft was without motive power. Otherwise, as most people who have tried it know, parachuting through cloud at night restricts your range of vision pretty well to the end of your nose.

Quite soon, however, there was a difference in the weaving void below him which was difficult to make out in detail, but he knew it meant that he was approaching the ground. He gripped the rigging lines, tensed himself and strained his eyes fiercely. Still nothing showed. Then suddenly he saw a tree and landed with heavy force, smashing through the thin ice of a shallow, frozen pond. Awkwardly, in the manner of a hooked fish, he rolled and plunged while his parachute dragged him about twenty yards clear of the pond before it lodged in a bush and collapsed. He staggered very shakily to his feet, released his harness and tried to get his bearings. He found the darkness almost as intense as it had been during his journey down through the cloud. He set out to try to take a straight path - in what direction he had no idea - and for the next hour stumbled in vague circles until at last a cottage loomed up in front of him. Subsequently he found that it was less than a hundred yards from the point at which he had landed. Not unnaturally, Baker was almost royally entertained by the good folk who lived in the cottage, directly he had knocked at the door and made his presence known. The nearest RAF station was contacted by telephone and he was given the glad news that all the rest of his crew had landed safely and were being cared for. Of the aircraft and the captain, however, he got no word until he had a night's sleep, when he was given the best and most amusing news of all.

Barnes, by a mixture of miraculous good luck and first-class skill, had managed to land the aircraft in the darkness, southwest of Anston in Yorkshire. The landing, as might be expected, had been spectacular. The big aircraft dug its nose into the ground, reared tail-up and then almost disintegrated upside-down. After which; when he could think clearly, the skipper found himself hanging head downwards in his harness. All who have tried it know there is one little difficulty about getting out of a safety harness when in an inverted position. This is to avoid dropping several feet on to one's head, thereby breaking one's neck, directly the release is effected. Nevertheless, Barnes managed it. After which, like Baker, he wandered in circles around the crash shouting and whistling but unable to find any form of human habitation in the darkness. Therefore with commendable good sense, he returned to the crash, climbed into what was left of the fuselage, collected seat cushions and anything else he could find and calmly settled himself to sleep. The crew of a roving tender from the nearest RAF station found him in the clear light of day, woke him up and carried him off to a good breakfast, no worse for his night's adventure. [22]

Flight Lieutenant Bill Barnes DFC was ill when on the night of 29/30 June 1942 Bomber Command returned to Bremen. Warrant Officer Len Collins RAAF, a Stirling WOp/AG on 149 Squadron at Lakenheath recalls: 'Having completed my tour I had been posted to an EFTS to train as a pilot. I volunteered to stand in for the mid upper gunner on Flight Lieutenant Bill Barnes DFC crew and fly my 33rd trip. Other than the 2nd pilot, Wing Commander [George William] Alexander, on his first trip to gain experience, the remainder of the crew were on their 30th. All were RAF. I was the only Aussie.

'As we assembled outside the canteen waiting for the flight bus to take us to our aircraft at the dispersal bay, we noticed several black limousines heading towards the squadron aircraft. On takeoff we were told that an adjustment had been made to each aircraft's IFF. This modification, after ten seconds warming up, was designed to make German radar feed inaccurate readings to its flak batteries.[23] I was ringed with cannon shells and injured in the leg by shrapnel. Owing to the electrical cut out which protected the tail of the aircraft from the mid upper guns, I was unable to fire on the fighter attacking us. Fortunately, the turret became jammed in the rear position, allowing me to vacate it. Forward, the aircraft was burning like a torch. I could not contact any crewmember. The position was hopeless. I felt I had no option but to leave the aircraft. My parachute was not in its storage holder. I found it under the legs of the mid upper turret with a cannon shell burn in it. I removed the rear escape hatch, clipped on the parachute and sat on the edge of the hatch. I pulled the ripcord and tumbled out. The parachute, having several holes from the shell burn, 'candlesticked' (twirled) as I descended and I landed in a canal.' Collins was apprehended the following day and he was taken to Leeuwarden airfield for interrogation. 'Here I met the pilot of the Messerschmitt 110 who claimed to have shot us down. I abused him in good Australian. He understood, having spent three years at Oxford University.'

'The trip to Bremen was uneventful. Conversing with the wing commander, I found he was most interested with the pyrotechnic display from the flak and the colours of the searchlights as we crossed the enemy coast. I predicted we were in for trouble when a blue one slid off our wing tip. However, either our doctored IFF did not work or the Germans were given a tip-off. Over Bremen we received a direct hit from flak on our inner starboard engine, killing Wing Commander Alexander and Pilot Officer Dellow and injuring the wireless operator Sergeant Hickley. The bombs were dropped live; a photo taken and we headed for home on three engines. Over the Zuider Zee a night fighter [Bf 110 flown by Leutnant Bethel of II./NJG2] attacked us [and the Stirling was shot down at 0204 hours, crashing in the Ijsselmeer near Wons just south of Harlingen]. I can still recall the flash of his windscreen in the darkness as he opened fire. As I was speaking to Sergeant Gallagher, he was blown out of his rear turret.[23] I was ringed with cannon shells and injured in the leg by shrapnel. Owing to the electrical cut out which protected the tail of the aircraft from the mid upper guns, I was unable to fire on the fighter attacking us. Fortunately, the turret became jammed in the rear position, allowing me to vacate it. Forward, the aircraft was burning like a torch. I could not contact any crewmember. The position was hopeless. I felt I had no option but to leave the aircraft. My parachute was not in its storage holder. I found it under the legs of the mid upper turret with a cannon shell burn in it. I removed the rear escape hatch, clipped on the parachute and sat on the edge of the hatch. I pulled the ripcord and tumbled out. The parachute, having several holes from the shell burn, 'candlesticked' (twirled) as I descended and I landed in a canal.' Collins was apprehended the following day and he was taken to Leeuwarden airfield for interrogation. 'Here I met the pilot of the Messerschmitt 110 who claimed to have shot us down. I abused him in good Australian. He understood, having spent three years at Oxford University.'[24]

Two months' later, on the night of 17/18 August, 'Douggie' Baker was captain of Stirling I W7589 when 139 aircraft of five types were detailed for the raid on Osnabrück. Baker took the Stirling off from Lakenheath at 22.46. The target was identified and their 1950 x 4lb incendiaries were seen to ignite north of a fire in a built up area. Six bundles of 'Nickel' were also dropped in this area. Altogether, 111 crews reported accurate bombing. Five aircraft - three Wellingtons and a Lancaster - were lost. Baker's Stirling was attacked on the return by a German fighter and he returned from the Dutch coast on two engines, crash landing south of Southery in Norfolk near RAF Feltwell at 04.40 in 5/10ths cloud, base 9,000 feet. The crew reported that the 'English searchlight assistance was of great moral and material significance'. There were no injuries to the crew. Two nights' later, in the Sergeants' Mess at Lakenheath, Sergeant H. Williams the wireless operator sat down and wrote to his wife.

'I am sorry about the previous letter, but I had got it half written and intended finishing it just before going on another trip, when things were rushed up and I carried the half finished letter in my pocket and found it still there after many fateful and varied incidents. I will tell you of these now, it was the night before last. The trip to Osnabruck again (Germany). We got there, arrived rather late, found our target and dropped our stuff and then went round and photographed it. Then the guns caught us and at first go with the searchlights got one of our engines, almost lifting us out of the sky. A fighter came after us and luckily didn't persist so we limped on and then when we got into Holland another of the engines went for a Burton. It is practically unknown for one of these kites to go on two engines so we were all prepared to bail out. I realised one of a Wireless Operator's ambitions and banged out those fateful SOS's.

We struggled on to the sea, to come down there because one of the two remaining engines was going half cock-eyed. We were losing height all the time and very quickly. So while Douggie was doing a marvellous job of work nursing the kite along over the sea, myself tapping away on the wireless, the others were throwing all the loose fittings out of the kite, chairs, ammunition etc. We were all certain that a chance to show our rowing skills had come at last. By this time we only had one and a half engines, but we chugged on, on what we thought was a losing battle and eventually came into sight of the English coast.

It was grand, the searchlights out, trying to help us along, we had asked them to. So we thought we would make Base. But 12 miles before Base the petrol ran out, it was all very sudden, we had to come down and take our chance, it was still dark. We took up our positions on the floor, bracing ourselves. We came down batting away at 200 miles an hour. Douggie saw a cottage looming up and managed to get over it and then we hit the deck, ploughed along a corn field, hit a concrete road running through it and finally finished up in a potato field. Out of the dust, haze and soil we scrambled out of the kite, over the wings and did a war dance of joy. The kite lying on its belly was pranged good and proper, nobody hurt just superficial scratches etc.

'We were torn, dirty but very happy. We had been flying for six and a half hours. It was a marvellous feeling to get away with it after thinking all was up. We walked along the road, it was just breaking dawn then and then the populace of the surrounding farms started turning out to meet us, a bit timid at first, thinking we might be Jerries, but we soon got over that and then into the various cottages and being plied with food and drink. Everyone was fine towards us and you can imagine how we felt. You know how I dislike rum, but when we were offered a cupful each I didn't have any qualms about knocking it back. Then the Group Captain and everybody motored out to us and we finally arrived back at camp at nine o' clock, twelve hours after starting out and so to bed.'[25]

A few nights' later, on the night of 24/25 August, 'Douggie' Baker captained Stirling W7572 OJ-R for the raid on Frankfurt when 226 aircraft

- 104 Wellingtons, 61 Lancasters, 53 Stirlings and eight Halifaxes were dispatched.[26] The main point of interest about that summer night was its beauty. The sky was absolutely clear as Baker's Stirling, having completed the operation, crossed the border between Germany and Belgium on its course back to Lakenheath. High above, the full moon hung like a great silver ball spreading its soft radiance over the sleeping world and the crew hated every square inch of it. This was because a full moon in a clear sky was just about the most dangerous thing that any bomber crew could encounter. It made their aircraft a silhouetted dead-duck target for any fighters approaching from below. Moreover, it was almost impossible for the bomber's gunners to pick out the small shape of a fighter rising from the green-grey expanse of the ground below until it had got perilously close.

Baker therefore was taking his crew home with 'the wicks turned fully up' and with everybody tense and the gunners alert for trouble. When trouble came none of them actually saw Oberfeldwebel Reinhard Kollak's Bf 110C fighter of 1./NJG4 which launched it, aided by the prevailing fine weather with good visibility, an almost full moon and no cloud. With a nice, clear target in his sights Kollak must have enjoyed himself as he came up for his first attack from below and dead behind. Even so, he seems to have been a little over-confident, for his first burst did no more than put Sergeant T. J. Jenkins' rear gun-turret out of action, produce a small fire and an equally warm stream of remarks from the flight engineer, Sergeant F. J. Berthelsen RNZAF, who jumped violently and winced over a wounded arm. Baker, at the controls, immediately flung 'R-Robert' into evasive action, but within his heart of hearts he knew that he hadn't a hope. Once again Kollak came into the attack and once again the Stirling shuddered as a burst of cannon shells smashed into the starboard wing-tanks, setting up a blaze of fuel which whipped back in the slipstream. Baker now had to make a decision. It was obvious they would have to abandon aircraft, but it would be best for all concerned if they could get as near home as possible before doing so. Meanwhile, the fire was gaining, so he had to decided how long the wing structure would stand up to the terrific heat before it finally collapsed and put the aircraft into a spin from which it might be impossible for anybody to get clear. However, the only thing to be thankful for was that Kollak had sheered off, obviously satisfied now that his 'kill' was burning.

For about five minutes Baker kept on course until he felt that the wing could not possible stand up to the strain much longer. He gave the order to abandon ship, but, to his horror, discovered that the intercom had failed and it was therefore impossible to communicate with his crew. In that moment of helplessness Baker sat rigid...and sweated. The fire was gaining and he knew that at any minute the wing might collapse. The lives of his comrades hung upon his ordering them away, but there was no way of passing this order. He wondered wildly what the hell to do - and then miraculously, the intercom suddenly 'came on' again. Baker gasped and shouted his order.

'Bail out, chaps' he yelled. 'Jump everybody. Make it snappy. Get away as fast as you can.' As he spoke the last word he realized that the intercom had crackled and gone dead again. He had no time, however, to relax in this moment of relief. He put 'George', his automatic pilot, into action and as his crew came tumbling forward to go out through the escape hatch, he unbuckled his safety harness and heaved himself out of his seat. Then he went aft along the fuselage to make a final check and satisfy himself that all of them had got away. Sergeants J. B. Downing, 2nd pilot and G. Robinson and Flight Sergeant V. S. Wood the MUG, who broke his ankle on landing, were taken prisoner. Berthelsen, Williams and Jenkins evaded capture.

Robinson said: 'I came down three miles southeast of Leuze, hid my parachute at the corner of a wood and walked towards the French frontier. About daylight I hid in a potato field but a dog began to bark and a farmer discovered me. I told him who I was and he brought me food throughout the day. He got in touch with a friend, who put me into an empty house a short distance from Leuze. I remained there from the 25th to 29th August and local farmers brought me food and water. On the 29th I was moved to another house in Leuze, where I remained 'till the 4th September when I was supplied with new clothes and shoes and I cycled to Tournai, where I saw Jenkins and Berthelsen. I spent that night at Herta on the Belgian side of the frontier and the next day I was taken to Lille.'

Probably, Berthelsen came down near Thieulain and he walked until about 07.00 hours. 'I then lay up all day in a bush and started to walk at night. After two hours I was threatened by two men with clubs who found me picking currants in a garden. I had a revolver with me and stopped them from attacking me. When I explained who I was, they suggested a bottle of pale ale and took me to a field, where there were about 15-20 men. They then took me to a farmhouse near Vezon, where I got civilian clothes and shelter for the night. As the whole village knew of my presence, I was moved to Fontenoy, where I remained until 31 August. I then cycled to Tournai, where I was handed over to an organisation.

By this time the fire was just starting to eat its way through into the fuselage, so Baker hurried back forward again and took a brief glance at the altimeter, which registered 12,000 feet, before he went to the escape hatch and rolled himself headlong into the night. For the next few moments he rolled over and over, the sky gyrating about him before he was jerked upright by the opening of the parachute canopy. In his own words: 'At some moment unknown to me I had pulled the rip-cord, but what I had done with it I never afterwards knew.

When I found myself swinging safely on the open parachute the ring was no longer in my hand. I think in that moment all I felt was regret that this souvenir was lost. Above me was my parachute billowing gently and singing softly in the still night air. Below was the silvery landscape, trees, rivers, fields and houses; everything I had seen so often from the aircraft, but now its beauty enhanced by the utter stillness. As I seemed to hang unmoving above it all I tried to turn myself this way and that to see what had happened to the others who had left the aircraft. But I could only hope that the rest of the chaps had landed safely. Then the thought suddenly came to me that very soon my parents would receive that grim telegram: 'The Air Ministry regrets,' I knew what a multitude of fears that terse announcement of 'missing' could carry to parents and what unpleasant visions it might cause. Yet there was I, enjoying the incomparable beauty of an August night over Belgium and in, in one sense, thoroughly enjoying it.'

Baker's descent took a long time since he had bailed out at considerable height. He saw the abandoned aircraft crash (at Thieulain in Hainaut) and landed quite close to it; so close that he could make out the figures of the local inhabitants around the wreck and heard their excited voices as they talked and called out to each other. Apparently, however, they did not think of looking up above them and it seems certain that none them saw him as he drifted down not far away and settled into the trees of a pine wood. He tried to spill his parachute in order to avoid the wood, but could not manage it. Therefore he held his feet tight together and shut his eyes just before he felt himself breaking the smaller outer branches.

With a fairly heavy thud, he found himself rolling over on the pine-needle floor in the middle of the trees and staggered to his feet, virtually unhurt. Baker scraped a hole for his parachute in the pine needles and made sure that it was well hidden. Subsequently, he found that the spot he had landed on was about twenty miles south of Brussels. Meanwhile, since it was his object to evade capture, he set off at a brisk pace to put as much distance between himself and the crashed aircraft as possible. 'I walked in cover of the woods until about dawn' he recalled. 'I got a meal at a farmhouse, but the people were afraid to keep me, so I went back to the woods and slept there all day. At night I walked southeast, again in the woods. I rested at dawn near an isolated farmhouse, where I was later given a meal. The farm people hid me in the woods and brought me meals regularly for the next five days and allowed me to sleep in a barn at night. I was then taken to Vezon where I was sheltered for four days. On 5 September I cycled to Tournai, where I was handed over to an organization.' In less than eight weeks with thanks due to the 'Pat O'Leary Escape Line', Baker, Berthelsen, Jenkins and Williams eventually reached Gibraltar where they were put aboard the S Class submarine, HMS *Seawolf* on 12 October for the sea-crossing to England. The submarine docked at Poole on the 19th.[27]

Endnotes

22 *Adapted from Chute Open - Inside the Aircraft, Jump for it!* by Gerald Bowman. Three Wellingtons and a Hampden were lost on the Hamburg raid and eight aircraft in total crashed in England. *The Bomber Command War Diaries; An Operational reference book 1939-1945* by Martin Middlebrook and Chris Everitt (Midland Publishing Ltd 1985, 1990, 1995).
23 Sergeants Philip Frank Hickley and Gallagher and Flight Sergeant Leslie Wiltshire and Sergeant Leslie Shearer were killed.
24 Flying Officer William George Barnes DFC and crew were KIA on 29/30 June 1942 on the operation on Bremen.

25   Courtesy of Mrs. V. Wright, daughter of Sergeant Williams.

26 Sixteen aircraft - six Lancasters, five Wellingtons, four Stirlings and one Halifax were lost on the raid on Frankfurt. Five Pathfinder aircraft, including that of Wing Commander John Morland Shewell the CO of 7 Squadron, were among the aircraft lost.

27 *Adapted from Chute Open - Inside the Aircraft, Jump for it!* by Gerald Bowman.

Chapter 10

Odour Cologne

Every time we beetle down the runway I'm wondering if we're going to make it back. I guess I've seen too many guys go for a Burton this past year. 'Gone for a Burton' meaning, in barrack room language, 'gone for a shit'. A Burton being a strong ale which caused one's bowels to move rather freely, necessitating a quick trip to the can.'

Pilot Officer J. Ralph Wood DFC CD RCAF,
76 Squadron Halifax navigator, 1942.

Sergeant G. H. 'Dixie' Lee on 102 Squadron had a nice singing voice. He loved light music, especially of the blues type and since that form of melody was generally approved by RAF personnel, 'Dixie' not only won a nickname, but was much in demand when anyone was around who could agitate a piano. Also, since he was a cheerful creature who didn't believe in letting things get him down, he usually whiled away the time he spent in his rear-gun turret by bursting into song. For once in his life, however, 'Dixie' did not feel like warbling sweet strains about the Swanee River when in the turret of Halifax W7653 DY-A, which, on 27 April 1942, was taking off from Dalton airfield in Yorkshire with a heavy bomb-load scheduled for Cologne. It was the second operation since the squadron had converted from the Whitley bomber to the Halifax. Twenty-two-year-old Flight Sergeant Lawrence 'Larry' William Carr, who was from Green Walk in Crayford, Essex and his crew - all sergeants - were one of 97 aircraft - 76 Wellingtons, 19 Stirlings and two Halifaxes detailed for the raid.[28] Before converting to the Halifax Carr had been a second pilot on Whitleys and had survived an explosion prior to take-off for Essen on 31 August 1941 when he and the others on Pilot Officer B. B. P. Roy's crew were able to run clear before the explosion and escaped injury. On 27 April none of Carr's crew was feeling light-hearted. Carr had found that the aircraft would not unstick when he was too far down the runway to do anything about it. One way or another, things had been 'dicey' for the boys on 102 Squadron for some days past. The Squadron had operated its Halifaxes for the first time on 14/15 April, sending two to Dortmund as part of a force of 208 aircraft. The new aircraft proved too heavy for their own grass airfield at Topcliffe and sank their wheels up to the axles in the mud which had resulted from the April rains. Therefore the aircraft had been moved to the satellite airfield where there was a concrete runway. But even this seemed hair-raisingly short for a bomber of the type, especially when the wind was blowing across it at an angle, as it was on the night of 27/28 April, the Squadron's second night of operations on the Halifax. It was the very first night Carr's crew had set off on a major operational trip in a

Halifax and it was his 14th operation since joining 102 Squadron.

With his engines wide open at full boost, Larry Carr tried to make 'A-Apple' take off and saw that he was running out of runway fast. It was not until disaster seemed absolutely certain that he felt the wheels sluggishly leave the surface. Even so he had an uncomfortable feeling that they were going to hit the boundary hedge which was racing towards them. He was right. They did. With a shudder the big aircraft bashed its undercarriage wheels through the aerodrome hedge, sending up a spectacular shower of broken bushes and twigs in the slipstream. This interesting display was observed at close quarters by 'Dixie' Lee in his rear gun-turret. He was the first man on the tense crew to break silence since the aircraft had started rolling.

'I don't suppose they *wanted* that hedge anyway' came his voice over the intercom. 'Still, Skipper, I'd rather take a *return* ticket to Cologne if it's all the same to you.'

'A-Apple' kept on level keel and since it had not lurched down and crashed into the ground, 'Dixie's cheerful loquaciousness could be understood. But he was in the rear of the aircraft, looking back, so he naturally could not see what his Skipper could see dead in front. The view before the Sergeant was still depressing. Directly ahead were the vast, dark shapes of a group of hangars of the parent airfield which seemed to rise higher than the heavily loaded Halifax was flying. Carr hadn't any hope of making a turn. As the hangars raced nearer and nearer he tensed himself at the controls, feeling quite certain that the aircraft was going to crash straight into the roofs. But the Halifax just made it. By how many inches he cleared the danger, Carr never knew. At one moment he was sure of death; and at the next the great, black shapes had flicked by without the wheels actually scraping them. Then there was only the broad clear acreage of the Yorkshire Wolds stretched out in front. Carr relaxed and perspired. Now that the worst was over he was able to offer up thanks for good luck. When he selected 'wheels up' he felt the comforting click as they retracted and locked correctly in place. He found that the aircraft would climb reasonably well and with the altimeter registering comfortably, he flew dead on course for the North Sea and his destined target. In the rear gun-turret 'Dixie' Lee began crooning a blues. In the navigator's position, Sergeant Ronald B. 'Ronnie' Shoebridge, from 1 West Way, Shirley in Croydon, Surrey, indicated the general relief with a cheerful remark. 'Well' he said, 'Cologne may be a stinking target but the stink will smell nice to me when we've pranged it up and turned for home again.'

'Odour Cologne,' said someone else. 'Listen to the sound of broken glass when we shake up the scent-bottles.'

By that time the Halifax was crossing the French coast at about 12,000 feet and the moon above was shining, silvery and serene. 'Dixie' noticed that there was hardly anything coming up in the way of flak and that there were only a few searchlight beams. He didn't care for it and stopped singing to speak to the 21-year old mid-upper gunner, Jimmy Garroway, who was from Glasgow. 'Jimmy, I don't like this much' he said. 'They're too quiet down below and that bloody moon's too damned bright. Better keep your eyes skinned for fighters.'

He had hardly finished speaking when a black shape flicked across the moon and he saw the unmistakable silhouette of a fighter about 600 yards away. Jimmy also spotted it. Both yelled 'Fighter to starboard, Skipper' at the same time and swung their guns. But Larry Carr at the controls tossed the big Halifax into weaving evasive action at their warning and in a minute or so it seemed that he had shaken the enemy off. Even so, 'Dixie' felt that it was only a foretaste of plenty of bother to come. The brilliant moonlight conditions were all in favour of any attacker since the slower moving bomber was illuminated almost as clearly as by day and the vast dim cavern of the sky would give an attacker every chance of making an unexpected pounce; which was exactly what happened a few minutes later.

Tense, keyed up and straining his eyes 'Dixie' Lee suddenly saw a Bf 110 whipping out of the void and diving straight upon them. Their attacker was Oberleutnant Reinhold Eckardt of 7./NJG3. On the night of 27/28 June 1941 he had destroyed four bombers in 46 minutes during a Helle Nachtjagd sortie in the Hamburg area where five bombers fell to night-fighters. 'Dixie' Lee yelled a warning to Carr, who again threw the Halifax into a violent weave, but the approaching Eckardt knew his business. He kept dead on his target and when he was about 350 yards both he and 'Dixie' Lee opened fire at each other almost at the same instant. Amidst the terrific din that filled 'Dixie' Lee's gun turret he was suddenly half-blinded by a brilliant flash. At the same time he felt a sharp, stabbing pain in one foot. One of the 110's cannon shells had scored a square hit on the turret, striking his ammunition feed. But the rest of the burst had also scored. A matter of seconds later the whole port-side of the Halifax was a roaring mass of flames which swept back in the slipstream. The shaken and wounded 'Dixie' heard Carr shout the order over the intercom for the whole crew to bail out. At the same time he realized that the aircraft had gone into a headlong dive. Dazedly he groped for his parachute pack, but as he did so he suddenly saw that the 110 was coming in for the kill. As was so often the case in actions of this kind, Eckardt was over-confident. He flew in dead close, thinking that he could be in no possible danger from his falling and blazing victim. But 'Dixie' Lee was ready for him. As Eckardt closed in Lee had his gun-sights dead on and let fly with a burst that poured squarely into the approaching German. The fighter immediately burst into a blaze and spun over, to dive earthwards.[29]

During this time, with the prescience that sometimes comes to a man in fierce emergency, 'Dixie' Lee had heard Sergeant Thomas Kenneth Robinson the flight engineer and ex-Halton 'Brat' and the second pilot, Flight Sergeant J. William Ralston RCAF from Dartmore, New Brunswick, ordered away in their parachutes. He felt the aircraft give a terrific jerk and guessed that the skipper had also gone' leaving the control stick free. For the second time Lee groped for his parachute pack, found it and slammed it into his harness clips. But while he was doing so there was uproar of approaching cannon fire - he thought it was the first of the two fighters which had returned - and again he grabbed for his guns. This time he could only fire at random and had no idea if he had hit anything. Meanwhile, he knew that the Halifax had been whining down the sky in a dive and he had no idea as to just when it would smash into the ground and obliterate him. The thought came into his mind that the hydraulic mechanism which rotated his turret had been shot to pieces. The only way to get out of a Halifax rear gun-turret was to revolve it round and escape through the doors.

'Dixie' Lee did the only thing possible and set to work to revolve it by hand, having no idea whether he was at 500 feet, 5,000 feet or only 50. At last he got it round far enough so that he could heave up and start forcing himself through the turret doors, but then found his legs jammed. He plunged and struggled but somehow his trousers had got caught in the turret mechanism. As a last resort he decided to pull the release-ring of his parachute, hoping that as it streamed out and cracked open it would forcibly jerk him from where he was held. At which point he found that he had put his parachute on the wrong way round. This actually proved to be such a lucky mistake that saved his life. His right arm was so jammed that he would not have been able to get at the release-ring had the parachute pack been put on correctly. As it was he found the ring with his left hand and gave it an almighty wrench. The next thing he knew was a terrific jerk on his body harness, a wrenching pain from his wounded foot and he was out in the open air.

Almost immediately afterwards, it seemed, two things happened simultaneously. There was a roaring explosion as the aircraft smashed into the ground and, as he swung like a human pendulum on his parachute rigging, 'Dixie's' feet clattered through the twigs of a tree-top. Just what the height was when he finally got out of the blazing Halifax he naturally did not know, but at the most it must have been only a few hundred feet from the ground. A second or two later he landed and rolled over in the middle of a field, knocked half-dazed by the thud of meeting the earth. He managed to free himself from his parachute harness and then picked himself up, finding himself not far from the crashed bomber.[30]

At that time, of course, 'Dixie' had no idea of what had happened to the others. Jimmy Garroway, Thomas Robinson and Sergeant Iorweth Edwards the 22-year old tail gunner who was from Portmadoc, Caernarvon had died in those few minutes of action. Ronnie Shoebridge, Ralston and Larry Carr, who had bailed out at low altitude; his parachute barely opening before he hit the ground near Hamois in the Belgian province of Namur, less than a kilometre from the remains of W7653, had survived. 'Dixie' Lee got himself to the village and was there befriended by some of the inhabitants. Soon afterwards however, he found himself in German hands because one of the villagers, a collaborator, had given him away. Ironically enough, his capture by a party of German soldiers was witnessed by Larry Carr who had also managed to get to the village and had obtained a suit of civilian clothes.

Carr immediately buried his parachute and life-jacket and started to head south for an hour and a half, away from the wreckage of his aircraft using his collar and stud compass. As he crossed a track two Belgians - Mauritius Wilmet and Constable Louis Massinon, a gendarme commanding the Brigade Hamois, who were members of the Comète Line,[31] asked him if he were English and did he want to return to England. Answering 'yes' to both questions Carr was taken to Wilmet's house in Hamois where he would be hidden in the basement. While he was having a meal Massinon dutifully telephoned the Germans to tell them that there were no survivors! Later, his host, François Devaux led Carr to a farm near Bormenville, five or six kilometres away, where he exchanged his uniform for civilian clothes and was able to rest. He was told that 'Dixie' Lee had been betrayed to the Germans, apparently by a Belgian Rexist. Carr was already starting the long journey to the Pyrénées and into Spain so he could only watch the arrest, powerless to do anything to help. On the morning of 29 April Wilmet and Carr left on a slow train from Bormenville to Ciney where a 20-year-old woman, Fernande Pirlot ('Pochette') met them before taking them on the express for Brussels.

Once in the Belgian capital, Carr stayed at a number of safe houses, meeting Ronnie Shoebridge and Ralston during his stay with the Lizin family. 'Pochette' acted as the courier and arranged for him to have photographs taken for an identity card. It was not considered safe for all three to remain together, so 'Peggy' (Margueritte van Lier), another young courier, collected Carr and took him to the house of Carl Servais and his wife in a residential suburb. On 7 May Carr heard that several of Comète's members had been arrested but Comète persisted with plans to get the airmen out. On 12 May Ralston and Shoebridge left together. Five days later they were apprehended at 112 Rue de la Victoire in Saint-Gilles in Lizin. Both men were sent to Stalag VIIIB Lamsdorf.[32]

At 7 am on the morning of 20 May 'Peggy'[33] returned to escort Carr to the Gare du Nord in the centre of Brussels, where she introduced him to Andrée de Jongh ('Dédée'), a slight young woman who appeared to know no fear. Dédée never asked or expected anyone to do anything she could not undertake herself and she made the double crossing of the Pyrénées 24 times, leading escaping airmen over the perilous mountain section into Spain. The route chosen may not have entailed serious climbing but the rough terrain, always traversed in darkness and sometimes in fog and appalling weather, was hazardous. All those who met her found it difficult to believe that such an innocent-looking girl could make such arduous physical journeys, in addition to the great presence of mind and courage that she displayed at every stage of the journey.[34] Not to show that they are travelling together, Dédée had a ticket to Ste-Quentin and Carr a ticket to Paris. Carr was given false papers and a railway ticket before they boarded the express for Paris. At the French frontier all the passengers had to disembark to pass through police and customs checks before the journey continued to the Care du Nord in Paris, where Frederic de Jongh met them. He escorted Carr across Paris to the Gare d'Austerlitz, where he received new forged papers allowing him to travel within the German-occupied area of France. Dédée and Carr boarded the night train for the Spanish border, arriving at Bordeaux at 6 am before continuing their journey south. They were due to leave the train at Bayonne in the south-west of France, but just before disembarking they saw 'Tante Go' (Madame Elvirede Greef of Anglet) on the station and she was able to warn them that increased security checks were in place on the station and they must remain on the train and disembark at Ste-Jean-de-Luz. Albert Edward 'Bee' Johnson, a 34-year old guide born in Farringdon, Hampshire met them when they left the train at Ste-Jean-de-Luz, but he told Carr to leave by a goods entrance since strict control was in force at the ticket barrier. After meeting up outside the station, they left for an apartment where Carr was equipped for the journey over the mountains and told to get some sleep. Late in the afternoon, Dédée and Carr left for the farm at Urrugne, where 'Francia' Usandizanga had prepared a meal for them. They were introduced to 'Florentino' Goïcoechea of Ciboure, a tall, sturdy Basque smuggler, who knew the routes to Spain like the back of his hand. Immensely strong and agile, he would carry some of the weaker or wounded airmen on his shoulders across the often swollen, fast-running Bidassoa River which formed the frontier.

But 'Florentino' was unable to take them over the mountains that night and a younger guide would escort them.

At midnight on 22 May the guide arrived and the three of them set off along mountain tracks into the Pyrénées dressed as Basques. The guide set a fast pace as they climbed the hills behind the farm to a ridge, which they followed before descending into the valley of the Bidassoa River. Crossing the frontier to the east of Irún with great caution and in total silence, they had to ford the fast-flowing river, cross the road and railway running alongside the river on the Spanish side and avoid patrols. Frontier patrols shot on sight and Spanish patrols finding anyone crossing from France would hand them straight back to the German authorities. Having crossed the frontier safely, it was necessary to keep out of sight until Carr could be handed over to the British Vice-Consul in San Sebastián. After crossing the border, they climbed up from the valley to the mountains, where they kept to the high paths until it was daylight, when they rested at a farm. It would have been too dangerous to have been seen walking in the mountains in the early morning. Later in the day the friendly Basque farmer wakened them. He provided them with a meal before they set off again once it was dark. They walked through the mountains all night, resting as dawn broke. The guide showed them the way down to a village at the end of the tramline to San Sebastián and then left them. Dédée and Carr walked into the village, joined the queue of workers and boarded tram 24, which they left near the centre of the town, where Dédée telephoned a contact, who arrived to take them by car to the garage of the British Vice-Consul. Carr said goodbye to the amazing Dédée de Jongh. He was soon taken to the British Consul in Bilbao, where he stayed the night at Seaman's Hotel and then to the Embassy in Madrid. Leaving the Embassy on 31 May in a Red Cross van, Carr arrived in Gibraltar on 1 June to learn that Bomber Command had just launched the first 'Thousand Bomber Raid'. He sailed from Gibraltar on 18 June on the aircraft-carrier HMS Argus, arriving at Gourock five days later. He was escorted to London to meet Lieutenant Colonel Jimmy Langley, Head of IS 9 (D), who was anxious to get the latest information of the threatened Comète Line and to get a detailed report of his experiences.[35]

Sergeant Jack Newton, a 'Wimpy' rear gunner on 12 Squadron at Binbrook, was among the first airmen that the Comète Line got away. Returning from a night raid on Aachen on 5/6 August 1941, Wellington II W5421 PH-G was hit by flak and, miraculously, Flight Lieutenant Roy B. Langlois, the pilot, landed the burning aircraft at an unlit Antwerpen-Dueme airport. There was no-one around at that moment and the six crew escaped. They organised themselves into two groups and, as luck had it; Jack's party was spotted by a Belgian Resistance member. At this point, the Comète Line took over and, on reaching Brussels, the three men were separated. After nearly five months, during which he was sheltered by 40 families and nearly came face to face with a German soldier over a hedge, Jack (accompanied by Dédée all the way to Spain) was returned to England where he became involved with air intelligence. His two companions were captured along with their helpers. The other three, who were on their own, were swiftly rounded up - all five spent the rest of the war in captivity.[36]

During late 1942, despite being infiltrated by the Germans, Comète still managed to smuggle several RAF and USAAF evaders along the escape line to the Pyrénées.[37] September was to prove to be Comète's busiest of the war to date and in October four groups of evaders crossed over the mountains into Spain. Among them was one of the few airmen to evade from inside Germany.

Flight Lieutenant Leonard Charles Pipkin DFM was the navigator and one of eight men on a 103 Squadron Halifax at Elsham Wolds flown by Squadron Leader Clive Saxelby that took part in a raid on Duisburg on the night of 6/7 September. Not yet 21, 'Big Sax' as he was known, was a second tour man, having completed his first tour on 75 New Zealand Squadron flying as second pilot and had then put in a year as an instructor.[38] The Halifax was shot down over the outskirts of the town while the raid was still in progress, killing Sergeant Charles Edward Benstead, 28, one of the air gunners. 'Bix Sax' and five others survived to be taken into captivity[39] but Pipkin, who bailed out as bombs were bursting around him, had other ideas. There were few people about, so that his actual descent by parachute was unnoticed. Losing a shoe as he descended, he managed to find it after square-searching for 45 minutes. Without drawing attention to himself, he was able to discard a good deal of his heavy flying kit and make his way unmolested through streets of blazing houses with bombs still crashing down. At intervals he was forced to take shelter in dark dug-outs crammed with people, who were far too terrified to notice the clothes of any individual. He reached the edge of the town before the raid ended and making his way as rapidly as possible past barbed wire entanglements, fences and other obstacles, reached a wood just before daybreak. Early next morning he neared the Rhine and heard soldiers massing on the road fifty yards from where he lay. Listening carefully to the orders being shouted, he realised that the search for him had begun and that he had probably been seen entering the wood. There was little time to hide, but Pipkin made the most of it. Selecting a small hollow, having first blackened his face with some dirt, he lay down and covered his whole body with leaves. Being almost invisible now as he lay on his back, he was able to see the soldiers as they came towards him. 'They came forward in a line,' he said,' about two yards apart and as they advanced they called out in English 'Come here, Tommy.' One German trod within six inches of his face but the line passed by without seeing him.

He waited all day before making good his escape. That evening just after dark, Pipkin emerged from the wood and started off westwards. Discovering in the light of day that he was barely 200 yards from a camp, he also saw several soldiers with fixed bayonets who were looking for him. A little later, on a lonely stretch of road, Pipkin was stopped by an unarmed German soldier who asked him for his papers. 'He tried to take hold of my arm and after inspecting my clothes as far as he could in the dim light, tried to lead me towards the camp for further examination. I was not prepared to be led and an all-in fight developed quickly.' For ten minutes the two men struggled desperately together. The German was the bigger and the heavier man and at first got the advantage, but never quite succeeded in reducing Pipkin to impotence. Both were in the last stages of exhaustion when by a lucky chance they slipped still locked together, into a ditch filled with water at the side of the road; the German undermost. 'I got the better of him and held his head under water till he was well out of the way. He was dead when I left him.'

Pipkin crossed the River Niers into Holland on the morning of 10 September and he made himself known to a farmer and his family near Reuver. A priest who had been summoned told Pipkin that 'everything would be all right.' On the 11th a Dutch guide took him across the Maas where two men with bicycles were waiting for the evader. 'We cycled fast for about an hour and a half to a farm were arrangements had been made with an organisation [Comète] to get across the frontier with Belgium.'[40] Finally, on 24 October, Pipkin reached Gibraltar. He was the 62nd 'parcel' sent along the escape line to successfully make a home-run'.[41]

On the same day that Pipkin reached Gibraltar, another navigator on 103 Squadron, 21-year old Warrant Officer Herbert John 'Dizzy' Spiller DFM awoke at Elsham Wolds, his nose pressed against the wooden wall of the aircrew dispersal hut. Short in stature, famed for his casualness, he was described as 'the untidiest man on the station', rarely bothering to wear his aircrew brevet or his chevrons of rank. On ops he carried the bare minimum of navigational instruments with him but was nevertheless one of the best navigators on the squadron. He had completed 49 operations; his 50th would mark the end of his second tour.

The saloon bar of 'The Dying Gladiator' in Brigg had certainly been jumping last night. Some party! Not the best time to have one in a busy Ops week, but things had been getting more dicey with a lot of the senior crews getting the chop. The skipper - Squadron Leader Sidney Horace Fox DFM - wouldn't like it; he didn't go much on pre-ops boozing, although he half accepted the tendency of crews to release their tensions that way. Narrow eyed and panther-footed, 'Sid' Fox commanded his crews' immediate respect. 'My head told me that he might be right. I painfully lowered myself out of bed and shuffled towards the crude window to check the weather. Lincolnshire was wearing a gown of fine mist.

'God, was it that time? 9.15am and breakfast 'up the Swanee' for a start. In the October half-light I peered across the room at the humped figure in the opposite bed. Chalky was still flaked out and ought to have been after flying for two out of the last three nights. Probably didn't get in until 4 am from last night's effort against Düsseldorf. I mused absent-mindedly, rocking to and fro in my bare feet, on my luck at having stood down for the last fortnight. One of the perks of being in the flight commander's crew, I suppose, or if you looked at it another way one of the disadvantages because your tour of ops was over an extended period, but at least you lived longer. Next time we went three of us would finish our second tours with fifty up each; old hands who were considered to be lucky to fly with. If you got that far 'Nebby' or the Good Lord or whatever you called him must be on your side. Experience helped, of course, but there was no flak shell that couldn't blow up the best. The nightly lottery in the barrages high over the Happy Valley of the Ruhr and elsewhere, proved that. Mentally I gave myself a 'kick up the trousers', my inner voice telling me to move down some other line of thought; maybe a cold shower would help.

The ablutions hut wasn't as empty as I had reckoned. Jock and Phil [Flight Sergeant Norman Alexander Mercer, rear gunner and Sergeant Philip Charles Heath, mid-upper gunner] and a few others were shaving and generally washing away the ravages of another thrash in Scunthorpe - 'The Oswald' more than likely; the 'Sods Opera' cabaret there was popular with the troops. Choruses of 'You look rough!' and 'Not time for the annual shower is it?' vibrated on my sensitive ears as I shambled towards the shower area. Later I would singe their ears but survival was the priority now and I needed that shower to feel alive. As the healing waters poured out of the battered shower head I dreamily reflected on the lads outside.

Jock, a laconic Scot from Aberdeen, swarthy, slim and energetic and Phil, a genial London lad from Putney, nearly six feet, heavier built and slow moving, were both gunners in our present crew, tail and mid-upper in that order, highly efficient and keen and happy to be with us. With luck they wouldn't have much trouble finishing their first tour after Sid, 'Woolly' [Pilot Officer Geoffrey Wollerton, wireless operator] and I had stepped down. Some crews came from Operational Training Units together and lived and shared their off duty hours as a family, but we had been assembled from various backgrounds and were individuals within a team. Strange that we shared the same enclosed airspace in our Halifax and experienced together the same mouth-drying death dance over a growing number of burning towns and yet each had his own private life, personal friends and pursuits when we were not flying. I really didn't know them at all well, but I knew one thing for sure: that up there, they would be protecting me at all times, if necessary placing their own lives at risk. The bond between us was a professional one but it had that element of light-heartedness that covered any inner anxiety that might come over to the others as fear or panic. If courage had any definition at all, that was it. It was the professional determination to do the job for which you were trained despite whatever difficulties arose. Sid and I had already been given gongs after our first tours for just that; no conspicuous gallantry, just dogged determination and the will to go on.

I turned off the shower as someone hammered on the door of the cubicle and shouted.

'Dizzy?'

It was Mac, a 'B' Flight wireless operator and bosom drinking chum.

'Yeah?' I gurgled still with a mouthful of water.

'You're wanted in the flight commander's office right away!'

'OK, Mac.'

'Time for a shave yet, even if the balloon has gone up.'

Looking at himself in the shaving mirror he saw a chubby pink face, dark brown wavy hair; a straggle of hairs on the upper lip and two front teeth missing, long since taken out by an RAF dentist, having contracted frost-bite in the upper front gum after flying in a Fairey Battle with the rear hood open trying to see how long he could go without an oxygen mask at 22,000 feet. His career as an air observer had nearly come to grief on that, but for an understanding commanding officer.

'Seems to be a lot of engine noise out at dispersal, maybe we go tonight. Looking at myself in the shaving mirror I shook my head at my reflection and quickly cleaned the teeth I had left and strode out of the ablutions hut feeling much better.

'On the way to the hangar with the camp roads bustling with airmen and airwomen moving in all directions, I had the feeling that Elsham Wolds had a separate life in which the flyers took no part other than as temporary interlopers with an existence limited by their luck in the air war. Their life was so unnatural, changing within hours from the safe comfort of the mess bars and chairs to the ever nearness of death in the concentrated barrages on target approaches, topped only by the sheer terror of being coned by searchlights and attacked by a night fighter. And then back again to the peace and comfort they had known, if they were lucky, to await another round of aerial roulette. Even the phrase 'Survival of the fittest' didn't apply. You lived for the day, or maybe a day, but the camp went on. I finished soliloquizing and reached the hangar. Most of the effects of the previous night had gone and I felt that the skipper could be faced with a fair chance of my escaping a reprimand.

'So you managed it at last!' Sid was in curt form as I appeared in the doorway.

'Sorry sir. Overslept, I'm afraid.' I really didn't sound convincing.

'Because of what, is more important,' Sid countered. 'You had better be sober, we're flying tonight.'

'I'm as bright as a button, sir. Had a fairly quiet night for me!'

Sid narrowed his eyes and smiled. I'm off the hook then.

'Navigator's briefing is at 1300. I'll look in shortly afterwards.'

'OK, sir,' I said crisply and gave him a smart salute, totally out of character but decidedly out of relief.

We had done twelve ops together now with 103 Squadron and knew each other's strengths and weaknesses. Looking at him now, dark hair, piercing eyes, mid-height but lithe as a panther, to me he was the epitome of the bomber captain, keen, pugnacious and overtly fearless. A squadron leader now, he had come up from the ranks and was the complete commander. His weakness? Well, he suffered from sinus trouble and hated to fly high and because of this we were mostly forced to carry out our ops somewhere in the 6,000 to 8,000 feet band with the main force sometimes the same distance above us. It made for an exciting life, but as a crew we never referred to it or made a fuss. We had the best pilot on the station and had utter confidence in his ability. In his own way, I believe he felt the same about us, which probably accounted for the fact that he never considered changing any of the crew. Twice he stood down to let the station commander take us on thousand bomber raids and he once said he was proud that his crew had been chosen, although he would have dearly loved to have gone himself.

The crew room was filled with a number of apprehensive crews excitedly discussing the lists of those picked for the night's operation; the relief in the eyes of some was hardly disguised. For them lay ahead twenty-four hours of more or less guaranteed survival and all the joys that could be packed into the off-duty hours. They usually left after a short while, strangely feeling that they were not part of the small community who would now prepare for the serious business of ensuring that such problems that can befall the sloppy and unwary airman did not have the opportunity to arise. Small groups began to break off to go to dispersal to check their aircraft and to make sure that their equipment was complete and working. The more experienced among them knew that the routine of check and double-check was the thin dividing line between a successful return and the prospect of eternal hallelujahs.

I was digging out my navigation bag from the crew locker as 'Woolly' and 'Peewee' [Flight Sergeant Rowland Maddocks, bomb aimer] broke through the milling throng.

'We're off to dispersal, 'Diz'. Any gen on the target yet?' called 'Woolly'.

'You should know better than that,' I countered.

'Woolly' our wireless operator, was recently commissioned after his first tour. Fair curly hair, angular, a Lancastrian without any side, he didn't attempt to stand on rank. He knew radio work backwards and was a treasure to have aboard an aircraft. 'Peewee', a broad Scot from Edinburgh, tall and talented not only as an aircrew member but also as an artist in oils. He had done several pictures already of scenes around the camp and in flight. His long jutting chin, spilling out of a flying helmet gave you the assurance that here was a determined character and on your side, to boot.

'Oh well. If you haven't anything to tell us we'll see you over at dispersal. Hope it's not the Big City.'

'Woolly's voice tailed off as an anxious prayer. You and me both I thought, Berlin is no place to finish off a tour. Perhaps we were getting edgy, the last hurdle and all that; life was beckoning at the end of a dark tunnel filled with flak and shouting.

Everything seemed to be in order in the navigation bag apart from my stock of pencils that needed sharpening and I busied myself in the crew room putting new points on them. Navigators over Europe worked through a series of immediate crises as aircraft stumbled their way against a host of distractions avoiding surprise fire and the ever present beams of searchlights. The course of the aircraft changed many times and each time frenzied fresh calculations were necessary. It may seem inconsequential but sharpened pencils were a life-line to me and I placed them here and there around the navigator's table so that at least one would be available in a flap.

Satisfied, I wandered out of the hangar to catch a transport to dispersal where I found 'Woolly' and 'Peewee' engrossed in their routine checks. Jock and Phil had been there some time and so had 'Fitz' [Sergeant Lawrence Fitzsimmons] our flight engineer. On him rested the operational efficiency of the aircraft and the sight of his short and slight frame topped with frizzy hair bent over the instrument panels in deep concentration, always gave me an almost divine assurance that we would be OK. I struggled through the front hatch past him to my own 'office' and went through my own checks, not forgetting to place my pencils, apart from those I would need for the briefing.

With our checks done and wolfing through teas and 'wads' at the mobile NAAFI wagon, we ruminated on the various factors which would comprise our evening's entertainment, target, bomb load, weather and aircraft numbers, but we had no real idea as yet. Individually ruminating, we returned to the hangar in an unconsciously agreed silence; the visit to the aircraft and the preparations going on had begun to have an effect on nerves, however subtle and until we had returned from wherever it was any humour would be forced and any conversation would be half-hearted unless it related to the job in hand.

On an impulse I checked the parachute list and found that my own was two days overdue for re-packing. It was just as well that I had seen it, although it wasn't really a hazard. In any case it gave me a chance to chat up Brenda, the WAAF packer, whose charms were not for all and sundry and you were made aware of it if you tried it on a little too cheekily.

Facing her across the enormously long parachute packing table I tried a 'How about coming to Brigg or Scunthorpe with me if I get back from the gates of Hell?'

Her smile was a little too sweet. 'The only pulling you'll do is on that rip ring on the chute.'

She meant it, so I complied with a sigh. As if by magic out blossomed yards and yards of pure white silk; what a wonderful art it was to get it all back in a parachute pack.

'On your way. It'll be ready at three.' Her tone was imperious and final. Disappointed, I slouched towards the door of the hut only to catch her voice saying, 'Dizzy.' I turned questioningly. 'Be careful,' she added.

Her eyes and voice were tender. She had seen a good many go, including her husband and knew what the risks were. She and her like, all the ground-staff who worked sometimes at all hours so that we could take the hero's part and strut about when all went well, were the salt of the earth and any flier who did not recognise that was not worthy of the name.

Hunger was getting the better of me now and I turned towards the mess hoping to get into the first sitting for lunch. Usually pre-operational inner tensions reduced the natural desire to eat, but I had had nothing much for a whole day apart from the 'wad' at dispersal and I felt the need. Through the mess door I could see Jock and 'Peewee', the two flight sergeants and Phil and 'Fitz', the sergeants, propping up the bar. As I approached, Jock was already buying a pint of shandy for me to match the others on the counter. This was the traditional glass we took together on these occasions and all that we would allow ourselves, bearing in mind the skipper's aversion. Not all crews did the same, some brazened it out and had a few drinks and a few went to their own quarters for a private tipple. The old hands knew better; a clear head kept the balance in your favour.

'We missed the first sitting,' purred Jock. 'I'm no hungry anyhow.' The Aberdeen lilt was strong in his voice. We moved away from the bar and flopped in the handiest armchairs. Apart from a desultory dart game the mess was virtually empty.

'Just like a morgue,' Phil was making a rare observation. 'Typical ops day, not a happy soul in sight,' he finished.

'Roll on briefing,' added 'Fitz'. 'These hours before take-off are pure murder.'

'So are the ones afterwards,' 'Peewee' croaked. 'I could do with some leave.'

Our reverie over the shandies were broken as the mess began to fill up again with satisfied eaters and the bar became noisy with false laughter. We looked at each other and shrugged and moved off to the dining room.

Lunch over, I returned to the hangar to pick up my navigation bag and was one of the first to enter the briefing room. The target information was still covered up but the board was set up long ways instead of sideways; well, well; we've got a target to the south then, could be Stuttgart or Munich I suppose. Looks a long 'un. Jostling started for the best position as more and more navigators crowded in. The operations officer and the weather man were already busy with their portfolios and charts when the Wing Commander entered. His tall figure and long dark countenance and chin reminded you of Basil Rathbone and his dark piercing eyes broadcast to all and sundry that here was a man born to authority who would expect 100 per cent effort and get it! Yet he was disliked by a number of crews who would, however, gladly have flown into oblivion behind him because they respected his skill and judgment. As an operational pilot he came close behind Sid.

A brief nod from him and the operations officer took off the wraps from the board. A chorus of whistles went up as the eager eyes around the room saw the red cord of the target route snaking down towards Italy. The final destination was still unknown as the cord hung limply across the Alps, purely as a security measure, so that no unauthorised person could discover the target. Very cunning. A further nod and the operations officer faced the assembly.

'The target for tonight is Milan,' he calmly said, moving to the map and placing his yellow board pin on the centre of the city and then winding on his red cord to complete the route. 'The route chosen is Base - Dungeness - Le Treport - Target, returning direct to Le Treport and landing at Tangmere.' A low murmur of voices was cut short by the Wing Commander. 'Main briefing is at 1445, when you will be informed of bomb loads, fuel loads and any gen about ancillary operations to divert the enemy. Now for the weather.'

The met man rose almost apologetically. 'A bit like the curate's egg tonight. There will be a great deal of cloud on the outward journey and you will need to fly through a fairly huge front over mid-France. From there, things get a lot brighter and you should find no cloud over the Alps and very little in the target area. I have prepared the provisional wind forecasts etcetera so that you can get ahead with the flight plans and you will have a further up-date at main briefing.'

Papers began to filter down as he was speaking and I could see why we were finishing at Tangmere. There was a distinct prospect of head winds on the way back and petrol would be at a premium. The south coast aerodrome would be a welcome sight.

'That's all, chaps,' rang out the Wing Commander's voice.

I could hardly contain myself. What a way to finish a tour. A lovely doddle over the centre of France, the Alps in moonlight, an easy Eyetie target and a warm bed at Tangmere with the additional perk of a fighter command mess. Sid tapped me on the shoulder, breaking my train of thought.

'Get on with it; you've only got an hour.' He had been busy in the flight commander's office and had just dashed over to check the route.

'OK, sir. What do you think of it?' I asked.

'Could be worse. See you at the main briefing,' was all I could get out of him. The charts were now being handed out and I settled down to my calculations. The new boys used Dalton computers for their navigational work, as did most of the others and I looked a little like Noah with my old-fashioned course and speed calculator. Be that as it may, I was always there amongst the quickest finishers. With my old instrument I could have a new course calculation in a fraction of a second, a vital factor over enemy territory. By the look of it the trip would last somewhere in the region of 8½ hours, long enough in rough weather. Calculations over, I left my bag in the careful keeping of the operations officer and wandered off to my room for a half hour siesta which I knew would not really lead to sleep. Fortunately I avoided seeing any of the crew so I wasn't subjected to their curiosity as to the night's destination.

Lying prone on my bed was as much as I was going to get in the way of rest. My mind was turning over with all the possibilities that could happen both during and after the flight. Fatal really, because nothing ever happened the way you envisaged it. Perhaps I'll do another stint as an instructor or try to get on the Atlantic Ferry. A film at the camp theatre had sparked off this idea, a sugar-coated American view of the life of crews ferrying Lease Lend aircraft over the Atlantic; the unreality of it appealed to our death-sensitive sense of humour. Ah well, let's get back first. My wrist chronometer told me I had about a quarter of an hour before briefing and I moved up to the mess kitchen to get a cup of tea, one of the perks of being a warrant officer. I milked that dodge quite a bit, helped by the fact that the middle-aged WAAF cook had a soft spot for me. The hot bitter brew chased away the remnants of last night's after effects. I left the empty cup and saucer on top of the hot plate, hugged her shoulder and wandered up to the briefing room.

Already the rows of seats were filling up with an excited gabbling throng, talking mostly about any other thing than the matter in hand. 'Peewee' and Jock had saved a seat between them and looked expectantly as I sat down.

'Well then,' came a gruff Scottish whisper, 'what is it to be to nicht?'

I smiled and said, 'Wait and see. It's a doddle.'

'Peewee' looked strained. 'Oh my God, it must be Hamburg, the way the wee man is smiling.'

'Jock' flashed a sympathetic glance across me and added, 'Well, we've no been there very much.'

'Sid' and 'Woolly' slipped into their seats straight from the officers' mess and nodded their hallos and quickly behind them came the Group Captain [Hugh Constantine the 34-year old Station Commander] and the 'Wingco'. An immediate hush exemplified the unconscious discipline under which we lived, a curious thing really as aircrews were notoriously high spirited, extrovert and devil may care, yet under certain circumstances both on the ground and in the air they reacted to discipline immediately without thinking. Much of it had to do with the need for such control to enable you to stay alive in tight corners and there had been some heroic examples of that in the war so far, not to mention our illustrious forerunners in World War I.

The Wing Commander broke the silence from the small rostrum on which the senior officers sat.

'Gentlemen, the target for tonight.' A nod to the operations officer who peeled back the covering from the target board. 'Milan.'

The initial inrush of breath from a hundred mouths quickly turned into delighted chuckles and chit chat. Immediate quiet again as the Wingco held up a restraining hand.

'We are sending eleven aircraft on our longest mission to date which involves a flight over the Alps in moonlight and a round trip of eight hours.[42] I've no doubt you will find it interesting but don't write this trip off as a milk run. You have some difficult French territory to fly over in terms of vulnerability to night fighters and you may find the Italians a little more aggressive than their colleagues in North Africa. In view of the length of the journey you will be taking second pilots and these will be allocated by the flight commanders. Take-off is at 18.30 and you should be at the target at 22.30. The operations officer and technical officers will now brief you in detail as to target material, fuel and bomb loads and of course the weather man will give you the latest run down on what to expect en route. You have your first chance to take the offensive to the other half of the Axis. Do it well and good luck.'

The rest of the briefing lost none of its interest as each speaker explained in fine detail what was expected of us and what we would be supplied with to carry out effectively the orders of Bomber Command Headquarters, perhaps the personal orders of 'Butch' Harris himself. An air of grimness was now beginning to pervade the assembly and the serious work of absorbing the information supplied was eroding the inner joy that the first news of the target had evoked in each mind. This was going to be some trip! It looked a piece of cake, but no chances please!

As the last of the confidential documents and information was being handed out, the Group Captain rose from his chair, sporting the DSO he had received after the thousand bomber raids he had made with us. His stock was very high with the aircrews, an old man by their standards, but he had been a rugger international and a pilot of some distinction in the peace-time Air Force. In their eyes he had earned his laurels and they were quite happy to serve under him.

'Gentlemen, tonight's effort has a great deal of significance to your squadron. Not only is it the first time that you will have flown over Italian soil but also, that this will be the last operation using the Halifax. Some of you, I know have already become endeared to the aircraft but higher powers than ourselves have decided that every effort must be made to increase the attacking capacity of the Command and the changeover to the Lancaster is therefore inevitable. Sufficient aircraft will be arriving in the next day or two for the station to remain operational without much loss of time. In a way you are at a turning point in history. Put your especial seal on this trip. Good luck.'

With that, the senior officers left the briefing room, whilst the general excitement again burst out of a hundred mouths. The hubbub remained for several minutes until the flight commanders managed to restore order and to inform everyone that the pre-flight meal would be at 16.30 with a final briefing at 17.30 when any deviations from the main briefing would be passed on. We bustled from our chairs throwing off asides and jokes to others around us.

The gunners shot off to make a second check that their heated suits were operating fully. I think that the prospect of the temperature over the Alps was the main factor. 'Fitz' made another visit to dispersal to watch how the maintenance of the aircraft [Halifax W1188 PM-D 'D-Donald'] was going, I repaired to the mess picking up my parachute on the way and Sid and 'Woolly' returned to the flight office to tie up the odds and ends which fall to a flight commander. The next few hours, the waiting, would be the worst although it would be hard to detect on the faces of the more battle-hardened crews.

Hardly anyone but the odd navigator was in the mess. Those not flying were no doubt busy with one or other of the emergency drills, practice shooting, simulated bombing runs (using a room fitted with the latest mechanical devices to produce a reasonably life-like representation of flying over enemy territory), or non-flying duties which were designed to hone up one's skills and reflexes. Ground staff were without doubt hard at it, as they always were, whether we were flying or not and the remainder of the crews were filling up the time before take-off in their own particular way, some even in prayer.

One of the male cooks was passing time on the snooker table and I joined him for a game, neither of us concentrating and almost content to play it out in desultory fashion. He left after a while to help prepare the pre-flight meal; obviously dying to ask where we were heading for that night but prudent enough to know when to keep silent. The snooker table had lost what interest I had in it and I was glad that I had only leafed through one picture magazine before the lads came in. Maybe it was getting to me too and I was supposed to be the intrepid one. We placed our chairs in a circle and smoked and chatted away the moments, not really listening to each other but just gaining strength from our communal relationship and sensing the importance of oneness in the next few hours. The meal was a complete contrast, the die was cast, we were mentally prepared for all that might lie ahead and all nervousness appeared to have vanished. We ate ravenously quite differently from the earlier meal when we had no idea of the target and jokes came thick and fast. The next half hour we would spend in our own quarters, either on our backs, or writing a 'last' letter, or meditating on the odds of seeing tomorrow.

The time soon passed and I began to dress for the evening's entertainment, not forgetting my thick silk vest and 'long Johns' which would be indispensable for this trip. A quick check of my good luck charms, a WAAF scarf and a cap badge of the French Tank Corps given to me by a poilu during the Battle of France in 1940 and I was ready but not before I had looked in all pockets for any items which would betray my British origin if I happened to be captured. Satisfied, I moved off to round up the lads and we made the pilgrimage in silence up to the flight hangar, except 'Peewee' who was humming a lesser known Scottish air. It helped.

All the crews gathered in the crew room to hear that no changes had been made to any of the briefing material apart from a slight increase to the petrol load which was always handy. Sid allocated the second pilots to each crew and this was the first we had heard of ours, a Sergeant Wood [Henry Frederick Wood] who had just arrived on camp. In fact his luggage was still in the guard room to await his return. Jock and Phil raised their eyebrows but Sid knew what he was doing and after all he was the ideal captain to ease a 'sprog' through his first operation.

To make him feel at home we quickly singled him out and introduced ourselves. He was fresh-faced and chunkily built and looked extremely useful and he was quite happy to have fallen in with such an experienced crew. Maybe he could take the lads over when Sid, 'Woolly' and I had finished. Why not, but they would need to see first how he coped when it got dicey. Sid had sorted him out some flying kit and while he busied himself adjusting it to suit himself, we went to our own lockers to finish togging-up. Quite a number used Irvin Suits, heavy leather and sheepskin, although I still preferred the Sidcot flying suit, really an overall with a number of useful pockets. Across the left breast of mine I sported a pair of wings with a beer glass in the centre instead of the 'RAF' letters and the motto 'The Flying Pint'. Another lucky charm from the Battle of France days and an ever reminder of our Dawn Patrol life during the early summer of 1940 in French airfields.

All that remained was for the crews to be allocated transport to take them to their dispersal points, Sid gave a short homily and wished everyone good luck and the Wingco popped in to give his final 'blessing'. We staggered out into the darkening outside world clutching our paraphernalia and boarded an open wagon reserved for the flight commander; another perk. You could just make out the fixed smiles atop all the bulky figures in the melee around the various kinds of transport and you were for a brief moment caught up in the melancholy that some of these might never return. A quick jerk of the clutch and you were back to reality, the hubbub receding in exhaust fumes, to be replaced in very quick time by the eerie silence and loneliness of the dispersal point with its huge black shape pointing ever heavenwards. Several of the ground crew appeared from the gloom to give us a hand with our equipment and to reassure us of the serviceability of 'D for Donald'. We knew them well enough but somehow we never seemed to have the opportunity to show our appreciation apart from an odd glass or two in the mess or the village local. Our working relationship was very simple, we borrowed their aircraft from time to time and woe betide us if we damaged it in any way by our foolishness or inexperience. Although they disclaimed emotion, it was they who showed the most anxiety if we were overdue and their joy when we returned after each operation was incapable of being hidden. They and all like them were superb.

The evening air was cold enough to cut down any lengthy attempts at conversation, Sid seemed anxious to board and get the early checks done since we were the first away. Almost mechanically, Jock, Phil, 'Peewee' and I moved down to the tail-wheel and ceremonially relieved our bladders over it. Yet another superstition. Relieved in one sense we climbed aboard and settled ourselves down in our various parts of the aircraft, stowing parachutes and plugging in to the intercom as we went. Moving around the front of the aircraft was going to be slightly more difficult as the second pilot's seat now bridged across the forward passage way leading to the wireless operator and bomb aimer, which meant a dip and a duck every time.

I gave Sid the first course to be flown which he transferred to the main compass and returned to my own 'office' to run over previous calculations. Apprehension had completely vanished, we were now operational. Jock, Phil and 'Peewee' confirmed that all was in order in their turrets and 'Fitz' then checked over the 'works' with Sid.

Another look at my wrist chronometer. Time to start up. Sid gave silent commands with his hands and the ground crews went into their normal drill. One by one the big Merlin engines burst into life to be joined like some huge Chinese cracker by similar explosions on other sides of the aerodrome. 'D for Donald' began to tremble, sometimes I thought with anticipation. Final engine checks done we peered into the gloom to pick up the duty pilots signal from the control hut near the runway. The correct flash from the Aldis lamp and Sid signalled for 'Chocks away'. We rumbled majestically around the perimeter and stood at the end of the runway all eyes looking for the green light. There it is and with it a lusty roar as D for Donald leapt forward snarling defiance at the Third Reich and gently leaving Lincolnshire for the upper air.

The ground had hardly slipped away before I made sure that the oxygen supply to my mask was working. Another vital matter, because Sid's sinus trouble would have to go by the board. We would have to be well over oxygen height before we cleared the Alps. The oxygen smelt a little stale, mixed as it was with facial perspiration on the mask and I quickly pulled the mask so that it hung solely on one button; the microphone which was incorporated would always be held over the mouth if I needed to pass a message.

Pushing my way past 'Fitz's engineer's area I could spasmodically make out the odd light on the ground through the second pilot's side window. This was

going to be no joy at all trying to pick up landmarks with the bulk of a second
'dickey' blotting out most of the window space. Sid banked the aircraft and the
single line of runway lights came into view and the familiar flashing beacon
monotonously winking out the airfield code.

The aircraft straightened up and Sid looked over, pointing to his mask. I
lumbered to the navigation table and plugged in: 'Hallo, captain, navigator here.'

Sid's voice came back loud and strong: 'Hallo navigator. On course. What's our
ETA at Dungeness?'

I didn't need to look at my flight plan. '19.31 and we should be at 8,000 feet,
climbing from there to 12,000.' I smiled to myself. Sid would stay below 10,000
feet until the last minute. I went on: 'Cloud should be about 5/10ths and we should
get a good pinpoint.'

'Okay navigator. Keep me informed of any wind changes.'

Jock and Phil piped up on the intercom together both asking about gun testing.

Sid's voice was brisk: 'One at a time. Watch your intercom procedure. You can
test the guns over the Channel not before. Wait for my command.' Sid was doing a
good training run in front of the sprog. To mollify Jock I asked him to see if he could
get me a drift bearing using his turret to follow a ground feature or light and reading
off a scale before him. There was rarely a hundred per cent blackout in wildest
Lincolnshire and there was always something on which to get a bearing. I didn't
really need it so early in the flight but it gave Jock something to do; he called up
later to give me the aircraft's drift which tallied perfectly with the calculated one.
So far so good. We crossed the western corner of the Wash with East Anglia spread
out before us. There were plenty of beacons and what looked to be quite a lot of
ground activity on the airfields of 3 Group who were joining us in the party.

Phil broke the silence to inform Sid that a Lancaster had passed below us on
the port beam. Good luck, son, I breathed. There would be more than a few in a
quarter of an hour's time.

Cambridge was somewhere away to starboard but fairly anonymous in the
blackness and a little later Chelmsford slipped by. Ahead the first glimmer of the
Thames and the bulky twins of the Isle of Grain and the Isle of Sheppey where we
had spent some uncomfortable days during the Battle of Britain operating our
Fairey Battles against the Channel ports. We were at height now and fairly
skimming along over the Kent downs, feeling a sense of history and the aura of
victory which the fighter boys had left behind them and which we were hopefully
carrying on our steadily mounting raids against the enemy.

The night's wind was certainly in our favour because we hadn't wavered from
our pre-selected track and we were hitting all the landmarks spot on. Dungeness
proved to be no different and apart from cries of discovery from the gunners as
they confirmed the position, we slipped into the darkness of the Channel, a sinister
shape on a sinister errand with the first butterflies beginning to take form in the
stomachs of the crew members and the dryness of the throat calling for a hasty
sip of whatever was contained in the crew flasks.

From now on the chips were down and everyone was on the look-out for the
slightest sign of danger, or anything that was not germane to the normal conduct
of the aircraft in flight. All nerve endings were vibrating and each one was
mentally alert to the highest degree. The second pilot passed down the aircraft to

make the first visit to the 'tube', a pipe and funnel device for errant bladders. The pipe leading to the outside of the aircraft dispensed its contents freely and impartially. Apprehension maybe, first trips were especially edgy, but no one would rib him about it. He would be that much more on his toes when the dull ache had gone.

'Captain to all gunners. You may now test guns. Short bursts only.' Sid was continuing his training routine impeccably. The French coast would be coming up soon and there was no point in giving our position away to any roaming night-fighters. Jock, Phil and 'Peewee' went through their test drills and reported that all was in order; their gunfire was hardly noticeable against the pulsing roar of the four Merlins just a few feet away. Sid checked the estimated time of arrival at the French coast with me and reminded all the crew not to use the intercom unnecessarily. We were flying in and out of cloud now but it was still sufficiently broken to pick up a landfall. Someone ahead had run into some light anti-aircraft fire, probably the gun cover for the airfield at Le Treport. I called Sid:

'Hallo, captain, navigator here. Do you want a course to avoid the flak ahead? We could cross slightly north of Le Treport.'

He was very calm and in control. 'No. We'll keep to track given. You'll get a similar reception anywhere along this part of the coast.'

'Woolly' looked round the edge of his partition smiling broadly. Sid wasn't one for dodging hot spots. 'Peewee's drawl came booming into the earphones:

'Front gunner to navigator. Coastline ahead, could be anywhere.'

Before I could reply, Sid ordered the crew to keep their eyes peeled for a pin-point, vague remarks like 'Peewee's sometimes got up his nose. It wasn't necessary in the end; one of the leading aircraft had been coned with searchlights through the gaps in the cloud and the reflected light was enough for us to confirm that we were definitely on course for Le Treport.

Minutes later we were being buffeted by the German gunners with Sid threading his way through the glowing streaks of cannon fire, deceptively slow until they suddenly burst past you in savage swift arcs cracking and thudding their exploding pieces against anything that dared use the same airspace. Weaving through with careful skill Sid waited until the noise had abated somewhat, checked his course with me and that everyone was all right.

'Keep a constant lookout gunners. This is night-fighter country.'

His command, though accepted, was really superfluous. I could guarantee that those three lads were pushing their eyeballs out on sticks!

Cloud began to thicken as the coast began to recede into the distance. Ice would be the hazard until we passed through the frontal system lying across mid-France, already we could see cloud ahead, building up to several thousand feet above us.

'Captain to navigator, I'm climbing up to just below 10,000 feet.'

'Woolly' appeared around his partition smiling again. I think he had in mind that Sid would quite likely find a route through the mountains rather than tempt his sinuses.

'Navigator to captain, alter course at the new height to 135 degrees.' Sid would tell me when he had levelled out and I was quite sure that he would be sticking to the laid down route tonight. Rain was forming on the windscreen and we were well into cloud now; this was the time when you entered the unknown, nothing apart from the instruments to tell you what lay ahead. You just prayed that no other aircraft was in your vicinity; the uncertainty heightened the suspense and tongues felt uncomfortable in dry mouths.

Happily the cloud level in our area reached only 9,500 feet and we broke cloud into clear air with a thin rim of moon showing bleakly above. Great! If there was any trouble we could always slip quickly back into cloud. By the look of things ahead we might have to climb over another ridge of cloud but there was some time to go yet. No one was offering any resistance from the ground below apart from the occasional individual searchlight under the cloud base and the Midi of France stretched interminably on. Ample time for recalculation and musing on the uplift you were giving to the French people, the audible sound of the engines telling them that the struggle to free them was continuing. Lulled by the ease and quietness of the journey we drifted on, revelling in our luck to have clicked for a 'doddle'. The attack [by Oberleutnant Gerhard Friedrich of Stab 11/NJG4 at 21.50 near Bar-le-Duc in the Meuse] when it came was sudden and incisive.

An incandescent missile zinged across the navigation table and ricocheted off the thick steel panel between my position and the wireless operator's compartment. At the same time the aircraft gave a series of shudders and began to yaw to port, in a slow diving turn. The angle made it difficult for me to rise to see what was happening and as I pulled myself upright using one of the fuselage stanchions I heard Sid broadcasting to the crew in measured tones that the aircraft had been attacked and that the port engines and wing were on fire. He was losing height in an attempt to put the fire out.

'We will be able to maintain height on two engines but standby to abandon aircraft if need be.'

It all seemed pretty well under control, but there had been no warning or word from the gunners. I moved up to the pilot's position leaving 'Fitz' to assist in the closing down of the engines and the extinguishing of the engine fires. The front cabin was brilliantly illuminated by the flames and Sid's grim silhouette was bent over the controls; he was glancing over at the second pilot and obviously passing commands in a desperate effort to keep us in the air. The dive to port became steeper and I reached for one of the forward intercom sockets to plug in for any order affecting me. The immediate priority was to get on an even keel, navigation would have to remain in abeyance, but I would have to have a course ready for us to fly a return leg home. Before I could connect the plug 'Fitz' hammered on my back and pulled the side flap of my helmet away.

'We've got to bail out!' he shouted against the roaring whine outside.

My intercom plug went home and I could hear Sid's voice high and strident: 'Abandon aircraft. Abandon aircraft. Immediately.'

I pushed my way under the second pilot and saw below me 'Woolly' and 'Peewee' crouching round the escape hatch, parachutes already attached and helmets off. The angle of the aircraft was becoming steeper by the second. I tore my helmet and scarf off and lurched towards the crouching pair and 'Peewee' cupped his hand over my ear. 'The bloody hatch is jammed,' he was screaming.

'Woolly' pushed 'Peewee' to one side and sat on the floor just before the hatch and gave an almighty kick; it needed about three but it eventually flew out. Moving behind them and pushing over to where my own and 'Fitz's parachute was stowed I watched them both disappear into the night. I clipped on my own chute and clawed my way to the hatch to discover in a blinding flash of horror that I had clipped it on upside down; I could see myself clawing away for the rip ring with the wrong hand. It had to be unclipped and put round the right way.

Fractions of a second were passing and I held on to 'Woolly's seat re-clipping whilst 'Fitz' got his chute and bent by the escape hatch. He would have gone but parachute drill was ingrained in us all: 'Woolly' out first and then 'Peewee' and then me and then 'Fitz'. He waited and I rolled to the hatch looking back into the pilot's compartment with its eerie bright red light, Sid's stony face almost gargoyle-like and Sergeant Wood's wide open eyes above a countenance serious with concentration. 'Fitz' tapped my head and put his thumb up. I sat over the hatch, dropped my legs outside in a tremendously tugging slipstream, placed my right hand round the rip ring and went. The change to complete silence was immediate and I turned over in a cartwheel feeling the dampness of cloud all about me. Semi-consciously counting I pulled the rip ring as if in training.

The damp cloud was still all around me as I swung first one way then the other. I felt a little sick and realised that my head and face were aching badly. It then dawned on me what had happened. I had looked down when pulling the rip ring instead of turning my head to one side and my face had taken the full force of the opening parachute clipped to my chest which had knocked me unconscious. Stupid thing to do, my neck ached as well.

Peering down at my feet I could see no breaks in the cloud; I was floating it seemed for ages in a strange silent world getting wetter all the time and beginning to feel the cold eating through my Sidcot suit. Then, as if by magic, the cloud disappeared and the dark earth lay below, an odd light showing here and there. No way of telling what sort of area I would land in, I would have to trust to luck. It was coming up pretty fast now and as the last few feet dissolved I felt a fresh flash of pain as I finally made contact.'

'Sid' Fox, Henry Wood, 'Fitz' Fitzsimmons, 'Phil' Heath and 'Jock' Mercer were killed. 'Peewee' Maddocks was captured the day after bailing out and spent the rest of the war in prisoner of war camps. 'Woolly' Woollerton also was captured shortly after bailing out. He remained a prisoner of war for the duration and on his release returned to the RAF which he eventually left in 1975 with the rank of squadron leader.

At Elsham Wolds there had never been any lectures on escape and evasion or how to make contact with the Resistance or how to get out of an area, how to hide, what to avoid but Spiller reached Paris where he confided in an abbe in a church who, as luck would have it, had friends in the Resistance. Once accepted by the group time passed slowly while the route south seemed barred to him so he was taken by train to Belgium and hidden in the countryside before crossing the border into Holland. A month passed before he was woken one night to be told it was time to go. The pretty teenager sent as his guide was enough to calm his fears. 'Never unhappy in the company of an attractive young lady, I set off with mounting anticipation of a successful run home.' Now he was fed into the Comète Line, passed from pretty girl to pretty girl. He got a kiss from Emmeline when she handed him over to Constance and played the sweetheart with Nounou, arm in arm, as they swept through the barrier at Brussels station.

Spiller travelled south with Sergeant R. P. 'Smitty' Smith, a Canadian Wellington pilot on 115 Squadron at East Wretham who had been shot down on the raid on Turin on 9/10 December. In Brussels the two airmen boarded the train to Paris disguised as Dutch students with Dutch cigarettes and coins in their jacket pockets. They were to rendezvous with Dédée de Jong whom they had kept hearing about. It was Smith who discovered that she was a woman and not a man as previously thought. 'Boy' thought Spiller 'she must be some sort of Valkyrie to run such a successful and professional organisation.' Entering the salon in Brussels with some trepidation they were astonished to see an attractive young woman, not a classic beauty but nevertheless fresh and vibrant. Her slim figure dressed in a simple blouse and skirt made her look like a teenager and her short bobbed hair and clear eager blue eyes did the same. 'Hallo' she greeted the two airmen. 'I am Dédée' she said. She shook their hands with a wide smile and with a wave of her hand towards the table said, 'Please sit down'. The immediate impression was that here was someone every much in charge whose instructions were explicit and were to be followed without question.

Within hours the two airmen were on the overnight express to Bayonne. Then it was out to 'Tante Go's house. In the book she kept recording all the airmen who had passed through on their way to Spain he counted the names above his. He was 'parcel' number 82. Some names he knew. There was 'good old' Jack Newton, a friend on 12 Squadron and Pipkin and Mellor; both navigators.[43] Knowing that they were now probably back in England gave him 'a tremendous boost of confidence.' Spiller and the others in his party of eight led by Dédée were put on the train for Ste-Jean-de-Luz, where bicycles were waiting for them. Soon they left the bikes and began to trek uphill on foot. In the cottage at Urrugne they dined on hot milk and bread around a roaring fire. Dédée ordered that there was to be no smoking, no talking, no coughing and no lagging behind on the twelve-hour journey ahead and any orders must be obeyed without question. 'Florentino' Goïcoechea pushed through the door in his dark blue fisherman's smock and he examined the evaders' feet, applying bandages and tying on their espadrilles. He checked everyone's clothing, telling Spiller to put his jacket and trousers on inside out so that the black lining would make him all but invisible in the night. Finally, after a last meal of some meaty soup, they left with 'Florentino' and Dédée for the arduous trek to the Pyrénées. They made it and for Spiller his ordeal was over. He felt safe. A warm glow came over him; there were fond kisses on the cheeks for 'Florentino' and demurely on the hand for Dédée before his emotions got the better of him and he hugged her and planted kisses on her face. Thanks to her, 'parcel' 81 and 'parcel' 82 had been delivered safe and sound.

They were joined by 'parcel' 78, Sergeant W. McLean an air gunner and the only survivor on a 7 Squadron Stirling which crashed in Belgium on 6/7 December 1942 on Mannheim. All three men spent a 'jolly' Christmas at the British Embassy in Madrid before they were smuggled out of Spain aboard a British orange boat that took them down the River Guadalquivir from Seville to Cadiz and on to Gibraltar. From there, aboard a captured French liner built solely for the Mediterranean, they set sail for England. It had a flattish bottom and the skeleton crew of Royal Navy men told them not to worry as any torpedo fired at them would pass underneath! They took turns on watches, finding the heavy seas a little overwhelming both in the continual spray and in the exaggerated pitching of the vessel which returned quite a few meals to the deep. The French liner docked at Gourock in Scotland on 26 January 1943. After de-briefing in London and two weeks' leave 'Dizzy' Spiller reported back to RAF Uxbridge for re-posting. Since he was returning from the last operation of his second tour he was given the option to choose where he might be sent. He plumped for Ferry Command and he was ordered to report to RAF Lyneham to be told that he was attached to a flight transporting VIPs to the Middle East. At that time Transport Command had not been formed. After a crash refresher course of astro-navigation, he was once again in the air, en route to Cairo and he landed in Gibraltar five weeks after leaving it by ship, on the way to take part in the desert war.[44]

In its three years of existence, the Comète Line was betrayed or infiltrated at least three times. In the worst of these disasters, in November 1942, the organisation was penetrated by two German agents masquerading as Americans serving with the RAF. Andrée de Jongh ('Dédée') was betrayed and arrested at the farmhouse in Urrugne on 15 January 1943 together with 'Francia' Usandizanga of Urrugne, who would die in the horror of Ravensbrück on 12 April 1945 aged 36. Twenty-three members in the Comète Line were shot.[45] They included Dédée's father Frédéric 'Paul' / 'Kiki', a headmaster, who was arrested on 7 June 1943 and was executed on 28 March 1944 at Mont-Valerien, Paris, by firing squad. Some 130 did not return from German concentration camps.

Like 'Dédée', one of the first courier volunteers, Andrée Dumont, known as Nadine, ended up in Ravensbrück. She was just 18 when her country capitulated to the Germans. By day she worked in the office of an organisation that looked after the needy, but it was not long before she had an evening job as well. Her parents were among the first to join the official resistance and Nadine made herself useful by delivering copies of a banned underground newspaper, even though she knew she would be severely dealt with if captured. She quickly came to the notice of the Line and, after a spell of carrying messages, was entrusted with leading Allied airmen and the occasional Belgian fugitive on the long journey south. She made 20 such trips but, along with a handful of others in Brussels, was betrayed and arrested. She especially remembers the last time she saw her father, a doctor, who was also taken prisoner. 'It was during the train journey to Germany. He was sent to a place called Groß Rosen where much later, with liberation imminent, the inmates were set free. But my father stayed on to look after the sick and, acting on last-minute orders, the Germans torched the camp - and all its remaining occupants.' She was another who gave nothing away during questioning, despite the beatings. 'I admitted that I was a courier at Brussels Gare du Nord station but then they knew that.' What they didn't know was that I actually used the station at Lerven, but to keep the Germans guessing, I gave them descriptions of non-existent people at the Gare du Nord...'[46]

Andrée Dumont was replaced by her sister, Micheline (aka 'Michou'); who was 15 months her senior but looked much younger. And it was 'Michou' (who later married Pierre Ugeux, a major in the Special Operations Executive in France) who unmasked the traitor who seriously damaged the Line in the summer of 1943, causing Dédée's father, among others, to be captured. Martine Noël, one of those arrested in this latest setback and thrown into a Paris prison, knew the identity of the traitor, so, as cool as you like, 'Michou' went to the jail and screamed at the top of her voice for Martine to be brought to a window. Minutes later, the traitor's identity was revealed, only for 'Michou' to be apprehended for trespass and marched to the prison commandant. 'Luckily, he believed my story that I was only 15 and that I had gone there to see if I could do anything for my dentist who had been arrested. He asked what I thought I could do and I told him that no doubt my mother would have liked to send her a parcel - and he let me go with a warning.' Her action saved the southern end of the Line and one of the key figures, Elvire de Greef, (aka 'Tante Go'), along with it. Although arrested at one time and released, she never gave up her work for Comète and stayed in her villa until the end of the war.[47]

Miraculously, 'Dédée' de Jongh and Andrée Dumont survived their horrific ordeal in Ravensbrück. They had spent two years in the notorious concentration camp and were both seriously ill. Such was their condition that when they were liberated by the Allies that one English nurse could not believe that they were still alive. An English doctor told them: 'You should be dead. But happily this is not the time for you to join the angels.'

The courage of the women of the line like 'Dédée' de Jongh and Andrée Dumont was recognized by the award of the George Medal, the highest decoration that can be awarded to a foreign civilian for bravery. Other recipients included Elvire de Greef and 'Michou'. Her sister Andrée was made an OBE and was awarded the King's Medal for Courage. But the 'decoration' that gave Andrée the most pleasure was the pilot's wings given to her by the RAF. 'Florentine', who saw several hundred airmen over the dangerous route to Spain, also received the George Medal, together with the King's Medal for Courage. He was severely wounded in the leg in July 1944 but survived the war. He died in July 1980 and is buried at the foot of his great love, the Pyrénées. Louis Massinon did not survive the war. He was arrested on 10 August with Fernande Pirlot after the Germans had infiltrated the network and he disappeared in Groß Rosen in February 1945. Mauritius Wilmet evaded the Gestapo by hiding in the cellar of his own house for over two years before the Liberation. His wife kept him hidden and supplied with food and successfully led the Gestapo and all his friends to think that he had fled to avoid capture. He never fully recovered his health and died in 1960. Carl Servais avoided capture until just before the liberation of Brussels, when the Gestapo arrested him and many others. They were all put on a train, but railway workers took advantage of the confusion and managed to divert it around the capital until the British captured it.

Andrée de Jongh recovered to return to nursing and devoted herself to caring for lepers in the Congo, Cameroon, Ethiopia and Senegal. Among her many awards was the George Medal, which she received from King George VI in 1946.

Next to Mary his wife, 'Dédée' became the most important person in Jack Newton's life. 'After the war, the British awarded her the George Medal, conferred on civilians for acts of great courage. In my opinion, she should have been given a string of them, not just for what she did for me and the others but for constantly risking her life as well as experiencing at first hand the horrors of a concentration camp and, through the cause, losing her father and so many of those that she loved. Without the remarkable Dédée and her friends, there is just no way that I would have got back.'

In later years the King of Belgium made Andrée de Jongh a countess.[48]

Endnotes

28   *The Bomber Command War Diaries; An Operational reference book 1939-1945* by Martin Middlebrook and Chris Everitt (Midland Publishing Ltd 1985, 1990, 1995).

29   Eckardt was KIA on 29/30 July 1942 near Melsbroek in air combat with a Lancaster. He had scored 22 night and 3 day victories at the time of his death.

30   Six Wellingtons and the Halifax W7653 on 102 Squadron FTR. *The Bomber Command War Diaries; An Operational reference book 1939-1945* by Martin Middlebrook and Chris Everitt (Midland Publishing Ltd 1985, 1990, 1995).

31   The *Reseau Comete* was a resistance group in Belgium and France that helped Allied soldiers and airmen return to Britain. The line started in Brussels where the men were fed, clothed and given false identity papers, before being hidden in attics or cellars. A network of people then guided them south through occupied France into neutral Spain and home via British-controlled Gibraltar. A typical route was from Brussels or Lille to Paris and then via Tours, Bordeaux, Bayonne, over the Pyrénées to San Sebastian in Spain. From there evaders travelled to Bilbao, Madrid and Gibraltar. There were three other main routes. The Pat line (after founder Pat O'Leary) ran from Paris to Toulouse via Limoges and then over the Pyrenees via Esterri d'Aneu to Barcelona. Another Pat line ran from Paris to Dijon, Lyons, Avignon to Marseille, then Nimes, Perpignan and Barcelona, from where they were transported to Gibraltar. The third route from Paris (the Shelburne line) ran to Rennes and then St Brieuc in Brittany, where men were shipped to Dartmouth.

32   Later, Ralston was moved to Stalag Luft III at Sagan.

33   Peggy van Lier later escaped to England, where she was awarded the MBE - later she became Mrs Jimmy Langley.

34   Andree de Jongh was 20 in 1940 and lived in Brussels. She was the younger daughter of Frederic de Jongh, a headmaster and Alice Decarpentrie. A heroine in her youth had been Nurse Edith Cavell who was shot in 1915 in the Tir National in Schaerbeek for helping troops escape from occupied Belgium to neutral Netherlands. In August 1941 Andree de Jongh appeared in the British consulate in Bilbao with a British soldier (James Cromar from Aberdeen) and two Belgian volunteers (Merchiers and Sterckmans), having travelled by train from Paris to Bayonne and then on foot over the Pyrénées. She requested British support for her escape network (later named 'Comet line'), which was granted by MI9 (British Military Intelligence Section 9), under the control of an ex-infantry major Norman Crockatt and Lieutenant James Langley. Langley had been repatriated after losing his left arm in the rearguard defence of Dunkerque in 1940. Working with MI9 de Jongh helped 400 Allied soldiers escape from Belgium through occupied France to Spain and Gibraltar. ('Dédée'De Jongh escorted 118 airmen on 218 journeys over the Pyrenees herself.

35   Following his evasion, Larry Carr was awarded a Mention in Despatches. He was commissioned on 19 June 1943. After some leave, he returned to flying duties, but his detailed knowledge of the helpers and the escape lines prevented him from returning to operational flying and he flew with the Airborne Experimental Establishment and later with a communications squadron, ending the war in Norway. *RAF Evaders: The Comprehensive Story of Thousands of Escapers and their Escape Lines, Western Europe, 1940-1945* by Oliver Clutton-Brock (Grub Street 2009). 'Dixie' Lee spent the rest of the war a prisoner, varying the tedium by making several fruitless attempts at escape. At last came the end of the fighting and his repatriation. The quisling who had caused his capture by the Germans was put on trial by members of the local Underground Movement, sentenced and quietly executed.

36   Langlois, Sergeant J. W. 'Pat' McLarnon, second pilot; Sergeant Harold J. E. 'Burry' Burrell, navigator; Flight Sergeant Richard A. 'Titch' Copley, wireless operator; and Sergeant R. D. 'Doug' Porteous RNZAF, usually the front-gunner. *See Heroism Right Down The Line* by Roy Johnstone and *Evader* by Derek Shuff (Spellmount 2003 & 2007).

37   After November 1942 the escape lines became more dangerous, after southern France was occupied by the Germans and the whole of France came under direct Nazi rule. Many members of the Comète line were betrayed; hundreds were arrested by the Geheime Feldpolizei and the Abwehr and, after weeks of interrogation and torture at places such as Fresnes Prison in Paris,

were executed or labelled Nacht und Nebel (NN) prisoners. NN prisoners were deported to German prisons and many later to concentration camps such as Ravensbrück concentration camp for women, Mauthausen-Gusen concentration camp, Buchenwald concentration camp, Flossenburg concentration camp. Prisoners sent to these camps included Andrée de Jongh, Elsie Marechal (Belgian Resistance), Nadine Dumon (Belgian Resistance), Mary Lindell (Comtesse de Milleville) and Virginia d'Albert-Lake (American).

38 On Operation 'Millennium', the 1,000 raid on Cologne on 30/31 March 1942, as Saxelby and his crew crossed the Dutch-German border and were approaching Eindhoven their Wellington was attacked twice by a night-fighter, which raked the fuselage with cannon shells and set the aircraft on fire. Pipkin was nearest to the flames. He had no gloves on but he attacked them immediately with his bare hands. Flight Sergeant W. J. McLean the wireless operator helped Pipkin and between them they managed to extinguish the fire. Saxelby was having great difficulty keeping the aircraft airborne. Locked in a spiral, the ground was coming up fast. Pipkin disappeared and then came back with a rope, which he tied round the control column. Saxelby noticed that the skin on Pipkin's hands were shrivelled and burnt. Pipkin lashed the stick back and the Wellington levelled out. They made it back and force landed at Honington.

39 Saxelby was sent to Stalag Luft III and was one of the officers who took part in 'The Great Escape'. Whilst waiting in the tunnel close to the foot of the final ladder, shots were heard, upon hearing them the waiting party turned and went back along the tunnel expecting to be shot at any moment. He was not one of the fifty who were murdered by the German's following the escape, Clive Saxelby died on 22 March 1999.

40 Gertrude Moors, one of his anonymous helpers, who kept a safe house in Maastricht, was arrested on 18 June 1943. After months of torture, she was condemned to death on 2 July 1944 and died in Auschwitz.

41 Pipkin was flown to Mount Batten the following day. He was awarded the DFC on 10 November. Squadron Leader Pipkin died in a shooting accident on 30 August 1944. See *RAF Evaders: The Comprehensive Story of Thousands of Escapers and their Escape Lines, Western Europe, 1940-1945* by Oliver Clutton- Brock (Grub Street 2009).

42 On 24/25 October 1942 71 aircraft of 1 and 3 Groups and the Path Finders were detailed to attack Milan.

43 Flight Sergeant Gordon H. Mellor had been shot down on Halifax W1216 PM-Q on the raid on Aachen on 5/6 October by a Bf 110 piloted by Leutnant Hans Autenrieth who badly damaged the aircraft and set the wing on fire. Three of the eight-man crew were killed, including the pilot, Warrant Officer Kenneth Fraser Edwards. Four men were taken prisoner. Gordon Mellor evaded capture. In Paris he was met by Dédée and was taken to Bayonne and St Jean-de-Luz where he and three other evaders, led by 'Florentino' Goïcoechea and Albert Johnson, made it across the Pyrénées on 19 October. The airmen were taken into San Sebastián and transported to the British Embassy in Madrid before being put on an aircraft at Gibraltar and flown home on 31 October, arriving at his home in Wembley on 1 November; his birthday!

44 *Ticket To Freedom* by H. J. Spiller DFM (William Kimber 1988).

45 Monique de Bissy was arrested in March 1944, freed in September 1944. Baron Jean Greindl, (aka Nemo), Head of line in Brussels, was arrested on 6 February 1943 and killed on 7 September 1943. Jean-Francois Nothomb, (aka 'Franco'), succeeded 'Dédée' in France. She was arrested on 18 January 1944, surviving several Nazi concentration camps and was awarded the DSO. Comte Jacques Legrelle (aka 'Jerome'), organised and operated line in the Paris area and linked the Belgium part of line to the South of France. He was captured, tortured, sent to concentration camps and survived. He was awarded the George Medal. Comte Antoine d'Ursel (aka 'Jacques Cartier') succeeded Nemo in Brussels. He died crossing the Franco-Spanish border on 24 December 1943.

46 See *Heroism Right Down The Line* by Roy Johnstone.

47 See *Heroism Right Down The Line* by Roy Johnstone.

48 *Shot Down And on the Run; True Stories of RAF and Commonwealth aircrews of WWII* by Air Commodore Graham Pitchfork (National Archives 2003. Andrée de Jongh's story is admirably told in the book *Little Cyclone* by Airey Neave. The authors of the official history of MI9 cite 2,373 British and Commonwealth servicemen and 2,700 Americans taken to Britain by such escape lines during WWII. The RAF Escaping Society estimated that there were 14,000 helpers by 1945.

Chapter 11

Lonesome Road

George R. Harsh RCAF

On 5 October 1942 as the dawn began to break over the fields of England Flying Officer George R. Harsh RCAF, the 102 Squadron Gunnery Officer, with cold and trembling fingers, fumbled amidst the straps and buckles and flaps of his flying gear and extracted the flask of brandy from his hip pocket and took a long, gurgling belt of this time-tested restorative. Described as 'grey as a badger' and looking like a 'Kentucky colonel; a wild, wild man with a great spreading nose and a rambunctious soul', Harsh was an American born in Milwaukee and educated in North Carolina and at Oglethorpe University in Atlanta. Having found and circled over their home base at Pocklington in 4 Group in the county of Yorkshire, the Halifax crew spotted the operations officer standing at the end of the runway, signalling with his green Aldis lamp the call letters of the squadron and their aircraft; 'O-for-Orange'. With the four magnificent Merlin Rolls-Royce engines straining against the lowered flaps, the crew settled in for the touch-down. Then, having taxied to the dispersal site the pilot shut off the engines and the sudden silence tore at their ear drums. One by one, they dropped out of the hatch and walked slowly over to the waiting lorry. Harsh wrote that, 'the birds would just be starting their cheerful greetings to this new day and for some reason the sound always startled me, as though I thought those birds had no right to be any part of this crazy business. And yet I loved that sound, for I knew they were English birds and that once again I was on friendly soil. The same WAAF who had seen us off the night before and had watched unconcernedly as we each in turn had unbuttoned and peed on the port wheel for luck would be standing beside her lorry waiting for us with a big cheerful smile on her English-complexioned face. We had taxied out of the dispersal site and she had seen us off with that big smile and her arm held aloft and her fingers giving the Victory sign and this morning the smile was still there and so was her unvarying greeting: 'Morning, chaps: Have a nice trip ?'

'And the reply would come from my polite British fellow crew members, as though we had just returned from a holiday cruise to the Caribbean. 'Veddy nice, thenk you.' [49]

Life had started out with great expectations for George Harsh. He lost his father when he was twelve but at his death a half-million dollars was put in trust in his name. Then at age 17 Harsh shot a man in a hold-up, for kicks. He was sentenced to die in the electric chair but at age 18 his sentence was commuted to life in prison and he spent the next twelve years on a Georgia chain gang. Harsh wielded a shovel for 14 hours a day; slept in a stinking cage; fought off the sexual attacks of other prisoners and learned how to survive a hell that would have killed most men. He was pardoned when he saved the life of another prisoner by performing an improvised appendectomy. Less than a year later Harsh had volunteered for the flying service in the RCAF.

At 4 o'clock on the afternoon of 5 October, all air crew members at Pocklington were ordered over the tannoy system to report to the briefing room. The target for over 250 aircraft was Aachen, though George Harsh was not scheduled to fly that night. At take-off time he stood at the end of the runway, with the operations officer, enjoying this brief respite from what the American called 'this orgy of killing'. During the past two weeks 102 had taken more than its usual share of casualties. The operations officer with his Aldis lamp signalled the aircraft and got them airborne, one following right on the tail of the other. W7824, the third-from-last Halifax II was standing poised, waiting for the 'go' flick of the light when suddenly the pilot signalled us. In a dogtrot they hurried over to see what the trouble was. The pilot, Warrant Officer Frederick Arthur Schaw RNZAF, with a frantically jabbing finger was motioning them towards the rear turret. Schaw's was one of the green crews that had been sent to the squadron from the replacement depot. In fact this was the first combat operation for this crew. Running around to the rear turret and motioning with his hand because of the wash of the props and the tinny roar of the engines, Harsh got the gunner to understand that he wanted him to swing the turret around and open the door. 'What's the problem?' Harsh bellowed at him over the noise. 'The gunner, a huge farm boy from Yorkshire, held out his hand; and there, nestling in the great palm, were the remains of what had once been a finely adjusted gun-sight. 'It coom apart in me 'and!' he shouted in his Yorkshire accent. It was as though a bear had got hold of a fine, jewelled Swiss watch.

'Get the bloody hell out of there!' I roared at him and as he extricated his lumbering bulk from the turret. I snatched off his parachute harness and buckled it on myself over my best uniform. That plane had to go on the mission and there had better be someone in the turret who could hit a target without the aid of a gun-sight. Perhaps I could do something with the help of the tracers.

'As we got airborne and headed out across the Channel, the realization of how stupid I had just been crashed into my mind - and it was that parachute harness which acted as the catalyst. For some reason known only to himself the ploughboy had been wearing an unneeded sheepskin-lined leather flying jacket and the harness had been adjusted to all that bulk. There was now enough slack in the harness to hang a horse and it was all hanging down between my legs. If I had to bail out and the parachute opened, that slack would snap taut right into my crotch! With this sickening picture in mind I reached behind me for the adjusting buckles but in the cramped quarters I couldn't do anything with them, so I pulled the slack up around my chest and offered a small prayer. By now I was beginning to feel that I had used up all my luck; but maybe it would hold for one more time.

'For an hour or more we droned along uneventfully. We had not run into any heavy concentrations of flak and miraculously no night fighters had challenged us. Intelligence had assured us the flak would be light. Suddenly a cold thought entered my mind: for the past half-hour I had not noticed any other bombers flying in our direction and this despite the fact we should have been right in the middle of the bomber stream. Slowly I swung the turret in its full arc - nothing out there but an occasional fleecy patch of white cloud, shimmering in the bright moonlight. And then I looked down at the ground 8,000 feet below us. Oh, no! But blinking my eyes wouldn't make it go away. The Kölner Dom! The majestic twin spires of the Cologne Cathedral were pointing into the sky at me. The bulk of the old Gothic edifice was bathed in moonlight and the moonlight was shimmering from the waters of the river as it made its unmistakable bend around the church. There we were, right on top of Cologne... alone.

'The pilot must have instinctively sensed that something was wrong, for I heard a microphone click on and then his voice crackled in the earphones. 'Hullo navigator! Where are we?' For what seemed interminable seconds there was dead silence and then the well-bred, English-public-school accents of the navigator came over the intercom. 'I'm fucked if I know old boy.'

'The groan of despair did not even have time to escape my lips before everything seemed to begin happening at once. The eerie purple light of the radio-controlled searchlight, the master searchlight of the Cologne air defence system locked onto us and having seen this happen to other bombers I knew there would be no escaping it. No manoeuvring, no 'jinking', no diving nor turning nor any amount of speed would shake off that relentless finger. With the range signalled to them from this automatic light the entire searchlight complex now locked onto us and we were 'coned', the most dreaded thing that could happen to any bomber crew. The sky around us and the aircraft itself were lighted up like Broadway on New Year's Eve and then it came. The German gunners had a sitting duck for a target and all they had to do was pour their fire up into the apex of that cone and there was no way for them to miss. In the bright, blinding light there was no flashing coming from the flak bursts now but suddenly our whole piece of illuminated sky filled with brown, oily puffs of smoke. Pieces of shrapnel began hitting us and it sounded like wet gravel being hurled against sheet metal. Then we started taking direct hits and the aircraft jumped and bucked and thrashed and pieces of it were being blown off and I could see them whipping past me. Then the fire started and I could smell it and see the long tongues of flame streaming out from the wings. The intercom was now dead and so was the hydraulic system that operated the turret but with the manual crank I quickly turned the turret around, opened the doors and was preparing to push myself backwards out into the sky when a burst of light, fine shrapnel sprinkled my whole back. It felt as though the points of a dozen white hot pokers had suddenly jabbed into me. My one prayer at that moment was that the flak had not cut the parachute harness draped over my back. The parachute harness! Oh, God... get that slack out of your crotch! I dropped, clutching the slack around my midriff with my left hand and pulled the rip cord on my chest pack with my right. I was now conscious of the dead silence through which I was falling. Gone was the aircraft with its roaring engines and miraculously the flak had stopped. But one searchlight glued itself onto me and began following me downward. Then the chute opened and my fall was suddenly, jarringly halted and I bobbed upward like a yo-yo in the hand of some idiot giant. With a tearing, rending noise the slack snapped taut around my chest and I felt my whole rib cage cave in. Then I passed out.' [50]

George Harsh spent two weeks in a hospital in Cologne before being incarcerated in Stalag Luft III. Harsh had charge of tunnel security in the 'X Organisation'. 'Home for Christmas' was the standard joke in prisoner of war camps but tunnelling went so smoothly at Luft III that Harsh said thoughtfully one morning, 'You know, this time it might really be home for Christmas for some of us' and for once nobody laughed. [51]

Endnotes
49 *Lonesome Road* by George Harsh (Sphere Books London 1972).
50 *Lonesome Road* by George Harsh (Sphere Books London 1972)
51 *Lonesome Road* by George Harsh (Sphere Books London 1972). Fellow American 'Junior' Clark, a 'gangling, ginger-headed youngster in his twenties and a lieutenant colonel already' was chief of security and known as 'Big S'. At the beginning of March 1944, just before the 'Great Escape' took place, George Harsh and 18 other PoWs were ordered to pack and they were marched out of the gate at Sagan to a compound at Belaria five miles away. The move probably saved George Harsh's life and that of some of the others, including two of the tunnellers and Robert Stanford Tuck, who all worked in the escape organisation and would have been among those at the head of the queue when the 'Great Escape' took place on the night of 24 March. *The Great Escape* by Paul Brickhill (Faber and Faber).

Chapter 12

Yvonne

W. Newton MBE

I was a Secret Agent who early in 1942 was parachuted behind enemy lines. For a whole year I went about France doing my job peacefully and undisturbed, blowing things up and derailing German trains. But even the best of things come to an end and one day a double-agent crossed my path and betrayed me to the Gestapo. The betrayal was followed by a man-hunt which lasted three months, with gun battles and narrow escapes which would have made the toughest American gangster-film audience smile with incredulity.

One night I was trapped, overpowered, captured and taken to the dreaded Hotel Terminus in Lyons, Gestapo HQ of the region. The very next morning, not liking in the least the company of the Gestapo gentlemen, I made an escape bid which at the time caused quite a sensation and was highly disapproved by my hosts! However, I soon discovered that the double-agent who had betrayed me had been able to tell the Gestapo very little about me or my activities. As a matter of fact, the Germans knew that I was a British agent and that was about all! They did not know what I had been up to, or what amount of damage I was responsible for! As I was not the friendly and talkative type, they tried to make me spill the beans! But when they realized that they were wasting their time and energies they switched their tactics to a more primitive type of method: Hunger!

To punish me for attempting to escape they kept me chained to my bed for three months, with an armed sentry at the foot of the bed day and night. That was at Fort Mont-Luc. Then I was transferred to Frèsnes Prison in Paris and thrown into (booted into, would be the correct wording) a small cell with a planned starvation-diet which they hoped would loosen my tongue. The ordinary German prison diet is known to be reduced to a minimum, but I had the privilege to test for myself what really is the strict minimum on which a man can exist. At first I suffered agony and wondered how long I would be able to stand it and keep my mouth shut; but after long weeks of the experiment my stomach contracted and the hallucinations of food were replaced by a lethargic state caused by weakness. Long days and nights went by with only one thought in my mind: to have a little more to eat and not to give in! But I was not the only hungry one; more than a thousand other prisoners in Frèsnes were also starving.

Lonely days and hungry nights went by and my solitude was only disturbed by the tantalizing thoughts of a juicy 'Roast-and-Yorkshire' or by the visit of the Stabwebel in charge of the wing.

The Stabwebel made me an unofficial daily visit, a hatred-visit! He barged into Cell 347 every morning and, without a word, stared at me. He sometimes came up so close to me that I could feel his foetid breath on my nose and cheeks. For a while his cold, grey eyes fixed me and then with a loud sniff, he walked out of the cell. After a few weeks of this silent comedy he would growl: Englischer Schweinhund, du! I reached the stage where I had black dots constantly in front of me. Sometimes I fell to my knees and I could not get up again without an effort which was such a strain that it often made me pass out. One afternoon, a Thursday to be precise, the bolt of the cell door snapped back with such violence that it startled me and, contrary to my expectation, it was not the Stabwebel coming back the same day for a second dose of hate-the-British, but an ordinary German soldier who carried a small wicker-basket tied up with string. He looked at me blankly and said inquiringly: Alfred Norman? Paket! Then added in bad French: 'Food parcel!'

If the Germans had succeeded in making me a physical wreck, they had not yet succeeded in dulling my brain and for a few seconds I did some very fast thinking. My first reaction was: Caution, Gestapo trap! None of my friends would be mad enough to admit knowing me and getting themselves into a similar pickle! But something told me it was not a Gestapo trap. Who, then, would send me a parcel? The German soldier opened the little wicker-basket and took out the contents, examining closely every item. There was a little piece of stale bread, a little piece of Camembert cheese and an empty tomato-puree tin filled with jam, a slab of potato-and-rice cake and two apples! Humble home-made potato-and-rice cake, how appetizing and filling you appeared to me! The German soldier smiled at me and said: *This food is confiscated. You are a spy and must be punished.*' He then proceeded to replace the contents back into the little wicker-basket and the door of the cell closed behind him, leaving me to ponder with a watering mouth on the mysterious sender of the parcel. It was mystery sure enough and I could make neither head nor tail of it. Regularly at fortnightly intervals, on the Thursday, a soldier appeared with the little wicker-basket. The contents varied, but were always of the same home-made and humble brand. What never varied was the sentence: 'This food is confiscated!'

One Thursday, although the contents had been shown to me and taken away as usual, the German left behind him a delighted prisoner. For the first time I was able to have a glimpse at the name on the attached label. It read: Mademoiselle Yvonne Baratte. I was delighted. Yvonne! But I knew no Yvonne's and I was no nearer to solving the mystery. Another time I was able to read the address of the sender. It still meant nothing to me! The little wicker-basket came and went for almost a year and on a cold January morning I was yanked out of my cell on my way to Buchenwald Concentration Camp.

I suppose I am one of the lucky ones! As I am one of the only four British agents who survived and returned from Buchenwald with enough life to tell a story! On my return to England I had not forgotten the mysterious little wicker-basket, nor the name and address of the sender. As soon as I was fit enough to make the journey I jumped into a plane bound for Paris. I had to solve the mystery. I wanted to know! From Le Bourget airport I went straight to the address I had so carefully memorized. At long last I was going to know!

A maid answered my ring and looked very surprised when I asked to see Miss Yvonne. Presently she returned and ushered me into a large living-room and I found myself staring at an old lady. 'Mademoiselle Yvonne Baratte?' I asked. 'My name is Alfred Norman!' But the reaction to my introduction was not the one I expected, for the old lady had tears in her eyes. I looked around me embarrassed and noticed a portrait of a very beautiful young woman. The portrait was draped with black crepe and a vase with roses stood before it. I fumbled for words and finally stammered: 'I have come to thank Mademoiselle Yvonne for the little wicker-basket...'

'You are too late, monsieur,' said the old lady sadly. 'Were you a friend of hers? Did you know her?'

'Only by the little wicker-basket, Madame. But tell me, how did she know I was at Frèsnes? How did she get my name?'

The sad old lady waved her hand resignedly and explained. 'How did she know of the others she sent parcels to? Somehow she got the names of British airmen and French patriots imprisoned at Frèsnes and she went about scrounging a little flour and sugar here, bread and a little cheese there, spending all her money on black-market jam, going short of her own meagre rations to make up little food parcels. She said that was her way of contributing to the allied cause!'

I did not tell the old lady how vain her efforts had been in my case, for the motive remained sublime. I was so accustomed to death; I had seen so many people die a horrible, shabby death, that death itself left me unmoved and very often I had looked upon death as a friendly relief and good thing. But Yvonne's death saddened me beyond words; I sensed immeasurable tragedy and misery. My silence encouraged Yvonne's mother to continue.

She was constantly on the job, either collecting the food and preparing it, or travelling to and fro to Frèsnes Prison with a little handcart to deliver her parcels. She was wearing herself out, but she was happy to relieve the hunger that went on at Frèsnes.'

'Yes...'

'The Germans started to frown on her activities and she knew that she was running into danger, but that did not stop her. She never thought of herself.'

'Then one day,' the old lady sobbed, 'one day the Boches arrested her and accused her of working for British Intelligence and they tortured her to make her talk, but she could not say anything, for she did not work for the British.'

The light was fading in the room and I could hardly see the old lady's face, only her voice reached me, but it was almost a whisper now. 'It was horrible what they did to her, poor child, how she must have suffered. Then they sent her to Ravensbrück Concentration Camp, as a slave-worker to dig trenches and level out fields. That is where she died and the irony of it, monsieur, is that she died of starvation.'

The room was dark now and Yvonne's mother gave way to desperate sobs. I tiptoed out of the room, leaving the old lady to her sorrow. Words of comfort were meaningless before such grief. She was best left alone with the memories of her brave daughter. Out in the street, I hastened my step toward the bright lights of a bar. I had a lump in my throat and badly needed a stiff drink. I was sad and angry. The irony of the girl's fate made meangry and I was sad because Yvonne's sacrifice and courage would be known only to her family and a few friends. Her personal contribution to the allied cause would receive no praise or official acknowledgement. The story of her gallantry, like that of so many others, alas, would never be told and would forever remain unknown.

Chapter 13

Annette

Yvonne Cormeau was born Beatrice Yvonne Biesterfeld on 18 December 1909 in Shanghai, China, the daughter of a British consular official and Scottish mother. When he died in 1920, the family moved around France, Belgium and Scotland, where Yvonne was educated. Yvonne was living in London when in 1937 she married Charles Edouard Emile Cormeau, a chartered accountant who was a second generation French immigrant born in England. They had one child, Yvette; a daughter. Yvonne's husband enlisted in the The Rifles and in November 1940 he was wounded in France and was sent back to England. Shortly afterwards he was killed when their London home was bombed. Amazingly Yvonne's life was saved by a bath which fell over her head and protected her. Newly widowed she decided to 'take her husband's place in the Armed Forces' and in November 1941 Yvonne joined the WAAF as an administrator. Being bilingual in French and English, whilst serving at RAF Swinderby she answered an appeal on the notice board for linguists and was recruited by SOE and trained as an F Section wireless operator on 15 February 1943. She was promoted to the rank of flight officer. Yvette, was only two years old at the time and was placed in a convent of Ursine nuns in Oxfordshire where she remained until she was five. She volunteered to 'do something and save France from the Nazis'. She did her SOE training in radio, photography, codes, ciphers and some parachuting with Yolande Beekman, Cecily Lefort[52] and Noor Inayat Khan.

Yolande Beekman was born 7 November 1911 as Yolande Elsa Maria Unternahrer to a Swiss family in Paris. As a child, she moved to London and grew up fluent in English, German and French. At the outbreak of war, she joined the Women's Auxiliary Air Force and trained as a wireless operator. Because of her language skills and wireless expertise, she was recruited by the Special Operations Executive (SOE) for work in occupied France, officially joining the SOE on 15 February 1943. In 1943, Yolande Unternahrer married Sergeant Jaap Beekman of the Dutch army, but a short time after her marriage she said goodbye to her husband and was flown behind enemy lines in France. Beekman was dropped into France on the night of 17-18 September 1943, flown in an aircraft piloted by Squadron Leader Austin of 624 (Special Duties) Squadron. In France, Yolande Beekman operated the wireless for Gustave Bieler, the Canadian in charge of the 'Musician' Network at Saint-Quentin in the departement of Aisne, using the codename 'Mariette' and the alias 'Yvonne'. She became an efficient and valued agent who, in addition to her all-important radio transmissions to London, took charge of the distribution of materials dropped by Allied planes. On 13 January 1944 she and Gustave Bieler were arrested by the Gestapo while meeting at the Cafe Moulin Brule. At the Gestapo headquarters in Saint-Quentin the two were tortured repeatedly but never broke. Separated from Bieler (he was later executed), she was transported to Frèsnes prison in Paris. Again she was interrogated and brutalized repeatedly; she shared a cell with Hedwig Muller (a nurse arrested by the Gestapo in 1944). Muller said after the war that Beekman '... didn't leave her cell much as she suffered badly with her legs'. In May 1944 she was moved with several other captured SOE agents to the civilian prison for women at Karlsruhe in Germany. She was confined there under horrific conditions until, sharing a cell with Elise Johe (a Jehovah's Witness), Nina Hagen (arrested for working as a black marketeer) and Clara Frank (jailed for slaughtering a cow on her family farm without permission). While imprisoned, Beekman drew and embroidered. She would take a needle and prick her finger to use the blood as ink and draw on toilet paper as there was no paper and pencils. She was identified from drawings made by Brian Stonehouse after the war.

After training, Yvonne Cormeau went to Tempsford and she was given a powder compact by Colonel Maurice Buckmaster before leaving for France. Her role was to work as courier and wireless operator on the 'Wheelwright' Circuit in Gascony. On the night of 22 August 1943 she was flown to France in a Halifax piloted by Wing Commander Len Ratcliff. Yvonne parachuted into Ste-Antoine-du-Queyret, northeast of Bordeaux and soon began work on the 'Wheelwright' Circuit with George Starr, 'Hiliare', who she had known before the war when living in Brussels. Whilst carrying out her secret operations in Occupied France she used the code names 'Annette', 'Fairy' and 'Sarafari'.

'Annette' Cormeau sent over 400 transmissions back to London, which was a record for the F Section. She made arrangements for arms and supplies to be dropped for the local Maquis. She also assisted in the cutting of the power and telephone lines, resulting in the isolation of the Wehrmacht Group G garrison near Toulouse. She was almost arrested by the Germans after being betrayed by an agent codenamed Rodolph. However, she continued to operate, despite being confronted by 'wanted' posters in her neighbourhood which gave an accurate sketch of her appearance. Her success was possibly owed to the fact that she used car batteries rather than mains power, making it more difficult for the German D/F vans to find her. Famously, Cormeau was stopped at a German road block whilst with Starr and the pair were questioned while a gun was held in their backs. Eventually the Germans accepted her story and ID that she was a district nurse and she succeeded in passing her wireless equipment off as an X-ray machine.

She worked for 13 months and evaded arrest despite some narrow escapes. Whilst operating in France Yvonne was shot in the leg by a German patrol, but managed to escape.[53]

'I would stay three nights only in any one house, never stay longer than that, because the signals could be traced. This went on for quite a while. I had to be philosophical about the danger of being caught, it was no use having tantrums and nerves and trying to do things too quickly. I had to be calm in all situations and that's how I got out in the end. A member of the team which received me on my arrival in France gave us all away. But luckily the Germans never caught up with me. I needed a lot of places, as my area covered from the Pyrénées to the Dordogne, from Bordeaux to Toulouse, so I had several houses I could stay in regularly. French people were very helpful and the women were especially courageous. They never got the thanks they really deserved. They had to keep up appearances all the time, while the men could go off to work. The women had to be at home and they had to receive the Gestapo if there was a visit and quickly make excuses to be sure no one was caught.

If I was discovered to have been with any of these families, I would have endangered them - that's why I was so grateful to them. I go back every year. They not only gave me food (I could give them money, as I had no tickets for food), but they gave me a bed. And they knew, not only that I was English, but I had a radio transmitter. They were extremely brave and I know some of them got MBEs for it.

'I thought it might be better to learn a little patois while I was there, I didn't use it very much, but I thought it would be helpful if I was ever caught. I always worked alone as a security measure. I experienced some of the major operations during D-Day. Everything was prepared for D-Day. We had little stocks of munitions and weapons, dotted around the area. We heard 36 hours before D-Day happened and when we heard it had happened, I had to go and check everyone had heard their messages. After that I was on the air every day to let them know what we were doing - where we were located, for example.

'I also organised for people to escape through the south of France, over the Pyrénées and down into Bilbao, where I told them to go to the consulate. If they were caught by the Spaniards, they were put into concentration camps run by the Germans, but having told London to expect them, if they didn't turn up in three or four days, Consulate staff would go to camp and bail them out.

'There were so many incidents during my time in France, but on one occasion after D-Day my boss came to the farm and said: 'Come on, the Germans have traced you and are looking for you.' I picked up my radio set and my code book, no clothes or anything and got in the car. He explained they were coming up the road to the west so we went along the middle road, as he didn't trust them not to be coming up the eastern road as well. We had travelled about 10 kilometres on the middle road when up came a personnel carrier from the German Army and they stopped us and put us in the ditch. Luckily it was dry; we were back to back to start with and then two soldiers with pistols separated us. I could feel the pistol in my back and the same was happening to my boss. This lasted about an hour under terrible July heat, with flies buzzing around and we didn't dare move, even to brush them away. Then their airfield telephone went and an adjutant got the message that he had to get back to his people or risk being overrun, so he let us go. That was really a stroke of luck!

'I trained with Yolande Beekman and Noor Inayat Kahn ['Madeleine'] - we were the first three WAAFs as far I can make out. Unfortunately neither of them came home. Noor Inayat Khan with her dark Indian skin - and not very security conscious was kept an eye on and was eventually given away. We're not quite sure, but we think she was shot in Dachau at the end. Poor Yolande was caught too. As they got into the train, they recognised each other and they were transported to the final concentration camp.'[54]

Born in the Vasco Petrovsky Monastery of Moscow in pre-revolutionary Russia on New Year's Day 1914, Noor-un-Nisa Inayat Khan was the eldest of four children. She was of royal Indian descent through her father, Hazrat Inayat Khan, who was born to nobility and came from a princely Indian Muslim family (his mother was a descendant of the uncle of Tipu Sultan, the 18th century ruler of the Kingdom of Mysore). He lived in Europe as a musician and a teacher of Sufism. Her mother, Ora Meena Ray Baker (Ameena Begum), was an American from Albuquerque, New Mexico, who met Inayat Khan during his travels in the United States. Ora Baker was the half-sister of American yogi and scholar Pierre Bernard, her guardian at the time she met Hazrat Inayat Khan. Noor's brother, Vilayat Inayat Khan, later became head of the Sufi Order International. Khan was betrayed to the Germans, either by Henri Dericourt or by Renée Garry. Dericourt (code name 'Gilbert') was an SOE officer and former French Air Force pilot who has been suspected of working as a double agent for the Sicherheitsdienst. Garry was the sister of Emile Garry, Inayat Khan's organizer in the Cinema network (later renamed 'Phono'). Allegedly paid 100,000 francs, Renee Garry's actions have been attributed by some to jealousy due to Garry's suspicion that she had lost the affections of SOE agent France Antelme to Noor. On or around 13 October 1943 Inayat Khan was arrested and interrogated at the SD Headquarters at 84 Avenue Foch in Paris. Though SOE trainers had expressed doubts about Inayat Khan's gentle and unworldly character, on her arrest she fought so fiercely that SD officers were afraid of her. She was thenceforth treated as an extremely dangerous prisoner. There is no evidence of her being tortured, but her interrogation lasted over a month. During that time, she attempted escape twice. Hans Kieffer, the former head of the SD in Paris, testified after the war that she did not give the Gestapo a single piece of information, but lied consistently. Although Inayat Khan did not talk about her activities under interrogation, the SD found her notebooks. Contrary to security regulations, she had copied out all the messages she had sent as an SOE operative. Although she refused to reveal any secret codes, the Germans gained enough information from them to continue sending false messages imitating her. London failed to properly investigate anomalies which should have indicated the transmissions were sent under enemy control. And so three more agents sent to France were captured by the Germans at their parachute landing, among them Madeleine Damerment, who was later executed.

On 25 November 1943 Inayat Khan escaped from the SD Headquarters, along with fellow SOE Agents John Renshaw Starr and Leon Faye, but was captured in the immediate vicinity. There was an air raid alert as they escaped across the roof. Regulations required a count of prisoners at such times and their escape was discovered before they could get away. After refusing to sign a declaration renouncing future escape attempts, Inayat Khan was taken to Germany on 27 November 1943 'for safe custody' and imprisoned at Pforzheim in solitary confinement as a 'Nacht und Nebel' (condemned to 'Disappearance without Trace') prisoner, in complete secrecy. For ten months, she was kept there handcuffed. She was classified as 'highly dangerous' and shackled in chains most of the time. As the prison director testified after the war, Inayat Khan remained uncooperative and continued to refuse to give any information on her work or her fellow operatives.

On 11 September 1944 Noor Inayat Khan and three other SOE agents from Karlsruhe prison, Yolande Beekman, Elaine Plewman and Madeleine Damerment, were moved to the Dachau Concentration Camp.

Eliane Plewman was born Eliane Sophie Browne-Bartroli in Marseille on 6

December 1917, the daughter of an English father and Spanish mother. Elaine was educated in England and in Spain. When she finished college she moved to Leicester to work for an import company. After the outbreak of war, she worked for the British Embassies in Madrid and Lisbon. In 1942 she went to Britain to work for the Spanish section of the Ministry of Information. That same summer she married British army officer Tom Plewman. Later she joined the Special Operations Executive (SOE) and was given a codename 'Gaby'. On 13/14 August 1943 Eliane parachuted into France and joined 'Monk'; a resistance network of Charles Skepper. She worked as a courier in the area of Marseilles, Roquebrune and Ste-Raphael. When the network was betrayed in March 1944 Plewman was also arrested. The Gestapo interrogated and tortured her for three weeks at Les Baumettes Prison and then transferred her to Frèsnes prison.[55]

Madeleine Zoe Damerment was born in Lille, the daughter of the Head postmaster of Lille; following the occupation of France by the Germans in 1940, her family became actively involved with the French Resistance. The unassuming twenty-two-year-old Madeleine worked as an assistant to Michael Trotobas on the escape line set up by Albert Guerisse. She helped downed British airmen and others to escape France until 1942, when it is believed that one of her fellow resistance workers, Harold Cole, betrayed the group and she had to flee to England. Once in England Damerment volunteered to work with the Special Operations Executive (SOE). Trained to be a courier for the 'Bricklayer' network, on the night of 28 February 1944 she and agents France Antelme and Lionel Lee were parachuted into a field near the city of Chartres. However, they had been betrayed and the waiting Gestapo arrested them on landing. Shipped to Gestapo headquarters on the Avenue Foch in Paris, Damerment was subjected to examination and torture. On 13 May 1944 the Germans transferred the eight SOE agents being held in Frèsnes prison to the civilian prison for women at Karlsruhe in Germany.

On 12 September Noor Inayat Khan, Yolande Beekman, Eliane Plewman and Madeleine Damerment were among those who arrived at Dachau concentration camp, accompanied by three officials of the Karlsruhe Gestapo. They arrived at Dachau after dark and had to walk to the camp, which they reached about midnight. They spent the night in the cells and between 8 and 10 the following morning, 13 September, they were taken to the crematorium compound and shot through the back of the head and immediately burned in the crematorium.[56] An anonymous Dutch prisoner emerging in 1958 contended that Inayat was cruelly beaten by a high-ranking SS officer named Wilhelm Ruppert before being shot from behind. She was 30 years old. Yolande Lagrave wrote to Noor's brother Vilayat after the war. 'As for myself I was deported to Pforzheim and had the luck to return. I am the only survivor; all the others of my group have been murdered... At Pforzheim I lived in solitary confinement. There I could correspond with an English parachutiste who was interned and very unhappy. Her hands and feet were manacled, she was never taken out and I heard the blows which she received. She left Pforzheim in September 1944. Before that she was able to pass a message to me - not her real name, that was too dangerous, but a pseudonym...I took note of this as Nora Baker, Radio Centre Officers, Service RAF, 4 Taviston Street London.'[57]

A year after the end of the war, Annette Cormeau was demobilised with the WAAF rank of Flight Officer. She then worked as a translator and in the SOE section at the Foreign Office. She became a linchpin of F Section veterans and arranged their annual Bastille Day dinner. She was appointed MBE and decorated with the Legion d'honneur, Croix de Guerre and Medaille de la Resistance. She died on 25 December 1997, aged 88, at Fleet, Hampshire.

Endnotes

52   Cecily Lefort was born Cécile Margot Mackenzie in London on 30 April 1900 to a prosperous family of Irish descent. In 1925 she married a wealthy French doctor, Alix Lefort, who had an apartment in Paris and a villa near the fishing village of Ste Cast on the north coast of Brittany. Her husband remained in France after the occupation but in 1941 Cecily joined the WAAF in Britain in 1941 where her ability to speak French fluently brought her to the notice of SOE in 1943 and she was trained as a courier. She arrived in France by Lysander on 17 June 1943. She was apprehended by SS guards on 15 September 1943 and sent to Ravensbrück before the end of that year. She died in the camp in February 1945. *The Heroines of SOE F Section; Britain's Secret Women in France* by Squadron Leader Beryl E. Escott (The History Press, 2010).

53   The dress she wore on this occasion, complete with bullet hole; and the bloodstained briefcase she carried and her WAAF officer's uniform are on permanent display at the Imperial War Museum in London.

54   *The Women Who Lived For Danger: The Women Agents of SOE in the Second World War* by Marcus Binney (Hodder & Stoughton 2002). Yolande Beekman was abruptly transferred to Dachau concentration camp with fellow agents Madeleine Damerment, Noor Inayat Khan and Elaine Plewman on 11 September 1944. At dawn on 13 September, the day after their arrival in Dachau, the four young women were taken to a small courtyard next to the crematorium and forced to kneel on the ground. They were then executed by a shot through the back of the head and their bodies cremated. Beekman's heroic actions were recognized by the government of France with the posthumous awarding of the Croix de Guerre. In addition, she is recorded on the Runnymede Memorial in Surrey and as one of the SOE agents who died for the liberation of France she is listed on the 'Roll of Honour' on the Valencay SOE Memorial in the town of Valencay, in the Indre departement of France. See also, *The Heroines of SOE F Section; Britain's Secret Women in France* by Squadron Leader Beryl E. Escott (The History Press, 2010).

55   See *The Heroines of SOE F Section; Britain's Secret Women in France* by Squadron Leader Beryl E. Escott (The History Press, 2010).

56   At one point it was thought that Noor had been taken with Diana Rowden, Vera Leigh and Denise Borrel from Karlsruhe City Gaol to Natzweiler concentration camp on 6 July 1944 - and had been killed with them by lethal injection. An official announcement was made to this effect. It was only two years after the war had ended that the true circumstances of Noor's death finally emerged. Eliane Plewman is remembered on the Brookwood Memorial in Surrey and the F Section Memorial, in Valencay, France. She was posthumously awarded the King's Commendation for Brave Conduct and the Croix de Guerre 1939-1945 with bronze star. Madeleine Damerment was posthumously awarded the Legion d'honneur, Croix de Guerre and the Medaille de la Resistance.

57   Inayat was posthumously awarded a British George Cross and a French Croix de Guerre with Gold Star. The citation, dated 16 January 1946 and signed by de Gaulle, said: 'Falling into an ambush at Grignon, in July 1943, her comrades and she managed to escape after having killed or wounded the Germans who tried to stop them.' As she was still considered 'missing' in 1946 she could not be recommended for the Member of the Order of the British Empire but was Mentioned in Despatches instead, in October 1946. The citation for her George Cross, issued on 5 April 1949, commended Noor for her most conspicuous courage, both moral and physical, over more than twelve months. Maurice Buckmaster described her as 'A most brave and touchingly keen girl. She was determined to do her bit to hit the Germans and, poor girl, she has.' Inayat was the third of three FANY members to be awarded the George Cross, Britain's highest award for gallantry not in the face of the enemy. At the beginning of 2011, a campaign was launched to raise £100,000 for a bronze bust of her in central London close to her former home. It was claimed that this would be the first memorial in Britain to either a Muslim or an Asian woman, but Inayat was already commemorated on the FANY memorial in St Paul's Church, Wilton Place, Knightsbridge, London which lists the 52 members of the Corps who gave their lives on active service. The unveiling of the bronze bust of Inayat by HRH The Princess Royal Anne took place on 8 November 2012 in Gordon Square Gardens, London.

Chapter 14

Journey to Toulouse

W. H. Marshall DFC DFM

At 2235 hours on the night of 12/13 May 1943 Halifax II BB133 on 138 (Special Duties) Squadron piloted by Squadron Leader C G S Robinson DFC took off from Tempsford on SOE Operation Donkeyman 1/Roach 10 and Lime 16. After completing Lime 16, dropping five containers onto this target near the Swiss border, the Halifax flew over Romilly aerodrome approximately 30km NW Troyes (Aube), was hit by flak and set on fire. Robinson ordered the crew to abandon the aircraft and 22-year-old Pilot Officer J. T. Hutchinson, air gunner and 33-year old Sergeant W. H. Marshall the flight engineer jumped from between 6,000 and 8,000 feet, not seeing any other crew member bail out after the order had been given. The burning aircraft was seen falling and explosions were heard somewhere to the west of them. They heard that four members of the crew had been killed when the aircraft had crashed but this, however, proved not so although Flight Sergeant L. Martin DFM and Flying Officer R. R. Piddington had bailed out and were captured; they both landed uninjured close to each other and buried their Mae West, parachute and helmet. Robinson made a forced landing in a field west of Troyes. Although he was dazed and cut about the face coming out of the aircraft he and Sergeant John C. Tweed the second pilot, who sprained his ankles, badly damaged his hand and suffered a deep cut on his leg, pulled Pilot Officer R. G. Johnson, the bomb aimer clear and dragged him about 100 yards from the aircraft. Tweed was unable to help Flying Officer F. C. Jeffrey the navigator as he was pinned under the wreckage and he decided it was time make good his escape. The five men were taken prisoner. (Jeffrey and Johnson were repatriated from PoW camp in February 1945). Tweed, who had only just recently celebrated his 21st birthday, evaded capture and on 18 September he was flown back to England with two other men by a 161 Squadron Lysander piloted by Flying Officer Jimmy Bathgate and landed at Tangmere.[58] Hutchinson and Marshall also successfully evaded, as Marshall recalled:

There were Germans in their hundreds on the platform, many of them no more than boys in their teens, with - incongruously - a sprinkling of elderly veterans among them, probably of some Pioneer Corps. I noticed the loose-fitting, untidy uniforms and thanked the gods that I was not in the German Army. The train came snorting in; a big, black, ugly locomotive, greatly ornamented with pipes and pistons, enveloped us in smoke. This was the express to Toulouse. I got in and was lucky enough to get a seat near the window. A large, stout woman with a basket and a red, greasy face settled herself next to me, her ungainly body overlapping one of my shoulders. The train gathered speed. The stout woman rustled in her basket and took out some magazines. I remembered my journey to Paris and the embarrassment a girl hiker had caused me. I hoped that this old dame would occupy herself with the magazines and not try to hold conversation with me. I looked out of the window. Soon we would be out into open country. I would close my eyes and doze. When my neighbour had looked through one magazine she turned her big head and eyed me for a moment. I was leaning with my elbow on the window ledge, my cheek resting in the palm of my hand. My eyes were almost closed in sham sleep and all would have been well had I not sensed that the woman was scrutinizing my face. My eyelids gave an almost imperceptible flicker. She nudged my shoulder with her great sturdy arm and proffered me the magazine. My heart sank. Again I was cornered! Again I was to be pestered by another traveller. If this woman found I was a foreigner she might scream her information to the guard, or to the Germans at the line of demarcation! There came ten minutes of peace during which I browsed slowly through the unintelligible journal. I prayed that the woman would not trouble me again. It was possible, I thought, she might fall asleep with the rocking of the train. No. She began rustling in the paper bags in her basket and brought out two hard-boiled eggs.

I considered the other occupants of the compartment. All, except one, were looking at the stout woman as she shelled the eggs. The one, an old man with a beard, sat in the far corner, slobbering over a meerschaum pipe. His shrewd old eyes looked straight at me! Voulez-vous un oeuf, monsieur? said the woman, giving me another dig with her elbow. I took the egg because I was afraid to offend the woman. She held out a paper with some salt in it. I dipped the egg and started to eat, taking my time. This would have been an embarrassing situation for me in England; here it was ten times more so, with all the people opposite watching me with cow-like eyes, thinking about me, wondering who I was and guessing much of the truth. When the first egg was eaten the woman offered me another. Merci Madame I said, smiling a grim smile. I wondered why she didn't go to hell with those wretched eggs! When I had finished that egg, I decided, I would go to the lavatory and have a smoke. While I was away the woman might go to sleep. I swallowed the last large lump of egg and got up. I staggered past the people in the corridor and reached the lavatory.

There was an obnoxious smell! The place had no water. I lit one of the American cigarettes the Resistance had given me and stood puffing for a few minutes. The little place was hot. Flies crawled thickly across the floor. This was far worse than the woman with the eggs! When I got back the woman was dozing. I wriggled myself carefully into position beside her, rested my head on my hand and tried to sleep. For half an hour the compartment was silent. I felt certain that all the occupants of the compartment knew I was a fugitive, but there was no escaping the consequences of that: I was surrounded. I went to sleep and dreamt I was going on leave and changing at Crewe, with people jostling and pushing. There were so many foreigners in my dream. I sat up suddenly, my heart throbbing. The woman had nudged me again. 'C'est un voyage fatigant celui-ci, she yawned. She took out some sandwiches and I ate two of them. In the gloom of the compartment I could see the eyes watching me. When the woman talked I answered Oui madame quietly. She grinned. She knew me. She knew I was English.

It was a weary night of futile conversation, smoking, yawning, dozing, eating, muttering. The train began to slow down. At last we had reached the danger spot. It must have been one o'clock in the morning. The train crawled into the station.

Suddenly the Resistance guide appeared in the doorway. He nodded. The woman nudged me. It was an urgent nudge, yet, I felt, friendly.

'C'est ici qu'on devra passer le controle' she told me. I got up quickly.

'Get out, monsieur, quick - under train,' the guide whispered.

Without thinking of the stir I was making, I opened the door of the compartment and looked out. Another train came into the station from the opposite direction! Could I get out in time before the other train came alongside? I would have to wait until the engine passed the compartment. The driver would not see me then. Thank God it was fairly dark! Perhaps the train would shield me from curious eyes on the far platform. When the engine had snorted past I jumped down. There was steam, heat, dust and grit. I banged the door and sped a little way along the track between the two trains. Underneath it was dark, dirty and stinking. I could smell the wagon-grease. I got on to an axle and found an iron bar with my groping feet. My knees quivered with the excitement. My back soon began to ache. I clung on grimly. There was a great deal of shouting from the platform, with noise and lights being switched on. Then footsteps. There came a sound underneath the train as of gravel being shifted. I guessed it was my companion who had been travelling in another part of the train for security's sake. I wondered how long we would have to wait. I thought of my predicament. Supposing the train began to move? I could not hold on to this precarious position. I would fall to the ground on to the gravel. My body might be mangled. Was the floor of the train high enough to allow me to lie flat? I could not tell in the blackness. Even if it were, when the train had gone the policemen on the platform would see me. It was death or arrest: a mangled body or Stalag Luft. The thought that six weeks of hard freedom were to be thrown away was agony.

There was a crunching of gravel from behind me. Someone was coming, murmuring to someone else. The feet stopped. There was a tapping sound. The feet again, the tapping sound. Nearer and nearer - the wheel-tapper and some others! A light came dodging between the trains, over the sleepers. Feet, heavy, lumbering feet. Jackboots came tramping past, reflecting in a yellow streak the light of the lamps. My mouth was full of spit. I trembled and almost fell. The wheel-tapper was actually tapping the wheel of the axle I was on. I could feel the vibration through my back-bone! Then the men had gone past. I wondered about my companion. Then I realized how unbearably my back ached. My legs were stiff, knees cramped, arms hard with muscular strain. How long now? I can feel the horror of it to this day - waiting for the train to go, to tear me to pieces! To be harried into this danger after all our wanderings! I felt the sweat and tears of despair on my face.

The long minutes dragged on. Before much longer, I knew, I would collapse and fall unconscious on the ground. And then someone hissed. Someone whispered: 'Com', monsieur.' It was the stout woman with the red face! I crawled out, staggered back, following the woman. How she found the compartment in the dark I don't know. I climbed in and closed the door. I mopped my brow and sat down, trembling. They were all excited and very anxious. Someone gave me a flask of coffee. I drank it gratefully.

The guide was in the doorway again, like a genie of the lamp. 'That was very dangerous, monsieur,' he said. 'They have caught forty young men. You have been most fortunate, eh?' He smiled and went away. I sank back and felt myself against the soft arm of the stout woman. She murmured something and moved her weight in order to give my shoulder more support. She seemed a motherly, kindly old soul at that moment. When the train started everybody sat back, deeply relieved. The old fellow with the beard and the meerschaum wiped his mouth with a red handkerchief. 'Train late,' he said softly, looking across at me. 'No more big contrôle, monsieur.' I could only look at him and smile my incredulity.

Thenceforth the journey was pleasant, I had to admit. I was surrounded by so many friends who kept looking at me and smiling in sympathy. They whispered together and conjectured who I was. No matter, they were on my side, whoever I was. The train rolled into Toulouse, some hours later, puffing great clouds of smoke to the high, curved rafters.'

Pilot Officer J. T Hutchinson and Sergeant W. H. Marshall were in hiding in Paris on 2 July 1943, when 'the chief of the 'Burgundy' organisation - whose name we do not know - introduced us to a young Frenchman named Peter, who spoke perfect English.' Hutchinson and Marshall were taken by Peter and another Frenchman called simply 'Chief', but who had been in the French navy at Dakar, to catch the overnight train to Toulouse. It was very early on the morning of 3 July when the train was halted at the Demarcation Line. Peter and Chief learnt that the Germans were making their way through the train and rounding up young Frenchmen for their labour service in Germany. Seeing six young men being marched off under guard, Hutchinson slipped unseen from the train and hid underneath another one on an adjacent track. But then he was faced with a problem, for heading his way was a 'wheel-tapper', accompanied by a German guard, checking the carriages and peering underneath them. Drawing himself up Hutchinson managed to remain unseen and, just as the Toulouse train started to move off, he rejoined his companions. As it happened his departure was unnecessary, for the Germans never got as far as their carriage to test the false papers. Marshall might even have got through the control.

By late that same evening, Hutchinson and Marshall set out to cross the Pyrénées with their guides, but it was not until mid morning on 6 July that they arrived in Andorra. Resting until 11 July they set off across the Spanish border 'with two guides and a local tobacco smuggler'. Avoiding Spanish patrols they also walked to Manresa. It took them a week, but they finally arrived at the British Consulate in Barcelona on 18 July, where they were provided with clothes and accommodation. Surprisingly, told to report to the Spanish police, Hutchinson was advised to say that he was 19 and Marshall that he was 42. They were also told to say that they had escaped from a civil internment camp in France. Whether or not the police believed their stories, the two airmen were issued with ID cards and taken to a hotel, before leaving for Madrid on 22 July. They flew back to England from Gibraltar on 5/6 August 1943. Marshall was awarded the DFC on 15 August 1944 and was promoted flying officer.[59]

Endnotes

58   See *Agents by Moonlight: The Secret History of RAF Tempsford During World War II* by Freddie Clark (Tempus Publishing Ltd 1999) and *Shot Down and on The Run: True Stories of RAF and Commonwealth aircrews of WWII* by Air Commodore Graham Pitchfork (The National Archives 2003).

59   *RAF Evaders: The Comprehensive Story of Thousands of Escapers and Their Escape Lines. Western Europe 1940-1945* by Oliver Clutton-Brock (Grub Street, 2009).

Chapter 15

The Busy 'Reaper'
of the Ruhr

St. Peter, theologically is the keeper of the Gates of Heaven, with his 'Golden Chopper', with which he harvested the 'Good Boys' for Heaven. This was current Bomber Command mythology. Hence the expression to 'Get the Chop'.

J. Norman Ashton, the 30-year old flight engineer on the Lancaster crew skippered by R. J. 'Reg' Bunten arrived on 103 Squadron in early May 1943. Their base at Elsham Wolds was a wartime station and 'likely to be comparatively rough-and-ready, as indeed it was' recalled Ashton in *Only Birds and Fools,* his autobiography of those days.[60] 'We stood by the untidy pile of kit-bags, eyeing with dismay the Nissen hut which was to be our home for the next few months. Rather a come-down, we felt, after the luxury of previous billets. Still, we had the hut to ourselves and would be able to make it cosy. The kit was carried inside and we started to sort ourselves out. Beds were moved around until everyone was satisfied and then each wall-space was decorated according to individual taste. Pin-up girls and photographs of wives and sweethearts were in great favour, whilst I - the dedicated engineer - settled for a wizard cut-away diagram of a Lancaster.

'We had arrived at Elsham, fully prepared to be thrown straight into the maelstrom of operational flying. That, however, was not the case. The Squadron had been given a week's stand-down and this gave us the chance to settle in without undue haste. The Squadron, we learned, had been very busy and was now licking its wounds and preparing men and machines for an all-out assault on the Ruhr. 'Happy Valley', as it was known to the crews, had long been a popular spot with Bomber Command and the introduction of new radar aids now made possible the complete destruction of the main cities of the Ruhr, with all that that meant to the Nazi war effort.

'There was an air of keenness and vitality about the whole place, an ops 'drome of which we had heard so much during our training days. The trappings of war were all around us: long, low bomb trolleys trundling round the perimeter track; flak-torn aircraft under repair in the hangars; belts of operational ammo in the armoury; a recent battle-order pinned to the notice-board in the crew room; aiming-point photos displayed in the Intelligence Section; a sprinkling of medal ribbons on battledress blouses; rows of miniature bombs (denoting raids) painted on the sides of the aircraft; and the partially erased, but still readable, names of missing crews on the squadron crew-state board.

On joining a new unit, it was customary for members of a crew to report to their respective leaders and to meet the other boys in the section. They were then given all the latest gen and acquainted with the equipment and methods adopted by the particular section. At that time, however, this did not apply to flight engineers. They had neither leader nor section and the only person to take the slightest technical interest in them was the Squadron Engineering Officer. Usually, he was too busy with the maintenance of the aircraft to devote much time to flight engineers and they were left very much to their own devices. I soon realised that I would have to rely largely upon my own initiative and the advice of the more experienced fellows. I drew a kit of tools and a torch from the squadron stores; parachute, harness and 'Mae West' from the parachute section; transferred my flying clothing to the locker room; and was all set for action.

'Our early days on 103 Squadron were rather in the nature of an anti-climax. We were so eager to start operating and to make good as a crew that it never occurred to us that things might not work out according to plan. Our first flight, a 'Bullseye' exercise, had to be abandoned when we were forced to 'feather' both starboard engines over the English Channel. True, we did return to base in good order and made a fine landing, but we were very disappointed. The night of 23 May was the occasion of the heaviest raid of the war, up to that date, the target being the unfortunate town of Dortmund.'

After a nine-day break in Main Force operations, 829 aircraft were detailed for the raid on Dortmund. No less than 343 of the aircraft involved were Lancasters and the rest comprised 199 Halifaxes, 151 Wellingtons and 120 Stirlings and 13 Mosquitoes. There would be no element of surprise in their favour. A hot reception from countless radar controlled 88mm cannons was an absolute certainty. Strong forces of experienced night fighters would be out hunting for unwary bombers.

Warrant Officer Gordon Stooke and his crew on 460 Squadron RAAF at Binbrook made it all the way to the target.[61] Stooke, who was from the bayside suburbs of Melbourne, had volunteered for aircrew duties in 1941. By January 1943, at just 20 years old, he was pilot in a five-man crew at 27 Operational Training Unit (OTU), Lichfield, Staffordshire. Although it included some British and other Commonwealth aircrew, this was essentially an OTU for Australian aircrew. Later, with two additional crew members and after a spell at 1662 Heavy Conversion Unit at Blyton in Lincolnshire, the Stooke crew was posted in early May 1943 to 460 Squadron RAAF then located at Breighton, Yorkshire. Five of the crew were Aussie's - Sergeant Norm Conklin, the bomb-aimer, Warrant Officer 'Clarrie' Craven, the navigator and Sergeant Stan 'Rowdy' R. Nowlan, the rear gunner, all from New South Wales and Warrant Officer Frank B. Shaw, the mid-upper gunner, from South Australia; Flight Sergeant Colin W. Broadbent, the flight engineer and Warrant Officer Dennis T. Toohig, the wireless operator, were Londoners. By the middle of the month 460 Squadron had moved to Binbrook, which compared favourably with Breighton, being permanent, built with bricks, paved and warmer. Here the crew was allocated Avro Lancaster Mk I W4320, coded UV-D. For personal reasons Stooke identified the aircraft not as 'D-Dog', but as 'D-Donald' and that was how it stayed.

'As we approached Dortmund' says Stooke,' it was already alight from incendiaries dropped by waves of bombers in front of us. The visual impact was unbelievable, almost abstract. This large city was on fire and dozens of probing searchlights turned night into day. Down below, thousands of flickering lights pinpointed bomb strikes. The smoke balls from exploding anti-aircraft shells appeared an impregnable barrier. Over to my right I saw a bomber caught in a cone of searchlights. Suddenly it exploded.'

This raid was the first time that Bomber Command had delivered over 2,000 tons of explosives and incendiaries to a single target. For 460 Squadron, the contribution was 24 Lancasters and the cost was two crews; 14 men failed to return. The crew of 'D-Donald' returned safely to Binbrook from this initiation into Bomber Command. (Their first operation, on 18/19 May, when they were one of five 460 Squadron Lancaster crews to complete a mine-laying sortie in the Gironde River estuary at Bordeaux, was not considered as such by them).

'Dortmund was also to have been our first sortie' recalls Norman Ashton. 'To our dismay, we were not amongst those present. Complete failure of the flying instruments, whilst crossing the North Sea, resulted in a decision to jettison the bombs and abandon the mission. How different from those wonderful dreams of ours! We felt thoroughly dejected. Compare our effort with that of another new crew with whom we were very friendly. Kenneth Breckon and his boys were attacked by fighters when approaching the target but managed to shoot their way out, with the loss of one engine - pressed-on and bombed - were again attacked by fighters, one of which was shot down in flames by the mid-upper gunner, the American George Ferrell, but only after the loss of another engine - reached the home coast, when a third engine caught fire - finally making a crash belly-landing, without a single casualty in the crew. Both Ken Breckon and George Ferrell were awarded the DFM. That, we thought, was something like a first mission.

'After a good night's sleep we reviewed the whole thing in the cold light of reason and felt that after all, we had carefully weighed the circumstances and had made the right decision. We intended always to press home our attacks but, at the same time, realised that even in the heat of battle, valour must still be tempered with discretion. Bomber Command - and the cause for which we were fighting -would be better served if we lived to complete a tour of operations, than if we threw away everything in a single night of glory. Provided, of course that the choice was ours!

'Two nights later [25/26 May] we regained our self-confidence. The target was Düsseldorf and we had a good trip. We flew with all fingers crossed for luck and heaved a sigh of relief when we sighted the hundreds of searchlight beams criss-crossing the target area - no abortive sortie this time! The effect of that first glimpse of a town undergoing the agony of a saturation raid was shattering. The fierce red glow of bursting bombs, the white shimmer of incendiaries, the brilliant glare of target indicators, the blinding flashes of the photo flares, the red-gold strings of 'flaming onions' and the whole witches' cauldron of fire and belching smoke, was like hell let loose. My mind was bludgeoned by the impact of it all. It was all over in a few minutes: Reg made a good run-up; Corky Corcoran the bomb aimer picked out the target and pressed the bomb-tit; the aircraft shuddered as the bombs left the racks; Bill Bailey the navigator gave us a course and we turned for home. Our operational tour had started.'[62]

Two nights' later, on 27/28 May, 19-year old Flight Lieutenant Gordon Cammell RNZAF, a Lancaster pilot on 115 Squadron at East Wretham, Norfolk, flew the first of his crew's operations of their tour when the target for 518 aircraft - 274 of them Lancasters - was Essen.[63] His first operation was with another pilot and his crew, on which he flew as second-pilot on a bombing sortie over Germany to see at first-hand what was involved in this type of sortie and gain experience of being shot at by flak. 'We did indeed see plenty of flak bursts like hundreds of black puffs of cloud below us over the target, which was lit up like a bonfire, but we suffered no near misses from flak or from night-fighters. We were only one of at least 500 bombers that night, en route to the same target. For our next few operations I was the captain of my own crew and our targets were cities in the Ruhr Valley, Germany's industrial heartland, which we were attempting to destroy to hamper Hitler's war effort.

'On the night of 27 May, following a briefing for our target of that night, to Essen, we went to our aircraft, which were dispersed around the airfield. Tonight our machine was to be Bristol Hercules-engined Lancaster II DS655, painted in the unit's code letters, KO, with the individual code letter 'M for Mike'. As usual before taking off on a sortie, I felt rather nauseous, with butterflies in my stomach, but I knew that once we were airborne this feeling would disappear as my mind became occupied with the task of flying the aircraft. Tonight, therefore, was no different from those others when we had taken off on a sortie and had returned unscathed. There was no reason to believe that we should not return again.

'Take-off time approached fast and the crews of the first scheduled aircraft entered their machines. We stubbed out our cigarettes and climbed the steps to enter our Lancaster's rear door. I placed my parachute on the floor behind my seat and prepared to secure myself in the captain's position. I was wearing the normal parachute harness, which had two clips at the chest on to which my parachute could be attached quickly in an emergency. I then adjusted my seat, remembering that I always required two cushions to raise me to my desired position. Extra cushions were carried in most aircraft and I removed one from my navigator's seat to put on top of my own. As it turned out there wasn't another for him, so he suggested that I use my parachute pack under my cushion to give me the extra elevation I needed. I did so, not knowing that this action would help to save my life that night and returned his cushion to him.

'Settled comfortably in my seat and securely strapped in, I started the four engines one by one and felt more confident and calm as each one burst into life. We took our turn in line as the aircraft began to taxi slowly to the take-off point. Soon number one was airborne and then number two and so on until finally our turn came to take off in sixth position. I turned on to the runway, opened up the engines to full power, released the brakes and immediately the aircraft began to roll down the tarmac, increasing speed rapidly. The surge of power pushed me back in my seat and the big machine, laden down with a heavy load of incendiary and high-explosive bombs, seemed impatient to be on its way.

'Once in the night air we climbed in a wide sweeping turn around the airfield, holding our position some distance behind the previous aircraft, until the time came to set course for our target. My navigator gave me a heading and, having checked with each member of the crew that everything was in order, I settled down on course, still climbing for more altitude. Our navigation lights were extinguished as we crossed the English coast and no longer could we see any of the other 517 bombers that had taken off from England carrying thousands of tons of destructive power to the Reich's industrial belt.

'Through their early-warning system the Germans received plenty of warning of the approach of such a large force of bombers and their night-fighters would be active, searching for the lumbering aircraft as prey to their heavy-calibre machine-guns. Indeed, I had already seen two of our bombers go down in flames. It was impossible to see if anybody had got out.

'As we approached the target I briefed the crew to maintain a close watch for fighters, but none was seen; nor had we been bothered by any flak bursts. Everything looked good, but as I rolled out of a gentle turn to steady the aircraft on course for the final bombing run at 20,000 feet I heard a tremendous explosion just before everything faded to black. I do not know how long I remained unconscious; when I partly regained my senses I found that I could not see, but could hear both engines on the port side spluttering and banging. Everything was pitch-black and I must again have lost consciousness, for when I was next aware of my surroundings the aircraft was in a steep dive. I was still blinded, but I could hear what sounded like a loud scream as the air rushed by at very high speed. The oxygen mask that contained the microphone for communicating with my crew was hanging loosely from my helmet. Since I could not see the flight instruments I was unable to take corrective action to regain control, even if this had been possible. I had no alternative, therefore, but to instruct my crew to abandon the aircraft. I did not know what had caused the explosion, nor did I know how badly the Lancaster had been damaged. I was also unaware of the circumstances of my crew, but I hoped that they would still be in a position to get out and save themselves by parachute.

'I gave the order 'Bail out, bail out', but only one crewman answered. He replied: 'I can't; I can't get out'. Still blinded, I released my seat straps and removed my parachute pack from under my cushion, thankful that it was there, where I could reach it. I then tried to attach it to the two hooks on my harness and managed to connect one but could not secure the other. My efforts became increasingly frantic until I realised that there was really no point in continuing to struggle, since I would be unable to use the 'chute, even if I could get it properly attached. There were two escape hatches, one in the nose under the bomb aimer's prone position and the other in the rear, near the tail, neither of which could I reach. As an escape attempt seemed hopeless I resigned

158

myself to a sudden death. I felt quite calm when I came to terms with the idea that it would happen so quickly that I should know nothing about it.

'At that very second there was another tremendous explosion, which knocked me unconscious again. I do not know how long I remained in this state, but when I came to I was falling through space. I felt for my parachute ripcord and pulled it sharply; nothing happened and my fall continued unchecked. I struggled frantically with my 'chute, ripping and tearing at it in an attempt to get it to open. After what seemed an eternity it suddenly deployed and pulled me into a sitting position with a violent jerk.

'I imagined that the aircraft must be a flaming mass in the sky, but there was darkness everywhere. My sight had returned, though and when I looked up I saw my parachute. However, since it had been attached to my harness by only one hook the canopy was set at an angle, allowing air to spill out and causing me to descend at a much higher rate than normal. The one strap from which I was hanging seemed very insecure, so I grabbed it with both hands.

'We had been flying at about 20,000 feet when the aircraft was first hit. Since then I had been unconscious for two periods of time and therefore had no idea of my height above the ground. However, I was in my parachute for no more than 3-4 seconds before I hit a pavement with an enormous thump. My legs buckled under me and the force of the impact was taken at the base of my spine. I saw about a thousand stars and collapsed in a heap.

'Although the wind was knocked out of me I was surprised that I could stand up, although my balance was greatly impaired and I staggered like a drunk. When I tried to walk my back hurt a great deal, but provided I altered my position frequently I could bear the pain. I had landed at the corner of a road junction, less than 3 feet from a spiked iron fence. My parachute had caught on top of a tree, perhaps thereby helping to break my fall. I pulled my 'chute from the tree and shoved it through the fence in an attempt to hide it. Then I looked around to take stock of my situation.

'In one direction I saw that there were tall buildings along the road on which I was standing, so I moved slowly away from what appeared to be the business area. I was having great difficulty in walking and was staggering from side to side. In a short distance I came to a small field with a narrow dirt path crossing it. I emerged through a hedge next to a petrol station, opposite a road that ran between two rows of houses. I continued down this road, thinking that if I followed it I must eventually get out into the countryside.

'However, my plans were soon thwarted when I was accosted by a German standing in the doorway of his house. He called out loudly to me in German - I had no idea what he was saying. As there seemed no point in stopping, I continued down the road. Very soon he rushed after me to see who I was and I later discovered that it was against the law there to move about in the open during air raids.

'He pulled me about to face him, all the time speaking in German. When he saw my bloody face and torn foreign air force uniform he must have immediately recognised me as an enemy airman. His eyes opened to the size of saucers and he yelled to another man in the doorway of another house. After a quick conversation one of them decided to take me to the local police and he proceeded to pull me down another road, towards the tall buildings I had seen earlier. I was having great difficulty in walking at all, but this man was in a tremendous hurry to get me to the authorities and shouted at me, while I pulled against him like a mule. In this manner I began two years of my young life as a prisoner of war at the famous camp Stalag Luft III, in Sagan, Upper Silesia, Poland. Sadly all of my crew were killed and are buried in the Reichwald Forest War Cemetery in Germany.[64] At 19 years of age I was the sole survivor.'[65]

Gordon Stooke and the rest of the crew of 'D-Donald' flew four consecutive operations without damage. The last three were over the Ruhr; the 25/26 May raid was on Düsseldorf when 759 bombers were dispatched and the 27/28 May raid on Essen. The attacks were relatively unsuccessful. 'D-Donald's crew perhaps had the closest encounter with mortality during the Düsseldorf operation. A Short Stirling on the port beam, taking evasive action, corkscrewed to starboard and down as Stooke was executing the same manoeuvre to port and up. The avoidance of a collision was attributed more to luck than skill by the Lancaster pilot. So sure was Stooke that they were going to hit that, to this day, his overwhelming recollection of that moment is one of blank unconcern rather than fear. The realisation of what might have been was jolted into the Lancaster crew by the violent turbulence as the Stirling slipped beneath them. As with Düsseldorf on the 25th, the target was covered by cloud. Sky-marking, a means of aerial illumination of a point in the clouds over which the main force was to aim its bomb loads, was carried out by designated Pathfinders. Again, the double advantage of a large main force and 'Oboe' technology was lost to the weather. There was a pronounced tendency for many bombers to clear the target area as quickly as possible and this resulted in the phenomenon of 'creep back', with bomb loads falling progressively shorter of the target marker flares. Over half a century later, Stooke's vivid impressions of the Essen raid are confined to the 'filthy weather' and the 'flares'. Twenty-three bombers failed to return.

'For just over four months' says Norman Ashton on 103 Squadron at Elsham Wolds 'I thoroughly enjoyed myself. Life on an operational squadron had far exceeded my expectations; there was something about it which got into my blood.

'The Sergeants' Mess at Elsham could hardly have been described as palatial, but the social atmosphere and squadron spirit was terrific. The boys of '103' who crowded into the building transformed it into a home - a gay, exciting home. Sprawling in cane-bottomed chairs or pacing the well-worn carpets, they breathed life and adventure into every brick and slab of concrete. The Mess became a real home-from-home as the 'older' crews were screened and the crews with whom we were more familiar assumed the mantle of experience and dignity. It was then our turn to welcome new crews to the squadron and relate to them the stirring adventures of the past, pausing occasionally to point out such famous crews as Stoneman's, Chesterton's, Breckon's, Cant's, Drew's, Egan's, Steele's, Van Rolleghen's and, of course, Bunten's![66]

'Ches's kite was better known as *The Cank Box* and was famous for the amazing collection of lucky charms in the cockpit; for the poster pasted on the wall opposite the door, 'Is your journey really necessary?'; and for the wooden notice-board over the Elsan; *Passengers are requested not to use this seat whilst the train is standing in the station.* Van Rolleghen's kite was 'Z-Zebra' with its crossed British and Belgian flags. Drew's kite [Lancaster III ED731 AS-T2] known as *Dante's Daughter*, took its name from the painting on the side of the nose, showing a life-size nude, with a bomb in each hand, rising from the flames of an inferno.'[67]

Flying Officer Peter Lees DFM first met John Drew in December 1942 at 25 OTU (Operational Training Unit) at Finningley, Yorkshire when, as a newly trained sergeant pilot, he came up and asked him, a sergeant bomb-aimer also newly trained, if he would care to join him as a member of his crew. Lees accepted at once.

'There wasn't much option anyway as I was the only one of our draft of ten bomb-aimers not yet fixed up in a crew and he the only pilot of his draft still short of a bomb-aimer. Johnny was an American who had volunteered to join the RAF and his actual introductory words were, 'I guess we are the only two left, OK by you if we team up?' All the various members constituting the crew of a Lancaster bomber had been posted to the OTU in drafts of ten each. There we were left to mingle with the other drafts and sort ourselves out into crews during the next week or so. This was the normal method of crew formation and was far more effective than if someone had merely allocated names. It ensured that the bonding of the crew members was done by friendships and made for a harmonious working relationship. At that time Bomber Command losses were high, only one crew in three survived to complete a tour of operations over Germany, a loss rate proportionally higher than the other armed forces so a lot of luck was required to get through, but crew harmony helped to increase the chance of survival.

'Johnny soon roped in the other members also required. Sergeant Desmond Lowe, rear-gunner, Pilot Officer Harold Cooke, mid-upper gunner, a Canadian known thereafter as 'Cookie'; Sergeant Sid Pett, wireless operator; Harold Ellis, navigator and finally Ken Lewis, engineer. The moment that fate decreed Johnny Drew was to be my pilot was in retrospect the most momentous of my life because ironically our crew, consisting as it did of the remnants of the various drafts, turned out to be the only survivor of the original ten formed at OTU Johnny was not the Englishman's idea of a typical Yank; all talk and brashness. He was in fact very quiet and unassuming, but in the air and particularly on ops, there was never any doubt as to who was the skipper. Any unnecessary chatter over the intercom was swiftly cut short by 'Shut up you guys and keep your goddam eyes open'. His American background however was never far away. Our ditching drill on the ground for instance, when the pilot was meant to call out 'Dinghy, dinghy, prepare to ditch' became in his case 'Dinghy, dinghy, ditch you bitch' and his American style salute, exaggerated in its casualness, would have driven an RAF drill sergeant berserk.

'He was a very good pilot technically, but more than that he was

Stirling I N3752 OJ-O, one of three on 149 Squadron that were shot down on 'Gardening' operations off Denmark on the night of 17/18 May 1942. OJ-O crashed near Roderkro. Sergeant J. A. Jerman and his crew were taken into captivity.

For you the war is over.

Opposite page: A Westland Lysander which was used by SOE for agent delivery and pick-up. Inset: Noor Inayat Khan 'Madeleine'. On 11 September 1944 Noor Inayat Khan and three other SOE agents from Karlsruhe prison, Yolande Beekman, Eliane Plewman and Madeleine Damerment, were moved to the Dachau Concentration Camp and between 8 and 10 the following morning, 13 September, they were taken to the crematorium compound and shot through the back of the head and immediately burned in the crematorium. Inayat was posthumously awarded a British George Cross and a French Croix de Guerre with Gold Star.

35 Squadron crew at Graveley. Standing L-R: Flight Lieutenant Roger 'Sheep' Lamb, mid-upper gunner (PoW 19/20.2.44); Squadron Leader Gordon Carter DFC* RCAF, Navigator Leader (PoW 19/20.2.44); Squadron Leader Julian Sale DSO* DFC RCAF; Flight Lieutenant 'Bod' Bodnar DFC RCAF (PoW 19/20.2.44), H2S operator; Flight Sergeant 'Harry' Cross DFC DFM flight-engineer (PoW 19/20.2.44); and Flying Officer 'Johnny' Rogers DFC Wop (PoW 19/20.2.44). Kneeling in front, the ground crew of their Halifax. Julian Sale survived the shoot down on 19/20 February but he died of his wounds on 20 March 1944. This was the second time Gordon Carter had been shot down. On the first occasion, on 13/14 February 1943 contrary to reports, he was very much alive and safely in the hands of the Resistance. During the time Carter spent with the French Resistance he met and fell in love with 22-year-old Mademoiselle Janine Jouanjean (pictured, next page).

Gordon Carter and Janine fell in love but Carter had to be returned to England. The RAF navigator wanted to take Janine with him but it was far too dangerous and it was obvious that she would have to remain behind. Carter returned to France at the end of the war and was reunited with Janine.

Gordon Carter and Janine
married on 11 June 1945.

Sergeant Len Manning.

Len Manning with his mother and father in 1944.

Fahnenjunker (officer-cadet) Oberfeldwebel Herbert Altner of III./NJG3 at Laon-Athies who, flying Bf 110 C9+AS, shot down Flight Lieutenant John Alec Bulcraig DFM's Lancaster on 57 Squadron on the night of 18/19 July 1944..

Len Manning holding his lucky white rabbit with Sergeant McKensey, a friend (left) and Sergeant Tom Loughlin the wireless operator who was killed when Bulcraig's Lancaster was shot down.

Opposite page: Len Manning with 59 year old Madame Louisette Beaujard and her mother, Madame Beaujard. Lousette Beaujard was later awarded the Legion d' Honneur for her work in the Resistance. She died in 1973 aged 88.

Former adversaries Herbert Altner and Len Manning share a glass of champagne. It was only in 1991 that Len learned the name of the night fighter pilot who had shot him down. (Ralf Zweynert)

Some German officers look on as former American and British prisoners are evacuated from a Stalag.

Red Cross parcels being distributed.

Lancaster B.I R5868 S-Sugar on 467 Squadron RAAF at the USAAF fighter base at Kitzingen north of Nuremburg on 7 May 1945. On this date Sugar was skippered by Wing Commander I. H. Hay on a reconnaissance for Operation Exodus for the repatriation of British ex-PoWs.

Appel (Roll Call) at Stalag Luft III.

Lancaster B.I R5868 S-Sugar on 467 Squadron RAAF at the USAAF fighter base at Kitzingen north of Nuremburg on 7 May 1945. On this date Sugar was skippered by Wing Commander I. H. Hay on a reconnaissance for Operation Exodus for the repatriation of British ex-PoWs.

Operation Exodus. The war is over and ex-British PoWs file past Lancaster III PB035 on 635 Squadron at Lübeck on 11 May 1945 for repatriation.

completely calm during any form of crisis, a factor that spread throughout the crew. We had developed into a good crew during our training over the next five months, but more importantly perhaps we had all become close friends which, in view of the way we had been more or less thrown together was a fortunate outcome and this served us well when we reached the real thing, the operational squadron. This was 103 Squadron, No.1 Group at Elsham Wolds, Lincs.

'We were allotted Lancaster 'T for Tommy' which we quickly named *Dante's Daughter* for no particular reason that I can think of. The insignia of a naked woman rising from the flames was painted on the nose by the ground staff, a fine lot of lads who also became our friends over the next few months.

'Our first op was over Dortmund on 23 May 1943 and was followed during the next five months by raids on most of the major German cities to finally complete our tour on 2 October 1943 with a raid on Munich. During the tour Johnny showed that in addition to being a fine pilot and skipper he was a great tactician. He developed a strategy, when he saw another bomber caught in a cone of searchlights, of taking us immediately alongside but just out of the lighted area. We were a little dubious at first but, as he explained, we were more likely to get through undetected whilst the enemy were concentrating their attention on the other unfortunate bomber crew. It certainly appeared to work whenever the opportunity arose.

'We were lucky, very lucky, to complete our tour without any major incident, but I prefer to think that having Johnny Drew as our pilot perhaps gave us that slight edge towards survival. We split up after our tour, most of us to become instructors, but Johnny had, during the intervening period, been transferred to the American Air Force and given the uniform and rank of 1st Lieutenant, although continuing to fly with the RAF. It was stipulated however that he had to complete another tour before being allowed back home. He was posted immediately to a Pathfinder Squadron and we subsequently lost touch with him. I hope very much he survived, of all people he deserved to and I know these thoughts would be echoed by the rest of the crew.

Norman Ashton's next trip [29/30 May] was destined to become 'legendary'. 'The target was Wuppertal (the name given to the twin-towns, Barmen and Elberfeld), famous for its suspended mono-railway system. The route took us through the gap between the defended areas of Cologne and Düsseldorf. At least, we were glibly assured by Intelligence of the existence of a gap. As all crews present on that memorable night agreed, the 'gap' proved to be the concentrated aiming-point of the combined defences of both cities. We ran the gauntlet with faint hopes of getting through in one piece, the flak was so thick that we could almost have put our wheels down and taxied across! The 'Reaper' was busy on all sides but we managed to evade his chopper. The raid was very successful but the comments of returned crews were unprintable. Everyone felt that the Intelligence bods had really let the side down. [Paul Fulton] Chesterton's crew summed up the feelings of all engaged in the attack, when they introduced a little song with the apt title, 'Mythical Gap'. Sung to the tune of the Laurel-and-Hardy *Cuckoo Song*, it was soon adopted by the squadron.

*'Wuppertal. Wuppertal.
Mythical gap. Mythical gap.
'Twixt Cologne and Dusseldorf
There isn't a gap at all.*

*'We went there, one Friday night,
Oh, what a trip. Oh, what a sight.
Bags of flak and bags of light,
But there wasn't a gap at all.*

*'We'll go back, we don't know when,
Now we've got all the pukka gen,
Intelligence have boobed again,
There isn't a gap at all!'*

'We had done four trips when we got our first leave and I went home feeling quite a veteran. It was a common saying in Bomber Command that any crew completing four operations had an even chance of finishing their tour. Whatever the value of that statement, I did feel that we were showing progress and had got what it takes to make a good crew. On our return from leave, Reg went on a week's course to the Rolls-Royce works and the rest of us expected a nice scrounge. This did not materialise. The engineer of one of the new crews was sick and I flew in his place on trips to Cologne and Gelsenkirchen. Bob Cant had a good crew and I enjoyed flying with them but their aircraft, 'U-Uncle', with its pawnshop sign of the three brass balls, was a rather aged chariot which just managed to stagger up to 17,000 feet. Bob seemed quite satisfied with the altitude but I felt too near the deck for comfort - it seemed strange to be milling around in the company of Halifaxes, Wellingtons and Stirlings; usually, we Lancaster types were far above them.'

It was the policy of the command of 460 Squadron to allocate leave on a roster basis. After four operations Gordon Stooke was given ten days' leave, which he was able to spend part of it with family friends in Surrey. By 15 June he was back at Binbrook and was on the Battle Order on the night of the 16/17th for the raid on Cologne. The marking for this raid by a force of 202 Lancasters and ten Halifaxes of 1, 5 and 8 Groups was not by 'Oboe' but by 16 heavy bombers of the Path Finders fitted with H_2S. Fourteen Lancasters were lost. Approaching the Dutch coast, the bomber was targeted by a flak ship, without result. Ten minutes later 'D-Donald's intercom system went unserviceable. As they pressed on, the engineer was forced to shut down the overheating number four engine. Without intercom, running on three engines and with the mid-upper turret's hydraulics gone because its pump was driven by the dead engine, the crew of 'D-Donald' turned back on a reciprocal course for Binbrook. As it was forbidden to land with the 4,000lb 'cookie' blast bomb that was part of their load that night, this was released beyond the Dutch coast, aiming at the flak ship. Their claim at debriefing for one destroyed flak ship was ignored.

The crew was on the Battle Order for the next Ruhr raid, this time to Krefeld just inside Germany near the frontier with Holland on the night of 21/22 June before the moon period was over. For this operation 460 Squadron despatched 20 Lancasters in a total force of 705 aircraft.[68] Visibility was good. In order to saturate the German fighter defences along the route of the attack, the bomber crews kept together in a concentrated 'stream'. Amid full concentration just after take-off, Stooke suddenly became aware of someone at his right shoulder. The 'stowaway' was one of the ground crew, Jim Nuttall, the same corporal who had so ably directed Stooke to the 'big house' a few weeks earlier. 'I just wanted to do one operation - just one', he yelled into Stooke's ear. To return early with a ground crew member was unthinkable. They pressed on.

Over the Channel the mid-upper turret went unserviceable, being able to fire but not to turn. It was decided to make for the target, a not uncommon choice. In spite of the best efforts of ground crew, the intensity of operations with such a complex piece of equipment as a Lancaster led to sequences of almost regular faults and failures in most aircraft. Upon reaching the Dutch coast the rear gunner reported seeing a Messerschmitt Bf 109 and, shortly after, a Focke-Wulf 190. The pilot kept up the violent evasive manoeuvres. The target was well marked in clear conditions, the moon period yet to finish. The bomb-aimer was able to bomb directly on to the green markers of the 'Oboe' Mosquito, in preference to the supporting red flares. As they left the target area the crew of 'D-Donald' made several more sightings of suspected enemy aircraft. They considered themselves fortunate to have returned to base; a total of 44 aircraft Bomber Command crews had not; 38 of them due to German night fighters operating mainly over the southern provinces of the Netherlands.[69]

The Path Finder aircraft produced an almost perfect marking effort, ground markers being dropped by 'Oboe' Mosquitoes being well backed up by the Path Finder heavies. In 53 minutes 619 bombers dropped 2,306 tons of bombs on the markers, more than three quarters of them achieving bombing photographs within three miles of the centre of Krefeld. The whole centre of Krefeld - approximately 47 per cent of the built-up area - was burnt out and over 5,500 houses were destroyed and 72,000 people lost their homes. Twenty thousand of these were billeted upon families in the suburbs, 30,000 moved in with relatives or friends and 20,000 were evacuated to other towns.

Gordon Stooke's crew on 460 Squadron was on the operation on the night of 22/23 June, when 565 bombers were detailed to bomb Mülheim, midway between Essen and Duisburg. In the twin towns of Mülheim and Oberhausen 578 people were killed and 1,174 were injured. Post war the British Bombing Survey Unit estimated that this single raid destroyed 64 per cent of Mülheim. Thirty-five bombers, twelve of them Halifaxes, failed to return. Of the eleven Stirlings lost, four were from 75 New Zealand Squadron at Newmarket Heath. Only five men survived from the 28 crew members on the four aircraft. With Mülheim's neighbouring city, Oberhausen, just to the north-west, the ground defences of these four areas were particularly fearful, an approach on one invariably producing flak from the others. Lancaster 'D-Donald' was within two or three miles of Mülheim when it was caught by one searchlight, then another and then more. This was the experience of being 'coned'. Within seconds Stooke had 'D-Donald' diving steeply, its engines screaming and the fuselage and wings shaking violently as the airspeed indicator approached 400 mph. The crew were very scared and very lucky. After a descent of perhaps 5,000 feet they broke free from the searchlights. Disoriented by the sudden change from black to blinding light to black, 'D-Donald's crew took some time to recover, but they subsequently completed their bombing run over Mülheim. An inspection at Binbrook the next day revealed how lucky they had been. The starboard inner fuel tank had been holed by flak fragments.

Norman Ashton received a letter that brought the dread news that his home-town friend of pre-war days was reported missing from the raid on Mülheim. This was Sergeant Jack Osborne's third operation from Holme-on-Spalding Moor and Ludford Magna, having previously been on the Wuppertal and Krefeld efforts on 101 Squadron. He had also volunteered for flight engineer and he and Norman Ashton had travelled down to No.4 School of Technical Training at St Athan, South Wales, together in late 1942. Ashton thought sadly of all the glorious plans that they had made. Although he was ten years older than Jack, they had a great deal in common and decided 'to stick together as far as the RAF, enemy and fate would allow'. They made great plans for the future and were confident that 'honour and distinction would be theirs in the fullness of time'. Jack Osborne had the bad luck to be delayed later at Heavy Conversion Unit Lindholme by illness and then, so soon after finally getting on to an operational squadron, had failed to return. Fate had struck a savage and early blow.

'The Red Cross organisation had recently informed Jack's mother that although the bomb aimer [Flight Sergeant E. A. Williams] was reported PoW the remainder of the crew had been killed and were buried in Holland. The bomb aimer had written from the camp to say that he bailed out and did not know what had happened to the others. In spite of this information, I felt that there was still an outside chance that Jack had escaped and was in hiding with the underground movement. There had been no further news of Jack Osborne when I visited his folks and I was forced to adopt an optimistic attitude for their sakes. My one remaining hope, however, was that he had managed to contact the underground movement in the Low Countries and was lying low until it was considered safe to make an attempt to reach England. There had been many instances of evaders taking months to return to this country and I had no doubts about Jack's ability to make the grade if he was still alive.'

The crew of 'D-Donald' had now completed five successful operations, plus one mining sortie and an early return over the Continent from the Cologne raid. The next operation went ahead on the night of 24/25 June. This time Wuppertal was the destination for 630 aircraft when Elberfeld, the other half of the town (unharmed on 29/30 May) was the target, the Barmen half of the town having been devastated. Stooke distinctly recalls that not one of his crew, himself included, imagined that they would not return to Binbrook that night. The Path Finder marking was accurate and the Main Force bombing started well but the creep-back became more pronounced than usual and thirty aircraft bombed targets in more western parts of the Ruhr.[71]

Gordon Stooke could see Wuppertal burning about ten miles ahead of him.

Suddenly, 'night was turned into day' as 'D-Donald' was held at the meeting point of searchlight beams. Airmen knew that to be coned over the Ruhr could be deadly. There were so many searchlights that more than 50 could seize on one black silhouette of a bomber and they operated over such a wide area. The master blue beam was particularly feared. Guided by radar, it did not have to wave about the sky in hope but could be switched on and instantly bathe an aircraft in its intense blue-tinged light. Other beams then fastened on the aircraft. The coned bomber might be attacked by night fighters, but over a target where the flak was thick and other hazards numerous the night fighters left the bomber to the gunners. They filled the cone with shells. Having been coned in much the same way as it had been over Mülheim two nights earlier, he reacted quickly, stopped weaving and dived. Still carrying bombs, the Lancaster quickly dropped 5,000 feet and built up speed to 400 mph. Stooke was following one of the standard ways of evading searchlights: dive to gain speed, throw the aircraft into a violent turn and escape into darkness or keep on making unpredictable movements. It did not work. Just before 'D-Donald' cleared the light, probably just east of Düsseldorf, not far from the target, two shells exploded on its nose and the number three engine immediately caught fire. Soon after, number two engine stopped. By this time the aircraft was down to 12,500 feet, directly over Wuppertal. With part of the incendiary load ablaze, the bomb load was salvoed. Now with its bomb bay doors unable to close and its starboard undercarriage half down, the Lancaster began to lose height. It also became obvious that the fuselage had been holed in several places. A course was set to track south of Cologne and then turn north-west for England. At around 0200 hours, with the aircraft by now over Belgium at an altitude of 3,500 feet, the number four engine lost oil pressure. At 2,500 feet, about 20 miles north-northwest of Liège, Stooke gave the order to bail out. His six crew bailed out at less than 3,000 feet over the Belgian countryside. Alone in the aircraft, Stooke stepped away from the controls and down to the already open nose hatch. At barely 2,000 feet he left the Lancaster. Against the odds, all seven crewmembers had parachuted safely.[72]

Gordon Stooke, Craven, Conklin and Toohig were at first helped by generous Belgians and then came under the care of what appeared to be the Belgian Resistance. In fact a Belgian group in the pay of the Germans collected a group of evaders and handed them over to the Germans in Paris. The one month of freedom ended in sudden arrest, tough interrogation and a month in appalling conditions at Frèsnes prison on the outskirts of Paris.[73] From there Gordon Stooke was sent to Oberursel (Dulag Luft) and then to Stalag Luft IVB at Mühlburg, where he remained for the rest of the war.[74]

'Until the end of my days' recalled Norman Ashton, 'the words, 'Elsham Wolds' and '103 Squadron' would bring back a flood of memories. In the main they would be happy memories but there would also be sad memories of gallant crews and true friends who had failed to make the return trip. I could never forget those grand lads skippered by Bob Cant, whose crew went down south of Luxemburg on the raid on Mannheim on 5/6 September; Ken Breckon, Johnny Stoneman and all the others.[75] Of the crews which had left Lindholme in such jubilation during the early part of May, bound for squadrons at Elsham, Binbrook, Ludford Magna and Waltham, so very few remained.

'The famous footprints on the Ante Room ceiling were pointed to with pride, almost as though we had been personally responsible for their presence. It was our privilege too, to claim acquaintance with the chap who could chew razor-blades and beer glasses - an accomplishment possessed only by the few. To see him drink a beer and then eat the glass was an unforgettable experience. The Ante Room, when empty, was almost bleak but when full it was the cosiest, friendliest place imaginable. Every chair occupied; card-tables surrounded by 'brag' and 'poker' fiends; energetic types knocking lumps out of the table-tennis table; the stock tunes, *You are my Sunshine* and *Maybe,* oozing from the radiogram; the piano dancing under the ministrations of Chesterton's wireless operator; the ever-smiling steward handing out drinks from the pigeon-hole bar; and above all, the incessant talk, laughter and good comradeship.'

One evening in mid-September, Norman Ashton was amazed to see a once-familiar figure come walking into the Ante Room. It was Sergeant Syd Horton MiD, wireless operator on the Bob Cant crew which failed to return from the raid on Mannheim on 5/6 September. He and Sergeant D. R. 'Bob' Parkinson were two Lancashire lads from Wigan. 'I had heard rumours from time to time that certain members of the crew were safe' wrote Ashton, 'but this was news in the flesh! Syd was not only safe and looking disgustingly fit, but had been posted to Seighford as a Signals Instructor. And what a story he had to tell.

'U-Uncle' [sic - Cant was flying Chesterton's ED751 PM-'S-Sugar' that night] had made her attack on the target and was settling down for the run home from Mannheim, when one of the starboard engines started misfiring badly and the aircraft became unmanageable. Bob ordered the crew to abandon aircraft. (Syd smiled at my puzzled frown and then whimsically explained that they had arrived at the target on three engines, had lost another over the target and the misfiring left them with only one good engine!) On the order to bail out, Syd made his way down the fuselage and departed with no little haste from the rear exit. He remembered to pull the string and the parachute opened perfectly; apart from a sensation of going up instead of down, the descent to earth was uneventful. After spilling and retrieving his 'chute, Syd sat down on enemy soil and waited for something to happen. Soon he heard the low whistling of a still lower song, Salome and the whistler could only be one of his crew mates. Syd crept on all-fours in the direction of the sound and saw the stocky figure of the rear gunner, unmistakable even in the gloom. Bob Parkinson had also made a good landing and after a futile search for the rest of the crew, both boys took counsel on their plans for the immediate future. They decided to stick together and make for home by the quickest route, so parachutes and harnesses were hidden in a ditch and stock was taken of their equipment. Like all good ops types, they each carried escape-kits and purses and had a good reserve of emergency rations. By calculating the flying time, speed and direction from the target, they were able to form a rough estimate of their position on the map and figured that they were in

Luxembourg. After checking direction by the aid of an escape-compass and the stars, they turned west and set course for home.

'I sat enthralled as Syd unfolded the story of their journey across Occupied Europe - not the complete story, of course, because the security people insisted on certain details being kept secret. There was, it seemed, reliable news of the remaining crew members; with the exception of the bomb aimer, Sergeant Dennis Teare, of whom nothing was known.[76] Bob Cant, along with Flight Sergeant G. Dicky Dickson, the flight engineer and Sergeant W. R. 'Bill' Milburn, the mid-upper gunner, had successfully evaded and gained sanctuary in Switzerland. A recent letter from them had conveyed the impression that a pleasant time was being had by all. The navigator, Tommy Thomas, had unfortunately been captured after a spell of freedom and was in a PoW camp in Germany.[77] I thought this was a terrific performance: five successful evaders out of a crew of seven and perhaps another to come! Not only was I glad to hear this wonderful news but I also felt cheered by its implications. If Bob and his boys were safe, why not a goodly number of the other missing crews? And what of the possibility of Jack Osborne being alive?'

Syd Horton and Bob Parkinson had set off in a south-westerly direction. After walking for about two hours they heard someone shout and ducked into a hedge. Two German guards approached, found them and took them to a house which appeared to be a sort of guardroom. They had not removed their tunics or chevrons. A German corporal who spoke quite good English took particulars from them. He then spoke on a telephone. He called out an escort of two men, youths of about seventeen or eighteen years of age and ordered the two prisoners to follow their escort. Noting that their guards somewhat casually kept their rifles slung over their shoulders, Bob Parkinson asked if they could have a cigarette and please could the guards give them a light? Permission was granted. When they were close to the Germans Parkinson hit out at one and Horton knocked the other one over. Bundling the unconscious guards into a ditch, which was very swampy, the airmen ran off into the woods.

After being helped at Rupt-Ste-Mihiel (Meuse) they walked to Villotte-sur-Aire and at around 2 o'clock on the morning of 7 September climbed to the top of a haystack that was under cover. They slept all that night and through the following day and the greater part of 8 September. Leaving at around 9 pm they walked the twenty or so kilometres to Bar-le-Duc (Meuse) under cover of darkness, making their way to the station when it was light in the hope of catching a train to Paris. Spotting a German guard there, however, they decided to return to their hiding place. On the way back they persuaded a passing cyclist to buy them the tickets for the Paris train, giving him money from their escape boxes. He returned in an hour with the tickets and shaving kit, shaved them and gave them fruit and wine etc. Later he returned in a car driven by a well-dressed man. In the car there were civilian shoes into which they changed.

Driven to the station, Horton and Parkinson were introduced to the ticket collector, station master and signalman as being English. As the train was not due until 0220 hours the following morning they were hidden in the control room of the signal box, where they slept until awakened at 0120 hours. Arriving in Paris at 9 am on 10 September their only plan was to head for the suburbs, as they had been taught to do in their escape and evasion lectures. They wandered about all day until; with evening drawing on they saw a priest and decided to ask him for help. The priest took them to a sort of school and fetched another priest who could speak English and who inspected their identity discs etc to make sure they were British. The second priest put them in touch with a woman who had to be persuaded of their real identity and who took them to a block of flats about ten minutes' walk from a race course. After one night there, 10/11 September, a young couple took them off through an underground-railway passage to the house of the girl's father who as they learnt later was a French officer. On 12 September they were moved to 57 Boulevard de Champigny, Ste-Maurdes-Fosses, Paris the home of Henri and Georgette Douley, where they stayed a further three nights. On the evening of 15 September Madame Douley took them to the Bastille station and handed them over to the French officer's daughter, Yvonne, who in turn introduced them to a girl who had tickets for them and travelled with them to Quimper, which they reached about midday on 16 September.

Now in Fan-Fan's hands, on 18 September they were driven in a van to what appeared to be a shipping office. The man who drove the van said he had expected to see five RAF personnel. At 1900 hours the van returned with five French officers in plain clothes and they were taken to Douarnenez and stayed till about 2345 hours in a fish warehouse. From there, actually a sardine factory, Horton, Parkinson and twenty-three others, including two American airmen, were smuggled aboard the *Ar-Voualc'h* at Rosmeur harbour (Douarnenez) at low tide. They stayed in the quarters aft until 5 am when they were hidden in the ice box until the vessel had passed the inspection point. They drifted about during 19 September pretending to be fishing and in the night set course for England. On 20 September, still sixty kilometres from the Cornish coast, a flight of Spitfires arrived and at 1.30 pm *Ar-Voualc'h* and her passengers were brought ashore at Newlyn harbour, Cornwall. [78]

Sergeant Keith Kent was another who had a very good try at making it back the hard way. He was a bomb aimer on 12 Squadron at Wickenby in the spring of 1944 on Wing Commander John Nelson's crew. On 10 April they were on stand down but the bomb aimer in Pilot Officer Frank William Richards' crew went sick and he Keith Kent was detailed to fly with them on 'M-Mother'. His own crew were decidedly unhappy about this. They were a superstitious lot and very often people got shot down flying as a 'spare'. But there was little they could do about it and that night Kent took off with the crew he did not know heading for the marshalling yards at Aulnoye on the Franco-Belgian border. 'M-Mother' bombed from 8,000 feet, quite a change for 12 Squadron bomb aimers who were used to operating at 20,000 feet over Germany and were ten minutes into the return journey when the Lancaster was hit. Keith Kent did not know if it was flak or fighter, all he remembered was an 'almighty crack' and 'choking smoke' filling the aircraft. He got back to the flight deck and Richards shouted to him to get out; he did not need telling a second time. Kent came down in bright moonlight and could remember the sound of the 'all clear' being signalled by a local siren. He landed in a ploughed field, buried his parachute and set about trying to remember everything he had been told in those escape and evade lectures. Out came the escape kit and, with the help of the small compass, he set off south. He wasn't far from Cambrai, scene of a famous battle in World War I and the dykes that criss-crossed the region hampered his progress.

As dawn broke he found an isolated house and, plucking up courage and summoning his best schoolboy French, approached the man outside. Fortunately, he had fallen amongst friends. He was taken inside, fed, given a warm bed and when he awoke found civilian clothes all ready for him. That night several men, including the local mayor, arrived to see him. He learned from them that his aircraft had come down 12 miles away. There had been no other survivors.

He was provided with food and left later that night heading south again, this time for Peronne. It proved to be a difficult night, spent dodging in and out of ditches to avoid German vehicles using the road. So the following day he decided to simply brazen it out, reckoning he would attract far less attention walking by day as he would if found walking by night. He walked through Peronne, detoured round Paris and kept on going south through Meaux and Melun, sleeping in barns or, when he was lucky, in the home of friendly French farmers. Sometimes his request for help was simply refused. He had kept his aircrew-issue white pullover and it proved a godsend during some of the cold nights he spent out of doors. It was a journey which seemed blessed with luck. Even the French gendarmerie who stopped him one night turned out to be delighted to help an escaped Allied airmen, even taking him to their HQ for a meal before telling him where to avoid all the German patrols in nearby towns. The journey south continued, Kent finding the silk escape map invaluable in plotting the route he eventually hoped would take him to Spain. In the town of Gien, a picturesque spot on the Loire, he was befriended by the Jouanneau family who in turn introduced him to the local schoolmistress, the first person he had found in France who could speak English. From their initial conversations, it was clear she was being asked to verify that he was really who he said he was. Once she was convinced he returned to the Jouanneau's home where he met his family plus a young man who turned out to be a French fighter pilot who had escaped from a PoW camp in Germany back into France.

He was pressed continually for news of the invasion everyone was expecting daily and he gave them what little information he could. They suggested he remain with them until the invasion came but he decided to press on for Spain. He did, however, leave his home address with them and asked the family to write to his parents once the liberation came. They kept their word and in September Keith Kent's parents received a letter from the Jouanneau family.

His journey went on, through Bourges, Chateauroux, Arenton and onwards south. In La Barre he met Monsieur and Madame Poulain and stayed with them for several days. While Monsieur Poulain mended his shoes, his wife bathed Keith Kent's badly blistered feet. His route took him clear of Limoges and by now he reckoned he had covered 400 miles in three weeks and estimated that he would need another five days to reach the Spanish border. That night he called at an isolated farmhouse where he was politely but firmly refused help. He spent the night in a coppice and set off early the next morning for Celles. As he was approaching the village he saw two civilians talking in the middle of the road, effectively blocking his path. They demanded his papers. He told them who he was and the older man introduced himself as the mayor of Celles and said that they had been asked to watch out by the Germans for a man answering his description. Kent was asked to accompany him to the village where he was given a good meal and collected by two German soldiers who took him by car to their headquarters in Angouleme. His walk had come to an end.

He was later to spend three weeks in Frèsnes prison, where Squadron Leader Yeo Thomas of The White Rabbit fame was incarcerated; the same prison which was to send more than a hundred of aircrew prisoners to Buchenwald. From there Kent was sent to the interrogation centre at Frankfurt-on-Main and then into captivity at Stalag Luft III, Sagan. It was here, to his great surprise, that he bumped into Flight Lieutenant Stan Hearn, navigator on Pilot Officer David Clerk Hill Maxwell's crew on 12 Squadron at Wickenby who was shot down on the raid on Dortmund on the night of 22/23 May. Hearn's pilot and the flight engineer, Flight Sergeant Peter Joseph Hyland had been killed and the others were taken prisoner. Hearn thought he was seeing a ghost as he had already written to Keith's parents expressing his condolences and returning his personal effects. They were to remain in that camp until the following January, by which time they could hear the rumble of Russian artillery to the east. They were marched for five or six days before finally being packed onto a train to take them to another camp south-west of Berlin. Conditions were very bad until the surprise arrival of a large quantity of Red Cross parcels in mid-March. A month later the camp was on the move again and everyone was packed onto a train. It didn't move. For two days they waited there until they were told to de-train and march back to the camp. Five days later, it was all over. The Russians had arrived.

One thing still puzzles Keith Kent about his final frantic days in Germany. The whole country was desperately short of all the basic necessities of life. Yet two parcels containing clothes, cigarettes, food and chocolates his parents sent to him at Stalag Luft III which had never reached him, were returned unopened in late 1945.[79]

On the night of 28 July 1944 Lancaster ME799 PM-K on 103 Squadron - one of 495 heavies from 1, 3 and 5 Groups - was heading for Stuttgart when it was attacked by a Ju 88 night fighter. The Junkers' upward-firing cannon damaged the starboard inner of 'K-Kitty' but the pilot, Flying Officer Robert 'Bob' Armstrong, managed to feather the engine. He warned the crew to prepare to bail out but the immediate danger appeared to be over. It was then that a second night fighter struck, raking the Lancaster with 20mm cannon fire. This time Armstrong, an experienced pilot who hailed from Glasgow, told his crew to get out.

Sergeant A. M. B. 'Bert' Cutting the mid-upper gunner was wounded in the attack but still managed to open his parachute and came down on the lawn of a French family near Baccarat in Alsace-Lorraine. His wounds were such that the local doctor was summoned and the German authorities picked him up the next day. Ten days later, while in hospital, he met his bomb-aimer Flight Sergeant A. A. 'Terry' Holmwood, who was from the Elephant and Castle area of London. Holmwood suffered facial injuries in his escape from the Lancaster and was on the run for ten days before being picked up. They all thought all their crew had got out of the Lancaster and were able to pass this news on to a British army major who visited them in hospital. He was a PoW himself and his son, Sergeant Keith Kibbey, had been in the rear turret when the Lancaster was hit. It was only after the war that 'Bert' Cutting learned that Keith Kibbey, along with Bob Armstrong and the wireless operator Sergeant Dougie Thomas had failed to escape from the Lancaster. Their bodies had been found by villagers in Glonville and buried in the Communal Cemetery in the village. That left two other members of the crew, the navigator, Flight Sergeant Cyril Shaw and the flight engineer Sergeant Malcolm E. T. Macrae. They had parachuted to safety in the thickly-wooded area and had been picked up by a French family, Madame Reb and her daughters Marcelle and Andrée. They were taken to their house in Deneuvre, near Baccarat and there they remained until the Allies reached this area of France in October 1944.

Endnotes

60 *Only Birds and Fools; Flight Engineer, Avro Lancaster, World War II*, by J. Norman Ashton DFC (Airlife Publishing Ltd, 2000).

61 460 Squadron - motto 'Strike and Return' - had been the third RAAF Squadron to fly in Bomber Command. (The first was 464, which was formed at Feltwell, Norfolk on 1 September 1942 in 2 Group. 466 Squadron was formed in 4 Group at Driffield in Yorkshire on 10 October 1942). 460 had begun to form at Molesworth on 15 November 1941 with four officers and 117 other ranks transferred in from 458 Squadron. Their first commanding officer was Wing Commander A. L. G. Hubbard, an Australian by birth but who had served with RAF squadrons prior to assuming his new posting. Initially, 460 became part of 8 Group but this had been changed later to 1 Group when they moved to Breighton. Soon 460 was the only one carrying the Australian name in the Command for early in 1942, 458 Squadron moved to the Middle East and 455 Squadron transferred to Coastal Command.

62 The raid on Düsseldorf was a failure, due to the difficulty of marking in bad weather and 27 bombers were lost - 21 of which, were shot down by night fighters.

63 Cammell had joined the Royal New Zealand Air Force at the age of 18 for pilot training. He earned his wings and was commissioned as a pilot officer, sent to England and went to No.15 Advanced Flying Unit at Leconfield to undergo further flying training. From Yorkshire he was then assigned to No.11 Operational Conversion Unit at Oakley in Buckinghamshire, which operated Vickers Wellington Mk ICs. Here heI met four officers and two sergeants who became his crew. In April 1943 they were assigned to 115 Squadron at East Wretham in Norfolk, where the Officers' Mess was located in an old mansion that had belonged to one of the English gentry.

64 Flying Officers Halford Douglas Pye RNZAF and David Stewart Williams; Sergeant Eric Gordon Fay Beaumont Baker and Flying Officers' George Albert Parker; George William Cooper and Robert Ryland Reid.

65 Adapted from *A Matter of Life and Death* by Gordon Cammell, writing in *Aeroplane* magazine, February 2011.

66 Sergeant Leslie Arthur Steele on 166 Squadron was KIA on 20/21 October 1943 on Leipzig. Flight Sergeant A. E, Egan RAAF was shot down on the night of 25/26 June 1943 on Gelsenkirchen and was taken prisoner.

67 Warrant Officer Paul Fulton Chesterton DFC was KIA on 166 Squadron on 27/28 September 1943

on the trip on Hannover in JA704 'A-Apple' which crashed at Mahlerten. The flight engineer and the rear gunner were taken prisoner; the others were killed.

68   262 Lancasters, 209 Halifaxes, 117 Stirlings, 105 Wellingtons and 12 Mosquitoes.

69   17 Halifaxes, 9 Lancasters, 9 Wellingtons and 9 Stirlings. Twelve of the losses were on the Path Finders; 35 Squadron lost six out of its 19 Halifaxes that took part in the raid.

70   *The Bomber Command War Diaries: An Operational reference book 1939-1945*. Martin Middlebrook and Chris Everitt. (Midland 1985).

71   Post-war estimates were that 94% of the Elbefeld part of Wuppertal was destroyed on this night. *The Bomber Command War Diaries: An Operational reference book 1939-1945*. Martin Middlebrook and Chris Everitt. (Midland Publishing 1985).

72   See *Chased by The Sun: The Australians in Bomber Command in WWII*, by Hank Nelson (Allen & Unwin 2006). Altogether, 34 aircraft were lost.

73   See *Chased by The Sun: The Australians in Bomber Command in WWII*, by Hank Nelson (Allen & Unwin 2006).

74   During August-September 1990 Gordon Stooke and his wife visited the village of Aiken in Northern Belgium, on the outskirts of which 'D-Donald' had crashed. He returned to Melbourne with revived memories and renewed friendships with those Belgians who had helped him in his bid to escape and a most remarkable souvenir: a spring and exhaust valve from one of 'D-Donald's Merlin engines, salvaged from the wreck by a local Aiken official and kept for 47 years. Adapted from Stooke's Saga by Michael Enright, writing in *Aeroplane Monthly*, January 1996.

75   Warrant Officer John Stafford Stoneman and crew were KIA on 2/3 August 1943 on Hamburg. Their Lancaster crashed near the target. Warrant Officer Ken Breckon DFM and crew were KIA on Leverkusen on 22/23 August 1943. Their Lancaster crashed at Heusden in Holland.

76   Denys Teare was still on the run a year later before being liberated by US ground forces. By this time he had become involved with the French Resistance and was living under the assumed name of Denis Lebenec. Several times schemes to get him back to Allied lines failed, including one abortive attempt to fly him out in a Lysander which was bringing in a British agent. Denys Teare later recalled his adventures in his book, *Evader*, which was first published in 1954 and has since been reissued.

77   Thomas made his own way south and west for the best part of 250 kilometres before he received any real help. He eventually 'joined a small multi-national group of civilians trying to escape occupied Europe. During the last week of October 1943 a guide led them high into the Pyrenees, pointed them towards Spain and then turned back, leaving the group to fend for themselves. Caught in a sudden blizzard, one of them died, the others surviving only by eating what little food they had and by scraping moss from the frozen rocks. Four days later, on 29 October, they were spotted by a German patrol and arrested. After almost three months in Fresnes prison George Thomas spent the next 18 months at Stalag IVB (Mühlburg)., Germany, having arrived there circa December 1943. *RAF Evaders: The Comprehensive Story of Thousands of Escapers and their Escape Lines, Western Europe, 1940-1945* by Oliver Clutton-Brock (Grub Street 2009).

78   *RAF Evaders: The Comprehensive Story of Thousands of Escapers and their Escape Lines, Western Europe, 1940-1945* by Oliver Clutton-Brock (Grub Street 2009).

79   See *Maximum Effort* by Patrick Otter.

Chapter 16

Twice Bitten

In Bronxville, New York at 10.18pm on 16 February 1943 the English parents of Flying Officer Carter DFC* RCAF, a Halifax navigator on 35 Squadron at Graveley, received a telegram informing that their son was missing in action. On 22 March the New York Daily News noted briefly that he had been reported missing on13/14 February; the night RAF Bomber Command bombed the German U-boat pens at the port of Lorient on the west Brittany coast. That same day another newspaper telephoned Mr. Carter telling him that they had learned that his son had been killed. Contrary to reports, he was very much alive and safely in the hands of the Resistance.

Gordon Henry Francis Carter had been born in Paris and they had lived in the suburbs there until he was thirteen. Then the family moved to the United States and they set up home in Bronxville, New York. He decided to cut short his studies at Dartmouth College in New Hampshire and went to Canada and enlisted in the RCAF as soon as he became 18 in June 1941. His first commanding officer considered him 'calm and confident, very mature for his age, intelligent, deep thinker, dependable, responsible, serious, very good background' and a commission followed. Then it was across the ocean to England. In a teashop in Bournemouth he listened intently to two Free French pilots at the next table discussing how to escape if they were shot down in France. He wondered if he would one day find himself in the same situation. Late in 1942 he was posted to 35 Path Finder Squadron, one of the elite squadrons that led the waves of bombers to their targets and marked them for the Main Force.

The operation on 13/14 February was Carter's fourteenth trip. He was the navigator on Halifax W7885 piloted by Flying Officer J. C. Thomas an American in the RCAF; one of seven aircraft that were lost on the raid on Lorient. Heavy flak destroyed the Halifax's port inner engine and Thomas ordered the crew to bail out. Sergeant William Joseph Freeman RCAF the tail gunner was killed. Three other sergeants on the crew - E. R. Turenne RCAF, R. Martin and D. C. Young - bailed out and landed within a few hundred metres of each other near Spézet in central Brittany. They were taken under the wing of Operation 'Oaktree' and soon found themselves together in a house in Châteauneuf-de-Faou. On 15 February Georges Jouanjean ('Geo', or 'Joe' to the English-speakers) split them up, but they met up again on the evening of

17 February at Carhaix railway station when Geo and Jean Bach, a passeur of the Pat O'Leary (PAO) Line, took them to Paris on the overnight train, being joined by their American Skipper, who had been staying with the Jouanjean family. Young, who had been suffering from a badly sprained ankle since his landing, went to stay with a French family in a PAO safe house in Paris but the home was raided by the Gestapo on 3 March and though Young made an escape via a back window, he was captured. Thomas was also staying at a safe house when it too was raided. He also made a run for it and helped by railwaymen from time to time, he succeeded in reaching Switzerland on the night of 12/13 March 1943. He remained in Switzerland for 18 months when, with France all but free of Germans, he returned to Allied lines, leaving behind his wife, who had married on 2 November 1943 and a young son, Peter, born on 28 August 1944.[80] Flight Sergeant J. H. 'Napoleon' Barry RCAF the mid upper gunner and Sergeants' R. Martin and Eddie Turenne meanwhile, were passed along the escape lines to Spain and they too reached England safely.

Gordon Carter meanwhile, having bailed out 'in the nick of time' had jumped into the dark void; his 'guts cramped with fear'. He landed in a field about fifteen yards from a house, beside a group of about thirty people. He and Barry, who had landed nearby, began walking south-east, having planned to make for Spain using a Michelin map Carter had brought with him. He decided that they should pass themselves off as French and he buried his escape kit to avoid having anything incriminating on him if searched. A family took them in but only because they said they were Canadian. They next fell in with a local Resistance leader who had a wireless link to London and a plan was made for them to be picked up by submarine on the northern coast of the Brittany peninsula. Finally, after many close shaves with German sentries and French policemen, they reached the beach and crouched behind rocks waiting for a signal from the sea but just one flash came and hours later they crept away, disheartened. For the next week Carter and Barry remained hidden in a Cistercian monastery, drinking plum liqueur. In Carhaix, the Breton town where he lived, Geo Jouanjean, newly recruited as the Brittany end of the Pat Line, arrived to guide them to Paris but the French capital was not safe and the route south was now all but impassable, with Pat O'Leary under arrest and many other 'Pat Line' helpers also in German hands. Carter has been described as 'tall, sleepy-looking, very dark, very handsome and very reserved'. During the time Carter was lodged at the house of Geo's married sister Lucette he met and fell in love with their 'attractive blonde' sister, 22-year-old Mademoiselle Janine Jouanjean. Carter would cycle along with Janine and her brother as two young men on their own might attract unwelcome attention and a girl with them made it seem more natural. Gordon was younger than Janine, just nineteen; quite handsome even in his shabby clothes. Barry was given civilian clothing but Carter was wearing civilian clothes under his battle dress when he was shot down and he could speak fluent French. He even went to the town hall in Ploermel, claimed to have lost all his possessions during the raid on Lorient and left with a replacement identity card in the name of 'Georges Charleroi', food and tobacco ration cards, clothing and shoe coupon books. [81] Gordon Carter and Janine fell in love but Carter had to be returned to England.

The RAF navigator wanted to take Janine with him but it was far too dangerous and it was obvious that she would have to remain behind. Carter was taken to Treboul, a small port near the tip of Brittany where he joined a party of a dozen Frenchmen trying to get to England to join the war. They left in an old 40-foot sardine boat captained by a local fisherman and his two-man crew under the noses of Armed German sentries who patrolled the quay. After a gruelling voyage dodging German shipping and braving fog and a Force 9 gale in the Channel they finally reached Coverack in Cornwall on 9 April after a Cornish crabber guided them through a minefield to the lifeboat slipway on Lizard Point.

When MI9 learned of his successful escape to England they tried to persuade Carter to return to France for a role in the 'Shelburne' escape line but he declined. If he went he would not be able to stay away from Janine, the girl he had fallen in love with and that would put her in great danger. His thoughts were always with her. Once back on 35 Squadron at Graveley Carter talked at length about his new girlfriend who he described as his fiancée. On operations, he had 'Pour Janine' painted on a 1,000lb bomb loaded on his Halifax for a raid. Off duty he would compose love letters, in immaculate French and send them in a sealed envelope his Aunt Dot in Haslemere, Surrey with instructions to send them to Janine once France was liberated if anything happened to him on operations.

Gordon Carter was promoted to Flight Lieutenant and he joined the crew skippered by 29-year old Ontario-born and Toronto-educated Squadron Leader Douglas Julian Sale DSO, who had returned to operations after he was shot down on the Duisburg-Ruhrort raid on 12/13 May 1943 when he was a flight lieutenant. Altogether, 572 bombers - 238 Lancasters, 142 Halifaxes, 112 Wellingtons and 70 Stirlings - were detailed for the operation. Sale's Halifax was shot down near the small Dutch town of Haaksbergen in Gelderland province near the German border by Oberleutnant August 'Gustel' Geiger of III./NJG1 flying a Bf 110.[82] Julian Sale was blown out of the aircraft when it exploded and he landed in a pine tree. Four of his crew were taken into captivity and the two others were killed. Sale clambered down the tree, but he was unable to recover his parachute and he decided to leave his life-jacket at the foot of the tree. He had lost one of his flying-boots during his descent, so he put both socks on the one foot before heading away. He knew he was near the Dutch-German border, so he decided to head west, since he was not sure if he had landed in Germany. As dawn broke, he hid in a thicket between two farms hoping to determine if he was in Holland, but no safe opportunity occurred for him to find out. Once dark, he again set off in a westerly direction along small tracks and minor roads, covering 20 miles before he took cover in another thicket. He had filled his water bottle with milk from a churn and he ate Horlicks tablets from his aids box. At dusk on 14 May he convinced himself that he must be in Holland, so decided to approach a farmer for food and some footwear. The farmer was friendly, but nervous and was able to understand who he was. He gave Sale some food and a pair of clogs, pointed out the direction for Arnhem, but asked him to move on because of his fear of the Germans.

Sale walked all night along secondary roads, passing through numerous villages, when he took off the clogs for fear of making too much noise. His feet were badly blistered, so he rested through the day before setting off again once it was dark. His feet were in poor shape so he had to abandon the clogs and by the end of that night he had walked almost 40 miles during the previous three nights, but felt that he could go no further without some shoes and food. Towards dawn on 16 May, he reconnoitred a farmhouse on the outskirts of the village of Linde. He knocked on the back door and declared himself by sign language before entering. He was well received and found he was surrounded by a most helpful, but very frightened, Dutch family. They gave him a complete outfit of clothes and a pair of socks and shoes. The son of the family brought a friend who explained that the Germans had discovered that local people had been assisting shot-down aircrew and there had been some arrests. He urged Sale to give himself up, but he refused. The family gave him a bed in the attic and fed him throughout the following day. Sale found the family 'intensely patriotic, Dutch Royalist and pro-British'. That evening, they gave him a large-scale road map and sent him on his way.

With good clothes, he decided to walk by day and use bigger roads, in order to make more distance. On one occasion, he helped a German officer to push his car, which had broken down. He decided to bypass Arnhem to the north and headed for Oosterbeek, where he hoped to find a crossing point over the Neder Rijn. At dusk, he had reached the Arnhem-Nijmegen railway bridge, which he thought was unguarded. He had just got on to the bridge when he was hailed by a soldier who then fired at him as he raced off the bridge and down the riverbank. Once it was dark, he looked for an unchained boat, but had no luck. He stripped off his clothes and bundled them in his overcoat, secured them to a plank of wood and propelled the plank across the 100-yard-wide river. By morning, he had reached the River Waal at Druten, where there was a ferry crossing. A friendly Dutch boy, who spoke a little English, told him that there were no controls on the ferry, so he exchanged a British half-crown for a few cents, which allowed him to pay the ferryman. After crossing on the ferry, he headed for the next obstacle, the River Maas, which he reached later that day. Some workmen helped him across on a private industrial railway. Once again he approached an isolated house, where a schoolteacher who spoke some English gave him food and some new socks. As he walked through a small village the next day, a Dutch policeman stopped him and asked to see his papers. Sale was explaining his situation when the policeman suggested in broken French that he was 'a Frenchman going home from Germany'. Sale assented eagerly, they shook hands and the policeman wished him good luck.

In Ste-Oedenrode, Sale knocked at the door of a house that he thought was a priest's house. Instead, he found three elderly ladies who invited him in to have some food and to meet three residents from the town. After two nights' rest, his new helpers gave him a new pair of boots, three days' food, a road map and a bicycle. They also briefed him on a safe location to cross the Belgian border. At 3 pm on 22 May he reached the border, where he asked a Dutch family if there were soldiers guarding the crossing and he was told that it was safe. He headed towards Antwerp, but was soon stopped by two policemen and identified himself. They were friendly, but advised him not to keep the bicycle since it had no Belgian licence plaque and the blue Dutch plaque was too obvious. Sale kept the bicycle and improvised a Belgian plaque from an old cigarette carton. He headed south through Belgium and by the late evening he had passed through Louvain and Charleroi and was close to the French border, having cycled over 100 miles in the day. The following day, a friendly Belgian farmer personally took him through the town of Grandneu on the frontier, thus avoiding the customs post. Sale had arrived in France 11 days after being shot down and during that time he had walked and cycled almost 200 miles - some of the journey without shoes.

Sale had some knowledge of French and his general plan was to head for Spain, keeping to the east of Paris. He hoped to make contact with 'an organization', but apart from being given some bread coupons, he had to press on alone. He cycled through the day, approaching lonely farms each evening, almost always gaining access to a barn. Few farmers accepted any payment for his food and he was regularly provided with enough food for his journeys. For two days, he had only one pedal on his bicycle and punctures became a regular feature as he progressed south through Laon, Chateau-Thierry, Sens and on to Bourges, where he arrived at the demarcation line. As he had no repair outfit, he pushed his bicycle until he arrived at a small town where he was able to get repairs. Throughout his journey, he used coloured card and tin to improvise a local licence plaque and he was very alert for police patrols whenever he entered a small town. The demarcation line between the Occupied and Unoccupied Zones of France was regularly patrolled and presented a major obstacle to the evader. Sale approached a landowner a few miles south of Bourges who helped him cross at an unguarded bridge. Safely over, he continued south, aiming to cycle up to 100 miles each day, which he achieved to reach Castres on 1 June. A day later, he reached the small town of Revel, where he stayed on local farms for almost three weeks. Since leaving the Belgian border eight days earlier, he had covered just over 500 miles.

Shortly after arriving in Revel, he met a young Frenchman who had tried to escape to Switzerland, but had been forced to return to Revel because of the tight security near the Swiss border. They agreed to join forces to make an attempt to cross the Pyrénées. On 21 June Sale abandoned his Dutch bicycle that had served him so well. He and his companion left for Toulouse, where they caught a fast train to Carcassonne before transferring to a local train that took them to Quillan. After a 15-mile bus ride to Belcaire in the foothills of the Pyrénées, they stayed at a small hotel where they were able to contact a mountain guide who had gathered a party of six others who wished to cross the mountains. The party set off early on the morning of 24 June, but the guide became lost, which resulted in an overnight stop in the open. They started climbing early the next morning and reached a point two miles from the frontier with Andorra by mid-afternoon when the guide refused to go any further. Sale and his French companion continued alone, crossing a 7,000-foot mountain and snow drifts to reach the frontier, which they crossed late on the night of 25/26 June. They stayed overnight in a shepherd's hut before walking into the small Andorran town of Canillo the next morning.

In Canillo they met a man who put them in touch with a Spanish smuggler who agreed to take them to Barcelona. A short car journey took them to the closely guarded Spanish frontier and that night they crossed the mountains on foot into Spain with the smuggler and some of his associates. Over the next ten days they descended from the mountains, reaching the town of Manresa after a 90-mile walk. Sale claimed that this was the most arduous phase of his journey. The guide left them to go ahead to Barcelona to make contact with the British Consul, who arrived on 7 July to take the two men to the Consulate, where they remained until their onward journey to Gibraltar could be arranged. Julian Sale left Gibraltar on 5 August, arriving in Liverpool five days later and three months after he had bailed out of his stricken Halifax. With the exception of three short train and bus journeys, he had walked and cycled over 800 miles without once being supported by any of the escape lines. Local Dutch, Belgian and French people had been his helpers along the route. It was one of the longest single evasions during the war. In October it was announced that Julian Sale had been awarded the DSO for his epic journey, an extremely rare award for such an action. The citation concluded: 'His unconquerable spirit of determination, great gallantry and fortitude have set an example beyond praise'.

Back at Graveley Julian Sale and Gordon Carter would get up at 4am and go for long runs around the airfield. They also practised penetrating the perimeter fence and attacking parked aircraft. they had two organized exercises where they were taken out in a lorry at night and dumped in the middle of nowhere to get themselves back to Gravely without being picked up by MPs. Sale and Carter took these exercises so seriously that they even set fire to the odd haystack to divert attention from where they were actually headed. Both men also took to carrying civilian clothes with them on operations.

On the night of 20/21 December 1943 Julian Sale was returning from Frankfurt with a fire in the bomb bay of his Halifax. Hung-up TIs had exploded as the aircraft came below their barometric fuse altitude of 1,500 feet. Sale ordered the crew to bail out but Flight Lieutenant Roger 'Sheep' Lamb the mid-upper gunner appeared beside him with a charred parachute so Sale dropped back into his seat, stuck his head out of the port window of the cockpit, which was filled with smoke and calmly brought the blazing Halifax in for a normal circuit landing at Graveley before roaring off the runway and crashing in a ball of fire. Sale and Lamb got away safely before the bomber exploded. The four other men who bailed out were safe and only the rear gunner suffered any injury. Sale was awarded a bar to his DSO for his action.

On the night of 19/20 February 1944 four of the missing Halifaxes on Leipzig were on 35 Squadron, one of which exploded over Gohre and another was abandoned near Brandenburg. 'J-Johnny' piloted by Squadron Leader Julian Sale DSO* DFC was hit at 23,000 feet near Beedenbostel in central Germany near Celle by a Ju 88 armed with Schräge Musik ('Oblique Music')[83.] This device, invented by an armourer, Paul Mahle of II./NJG5, comprised two

20mm MG FF cannon mounted behind the rear cockpit bulkhead of the Bf 110 and Ju 88 night fighters and was arranged to fire forwards and upwards at an angle of between 70 and 80°. 'J-Johnny's' port inner engine caught fire and Sale called 'Bail Out; bail out, bail out!' His highly decorated crew included the navigation leader, now Squadron Leader Gordon Carter DFC* who had also evaded capture, the previous February. Because he had been through it all before Carter removed his helmet because 'a lot of chaps were hanged by their intercom leads going out' and bailed out. He had on his back under the parachute harness, a pack of escape items such as wire cutters and some civilian clothes bought in France during his evasion. On landing in a lane in a forest in snow, he buried his parachute and he went into the trees and put the clothes on. He remembered that he was carrying a revolver that he had bought in Huntingdon in case he ever fell into a city where he thought that civilians might mob him. Carter decided that he had better get rid of it. Later he ditched his distinctive RAF Omega watch. He followed a track to a road. A sign pointed to Celle, a town between Hamburg and Hanover. The navigation leader was free for 48 hours and had travelled forty miles when he met some children, who, trained to report any strangers, ran off to tell a sailor shooting crows in a field. He did not believe Carter's story that he was a French factory worker and he pointed his shotgun at him. Bitterly disappointed that he had not got any further, Carter was taken to a Luftwaffe airfield where he was visited by Hauptmann Ludwig 'Luk' Meister who told him that he was the pilot who had shot him down [84] Carter, who was still wearing his French clothes, was asked, 'Were you trying to do what your Skipper succeeded in doing last year? Apparently the Hauptmann had read all about it in the Toronto ski club magazine. Carter opened his shirt and showed his interrogator his RCAF identity disc. Four others on the crew were also taken prisoner.

Julian Sale meanwhile had crash-landed the Halifax because Flight Sergeant Kenneth Knight, the 19-year old rear gunner had not answered the call to abandon the aircraft. Knight was found dead. Sale was badly injured and he died of his wounds in hospital near Frankfurt on 20 March.

Carter would spend the next fourteen months as a prisoner in Stalag Luft III. In Northern France on 6 June there was jubilation after the Allied landings in Normandy and soon most of the country was in Allied hands. That August the postman brought Jouanjean a huge bundle of love letters from Gordon Carter. She read them avidly while at the same time hoping that there might be news of her brother Geo and her brother-in-law who were incarcerated in concentration camps at Birkenau, Buchenwald and Flossenburg. When the camp was abandoned the inmates were marched 400 miles along forest roads in southern Germany under the watchful eyes of SS guards. Thousands of the Flossenburg inmates died on that notorious march, most of whom were shot as they fell behind, others committing suicide by dropping to their knees, stuffing dirt from the ground into their throats and choking to death. American troops and tanks arrived and saved Geo and many of his fellow prisoners. When he returned to Carhaix, his arrival coincided with a visit by Gordon Carter, who after his release received permission to make his way from England to Paris. He set off with a fourteen-day pass, taking the ferry from

Newhaven across the Channel and travelled on to Paris where he had been told that Janine had worked behind the counter in a pastry shop in rue Blanche. But she had long since gone back to Brittany and was working in her grandfather's tailor's shop in Carhaix. Carter took the next train the 300 miles to Morlaix on the north Brittany coast in a first-class carriage reserved for Allied officers. In Morlaix he learned that there was no connecting service to Carhaix, twenty-five miles away, until the next day but he was offered a lift in a car. An hour later he arrived outside Janine's grandfather's tailor's shop in Carhaix, unannounced and unexpected. The door opened. An aunt stood there. She looked at him and turned her head back inside. Janine,' she called out, 'c'est Gordon!' Gordon and Janine had not seen each other for about two and a half years. The last time he had been in a shabby French suit but now he was in full RAF uniform, medals and all. Her heart jumped when she saw him. She was overwhelmed. Unable to take it in she burst into tears.

Carter rekindled his romance with Janine Jouanjean and his proposal of marriage was accepted but her parents were not so sure and they were slow to give their blessing. His leave was running out and so he and his fiancée travelled to Paris where Carter persuaded an RAF air marshal to extend his leave by another fourteen days. Gordon Carter and Janine married on 11 June 1945. Just over a fortnight later she went with her husband to Buckingham Palace where Carter received a bar to his DFC from King George VI. Before he left for Canada to be demobilised he took Janine to Graveley and showed her where he had written her name above his bunk.

Endnotes

80 *RAF Evaders: The Comprehensive Story of Thousands of Escapers and their Escape Lines, Western Europe, 1940-1945* by Oliver Clutton- Brock (Grub Street 2009).

81 *Bomber Crew* by John Sweetman (Abacus 2004).

82 Hauptmann Geiger was KIA with his Bordfunker Feldwebel Koch on 29 September 1943, shot down by a Beaufighter on 141 Squadron. He had 53 victories and had been awarded the Ritterkreuz with Eichenlaub.

83 Schrage Musik was in fact a modernized version of a combat technique used in 1916 by Gerhard Fieseler, then a front-line pilot in Macedonia. His friends used to call it 'fieseling'. With this tactic Fieseler was able to stand up to overwhelming odds and won 21 air kills without receiving a single machine-gun hit. In spring 1918 when Fieseler was a pilot in 38 Fighter Squadron on the Balkans Front, he took a round-turreted Lewis machine-gun from a Breguet he had shot down and mounted it in the upper wing indentation of his Fokker D VII, in front of the pilot's seat, so that he could fire it upward at an angle. Each time he attacked he would fly underneath the enemy aircraft and his slanted MG rarely missed its target.

84 Meister assumed command of III./NJG4 in December 1944, leading it until the end of the war by which time he had been credited with 39 victories.

Chapter 17

The Spirit of JB601

Sergeant Pilot Roy Bradley,
106 Squadron RAF

For you the war is over.

Fallingbostel, which is where it all ended, seemingly. A fair sized Westphalian town steeped in the traditions of the German Princedoms, those regions of earlier extreme, which found it so easy to transfer allegiance to the later extremes of Nazism. Fallingbostel, in the sixties and we are well into a touring holiday, the family and I, which brings us to the outskirts of the town. Our motor-caravan stands a little way up the road. I stand facing the remains of the entrance to what is left of Stammlager 357. Through and beyond the concrete remnants I still see those grimly grey facades of a PoW camp, which forever conjure up visions at once typical of these unique communities. I see again the mixed expressions of despair and determination on faces belonging to bodies struggling with the rigours of a near-starvation diet. I hear again the trudge of weary feet pacing the 'compound circuit' and I remember where it all began. April 1944 and the crew and I are fresh into the world of 106 Squadron. With the sublime ignorance and enthusiasm of our kind, we enter into a world of young but established tradition with the almost routine air of nonchalance and without any pre- conceived notions of tomorrow.

Forenoon of the 26th April 1944 and Squadron Leader Murdoch, the New Zealander Flight Commander tells me that I am to be his co-pilot tonight.[85] He suggests that the afternoon might be well spent 'in the pit'. Come evening and the very air is charged as only it can be when 'there is one ON'. The corny jokes and the nervous giggles. The haze and the maze of the briefing. The studied confusion of getting the gear. The truck to the kite. The gathering dusk and JB601 in semi-silhouette she shows all the majesty of her breed. (No one should ever attempt a description of the Lancaster; I'm not - it would have to be more a definition, really).

JB601, the centrepiece in this moment of unspoken reverence and devoted activity. JB601 ZN-V and I take another look at the outsize rabbit painted on the nose - hindquarter thumping and ears bristling in the defiant 'V'. I wonder who painted it? It's very well done but in what seems no time at all, which happily cuts down the time for wondering what the hell I'm doing here, the engines are humming their harassed hymn of harnessed energy, the wheels are rolling and we are joining the line. Now we are turning onto the runway and with their given freedom the engines speed us towards a shadowy horizon. I look back and down. Could so much have really happened in these past few hours, down there within the scattered confines of what spells RAF Metheringham? Lying in the wispy band that rests between a darkening earth and a paling sky is the form of Lincoln and its cathedral identity. They say it is a sight permanently etched in the mind of so many of 5 Group.

We are still climbing. We are heading south. There is a lessening definition of view. The sky is filling up. By the time we are all en route, this is going to be some mighty aerial brick, of metal and men. But it's comforting to know you're in company.

So it's to be Schweinfurt. I've never heard of it before. Funny that. Can't even work up a feeling about the name. It hasn't the ring of the Essen's and the Frankfurt's. It isn't far from Frankfurt though. A couple of loops of the River Main to the eastward. And there are two Frankfurt's. Not that it matters very much. It seems a nice kite this. I wish I had a greater sentiment for it. Maybe if it were my own it would be different. These chaps have had it for some time. (Did somebody really say it was their 13th?) Judging by the bombs painted on her nose 'V-Victor' could tell a lot of people's stories.

It's quite black now. The others are still out there. We are still in company, but it doesn't give quite the same feeling of comfort now that I can't see them. Quiet enough. Not far now from the Southeast turn point near Paris. There's a long, long leg coming up then! We're on the long leg. Fair old amount of flak. Funny how it gives the feeling of a lot of little men down there flicking away at outsize cigarette lighters that won't light. No flak now. Uncomfortably close glimpses of exhausts. Hell, there's a few being knocked down. I wonder how many, if any, got out.

Now us! Now us! No. 4's on fire. Now 3! Is this it? Is this it? Then it comes: 'Jump, jump, jump, jump'.[86] Chute on…and blank…a sightless blank…is this what it's like to be dead? Or is it all happening to somebody else? I open my eyes. The blackness has gone. If I did die, I didn't know about it. But this is the earth I'm lying on. And that is a tree above me. The sky beyond is a pale blue. Now the blackness again…Hell, it's cold! My left leg looks a mess. Feel so stiff and sore all over. Can't stand! My flying boots have gone. Not surprising - those suede jobs are a pretty stupid design. Funny thing - first time I've worn them since early Flying School! This is real earth and that's a real tree all right. Did I come through that? The chute's here, strung out around me. I tear a length for a bandage. Somehow or other I haven't 'bought it'. Any of the others around I wonder? I call out. No response. The rising damp air carries my breath into the surrounding solitude. I bury my chute. I crawl away, slowly, painfully and cursing the rough foliage which defies my progress. And now, a grassy corridor. This is easier. It slopes away before me and down to a main road ringing to the crunch of marching feet materializing into a squad of soldiers. German soldiers, which doesn't exactly surprise me. They are out of sight now.

With alternating grunts and yelps I land at the roadside, cross on all fours and roll thankfully into the comfort of the ditch. It's getting a struggle holding off the blackness…More footsteps. A man and a girl. No time for ceremony or second thoughts. I raise myself up. I ask them to help me get to England. I ask them to bring a doctor. Then into the blackness again…

I'm being helped to my feet. The man and the girl again. And another man and a car. My luck's in. I give the girl the whistle from my blouse collar and the orange from my ration pack. Getting into a car was never like this before - and into the blackness again.

And now I'm dreaming. I must be. This man in white looms mistily over me. But I'm not dreaming now. This is a real stretcher I'm on and the green clad gents fore and aft aren't on our side! On into a hospital and into a small treatment room. My wrists and ankles are being strapped to the table. A mask is pushed to my face, possibly ungratefully, but understandably, I struggle. But the blackness wins.

I'm in bed. A small room - and a guard; several, in turn, who take typical Teutonic delight in displaying the family photographs. Now and then there is the medical orderly whose army service cut short his medical studies and who likes to reminisce about his days in lodgings in Lincoln. There are two visits from members of a local Gestapo unit who seem more confused about it all than I do. Thank goodness I seem to be in some quiet area in France where such gents may be less practiced.

A week has passed. I'm on the move. The platform name board tells me I am in Chaumont. My two escorts and I will probably pass more pleasant train journeys but not together I hope.

Paris! On the platform an old lady strokes my face and mutters, 'Poor boy'. She is impatiently brushed aside. I am locked in a small room in the station entrance hall. There is one other occupant, a civilian. In a thick American accent he wishes me luck and throws me a hefty roll of French banknotes. Almost immediately, the door opens and he is hustled outside. And then it's my turn. I drop the money in the gutter before being put into an ambulance. Maybe some Frenchman will pick up the money and put it to some better purpose than I shall have.

The Feldwebel speaks perfect French. He explains that he has a French mother. I wonder what she thinks of him; more than I do I hope.

L'Hôpital Beaujon, Clichy, Paris. This is an imposing building of some eleven floors. The huge entrance hall boasts the busts of Adolf and Herman. They tell me it is the latter's hospital for the Luftwaffe - and the likes of me. The ninth floor: corridors suitably caged and windows properly barred. Who do they think we are? Clipped-wing birdmen?

Rooms for two. I share with a young American bomb aimer, Otto P. Mathis, from Cleveland City. He seems in bad shape, but his main concern seems to be concealment of the 'D' which seems to be a family name.

9th May and it's my 22nd birthday. Overtures to the Sister for a bottle of beer or some like token of celebration bring no joy. But I have the feeling she's on my side somehow.

Well, I tried to spin it out…I'm on the move again and the treatment is a little less ceremonious. We pick up a few more aircrew en route to the Gare du Nord… Frankfurt and Dulag Luft… Stalag Luft VI, Heydekrug… Thorn, Poland… Fallingbostel, to become lodgers in the British Army PoW Camp,

Stammlager 357... and it's a singular routine of life with a plurality of interpretation to be told and pictured by so many, many times... and freedom...

That, then, is the story; but behind the story lays a story. The reality of people unknown to me at that time. Unknown and unsung people. Those who had so much at stake, with so much lost, with so much, which could still be lost. Those who were prepared to put their simple ways of life at risk in the service of persons unknown to them. Which takes guts. Such people, with whom I was unknowingly concerned, but who showed concern and compassion for me, perhaps played a small part in the greater picture but their particular part was a jigsaw which I had one day to piece together.'

In all Bomber Command flew 1,060 sorties on the night of 26/27 April. Some 206 Lancasters went to Schweinfurt with the marking provided by eleven Mosquitoes of 627 Squadron. Meanwhile, 493 aircraft went to Essen and 217 Halifaxes, Lancasters and Mosquitoes of 4, 6 and 8 Groups, attacked the southern end of the railway yards at Villeneuve-Ste-Georges. In all, 30 aircraft (28 per cent) were lost this night, including 21 Lancasters (9.3 per cent of the force) on the Schweinfurt raid, which was a failure. The low-level marking provided by 627 Squadron, which recently transferred to 5 Group from Don Bennett's 8 (PFF) Group, was inaccurate. Unexpectedly strong head winds delayed the Lancaster marker aircraft and the main force of bombers. German night fighters were carrying out fierce attacks throughout the period of the raid. The bombing was not accurate and much of it fell outside the city. A Victoria Cross was awarded after the war to Sergeant Norman Jackson, a flight engineer in a Lancaster of 106 Squadron, which was shot down near Schweinfurt. A German night fighter hit the Lancaster and a fire started in a fuel tank in the wing near the fuselage. Sergeant Jackson climbed out of a hatch with a fire extinguisher, with another crew member holding the rigging lines of Jackson's parachute which had opened in the aircraft. Sergeant Jackson lost the fire extinguisher and, as the fire was affecting both him and his parachute rigging, the men in the aircraft let the parachute go. Sergeant Jackson survived, though with serious burns and a broken ankle received on landing with his partially burnt parachute. The remainder of the crew baild out soon afterwards.

Roy Bradley's own crew was subsequently posted to 619 Squadron at Dunholme Lodge where they received a new pilot, Flying Officer Lawrence Ambrose Hall. On 9/10 August 1944 in Lancaster I ME866 this crew went on operations and were involved in a collision with a Lancaster of 50 Squadron over Châtellerault near Poitiers. Only Sergeant H. J. Cleland in Hall's crew survived and similarly, only one member of the 50 Squadron Lancaster survived.

The day of 26 April 1944 has been what has become almost a routine day in what now seems the accepted way of life for M. Galais. He puts his day at the factory behind him, as he makes his way to his simple lodgings in Gourzon, Haute-Marne, Those simple lodgings, which also serve, as his headquarters for his Resistance Group. Tonight, his group will be as ready and. alert as always. He is going to see what the night brings. He ponders the implications of the message from Dr. Rény in St. Dizier: that any wounded of the Allied Forces must first be brought to him.

M. Galais has already briefed people in the surrounding villages of the two basic things they must do: if ever an aircraft was heard to be in difficulties or crash, they must immediately take to the fields and lanes in search of survivors before local German forces came on the scene; and then, if questioned later, they must 'know nothing'.

It is around midnight. M. Galais has received reports that the German night fighter aerodrome near St. Dizier seems active. Overhead is the heavy steady drone of a RAF bomber force.

M. Galais looks up and his heart goes out to the crews so far above him. He can feel for them and with them. At the age of 44, he has behind him the memory and pride of 25 years as a professional soldier and four years underground…

And one is in trouble! M. Galais stands rooted, eyes piercing the darkness, ears cocked. In so many homes in Laneuville-à-Bayard and the surrounding farmhouses, many a breath is held and many hearts pound as the whine of disaster grows closer. There is an explosion, which seems to break about the listening ears and, in the swift eternity, which follows, there comes the sickening crunch of metal onto earth.

The sound of the crash comes from the direction of the canal. Gathering helpers, M. Galais hurries along the Route Nationale, to the church on the corner and over the bridge…

In Flornoy, among its few dozen inhabitants, the Geoffrin family, two sisters, one brother, have hardly dared speak. Mariette is the eldest; as a person of the land and so close to nature, she thinks with tender pride of those pigeons she has sent winging their way back to England, with those laboriously scrawled messages clipped to their legs. She has hidden and saved those boxes and parachutes by which they arrived and the contained instructions. That, then, has been her war, but now it is upon her borne on other wings…Pierre, the gamekeeper, reflects solemnly on 'the chase'. Marcelle, the youngest, thrills to the exciting fear of the moment with all the simplified objectiveness of a teenager, but saddened to tears for torment of the living.

There is no time to be lost. If there are survivors, then Pierre shall seek them in the neighboring land he knows so well. Marcelle demands that she keep him company.

They go out into the night. It is getting light. M. Galais gazes with mixed emotions at the wreckage of this Lancaster JB601 ZN-V. He feels the natural relief that comes from seeing the houses nearby still intact. He feels anger for the destructive forces, which wrought this disaster. He feels compassion, with all the depth of his race, for those who have perished this night. With tightening lips and eyes filled with tears, he turns away. The scene has been photographed. Items of possible interest to the Germans have been-removed. The bodies of the crew have been taken to nearby shelter. First arrangements for a fitting burial are already in hand…But there is evidence of another crewmember. The Germans will soon be on the scene…

Pierre and Marcelle take the Route Nationale out of Laneuville-à-Bayard in the direction of home. Their hopes are lowering. They do not feel the cold and their tiredness. To their left, the great Forêt du Val fringes and banks the roadside; within the trees, little of the new morning light penetrates. Already a German patrol from the direction of St. Dizier has passed them. They round the bend in the road. A voice calls to them from the ditch…

In the village of Laneuville-à-Bayard, the Germans conduct a noisy house-to-house check. With one accord, the villagers deny knowledge but say they hear of one, not in the wreckage, who is dead. Pierre and Marcelle return the few hundred metres back to Laneuville-à-Bayard.

Now suddenly the war has come to this village. The searching and questioning is in full swing. The confusion of the would-be Teutonic thoroughness. The cold but impassioned reaction of the villagers and all this on behalf of an unknown ally only Pierre and Marcelle have seen. They seek and find an old friend, who has a car. Yes, it should be all right to use the car; there are occasions for travelling to St. Dizier. And that is where they must go - to take the wounded airman to Dr. Rény's clinic…

As he looks down at the still form of the airman, Dr. Rény makes his decision. He has given the best treatment possible in these days of limited drugs and paper bandages. But this young man has lost a lot of blood and he will need close care for a few days. Further risks to all concerned will serve no purpose. The hospital at Chaumont, which is German-controlled, must be contacted. And so the long journey to Fallingbostel begins.

Others followed that touring holiday in the sixties, which provided the incidental opportunity to retrace my earlier steps. The first return to Chaumont. The meeting with Professor Henriot, local historian and geographer, who escorted us to Laneuville-à-Bayard. There, in company with the Mayor, M. Maillot, I stood between the Marne Canal and the village on the spot where JB601 had hit the ground. I spoke to the villager who had been the very first on the scene. Aging now, he recounted the detail with tear-stained face but in a voice pitched with all the excitement of yesteryear. I spoke to the villager, an old lady now, who could still recall her emotions of that moment when she felt that the aircraft was about to fall on her home - then told me of her relief and happiness that I was still alive. The walk to the little churchyard to gaze upon the grave surmounted by seven headstones.

We remained silently in an atmosphere born of the pride of those intimate strangers who stood beside me. Someone pressed a photograph into my hand. It had been taken at the actual time of the burial. Someone else gave me a battered hand-type fire extinguisher, which he had taken from the wreckage and cherished over the years as the memento of what had been a symbol of liberty.

By all manner of official means, the Germans had attempted to control manifestations .of sentiment for lost allies. How miserably they failed.

The first visit to Dijon and the home of M. Galais and our first meeting. Then, in 1967 he was '67 years young' and living with his wife in the modest house that had been his parents. His tears and his smiles, often together, seemed never to leave his face, as both families ate and drank and gossiped through long hours. He relived those darker days with a clarity and vigour that typified his kind and I was comforted, all over again.

In late 1969, M. Galais' wife died. I knew from his letters that he was becoming a changing man. Our letters became more frequent. In 1970 I achieved the deep satisfaction of receiving M. Galais into my home for a holiday I knew he must have. And the circle and bonds of friendship widened and grew. I can never forget taking M. Galais to what remained of RAF Metheringham. How smartly he came to attention to face the ruined hulk of the Control Tower. I watched him pick a small remnant of concrete from the rubble and gazing at it before, almost reverently, slipping it into his pocket. In my car, we drove down a length of lingering runway and the journey began all over again. Nor can I forget the visit to Lincoln Cathedral and the intensity and fervour of M. Galais' silent homage in the RAF Chapel…

There has also been the return visit to L'Hôpital Beaujon, in Clichy, Paris. The detailed tour conducted by the Hospital Secretary with the delicacy and savoir-vivre that characterize the French race.

In 1970, there was the visit to Dijon and the homes of M. Galais' family in Beaune and Chaumont. I had expressed a wish to revisit Laneuville-à-Bayard and place on the grave a portion of stone, which I had selected from the ruins of the old Control Tower of RAF Metheringham. Members of M. Galais' family took us by car from their home in Chaumont.

As we turned the last curve of the Route Nationale into the village, we slowed to a halt by the church and I felt as I had when I first was there in 1944: that it was all happening to someone else. The houses about me were ablaze with Tricolours and Union Jacks and the entire community crowded that one stretch of road. The Mayor and his Council came towards me. Through the blur of colour and words came gifts of mementoes and expressions of happy welcome. With a proud and solemn dignity, the Mayor led the way to the grave. The throng fell silent at the command of the Mayor. I was invited to speak, I did so. I barely remember what I said now. I was invited to place the portion of RAF Metheringham stone into a prepared hole in the gravelled surface of the grave. I did so. And, with a formality and quiet excitement that convinced me I was watching this from afar, the stone was ceremoniously covered and sealed with a marble slab with the golden inscription: 'Souvenir des camarades et de la RAF'. And our eyes turned to those other inscriptions ranged before us:

Sgt. Henry David Clark RAF
Pilot Officer William Frederick Collins RAAF
Flt Sgt William Frederick Evans RAF
Sgt Ernest Ambrose Hatch RAF
Sgt. Leonard George Alfred Izod
Squadron Leader A. O. Murdoch
Sgt John Howard Rees

Time has done little to change that corner of Haute-Marne, in sight or sentiment. There was the time I was able to spend a day at the home of the Geoffrin family, Mariette, Pierre, Marcelle, they insisted that it was they who had been honoured…There have been, there will continue to be, other visits and exchanges and M. Galais is and will continue to be, the head of a 'family' embracing countless people and relationships forging undeniable links to show that something good came out of it all.

At the wish of the Mayor of Laneuville-à-Bayard, I hope to achieve the 'twinning' of his village with Metheringham. That chapter has yet to be written. I hope it will be soon.

Fallingbostel. Perhaps it didn't all end there really; perhaps that was just a beginning.

Endnotes

85 Squadron Leader Anthony O'Shea Murdoch, who was from Christchurch had joined the pre-war regular air force.

86 None other than 22-year old Experte Oberleutnant Heinz-Wolfgang Schnaufer Ritterkreuztrager and Gruppen kommandeur, IV./NJG1, in a Bf 110 night-fighter had shot down 'V-Victor', one of his two Lancaster victims on the night of 27/28 April. All told, 106 Squadron lost five Lancasters this night. Sergeant Norman Jackson on Flying Officer F. H. Mifflin's crew was awarded the Victoria Cross.

Chapter 18

The Pilot Officer

At a recent briefing I noticed a bod wearing a scruffy old sports jacket instead of battle-blouse. RAF blue shirt, RAF trousers, but a civvy jacket! This to help evading if shot down. And have since learned that some, while not going as far as wearing a sports jacket at briefing (which I'm sure higher authority would frown upon) take one along with them on an op. Evidently, if captured, the Germans don't treat you as a civvy if you're wearing at least part of your RAF uniform and are wearing your identity discs. Well, I don't have an old sports jacket around and I'm certainly not going to buy one, so if I get shot down over France I'll simply have to dress off the country, so to speak. In mentioning this in the Mess, discovered that one character takes a black beret along with him, an item which I wouldn't think would be in short supply in France. And another says he's a good mind to take a bowler hat along. Says it would be good for a laugh if he has to bale out. Imagine descending by parachute wearing a bowler (if it stayed on, that is, which I very much doubt). God, the Germans would die laughing! No, on second thoughts I don't think they would; they'd probably regard it as particularly unfunny.

Vernon, my American pilot, has been told to watch his eating habits if he's shot down and manages to evade. Not a criticism of Vernon's actual table manners, but a warning to avoid conveying food to his mouth as he does in the Mess. Like nearly all Americans, he uses knife and fork to cut his food into mouth-size portions after which he transfers fork to his right hand and then uses it on its own. All Gestapo on the lookout for evaders have been briefed on this American eating habit and to eat this way in a restaurant is almost tantamount to be sitting there wearing Allied uniform. We have been told that quite a few Yanks, baling out of their Fortresses and being picked up by the Resistance, have given themselves away by eating thus.

Pilot Officer Campbell Muirhead, Lancaster bomb aimer on 12 Squadron at RAF Wickenby.

Unseasonably bad weather on the morning of Sunday 27 June 1943 meant that there would be no Main Force activity that night but at several bomber stations in Eastern England a few crews were alerted for mining sorties in the Frisians, off La Pallice and in the River Gironde in France. Small numbers of aircraft often made themselves useful sowing their 'vegetables' on 'Gardening' sorties to 'regions' that stretched from the French Atlantic coast to as far as the Kattegat. Each 'region' had codenames like 'Spinach' (the area off Gdynia in the Baltic); 'Geraniums', 'Tangerines', 'Sweet Pea' and 'Silverthorne'. At Ludford Magna or 'Mudford Magma' as it was known because it was still marshy although built on one of the highest stretches of the Lincolnshire Wolds, eight Lancasters on 'B' Flight on 101 Squadron in 1 Group were ordered up for air tests and three crews were selected for that night's mining operations to France. 'Gardening' was a useful way of initiating new crews on operations. Flying Officer Frederick Sinclair Buck and crew, who had only just arrived at Ludford from 1656 CU the day before were put on the Battle Order, which totalled fifteen Lancasters and 15 Stirlings in all. Fred Buck was a Canadian, from Toronto. His all-sergeant crew were, like the majority of crews in Bomber Command, from all walks of life. James Norman Sparkes, bomb aimer, was from Manchester. Sergeant Kenneth William Gadson, air gunner, was from Stoke Newington in London and Sergeant Geoffrey William Fuller, navigator, came from Croydon. Kenneth Boyd Coulter, WOp/AG, was an Irishman from Lisburn, County Antrim. Harold Thomas Clarke was the other air gunner and Kenneth David Selwyn Mordecal was flight engineer.

Each member of 'Q-Queenie's crew signed for the Escape Kit because of the money it contained: French francs, Belgian francs, German marks, Spanish pesetas, etc. It was quite a lot of 'ackers', said one crewmember 'which no one minded your using if shot down, but also which they don't want you to consider your own'. 'Intelligence types' said that if an airman made it to Spain and ran out of pesetas he could promise a genuine helper who actually got him to the British Legation a 'reasonable' sum of money and that this promise would be honoured. Intelligence did not specify what 'reasonable' amounted to. The Escape kit was enclosed in a kind of mica, but was supposed to be relatively easy to open.

The Intelligence Officer described the importance of the target and its heavy flak defences. Crews were warned of fighter airfields close to their route which took them near more heavily defended cities. The Met Officer warned of severe icing conditions and ten tenths cloud up to 20,000 feet. There was a danger of fog closing down base before the crews returned. The CO ended the briefing by re-emphasising the dangers and warned of the risk of collisions in the air. Finally: 'Any questions?'

There was deadly silence...and then a little Sergeant air-gunner stood up.

our escape kits Sir?'

'Yes Sergeant?'

'Is there enough foreign currency in them for us to have a bloody good piss up if we get shot down?'

Besides money the Escape Kit also contained pills for making water safe, some toilet paper and other pills to give you energy and a pack of three cigarettes and a small book of matches. The cigarettes were not Virginian tobacco for sure. Air crew surmised that they were probably Algerian tobacco because Virginian was unobtainable in Germany and Occupied Europe - at least for civilians - and walking along a street 'puffing away at a fag' containing Virginian could be a giveaway and lead to the airman's complete undoing.

Flying Officer Buck and his crew were to take Lancaster I ED377 SR-Q, better known as 'Q-Queenie' on 15 February for their Sunday night outing to France. A veteran of 186 hours and still flyable after damage in a recent crash landing had been repaired, Buck taxied 'Q-Queenie' out and headed for the

'Gardening' region off La Pallice on the French Atlantic coast. Probably the crew were in a state of high expectancy but this first operation was to be their epitaph. 'Q-Queenie' was the only aircraft lost on the night of 27/28 June. Oberleutnant Gollasch of 11./NJG5 shot the Lancaster down at 02.15 hours at 15,000 feet, 25 kilometres WNW of Angers for his seventh Abschüsse (victory). 'Queenie' crashed at Angrie, six kilometres EWE of Cande in the Maine-et-Loire. The six crew who were killed were interred later in the Pont-du-Cens Communal Cemetery in Nantes. Jimmy Sparkes was the sole survivor. He successfully evaded capture and went on the run; rather, he started walking. That night the exhausted bomb aimer found a pile of straw in a barn and he slept until morning when he was rudely awakened from his slumbers. The Resistance had been informed and Sparkes was taken away for interrogation. He had to prove that he was indeed an RAF airman on the run. Once this had been established to the satisfaction of the Resistance, Sparkes was literally wined and dined by his hosts. There were several 'escape lines' running through France at this time and as luck would have it, Sparkes had been taken in by members of the Marie-Claire escape line, which ran from Ruffec in Occupied France to Foix and on to Andorra. From there RAF airmen had to chance crossing the Pyrénées into neutral Spain and risk being held in the notorious Castillo de San Fernando prison at Figueras 20 kilometres south of the French border (or even the concentration camp at Miranda de Ebro) before making a 'home run' via Gibraltar.

The autumn of 1943 was to be a busy period for the Marie-Claire escape line. It had been established by Mary Lindell, an Englishwoman born of well-to-do parents on 11 September 1895, who had been a volunteer nurse at a hospital in Hertfordshire for a time in World War One before she went to France to join to join the Secours aux Blesses Militaires; 'the aristocratic division of the French Red Cross' and was decorated for gallantry under fire. She was awarded the Russian Order of St Anne by the last Czar of Russia and also awarded the French Croix de Guerre with Star. Mary married a French nobleman, the Comte de Milleville in 1922 and bore him two sons; Maurice and Octave (Octavius, known as 'Oky') and a daughter, Barbé. When France was invaded in May 1940, the Comte was away on business in South America and Mary was left to look after their three children. She decided that she must do what she could to help the many wounded French soldiers. With the fighting over, she returned to the family's Paris apartment, where she further decided that she and her children; Maurice 10, Oky 16 and her young daughter Barbe, would enable British army stragglers to reach Unoccupied France. An escape route via a farm at Sauveterre-de-Bearn (Basses- Pyrénées) in the south of France which straddled the new Demarcation Line between Occupied and Unoccupied France and reaching as far as the foothills of the Pyrénées was established and was regularly used throughout the war. In 1941 not only was Mary on Vichy's wanted list, but she had also been sentenced to death in absentia by the Germans in Paris and so she made her way to Lisbon disguised as an elderly governess and a flying boat took her, via Shannon in Eire to Poole in Dorset, where she arrived on 28 July 1942.

In London SOE/MI9 persuaded her to become an agent in the field. To avoid confusion with two other 'Maries' already in France she was to be known as Marie-Claire. On the night of 26/27 October she landed near Limoges with a SOE wireless operator in a Lysander to begin organising her escape line based on the Hôtel de France at Ruffec. When, on 9 May 1943 she arrived in Ruffec, she found that the few couriers employed on behalf of the Marie-Claire line were struggling to cope with the increasing numbers of evading airmen. Mary was asked if she could help Canadian Sergeant P. Whitnall RCAF, who had been flying on a 296 (Army Co-Operation Squadron) Whitley V that had taken off from Hurn in Dorset on the night of 17/18 April 1943 and was in hiding far to the north in Normandy. She agreed and at the end of August a girl from Lyon escorted Whitnall to Ruffec and thence by bicycle to a farm, about 25 kilometres south-east of Ruffec which Marie Claire used on her journeys. Four other airmen were brought to Ruffec at this time. One of them was Sergeant Sparkes. His companions were Sergeants A. H. Sheppard and C. F Trott on 115 Squadron who had been shot down on the same Lancaster during a Gardening operation on 19/20 June and Sergeant J. G. F. Sansoucy RCAF on 75 Squadron who was shot down at Moulines in the Calvados region of Normandy on another 'Gardening' operation on 14/15 June.

The Marie-Claire line operated by collecting evaders from many parts of France and moving them by stages to safe houses at Ruffec. Once a group of five to eight had been gathered, Marie-Claire would take them herself to the Pyrénées and hand them over to mountain guides. At the beginning of July 1943 Mary arranged for the departure of the party of airmen. On 9 September they left by road accompanied by Marie Claire, dressed as a police officer in civilian clothes and the driver of the truck, for Varilhes, 20 kilometres south between Pamiers and Foix Varilhes. They were handed over to a Spaniard and stayed in a shed until daylight next day, when the Spaniard hid them for the day beside a river. Leaving that night, the Spaniard took them for about two kilometres before he handed over the party to a Frenchman. The Frenchman took them about five kilometres that night to a farm at Ste-Jean-de-Verges, a few kilometres north of Foix in the mountains, where the airmen remained for two nights and three days waiting for a party of Frenchmen. Once the French party of twenty men arrived, they set off on the night of 12 September. Just short of the Spanish border, on 16 September, where the guides and all the Frenchmen left them, two guides came from Andorra to collect the party, which now included not only the RAF evaders but also a Polish family and two Polish soldiers. They arrived in Andorra on the morning of 17 September. Following the usual route via Barcelona and Madrid where they were helped by British consular staff, Sheppard, Trott and Sparkes arrived at Gibraltar on 1 October and on 4/5 October the RAF evaders were flown to Whitchurch near Bristol.[88] Successful evaders and escapers often merited the award of a medal and, as in the case of Sergeant Jimmy Sparkes, if non-commissioned, promotion to pilot officer.

Many returning evaders toured RAF bomber stations imparting their knowledge gained during their escapes to operational bomber crews. Often they were hard to win over. Many adopted a veneer of cynicism to disguise their innermost fears. Most wanted to believe that it would be the other 'bloke' who would get 'get the chop'; not them and anything that indicated otherwise was not up for discussion. This was certainly the case when Pilot Officer Sparkes addressed Lancaster crews on 12 and 625 Squadrons at Wickenby on 17 June 1944, as Pilot Officer Campbell Muirhead recalled in his diary.

'All crews were told to report to the Briefing Room at 10:00 hours, non-operational as well, so it can't be an op. For once we were there ahead of time, far less dead on it and sat ourselves in the front row. Wing Commander Nelson, that most likeable New Zealander, popular with all, appeared accompanied by one of the Intelligence types plus a pilot officer bomb aimer I had never seen before. We were in the process of shuffling into what might be termed, very loosely, as some form of attention when he motioned to us to sit down again. He next informed us that we might smoke: a wry smile as he gave this permission, mainly, I think, because about half of us were smoking already. He then handed us over to the Intelligence chap. I got the impression that Wingco Nelson was present mainly to ensure that this pilot officer, obviously the star of whatever show was going to be put on for us, was accorded a fair hearing, free from interruption and would be able to say whatever he had to say subject to the very minimum of wisecracks.

The Intelligence Officer now introduced the pilot officer bomb aimer who was from some other Squadron in No.1 Group. He explained that the pilot officer, who had to bail out over France, was able to contact the Resistance who were instrumental in spiriting him out of France into Spain from where he was able to return to England. He was sure we would find his experiences interesting: some of us might even gain from them if we ever found ourselves in a similar position. He ignored the remark, 'Not if I can help it', which came from somewhere near us.

The pilot officer kicked off rather well. He had obviously spotted my bomb aimer's flying badge; he could hardly fail to do so being almost opposite me. He smiled at me, nodded and observed, 'See you've got a moustache'.

'Enables me to keep a stiff upper lip in a crisis,' I informed him.

'Also helps to strain the gallons of beer he knocks back', amplified Horsfall.

'Well, I also used to have a moustache', continued the pilot officer, unruffled.

'How interesting!' murmured someone.

Our guest pressed on: 'But I shaved it off in France'.

'During your parachute descent?' This from the back of the room.

Wingco Nelson's deepening frown rose with him. 'All right, gentlemen' he ordered, 'Half-wit time over. We'll now listen in silence'. He sat down again and nodded at our visitor.

'Yes, I shaved it off. Because young Frenchmen don't as a rule wear moustaches. For you to sport one might attract attention'. He looked at me again. 'Might be a good idea to tuck a razor and a spot of soap into your blouse pocket'. I nodded at him and determined to do just that. [89]

No interruptions from now on: all listened intently. It was odd how this bod's experiences coincided, in the beginning anyway, with the earlier Intelligence lecture.

Dusk falling when the crew had to bail out: he landed in a field and hid his parachute and harness as best he could. He then started walking. Dark now and curfew time so he hid whenever he saw a vehicle approach. Eventually he came to a village and made his way to the church. There was a house beside it which he took to be the priest's. He knocked at the door. When the priest opened it he started to explain, in what he described to us as schoolboy French, that he was an RAF airman who'd been shot down. He got no further than that: the priest informed him that he couldn't assist him in any way; that he should surrender to the local gendarme. He added, helpfully, just before he slammed the door, that this gentleman lived just along the street there. The pilot officer walked off, but in the opposite direction: he told us that, as he did so, he could discern a slight movement of the curtains. A short distance away was a barn: he entered it, saw a pile of straw, burrowed into it and immediately fell asleep.

It was a slap on the face that awakened him and he found himself staring at a knife held uncomfortably close to his throat. Yes, so far, exactly as the Intelligence Officer had forecast in that earlier lecture of his. And then the penny dropped. Honestly, at times I think I'm remarkably slow on the uptake. It would be a month or so ago [sic] when our bomb aimer lecturer arrived back in England. And there he would be accorded a massive and intensive debriefing, every small detail, no matter apparently how trivial, being recorded. All of that written down, commented on etc and then issued to Intelligence Officers on operational units. Yes, what the IO had been recounting to us earlier had been based on this bod's experiences. On murmuring my 'discovery' to Horsfall [Pilot Officer Horsfall, mid-upper gunner on the crew] I was rewarded with just one word, 'Balls'. So I fell silent and continued listening.

The Resistance people had of course been told of his presence by the priest (whom, he said, he never saw again). They tied his wrists together behind his back, put a blindfold on him and thereafter took him on a long, stumbling walk. When the blindfold eventually was removed he found himself in a farmhouse kitchen. Still bound, he was thrust onto a chair. He opened his mouth to protest, but shut it again when a hand was raised to slap him. Shortly after, a tall, thin individual appeared. In quite good English he asked him for his name, number and rank, which he gave. Next he asked him his Squadron number and base. The pilot officer refused to give this. The slap from the interrogator was vicious. And it set the would-be evader off on a swearing spree which, he confessed to us, amazed even him. This, curiously enough, didn't fetch another slap. Instead, once the profanities and blasphemies had tailed off, his interrogator explained that he was a school-teacher and that it was up to him to decide whether or not their prisoner was a German agent-provocateur. This was too much for our pilot officer friend; he burst out laughing but stopped it in mid-stream when informed that, if he was, it would certainly be no laughing matter for him. The schoolteacher went on to explain what had happened when the Germans had dropped English-speaking men dressed in RAF uniform. And after it, once more asked for Squadron and station, which was given. Then he asked for rough details of home town, which was Manchester. These also were given. The school-teacher then disappeared. He didn't come back for two days during which the pilot officer continued to remain closely guarded. On his return, the interrogator had only two questions to ask. And they concerned tram routes in Manchester. Clever: it was most unlikely for a German to know details of tram routes in and around Manchester. I didn't take notes but if it had been me, the home town would have been Edinburgh and the two (comparative) questions would have been on the lines of the following: Q.1 'Does the No. 12 tram still run to Musselburgh?' Correct answer. 'No. It never did. It terminates at Joppa.' Q.2 'When does the last tram pass the Caledonian Hotel at night and what is its number? (Failing which, its depot?)'. Correct answer. About 11:40 pm. And it's the No. 4 (heading for the Portobello depot).

Quite clever really, the Resistance getting a wireless signal back to England saying they'd picked up a character claiming to be Pilot Officer so-and-so, whose home town was Manchester and asking what questions to put to him and receiving those over the space of a couple of days. But not so clever, I suppose, if the escapee concerned was one of those persons who wouldn't know his home-town tram service numbers even if tattooed all over himself. However, the answers satisfied his interrogator, aided, he surmised, by the fact that, when slapped, none of his outraged and profane outbursts had been in German. All friends now, bonds removed; food and wine. He was kept there another day and then passed down the line. He explained to us how careful he was not to remember names of people or of places so that, if the worst came to the worst, he would not be able to reveal them. Also that, while he divested himself of his battle-blouse in favour of a scruffy old jacket supplied courtesy of the Resistance, he retained his RAF trousers and blue shirt. This latter, he explained, to avoid being accused of wearing civvies.

I found all this very interesting, as I'm sure all the other crews did also. But what was even more interesting to absolutely everyone in that Briefing Room was the pilot officer bomb aimer's finale. Really, I'm sure he had worked hard on it, honing away until he had it polished to perfection. He informed us that the end of the French line, for him anyway, was a brothel in Paris. That, he intimated, was where the Resistance lodged him until he could be put on the train to Perpignan - a Paris brothel. 'Spare us absolutely no details, please', came crisply from the back. 'Any photos?' asked another.

'Right, right', ordered Wingco Nelson, making a downward motion with his hand. And indeed, no details were spared. Our visitor was listened to in complete silence as he described day-today and night-to-night life in the brothel. There were six girls there, he explained, some pretty, others less so. Three had the clap and they were reserved for the Germans (outburst of cheering at this choice piece of information): of the remaining three, two were reserved for their French regular customers (more but rather subdued cheering this time). And the sixth, who was also by far the prettiest, was and here our Pilot Officer paused for effect, reserved for him. (No cheering this time: only an observation from the body of the room that some bastards seemed to have all the bloody luck.)

Some nods and jealous murmurs as he explained, that, whenever the

German MPs raided the place, he would hop into bed with this girl and try to arrange his timing so that when the MPs burst into the bedroom he was, in his own words, 'performing'. The MPs would make what he took to be lewd noises, but would take no further action such as asking for papers and so on. He was kept in this brothel for about two weeks. He was then taken by the Resistance to the station to take the train to Perpignan. Now he came to his piece de resistance. 'I was told', he said 'that after Perpignan I'd have to make Spain by climbing the Pyrénées'. He paused, 'Christ, after a fortnight in that knocking shop, far less the Pyrénées, I could hardly climb the steps up into that fucking train'. This brought the house down; no doubt as it had at the other squadrons he'd visited. And Wingco Nelson suddenly found something of great interest to him in an adjacent wall-map.

The IO quietened the applause by inviting questions. But as those were all about the brothel and nothing else, he quickly thanked our visitor and drew the proceedings to a close.

PS. I should have noted that this Pilot Officer bomb aimer can never fly over Germany or Occupied Europe again. It is RAF policy not to allow anyone who has been in contact with the Resistance to do so. This because the Germans almost certainly know of his name and that he was spirited out of France and into Spain by the Resistance. If he flew operationally again and they got their hands on him they'd torture him until he revealed everything he knew about his earlier encounters with the Resistance. Evidently second time around no holds are barred by the Germans when they have the chance of exterminating as much of the French Resistance movement as they can accomplish.[90] Should maybe also note that I don't believe his spiel about three with the clap being reserved for the Germans. The Germans are not exactly stupid, they'd fasten on right away to where their people were picking up a dose (though I've heard that catching VD in the German Forces is such a serious offence that many with it go to extraordinary lengths to keep the fact quiet). Think, actually, he'd made that up; or that someone at the brothel had been having him on.'

In the last group to travel to Spain with Marie-Claire in late November was Flight Lieutenant Allen F. McSweyn, an Australian Wellington pilot on 115 Squadron who had been shot down on 29/30 June 1941. An inveterate escaper, he had finally managed to escape from Stalag Luft VIII at Lamsdorf on 19 September 1943.[91] The other men in the group were 21-year-old Flying Officer Michael H. F. Cooper, a Spitfire VI pilot on 616 Squadron of Nakuru, Kenya, who was shot down (for the third time) on 16 August 1943, landing in an apple tree in the Calvados region near the town of Lisieux; Pilot Officer Harry F. E. Smith RCAF and Sergeant Leonard F. Martin RCAF on 419 Squadron whose Halifax was shot down on 16/17 September 1943. All three men had been collected in by the Jean-Marie resistance network in the Calvados region of Normandy. They were kept in a safe house at Villers-sur-Mer until contact had been made with the Marie-Claire line and they were then taken via Paris to Ruffec. The last member of the group to arrive was Captain R. B. 'Buck' Palm DSO a South African Air Force Hurricane pilot who had been shot down in the Western Desert. He escaped while he was being moved from Italy to a PoW camp near Moorsburg, Germany, but was recaptured by the Germans near the Swiss border. He managed to escape again and reach France, where he was collected in by Marie-Claire line at Lunéville and taken to Ruffec.

The group with Marie-Claire plus four 'helpers' set out by train via Toulouse and Foix to Andorra. At Parniers (before Foix) they were warned that the line had been blown, so they all returned to Ruffec. Maurice de Milleville left for the Pyrénées region to make arrangements for a second attempt an ten days later the party left by train for Limoges and on to Toulouse escorted by Marie-Claire and two of her assistants. They then took a slow train to Tarbes, Pau, Oleron and Tardets where a French guide was waiting and he rushed them to a bus that was just about to depart for the foothills of the Pyrénées. The party were deeply upset not to have time to bid Marie-Claire adieu. They left the bus at a remote spot to walk a few miles to a house where they were fed and met their French and Spanish mountain guides. To their surprise and concern, the evaders had little time to rest before they set off into the mountains in a steady and cold drizzle. They travelled all night and just managed to cross a dangerous road in a steep valley before dawn. Setting off up the next mountain, Harry Smith collapsed with acute chest pains and had great difficulty carrying on. Cooper was also desperately tired and unable to help, but McSweyn and Palm dragged Smith up and over the mountain and into the next valley, where they had a brief rest and food at a remote house. The guides insisted on continuing, despite the worsening weather. The climb became harder and it started to snow, which soon became a blizzard. Progress was desperately slow as they tackled yet another mountain. Nearing the summit, they noticed that the French guide had disappeared, so McSweyn retraced their steps to find that he had collapsed and died in the snow. A few hours later and with Cooper in a state of near-collapse, they found a mountain hut, which they broke into. It was 24 hours since they had left the French house. They found some dry hay and were able to start a fire, which soon developed into a fierce blaze. It undoubtedly saved their lives, as all of them were suffering from the first stages of frostbite and were too exhausted to carry on. After a sleep, they headed down the mountain and stumbled into a small village, where a Spanish Garde Civile saw them and took them into custody. They had to endure a frustrating period of interrogations before they were collected by bus to be taken to Madrid. Five days later, they arrived in Gibraltar, where MI6 agent Donald Darling interviewed all of them to obtain details of their evasion. On 20 December they boarded a Dakota for Whitchurch airfield near Bristol, arriving in the early hours of the next day; 128 days after Cooper had parachuted into France. [92]

On 25 November meanwhile, Marie-Claire was waiting to meet a courier called Ginette who was escorting airmen from Ruffec to Pau. The weather was very cold and it was snowing. The train arrived at Pau station without Ginette and the airmen. Marie turned to leave and was confronted by two Gestapo. Later, after initial interrogation, Marie-Claire was taken by train to Paris. Whilst under escort by two Gestapo guards she feigned sickness, made her way to a toilet, saw an opportunity and threw herself off the train. The guards immediately started firing and she was seriously wounded in the head and neck, one bullet piercing her cheek and a second crashing into the base of her skull. She was returned to the train and taken to a Luftwaffe hospital at Tours. The German chief surgeon rebuilt her neck and saved her life in a four and a half hour operation. Six weeks after her operation Mary was transferred to Dijon prison on 15 January 1944 and she spent the next eight months in solitary confinement. Despite being extremely ill and running a high fever, Marie was deported to Ravensbrück concentration camp, arriving there on 3 September 1944. Mary contracted pneumonia and she was moved into the hospital at Ravensbrück where she was seen by the camp doctor who decided to save her life because he had an English grandmother! As a trained nurse, she remained in the hospital and survived. Mary was highly decorated by the French government, but Britain awarded this remarkable and wonderfully brave Englishwoman a mere Mention in Despatches. [93]

Endnotes

87 *Bread and Butter Bomber Boys* by Arthur White (Square One 1995).

88 *RAF Evaders: The Comprehensive Story of Thousands of Escapers and their Escape Lines, Western Europe, 1940-1945* by Oliver Clutton-Brock (Grub Street 2009).

89 Among the evaders moved along Marie-Claire line in 1942 were Major C. 'Blondie' Hasler and Corporal Wlliam 'Bill' Sparks, the two surviving commandos (otherwise known as the 'Cockleshell Heroes') of the Operation 'Frankton' raid by ten commandos on shipping in Bordeaux harbour. (Two of the Commandos drowned and the other six were shot by the Germans following Hitler's infamous 'Commando Order'). The commandos had been briefed to make for Ruffec and the Café du Paris. At this time Mary was in hospital having been deliberately run down by a car thought to have been driven by collaborators. Her son Maurice took Hasler and Sparks and hid them in a safe house in Lyons. When Mary met them she handed Hasler a pair of scissors and ordered him to remove his 'magnificent blond moustache'. In May 1943 Maurice was arrested and severely beaten in an attempt to obtain information about the Marie-Claire Line. He resisted and was eventually released. Later Oky was also arrested and like Maurice, beaten to obtain information. Oky revealed nothing and was deported to a concentration camp, never to be heard of again.

90 Some, like Sergeant D. Brinkhurst on 101 Squadron who was shot down on the Nuremburg raid on 30/31 March 1944 and made it to Switzerland, returned to operations. Brinkhurst flew a further twenty trips.

91 Driver Geoff Williamson RNZAS, his fellow escapee at Lamsdorf died from exposure while crossing the Pyrénées on 26 October.

92 Back in England by Christmas, McSweyn was awarded the Military Cross and served in Transport Command until returning to Australia in January 1946. After recovering, Mike Cooper returned to 616 Squadron to be one of the first RAF pilots to convert to jet fighters when the squadron was re-equipped with the Meteor in July 1944. He remained with the squadron, finishing the war at Lübeck. He left the RAF in June 1946 and returned to France with his wife Kitty to see his helpers, the Siroux, Coudrez, Touly and Barthelme families, who had survived the war. He remained in contact with these brave people, making a number of visits in the years ahead. See *Shot Down And on the Run; True Stories of RAF and Commonwealth aircrews of WWII* by Air Commodore Graham Pitchfork (National Archives 2003).

93 After the war, Marie-Claire became the Royal Air Forces Escaping Society's representative in France. A film of her WW2 exploits was made called *One Against the Wind*. The story of her life is told in a book, *No Drums, No Trumpets* by J. B. Wynne, published by Arthur Baker Ltd. Mary Lindell died in 1986 aged 92.

Chapter 19

Escape and Evasion

Flight Sergeant Len Manning

The debriefing officers were really professionals. They had to have a great deal of patience with aircrews who were tired, sleepy, cold, damp and generally cheesed off. A tremendous reaction sets in after successfully coming back from a raid and finally getting on the ground. However, the debriefing officers had questions they had to ask. Even though some of the questions might've been absurd, they were really just doing their job and that job was to extract every bit of information from us that they could possibly get. We used to get a shot of rum after every operation and occasionally, if you were good with the padre, you'd get a double. I certainly enjoyed my shot, but some of the crew who were not too active in the debriefing used to fall asleep after their sip and we'd have to wake them up. We were just anxious to get to the mess, have our bacon and eggs, then get to bed. We never did get any feedback about information we gave them, so we never knew if any of the information was helpful to the war effort or not.

Flying Officer Alex Nethery RCAF, a bomb aimer who flew 15 ops on 427 'Lion' Squadron RCAF on Halifaxes before being posted to 405 'Vancouver' Squadron RCAF where he flew 14 ½ trips as a radar-navigator on Lancasters; being shot down on 8 May 1944 on the operation on Haine St. Pierre. He evaded, returning to England in early September 1944.[94]

Twenty-six year old Flight Lieutenant John Alec Bulcraig DFM's Lancaster crew joined 57 Squadron at East Kirkby on the gentle southern edge of the Lincolnshire Wolds at the end of June 1944. Bulcraig had flown a first tour as a navigator on Hampdens on 50 Squadron; his DFM being Gazetted on Christmas Eve 1940. He and his crew did several training flights on Avro Lancaster IIIs before their first op on the night of 15/16 July when 222 Lancasters and seven Mosquitoes attacked railway yards at Châlons-sur-Marne and Nevers. Neither of the raids was successful. Three days later Bulcraig's crew took part in the attack by 1,032 bombers on five fortified targets south and east of Caen that were still holding up the Canadian 1st and British 2nd Armies. The raids, in support of Operation 'Goodwood', the imminent armoured attack by British Second Army, took place at dawn in clear conditions. The operations to break out from the Normandy beach-head were planned to take place in the latter half of July. The British attack in the Caen sector, known as Operation 'Goodwood' was designed to draw German armour away from the American sector so that their Operation 'Cobra' could strike swiftly south from the north of the Cherbourg Peninsula, which was by then in Allied hands. Bulcraig's 19-year old air gunner, Sergeant Leonard E. S. 'Len' Manning had a 'grandstand' view from the rear turret as they turned for home after dropping their bombs. 'The whole area was covered in smoke and dust to about 5,000 feet. It was also an amazing sight to see so many planes in the sky at one time.'

Four of the targets were marked by 8 Group Mosquitoes and Lancasters and at the target where 'Oboe' failed, the Master Bomber, Squadron Leader Keith Creswell of 35 Squadron and other Path Finder crews, used visual methods. At Colombelles 126 Lancasters of 5 Group and 64 Halifaxes and 33 Lancasters all in 6 Group, flew in at altitudes of 6,000-9,000 feet, dropping mostly 1,000lb bombs onto prepared positions of the 16th Luftwaffe Field Division. Almost simultaneously I and 4 Groups, each with more than 100 aircraft, attacked the area around Sannerville. The three remaining targets were attacked between 06.00 and 06.25 hours. Mondeville was attacked by 3, 5 and 6 Groups; 1, 3 and 4 Group attacked Mannerville; and 3 and 8 Groups attacked Cagny. In all, it was one of the greatest air bombardments of troops ever seen. Bomber Command dropped more than 5,000 tons and American heavy and medium bombers, 6,800 tons.

In one orchard, near the village of Guillerville, fifteen tanks and nearly all the motor vehicles of a company from 21st Panzer Division were destroyed, some of them being thrown into the air to land on their backs 'like struggling beetles'. Despite heavy flak around Caen, only six aircraft - five Halifaxes and a Lancaster - were lost and four more bombers were lost on their return over England.

One by one the Lancasters returned to East Kirkby past the familiar windmill at Old Bolingbroke and brushing its sails with their prop wash. Bulcraig's crew had taken off at 4am and on their return they were told that they were 'on' again that night. The 5 Group target was a railway junction at Revigny in northern France. [95]

Bulcraig took JB318 DX-L off from East Kirkby at 22.56 hours. At Revigny the illuminating flares went down over the 'brilliantly lighted target' but no target indicators followed. The crews could hear the Master Bomber and his deputy talking but a German night-fighter hit the Master Bomber's Lancaster and the marker flares 'went down all right'. A few crews bombed the flares in the burning aircraft but they were not in the railway yards. Fighter flares were then dropped, air battles broke out and 24 Lancasters (almost 22 per cent of the force) went down in flames. 619 Squadron at Dunholme Lodge lost five of its 13 aircraft taking part in the raid. The deputy Master Bomber called to abandon the attack. By the end of the night 'trains were still running through Revigny.' [96]

Fahnenjunker (officer-cadet) Oberfeldwebel Herbert Altner of III./NJG3 at Laon-Athies in Bf 110 C9+AS was one of the Nachtjagd pilots who was patrolling the night sky looking for the RAF bombers. Altner peered out of the cockpit windscreen of his heavily armed Bf 110 night fighter, scanning the sky for the sight of a Viermot, or four-engined heavy bomber. He listened impatiently but attentively to the long litany of instructions from his Bordfunker crouched in the cockpit of their Messerschmitt as they continued their night chase across the sky. The clock was approaching 01.01 hours when suddenly Altner and his two crew reacted with excitement and enthusiasm to information received that they were only a few kilometres behind a Dicke Auto ('Fat Car'). It was a Lancaster. Altner's Bordfunker picked up contact on his radar set. The Oberfeldwebel throttled back the two 1,475hp Daimler Benz 605B-1 engines, approached stealthily from von hinten unten (below and behind) and closed to fifty metres' range before opening fire. His guns recoiled. The Lancaster never stood a chance. As he fired the Schräge Musik upward 20mm guns he closed his eyes to avoid losing his night vision temporarily by a possible explosion of the Lancaster. 'I heard my crew exclaiming 'He's burning', whereupon I swerved off to the left and levelled off my good old 110 outside of the danger zone. I've conquered my first adversary of the night.'

Ten minutes' later Altner's Bordfunker announced that he had another Kurier near Coulommirers. It was another Lancaster, possibly DV304 on 61 Squadron flown by Pilot Officer Herbert Wright Cooper. Pauke! Pauke! ('Kettledrums! Kettledrums!') Altner announced. He was going into the attack.

'1000 metres, 800 metres, 500, 400, 300 metres!' Power off and minimum speed in order not to overtake him, Altner once again attacked 'von hinten unten'. Small, bluish exhaust flames made it easier to keep the target in sight. Four engines, twin tail, were recorded almost subconsciously. No sudden movement that might attract the tail gunner's attention. Flight Sergeant James Higgins Blane the rear gunner and Sergeant Kenneth Francis Merrifield the mid-upper gunner, probably never even saw their attacker. Calm now! Altner applied a little more power to the two Daimler Benz engines, approached cautiously and in the classic 'von hinten unten' tactic, blew the bomber to pieces. Horrido! ('Tallyho') exclaimed Altner to announce his second success of the night. All seven crew and Pilot Officer George Albert Davey, who was flying as a 'second dickey' died in the attack. DV304 fell at Marcilly in the Seine-et-Marne, ten kilometres north of Meaux. All the crew lie in Marcilly Communal Cemetery.

The clock was approaching 01.21 hours when Altner once more scurried into action. As he listened impatiently but attentively to the long litany of instructions from his Bordfunker crouched in the cockpit of their Bf 110 he could make out another Lancaster. It was JB318. 'Kuriere in sight' he announced.

Len Manning takes up the story.

'After crossing the French coast we were picked up by searchlights. During our evasive action we lost the protection of the stream and became vulnerable to attack by fighters. Having lost the searchlights we set a new course for the target. Shortly after this there was an enormous explosion in the port wing. We had been hit by cannon fire. Immediately flames were streaming past my turret, which had stopped working as the pumps for the drive supply for the hydraulic motor were powered by the port engine. I centralized the turret by hand and opened the doors into the fuselage and climbed in. Fred Taylor our mid-upper gunner was already out of his turret and was clipping his chute on to his harness. He struggled to open the rear door and jumped out into the night. By this time the fuselage was a mass of flame and molten metal and the aircraft was in a steep dive. My chute, which was stowed on the port side, had started to smoulder. I pulled it from its stowage and struggled to clip it on to my harness. This was difficult due to the force of 'G'. I managed to fix it to one of the clips but the other was impossible. With everything burning thought 'It's now or never' and leapt through the door into the night. As I fell I pulled the rip-cord and hoped that the chute would open. It did but I was hanging to one side. I felt something brush my face. It was my intercom lead, which was attached to my helmet and it had been whipped off when the chute opened. The lead had become entangled in the silk shrouds. I grabbed it and hung on. This probably saved my life as it helped to take my weight. My helmet should have been removed before I jumped. I looked up and saw that the chute was burning and I hoped that I would get down before it fell apart. On the way down there was a terrific explosion when the Lancaster hit the ground with the full bomb load still aboard.' [97]

JB318 had been hit in the port wing by Schräge Musik cannon fire from Altner's Bf 110. The Lancaster crashed in flames and exploded with its full bomb load at La Boue, Bassevelle in the Seine-et-Marne, 12 kilometres ESE of la-Ferte-sous-Jouarre. Bulcraig, Flying Officer Edward Chatterton Robson the twenty-year old bomb aimer, Flight Sergeant Norman Leslie Ernest Gale DFM the 24-year old flight engineer and Sergeant Thomas Loughlin the 21-year old wireless operator died. Gale had received his award for his actions on 31 August/1 September 1943 when he was a sergeant on a 106 Squadron Lancaster that crash-landed on Romney Marshes returning from the raid on Berlin when they were hit by flak. Two of the crew had been killed. Bulcraig and the others lie today in the cemetery at Basseville. Flying Officer E. H. 'Rusty' Ruston, navigator and Sergeant Fred J. D. Taylor survived; Ruston was taken prisoner and Taylor evaded. Len Manning hit the ground flat on his back which winded him.

Oberfeldwebel Altner had not yet finished his night's sortie. He attacked and destroyed his fourth victim of the night at 01.25 at Saulieu. '250, 200, 150 metres'. A slipstream shook the night-fighter. They were close! At 100 metres Herbert Altner fired his cannons. As they rattled and recoiled he saw hits and the Lancaster catch fire before diving away in flames.

His fifth and final Lancaster victory occurred west of Dijon at 01.34. The rear gunner did not return fire, so either he had been killed in the attack or he or his hydraulics had been disabled and he could no longer turn the heavy guns. Or it could be that he and the mid-upper gunner never even saw their quarry. 'After downing my fifth adversary without return fire' wrote Altner, 'I feel that I have stretched my airman's luck far enough and decide to head for base. We touch down in one piece at 01.59 at Laon-Athies. The main task for Karl Brown my Bordschütze (flight engineer) is now, as it is after each mission, to light one cigarette after the other and put them into my mouth, to steady my nerves again.' [98]

Altner had dispatched five Lancasters in the space of just thirty minutes for his 17th-21st Abschüsse. In the later stages of the war Leutnant Altner flew Me 262 jet fighters and he was the only Luftwaffe pilot to fly the two-seat version in combat at night.

Len Manning's chute had started to burn quite vigorously, but he quickly smothered the flames, bundled what remained into a hedge and staggered off into the darkness. 'I continued thus for about eight miles until I collapsed in the doorway of a farmhouse. The farmer must have heard me moaning as the burns on my face were giving me great pain. He took me in and with help from his wife got me into bed. The following morning I was given civilian clothes and was moved to another farm in the same village, La Sablonniere, where I was again put to bed. To my amazement, I was then interrogated by members of the Resistance to ensure that I was not a 'plant' and this was pretty frightening. The Germans came looking for me but the farmer convinced them that I had not been seen and in view of this development it was decided to move me on again.

'Lulu, a member of the Resistance, came and we travelled across country to dodge German patrols. At one stage my guide indicated that he was lost and would have to call at a house to ask the way. He pushed a Luger pistol into my hand, hid me in a hedge and told me to shoot if he had trouble at the house. He returned shortly with directions and we continued on our way until we reached a small cafe, in the village of La Tretois, owned by two elderly ladies, 59 year old Madame Louisette Beaujard and her mother. Neither lady spoke English, but I was made very welcome and given a room in their hotel across the courtyard on the understanding that if the Germans came, I would have to move into their room over the cafe, as officers used the hotel when in the village. Also on the premises were two young men on the run, trying to avoid deportation to Germany into the labour force. They were Albert Bertin and Jacques Gougnard. Later another chap appeared; Maurice Leterne. From time to time a young lady, Madeleine Fahey-Godard, would bring us cigarettes and money from the Resistance.

'I had the run of the orchard behind the hotel but the front of the cafe was out of bounds. I was warned not to be around when the postman came as he was suspected of being a collaborator. There were lots of furtive comings and goings by the Resistance. One evening a group of Germans came into the cafe for drinks while we were having our evening meal in the back room. Madame Beaujard came in to fetch some change and one of the Germans followed her. He stood by the door and looked around the room at the four of us. Madame gave him his change and he turned and left the room without a word!

'A few days later we were told that some tanks were seen coming towards the village, so I moved into the ladies' room over the cafe. The next morning I was roused by the noise and looking down saw that the courtyard was full of tanks with soldiers standing about, automatic weapons to hand and grenades struck in their belts. This was a very worrying time, but fortunately, later that day, the Units moved out and that was the last time I saw enemy troops 'in anger.'

'After a few more weeks some jubilant young Resistance men arrived riding a German motor cycle and side-car which they had appropriated. They said that the Americans had arrived outside the village and were setting up a Field Hospital. I went down and found an officer who agreed to give me a lift into Paris the next day. In the meanwhile he gave me a good supply of coffee and tinned food for my French friends.

'That night there was a big party to celebrate the Liberation and all the good wines came out of hiding. My charred battle-dress appeared having been darned and pressed!

The next day, after three months in France, I was driven to the Hotel 'Maurice' in Paris where the RAF had set up a reception centre for evaders. The following day I was flown to Hendon where I was once again interrogated, presumably to establish, beyond all doubt, my identity! I was then taken to a hotel in Marylebone where I made my report to Bomber Intelligence. A telegram was then sent to my home and I was given leave. Living in London, I arrived home before the telegram was delivered, so it was quite a shock to my parents to find me on the door-step having heard nothing of me since I was reported missing.

'After several medicals I was given nine months sick leave and discharged in 1945.

'In 1991 I learned the name of the night fighter pilot, who had shot us down, when a Christmas card arrived out of the blue. Our Lancaster, apparently, was not the sole success claimed by Herbert Alther and his crew that night. Within the space of thirty minutes they had despatched another four bombers.'

Lousette Beaujard was later awarded the Legion d' Honneur for her work in the Resistance. She died in 1973 aged 88.

Endnotes

94 See *Maximum Effort; The Big Bombing Raids* by Bernie Wyatt (The Boston Mills Press 1986).
95 Two Lancasters were lost on the raid on the Aulnoye railway junction, which formed part of the attack on Revigny, by a total of 253 Lancasters and ten Mosquitoes of 1, 3, 5 and 8 Groups. In all, 972 sorties were flown that night, the two biggest raids being oil plants in Germany by 1, 6 and 8 Groups. Five heavies were lost on the raids on the oil plants.
96 See *Chased By the Sun*.
97 Bomber Command Association Newsletter October 1983.
98 *Night Airwar: Personal recollections of the conflict over Europe, 1939-45* by Theo Boiten (The Crowood Press, 1999).

Chapter 20

Lancaster QR-K King is Missing

'Last night RAF Lancasters of Bomber Command carried out a successful attack on the Dortmund-Ems-Canal. Fourteen of our aircraft failed to return to their bases'. BBC wireless news programme on 24 September 1944 giving brief details of the previous night's bombing operation carried out by 5 Group.

Sergeant Charles Cawthorne had joined the RAF as a Boy Apprentice and volunteered for aircrew duties as a flight engineer. At age 18 he became part of Australian Warrant Officer Warren 'Pluto' Wilson's newly formed Lancaster crew at 1660 Heavy Conversion Unit (HCU) Swinderby. Wilson was said to have won so much gambling his way across the oceans, to face worse odds in the air in England, that he was known as the 'filthy plutocrat'. [99] In late March 1943 the crew were posted to 467 Squadron RAAF at Bottesford where they began their first tour on 2 April. Wilson's crew completed their tour in August 1943. The skipper gained the immediate award of the DFC and George Oliver the mid-upper gunner was awarded the Conspicuous Gallantry Medal for actions on the trip to Peenemünde on 17 August. All the remaining crew members received the appropriate DFC or DFM decoration at the end of the tour. Following two raids on Berlin the crew were awarded Tour Complete status by the Squadron Commander on 9 September 1943. They were the first crew to survive a tour of bombing operations on 467 Squadron RAAF since it was formed at RAF Scampton in November 1942.

After an end of tour leave 'Pluto' Wilson and Charles Cawthorne DFM were posted to 1668 HCU at RAF Balderton and later carried out staff engineer duties with 1660 HCU at RAF Swinderby. This was followed by ground instructor duties at the Lancaster Holding Unit at RAF Scampton. In July 1944 Cawthorne was called back to do a second tour of operations and he joined Flight Lieutenant Hugh Horsley's crew at 1661 HCU at RAF Winthorpe near Newark. They first flew together as a crew in a Stirling on 20 July. On 2 September they started Lancaster training at 5 Lancaster Finishing School, RAF Syerston and eight days later they were posted to 61 Squadron at RAF Skellingthorpe near Lincoln. On posting Horsley was promoted to Squadron Leader and immediately took command of 'A' Flight on 61 Squadron. On 17 September they flew their first operational sortie against the French port of Boulogne in veteran Lancaster EE176 *Mickey The Moocher* QR-M. It was the aircraft's 107th operation. Little did Cawthorne know that his second tour of operations was destined to end over Holland a week later.

On 23 September at RAF Skellingthorpe, preparation for the raid on the Dortmund-Ems-Canal near Ladbergen, just north of Münster started early in the day when ground crews on 50 and 61 Squadrons carried out routine maintenance and later loaded 14,000lb of HE bombs and 1,500 gallons of fuel aboard each aircraft. The main operational briefing for the aircrews started at 15.00 hours. They were told this was a 5 Group operation and the aiming point was the twin aqueducts over the River Grane where the level of the canal water is higher than the surrounding land. If the crews were successful in draining this section of canal it would halt the barge traffic for a while from carrying vital raw materials between the North Sea ports and the industrial Ruhr.

Take-off time for the thirty Skellingthorpe Lancasters was set to start at 19.00 hours and the route selected was a direct track of 350 miles on an easterly heading of 110°. This took the heavy bombers over the North Sea to the Scheldt Estuary and then across Holland to the target area in northwest Germany. One of the Lancasters taking part in the raid was 'K-King' on 61 Squadron, a comparatively new aircraft with only 45 hours flying time in its maintenance log, flown by Squadron Leader Hugh Horsley AFC. This was the crew's fourth operation together. After taking off at 19.17 hours they soon settled down in their crew positions on the first leg of the flight to join up with the main force of 135 Lancasters and five Mosquitoes heading out over the North Sea.

By the time 'K-King' had reached the Dutch coast it was flying at an altitude of 20,000 feet and ahead the crew could see occasional bursts of scattered flak and searchlights lazily roving across the night sky. Twenty minutes later in the Eindhoven area Sergeant Herbert William 'Bert' Jennings the mid-upper gunner saw a twin-engine night fighter coming in for an attack and opened fire with his twin Brownings while yelling out over the intercom: 'Skipper corkscrew port. Go!' Horsley immediately responded to the instruction by diving the aircraft to the left while the rest of the crew hung on in the blackness to whatever they could while the aircraft gyrated in this dramatic manoeuvre. Throughout this defensive action the two gunners reported the position of the fighter. Suddenly, after the fifth corkscrew, the Messerschmitt Bf 110 attacked again from the rear port quarter and opened fire with its 20mm cannon and machine guns hitting the vulnerable Lancaster in the centre of the fuselage and port wing. Inside 'K-King' the crew felt their aircraft judder from the fighter's devastating fire which left the mid-upper gunner and the wireless operator either dead or seriously wounded and a power loss on both port engines. Within seconds the Lancaster was coned by searchlights and this was quickly followed by a barrage of exploding shells from the Eindhoven flak batteries. Horsley responded to the danger by putting the Lancaster into a high speed dive to escape the searchlights and deadly flak. Unbeknown to him the aircraft had also sustained damage to the control system and it took all his strength to apply enough backward pressure on the control column before the aircraft responded and they were flying straight and level once again.

They were now down to 10,000 feet and after quickly weighing up the situation Horsley decided the best course of action was to abort the operation, lighten the aircraft and return to base. As navigator Flying Officer Jack Webber worked out a course for home, the bomb doors were opened and the bombs were quickly jettisoned over the Dutch countryside. Even after trimming the aircraft Horsley still found it difficult to control and with the two port engines shut down they continued to lose altitude at an alarming rate. The situation was now grave so Horsley had no alternative; he ordered 'GET OUT' and the crew abandoned the crippled aircraft. The first one out was Sergeant Reg Hoskisson the rear gunner, who was wearing a fighter pilot's parachute so all he had to do was unplug his oxygen pipe and intercom lead before rotating his turret to the right, opened its back doors and rolled out backwards into the aircraft's slipstream.

Meanwhile, up front in the nose, bomb aimer Flying Officer Johnny Wheeler jettisoned the escape hatch in his compartment and quickly disappeared through the gaping black hole. Charlie Cawthorne should have been the next man out but was having problems locating his parachute under a pile of 'Window' packages. In his panic a number of the bundles were thrown in the direction of Jack Webber who had just left his seat and was moving towards the forward escape hatch. Moments later in the darkness of the cockpit, he pushed past Cawthorne, who was in the process of clipping on his chute and rapidly departed through the hole in the bomb aimer's compartment floor. By this time Hugh Horsley had set the automatic pilot and was leaving his seat so without further delay Cawthorne pulled off his oxygen mask and helmet and dived head first through the hatch from the cockpit step and was quickly followed by his Skipper. 'K-King' crashed near the village of Deurne in southeast Holland at approximately 22.30 hours on 23 September. Jack Webber and Johnny Wheeler were taken prisoner. Flight Sergeant George Twyneham the WOp/AG and 'Bert' Jennings were killed.

Reg Hoskisson recalled: 'Ten minutes after the night fighter attack and our defensive 'Corkscrew' manoeuvres the Skipper gave the Bail-Out order over the intercom. I was fortunate because I was wearing a fighter pilot's parachute and all I had to do was rotate the rear turret, disconnect my oxygen mask and intercom, pull the lever to open the rear door of the turret lean back and the aircrafts slip stream sucked me out of the turret. The next thing I knew I was floating downward, everything was quiet and peaceful just faint hum of the wind in the shroud lines of the parachute. Looking down I noticed hundreds of small fires burning on the ground and concluded they must be the incendiary bombs and flares we had jettisoned. As I descended I could also see trees and hedges taking shape. I was not dropping straight down as I imagined but travelling over the ground at a very fast pace. At a height of about 50 feet I saw my first German soldiers running across a field towards me. I braced my legs in a forward position for the inevitable impact as one of the soldiers who had totally misjudged my speed came towards me. I hit him full in the face with my feet and his arms flew up in the air as he rolled backwards on the ground. The next thing I knew the wind had filled the canopy and I was rising again and travelling at high speed away from my pursuers. When I eventually touched down the ground was very soft and sandy, but before I could get free of my parachute another gust of wind filled the canopy and I was airborne again. Twice this happened but the third time I managed to run forward and fall on top of the canopy to prevent it becoming re-inflated.

'It was at this point the gravity of my situation hit me. Here I was all on my own in enemy territory. Now what was I to do? Then suddenly all those lectures in ice cold lecture rooms came flooding back and the Flying Officer Instructors saying 'Pay attention Cadet Hoskisson it might happen to you. Remember the first thing you do is bury your parachute.' Trying to gather up 60 yards of silk in a wind blowing about 40 mph was not as easy as the instructors had suggested but by lying flat out on top of it I managed to gather the chute underneath me and wrap the shroud lines round it, until it looked like a large bundle of washing.

'I began to walk and eventually came to a small hedgerow and on looking round the other side I discovered a ditch about 3 feet deep overgrown with weeds, it was a good place to bury my chute, in it went and I covered it up with dead leaves so nothing could be seen. Having disposed of my chute I began to look round and found I was standing on an overgrown cart track deeply rutted with the wheels of farm carts. I began to follow this track which eventually led me to the approaches of a small farm. Again my mind went back to the lecture rooms of RAF Training command "Be careful when approaching your first contact, make sure no Germany Army transport is parked there, check to see if the house is on the telephone while the occupant may appear to be friendly, making you coffee, someone else may be phoning up to the local German Kommandant'.

'I looked around the farm buildings, no German trucks, no telephone wires, the place was well isolated, not a chink of light from any window or door. I stood for some moments listening and decided to take a chance. As I was walking towards the house looking for a door, a dog began to bark. I stood very still but the dog knew his job and barked louder than ever.

'Suddenly the door opened and against the dimly lit background I could see a man standing in the doorway. Cautiously I approached the man and we looked at each other as if neither of us had ever seen a human being before. I asked him if he was Dutch, he drew himself up and said 'HOLLANDER'. I think he mistook my 'Dutch' for 'Deutch' and said 'Deutchland Kaput' and spat on the ground, from that moment I knew I was in safe hands. I pointed to the sky and said RAF, he came forward and almost dragged me into the house. The next few minutes were complete confusion, he told his wife I was a 'British Tommie' I think the poor chap thought the village had been liberated. Then a little girl about ten years old appeared 'Winston Churchill' she said and gave the 'V sign. The child was quick to grasp who I was and what I wanted. I produced my escape map of Holland and she pointed on the map to a place called Deurne, near Helmond quite close to the German frontier. I gathered from her that there were German troops in the area. I underlined Deurne and she took the pencil from me and in a few seconds she had marked swastikas all around the area. The pencil was a Venus, dark green with gold markings. She looked at the pencil with eyes wide open so I said she could keep it. Later I realised this simple act of kindness could have had fatal consequences for the family. She explained my situation to her parents and after a short discussion the girl told me her father knew someone who might be able to help me and would go to see him later. Meanwhile, his good lady produced a pot of coffee, bread, cheese and two hard boiled eggs. My contribution to this feast was a bar of chocolate from my emergency rations. I gathered from the little girl their family name was Hooning and she was learning English and listened to the BBC broadcasts, which was strictly forbidden by the Germans.

'After supper Mr Hooning put on his hat and coat and went out. While he was away doubts began to cross my mind. I really couldn't blame him if he turned me over to the Germans because after all he had a wife and child to care for and he knew the penalty for helping an Allied airman to escape was death. About an hour later he returned accompanied by a young man with a dark complexion. He came forward with an out-stretched hand and a large grin on his face. He introduced himself in quite good English 'My name is Jo. Welcome to our country'.

'In a few words I explained to him that I had bailed out of an RAF aircraft after a German night-fighter attack. He listened very carefully to my story asking what our target was, what type of aircraft and then as if checking every detail, asked me where my parachute was. I told him it was buried in a ditch alongside the cart track leading to the farm. He whispered something to Mr Hooning and then asked me to go with them to find it. I suspected he was a member of the Dutch underground movement and I had to prove to him that I was a genuine British airman and not a German plant. We soon found the parachute and Jo seemed much relieved as we returned to the farm house kitchen. Jo asked me if I carried the usual photographs, I said 'Yes I have three, which one do you want?' These photographs were part of an airman's escape kit. The photographs fitted exactiy into Dutch, Belgium and French identification cards. Full face for France, left profile for Belgium and right profile for the Dutch. Jo was obviously satisfied that I was an evader and began to outline his short term plans for me. He said I could only stay here one night otherwise the family would be put in great danger and the child might talk.

'The plan was that I would go to church with the family tomorrow morning dressed in Mr Hooning's best suit and shoes. Jo said I had nothing to fear from the Germans as they could be fooled all the time providing you behaved naturally. After mass he would take me to a safe house where he was staying, with other members of the underground. I found out later this was the headquarters of the local underground movement. I explained to Jo I carried Dutch currency and could pay if money was required. I produced a 200 Guilder note and asked whether I could give this to Mr Hooning for his suit and shoes. Jo said they were a very poor family and the note was a large denomination. If they spent it in the local shop it would attract attention in such a small village. However, he decided to give the note to Mr Hooning on the understanding that on no account was he to spend it until Deurne was liberated by the allies, as he might bring misfortune on himself and his family. After Jo left, Mrs Hooning and her daughter went to bed. Mr Hooning sat with me by the dying fire enjoying one of my Players cigarettes. I could not sleep or even doze for thinking about the rest of the crew, had they all managed to escape or by some strange freak had the Skipper got control of the aircraft and returned to base minus his rear gunner. I idly wondered if poor old Hugh could talk his way out of that but was sure he could as he was training to be a lawyer in civilian life.

Sunday 24th September.

'It was now early morning, the fire had gone out and it was cold. Mrs Hooning came downstairs and quickly relit the fire with kindling and logs and then made coffee. It was made from acorns and tasted awful but least it was hot and warmed me up. She then produced slices of ham, bread and cheese and pork dripping. I changed into Mr Hoonings best suit and although the shoes were a bit tight I managed to walk ok. My uniform and parachute were then burnt in the farmyard as nothing must be left to indicate to the Germans I had been there. Jo arrived at 6am and told me what to expect over the next few hours. He then asked me if I had given the family anything. At first I said 'no' but then remembered the pencil I had given to the little girl the previous evening. After examining it he pointed to the markings -Venus Pencil Co Made in England. He said 'if she had taken that to school everyone would want to know how she came by it'. The girl returned the pencil with tears in her eyes. I felt awful and although Jo gave her his own pencil it did not console her. Shortly afterwards we all walked to the church for mass. I must admit I felt very uneasy as everyone looked at me and wondered who I was. After the service Jo and I casually walked from the church with other villagers down the main street before entering a large house that stood close to the road. I was introduced to the owner of the house and his wife although no names were mentioned. I was then introduced to another man who spoke very good English. He asked me where I lived in England and when I said Birmingham, he immediately asked me to name the two railway stations. I said 'Snow Hill and New Street'. He smiled and then wanted to know which was the best football team in Birmingham. My reply 'West Bromwich Albion' produced a very blank look so I followed this by saying 'others would say Aston Villa but you did ask for the best team.' He then reached in his pocket and handed me a Dutch Identification card. They had given me the name Peter Van Loom. Jo then said, 'What is your name?' I repeated the name on the card in my Brumy accent and they all laughed at my pronunciation. Jo said 'you may fool the Germans but not the Dutch Police'. They assured me the identity card was genuine as it had been signed by both the Dutch Burgomaster and German Kommandant. I was then told my plane had been found and two of the crew had died in the crash. They were being buried that morning by a German troop with the usual military honours. I was assured the local people would look after the graves. The death of my comrades was a shock and I had to turn away and look through the window. The crew had been together for 12 months and we were all good friends.

'As I gazed out at the window I saw German soldiers coming down the road. The men looked haggard and drawn, dirty and unshaven just slowly moving along with a fixed stare. My new friends told me the troops were being withdrawn across the frontier as they could no longer be relied on to fight. These troops consisted of Latvians and Poles who had joined the German

Army when things were good, now they were no longer interested in the Fatherland and Hitler's New Reich. They had been without food and for the past 48 hours RAF Typhoons fighter bombers had wrecked their transports and petrol dumps. Apparently the road all the way to Eindhoven was littered with trucks and the local people expected Deurne to be liberated by the Allies within 24 hours.

'We sat down and drank more coffee and I watched the endless file of German troops pass by the window. As I watched a soldier made a dash towards a wood across a field throwing away his rifle in the ditch. The German NCO in charge raised his submachine gun and fired a short burst. The man fell without a sound and the troop kept walking, no one crossed the road to see whether he was dead or alive.

'At last the road was clear of German troops and at about 10.30am four British armoured cars came tearing down the road and stopped outside the house. Out stepped a sergeant in familiar battle dress and beret, he looked around waved to us and opening the rear of the scout car and pulled out an empty water container and then walked towards the house. I opened the door before he knocked in my excitement asked him how many cars were in his unit, 'just us four mate' then he realising I had spoken in English and asked who I was. I told him and he called back to an officer in one of the cars 'there's a bloody RAF bloke in this house.' Meanwhile it didn't take long for the local people to realise they were almost free of German occupation at last and I have never seen such excitement. They poured out of the houses and gathered around the army Scout cars and orange bunting and flags appeared from bedroom windows. The British soldiers had no alternative but to stop for a quick brew of tea and biscuits with the newly liberated people of Deurne. I was given 100 cigarettes and a mug of real tea with sugar while some of the locals exchanged eggs and milk for tins of army Bully beef. The unit was an advanced patrol of The Inns of Court Regiment, commonly known as Monty's Greyhounds.

'Suddenly the air was shattered by the piercing scream of a shell and earth blew up in field across the road. In a few seconds the scout cars vanished back up the road and we dashed back to the house and went down into the cellar. The Germans continued to shell the village until about mid-day and then German troops and tanks came down the road. I cannot remember much about the shelling because we settled ourselves in the cellar on some straw and I fell asleep.

'It was about 2 o'clock when I woke, German units continued to pour down the road all the afternoon. An hour later another noise started to rend the air and my Dutch friends told me this came from a German mortar battery situated a short distance away at the cross roads. Just before 4 o'clock three RAF Typhoons flew over and fired their rockets at the mortar position and the village fell silent once again. The German troops seemed to disappear and we celebrated with a meal of cheese, biscuits, tomatoes and apples washed down with more of that awful coffee. I shared out the carton of cigarettes and finally we all closed our eyes and went to sleep. At first light British troops appeared with tanks and scout cars and the infantry started to dig fox holes and set up machine gun posts, this time the Allies had come to stay. The news that an RAF sergeant was living in the village must have been passed on, for at about 10am two MPs arrived and said they had orders to take me to their headquarters for interrogation. I hardly had time to thank my Dutch friends for all their help but I did manage to get Jo's name it was Browers and I gave him my home address, he made one request which I couldn't refuse after all he had done for me, he wanted me to return the Dutch Identification card as a memento.

'My journey back was irritating, I was in civilian clothes unshaven, treated as a suspect by the Army, I was interrogated at the Army Headquarters by a major, 'what was my rank, name and number, what aircraft was I flying? Over and over. There were forms to fill in and then a colonel arrived and it all started again. I suggest it would be best to take me to the nearest RAF unit and let them establish my identity. I refused to hand over the rest of my escape money, saying I had signed for that at my Base and it would be returned there. Seeing I was going to be awkward, they put me in a jeep with two MPs and drove to RAF Tactical Air Command Headquarters at Hellmond. 'Name, rank, number'; here it all began again, what Squadron, who was my pilot, what was our target, number of aircraft, how had I obtained civilian clothes? At last I was taken to an office where two officers were present, one was my Skipper Squadron Leader Hugh Horsley all dressed up in uniform as if he was going on parade. The other officer turned to him and said 'Do you know this man Squadron Leader?' My Skipper turned and looked me full in the face and said 'Never seen him before in my life.' The other officer asked in surprise 'Are you sure he says he's your rear gunner.' 'Well I don't recognise him because I have never seen his face before; he always sits with his back to me in the aircraft.' We all had a good laugh and they congratulated me on my escape. A month later we were back on operations on 61 Squadron at RAF Skellingthorpe.' [100]

After diving head first through the escape hatch in the bomb aimer's compartment Pilot Officer Charles A. Cawthorne had no recollection whatsoever of pulling the rip cord. 'But do recall hanging on the end of my parachute and yelling frantically the name of our bomb aimer Johnny Wheeler and expecting him to be only a few hundred yards away. On reflection, I think my calling was not only in fright but in the realisation that I was alone and in a desperate situation. Somehow while exiting from the plane I had received quite a crack on my skull but under the circumstance this gave me no immediate concern. I recall the absolute quiet except the rushing of air through the parachute shrouds and looking down I thought the ground was coming up fast so I prepared to land. The expected impact didn't come and when I opened my eyes I found that I was falling through swirling cloud. Once through the cloud it really became pitch black and I had no idea of my height above the ground or in fact what country I was about to land in.

'Suddenly without warning I hit the ground with a terrific thump and lay there somewhat dazed for a few seconds. I soon recovered from the initial shock and after taking stock of the situation ascertained that while there were no bones broken I did have severe pain in my left leg when I tried to walk. My parachute had snagged on a barbed wire fence so I tried to haul it off but unfortunately it kept billowing up in the wind. After the third attempt to release it I heard dogs barking close by and immediately thought German soldiers would appear any minute. So I abandoned the task of trying to hide my chute and ran wildly across fields in sheer panic as I tried to get as much distance between myself and possible pursuers. While moving blindly along the edge of a field I tripped over some low barbed wire fencing and fell into the ditch and in my state of shock became terrified when some cattle I had disturbed started to stampede across the field. I staggered on and an hour later, utterly exhausted and panic stricken I found a secluded ditch covered in bracken where. I decided to rest. Then to my utter amazement I found a rolled up parachute in the ditch so without hesitation, immediately left the area and again travelled over fields to put as much distance between myself and the area where I had landed. Eventually I found a small wood where I hid and gained some rest. There I took stock of my situation and to my horror realised I had lost the package containing local maps and money out of my escape kit.

'Throughout the next day I stayed concealed and waited until late evening before venturing out. About half a mile away on the other side of the wood I saw some farm outbuildings. After a cautious approach I found the barn was full of hay and as I had not slept for 48 hours decided to try and get some rest.

'The following morning I was in better spirits and decided the best course of action was to try and look like a local farm worker. From my air force jacket I tore off my badges of rank brevet and medal ribbons and then pulled my white flying jersey over the top. Then I thought the jersey was too conspicuous so I decided to darken it with mud and anything else I could find. I then cut off the tops of my flying boots so they looked like ordinary walking shoes. To complete my disguise I found an old hemp sack in the barn which I slung across my shoulders and outside an old green enamel bucket which had a handle but no bottom. This I decided to carry and try to pass myself off as a foreign peasant worker if confronted by the Germans.

'At this stage I had no idea where I was so after leaving the barn I headed west keeping close to hedgerows or cautiously walking down narrow country lanes. As night approached I hid in a wood of fir trees and by this time was desperately in need of water. The problem was that I had no container in which to use my purification tablets with the water I found in the ditches. By morning I was becoming very dehydrated and decided it was imperative, whatever the risks, to find water quickly. After moving down the muddy cart track that ran alongside a wood I saw a small cottage with smoke coming from the chimney. After keeping it under observation for a while I saw an elderly lady dressed in a long skirt with a shawl over her shoulders. She came out of the cottage to collect some fire wood from a pile stacked close by the door and then went back inside. In desperation, I picked up a piece of wood to use as an offensive weapon if necessary and approached the door of the cottage. After a brief hesitation I turned the door knob and went inside and saw the old lady sitting in front of the fire. She was alone and I could see that my sudden entrance and unkempt appearance had frightened her. By outlining a parachute with my fingers and then with my forefinger writing RAF, she immediately realised that I was an airman and then became more relaxed and friendly. At this stage of events I didn't even know what nationality she was so I was still very suspicious and on my guard. After indicating that I needed a drink she immediately gave me what I thought was coffee but found that it tasted like turnips and couldn't drink it. She also offered me some very dark bread which tasted like sawdust and some dreadful goat cheese. Although I was most grateful for her generosity I just could not eat anything for want of water. Eventually after further sign language she responded by giving me a drink of cold water from a stoneware jar.

'Suddenly without warning a young man of around 16 years of age come into the kitchen and after a hurried conversation with the old lady went into another room. I thought it time to depart but as I made for the door the old lady intervened and pointed to the boy who had just re-entered the room carrying some old clothes. He placed an old cap on my head and helped me on with a short dark coat that covered my bedraggled uniform. I pushed the cap over the back of my head as worn in England but with a severe "Non, Non!" the young man made me put it on the fore part of my head. I must have looked rather ridiculous because the coat was too short to be an overcoat but too long to be a jacket but I did as I was told and we went outside. The young man then took me quite a distance from the cottage and hid me in a small wood that was well away from any roads.

That evening I heard voices and then saw dark figures approaching my hiding place and immediately thought I had been betrayed and the Germans were combing the wood for me. My panic eventually subsided when I saw they were civilians and led by the young man from the cottage. Apparently they were all from a nearby village and I had obviously become the centre of attention. Shortly afterwards they led me down a narrow lane towards a large house with a red panelled front door. After knocking several times, my companions suddenly started talking impatiently amongst themselves and as none of them spoke English I was becoming very unhappy about the situation and in a bit of a quandary about what to do next.

'Suddenly the heavy door was opened and we were confronted by a short stout man who spoke in a very aggressive and authoritative way. He issued orders to some of the men who were standing by my side and then proceeded to scrutinise me in a quite unfriendly manner. At the time I thought he was a German official like the Gestapo and wished I had been armed. It later transpired that he was a prominent member of the community and a leader of the local Dutch resistance movement. I was then escorted to another house in the village for a short while before being taken to a Convent where the nuns made me very welcome. After a wash they fed me with fresh eggs, potatoes and black bread. That night I enjoyed the almost forgotten luxury of sleeping in a bed with clean white sheets. Early next morning after thanking the nuns for their kind hospitality we were soon trekking once again across the dykes and flat fields of Holland.

'Just before midday my Dutch companions pointed to some army vehicles that were parked under a clump of trees and announced they were British. We waved and shouted to the soldiers as we crossed the field towards them but we didn't receive the kind of welcome that I had expected. One of my companions indicated to the troops that I was British and after bidding me a short farewell soon disappeared in the direction from which we had just come. I gave the NCO in charge of the scouting unit my RAF rank and serial number but was not treated at all well because I was dressed as a civilian and I had no means of identification. When I tried to explain that my aircraft had been shot down and I was an RAF officer they took one look at me and thought it was a huge joke. Evidently the reason for their suspicious attitude was because German troops had, a few days before, infiltrated the British lines dressed as civilians and played havoc with front line communications.

'Over the next two days I was passed from one army unit to another, each time I was interrogated but no one seemed to believe my story. Finally I was brought in front of the Commanding Officer and again I got the impression that he did not believe me. So I decided that enough was enough and swore at him like an old soldier for at least two minutes using every abuse I could muster. When I had finally exhausted my four letter word vocabulary, he said, "Blimey if you can swear like that you must be British". At last I was given a good square meal and later, cigarettes and a bar of chocolate.

'The following morning the CO of the army unit gave me the option of staying locally with a Dutch family until that sector of Holland had been liberated or travel with them. It was only then that I fully realised that it was the Dutch who had befriended me and risked so much to ensure my safety. Later I learned our aircraft QR-K had crashed near the village of Deurne in the south east of Holland. As I could not understand the local language I elected to stay with the army unit. I found out later that this same unit, the Inns of Court Reconnaissance Corps, had helped our rear gunner Reg Hoskisson back to the British lines. I travelled in a small armoured car where the driver sat amidships of the vehicle enabling him to drive fast in both forward and reverse directions. It wasn't long before I understood why this facility was necessary.

'Later that day we entered a small village and came across some British troops cooking a meal outside a schoolroom. We had just slowed down when there was a terrific explosion in front of us quickly followed by a series of smaller ones. Before I knew what was happening the driver had slammed the vehicle into reverse and soon distanced us from a very dangerous situation. The small explosions I heard were apparently smoke grenades being fired to hide our vehicle from some German tanks that had fired at us. Shortly afterwards the air was alive with low flying RAF Typhoon fighter bombers which soon dispersed the enemy tanks with rockets. Following this exciting episode I was quickly passed back along the British lines and had the great pleasure of being in Brussels a few days after the city had been liberated. Although I was dressed in a mixture of RAF trousers and an Army battledress top I was treated royally by the celebrating Belgians. Eventually an RAF aircraft flew me back to England and after further interrogation in London I was sent on leave and reunited with my family.

'On returning to 61 Squadron at Skellingthorpe I was told the sad news that two of our crew had perished in the crashed aircraft but the good news was that the skipper and rear gunner had also evaded and returned to the Squadron while Johnny Wheeler and Jack Webber were thought to be prisoners of war. Shortly afterwards I entered hospital to have my damaged left leg re-set and then came a period of rehabilitation and welcome home leave. As soon as I was fully mobile I journeyed up to John Wheeler s parents home and reassure them that Johnny was a prisoner of war in Germany and with a bit of luck would soon be home.'

On 1 February 1945 Nos. 50 and 61 Squadron's aircraft started to take-off for Siegen at around 15.15 hours. As usual a large number of Squadron personnel were standing by the flying control caravan, at the end of the runway, to cheer the kites off. At 15.42 hours Hugh Horsley taxied Lancaster NF912 onto the runway, received a green light from the flying control caravan and after he opened up the four engines the aircraft soon gathered speed and lifted off in a steady climb. The aircraft climbed to about 500 feet when some of the onlookers noticed the propeller on the port outer engine had been feathered. This was quickly followed by the feathering of props on the remaining three engines. The powerless aircraft was now in a slow diving turn heading back over the airfield. As it rapidly lost height it just managed to skim over QR-P 'Peter' which was still in its dispersal, before making what seemed like a perfect wheels up landing in the overshoot area at the end of the main runway.

Shortly afterwards tragedy struck when the underside of Horsley's aircraft collapsed under the weight of fuel and bombs as it skidded along the runway. Within seconds the friction detonated the unstable thin skinned 4,000lb Cookie and this in turn detonated the remainder of the bomb load. This resulted in a blinding flash followed by a loud explosion which resonated around the airfield. Some of the watching ground staff started to run towards the crash site to see if they could help the crew. When they got there they found a huge crater. The aircraft had broken up into small pieces of distorted metal scattered over a large area, except for the engines and the rear turret which was lying on its side a short distance away from the crater. By this time the station emergency services had arrived on the scene and found to their amazement that Reg Hoskisson was still alive sitting in his rear turret. As the fireman carefully extracted him from the wreckage, his first concern was for the rest of his crew. He was then taken to hospital suffering from severe shock and a piece of shrapnel embedded in his back. Reg Hoskisson was the only survivor of the crash. [101]

Endnotes

99 *Chased By The Sun; The Australians in Bomber Command in WWII* by Hank Nelson (ABC Books 2002)

100 On 1 February 1945 the Lancaster flown by Squadron Leader Hugh Horsley crashed on take-off. Reg Hoskisson was the only survivor. See *Thundering Through The Clear Air; No.61 (Lincoln Imp) Squadron At War* by Derek Brammer (Toucann Books, 1997).

101 The other members of the crew who died were Warrant Officer Henry Pyke, flight engineer; Flight Sergeant Samuel Fleet, navigator; Flight Sergeant Victor Douglas Merrow, bomb aimer; Flight Sergeant Leslie Chapman CGM, wireless operator; and the mid-upper gunner, Flight Sergeant Arthur Albert Sherriff DFM; a second tour man and died while acting as a replacement for a sick member of the Horsley crew. See *Thundering Through The Clear Air; No.61 (Lincoln Imp) Squadron At War* by Derek Brammer (Toucann Books, 1997).

Chapter 21

Behind The Wire

Flying Officer John P. Wheeler

The night fighter attack on QR-K-King on the night of 23/24 September 1944 and the following defensive corkscrew tactic was a terrifying experience and when the skipper finally gave the order 'Get Out' I quickly ejected the escape hatch in my bomb aimers compartment. In front of me was a black hole through which the slipstream whistled and an occasional flash of light could be seen far below. Time seemed to stand still as the emergency drill ran quickly through my mind: Don't bale out feet first as the slip stream from the aircraft could force the lower part of your body backwards and you could decapitate yourself as you left. Check that your parachute is securely attached to the harness. Head between legs, kneel at the side of the exit and roll out. If sufficient height left, a quick count to ten and deploy the parachute.

After clearing the aircraft the first sign that I might survive the night's traumatic events was the jerk on the parachute harness that indicated the canopy had deployed and I was floating serenely down to earth. Shortly afterwards I experienced an intense feeling of relief that I had managed to get out of the aircraft alive but at the same time wondered how the rest of the crew had fared. In the distance the sky was lit by searchlights and apart from sporadic flak the only noise I heard on the way down was the drone of Lancaster engines high above as the heavy laden bombers continued their way to the target. One advantage of bailing out in the dark is that all your muscles are relaxed as you hit the ground and therefore you minimize the chance of injury to your ankles. I landed quite safely in a field full of cabbages.

The main points of the aircrew Escape and Evasion lecture continued to run through my mind. We were told 'Once on the ground get rid of any evidence as to your whereabouts'. I quickly rolled up my parachute and harness and looked for somewhere to hide them. Close by I discovered a small pond so without further delay I hid the gear amongst the reeds and then weighted it all down under the water with large stones. I then moved away from my landing area as quickly as I could and hid behind a boundary wall and took stock of my situation.

Fortunately I had managed to get down without losing my flying boots. This was a bonus because I was wearing the older type of suede boot with a zip fastener which were notorious for coming adrift under such circumstances. In order to help me formulate a plan of escape I took out the escape kit from my pocket. Amongst the things in front of me were:

Small silk maps of the area we were flying over.

Currency - Dutch Guilders, German Marks, French and Belgian Francs.

Concentrated chocolate bars and Horlicks tablets.

Water purifying tablets.

Also one of my battledress buttons could be converted into a magnetic compass. The top portion of the button unscrewed and when turned over became free moving on its base. In order to evade enemy forces we were advised to walk by night and sleep by day.

As we were flying over Holland when we abandoned the aircraft I decided to try to join up with some of our Airborne forces still fighting in the Arnhem/Nijmegen region. I did not know that the decision to withdraw the Allied troops from Oosterbeek and Nijmegen sector had already been taken and the area was full of German troops.

I remembered we were flying over the city of Eindhoven when our aircraft was attacked by the night fighter so I estimated my present position to be about 20 miles south of Nijmegen. Feeling confident I set off north and hoped to get my bearings from the next village I came across. Unfortunately it was not to be because as I made my way down a narrow country road I was suddenly accosted by a German soldier who was on guard duty outside a small village. Although I did try to make a break for it without too many histrionics, I was surrounded by German soldiers within a few minutes.

After being searched and relieved of a packet of cigarettes by the guards, I was taken to a forward command post where I was interviewed by a young German officer. He asked me if I had anything to say to which I pointed out that my cigarettes had been removed. The guard who had them was still with me and he received quite a rollicking from his superior and the cigarettes were returned to me. Thank goodness I had been taken by front-line troops. My school language lessons were becoming very useful enabling me to reply to all questions in German with my name, rank and service number. I also quoted the Geneva Convention of 1926 as to what I was allowed to say as a prisoner of war.

After a short while I was taken under escort to German Headquarters in a large staff car. When we arrived, the place seemed to be in complete chaos and I began to think and hope that it wouldn't be too long before the Allied troops over-ran this sector. Unfortunately it was not to be and after further questions I was bundled into another staff car which took me at great speed from Arnhem to a civilian jail in Nijmegen. Artillery and small arms fire could still be heard in the vicinity of the Nijmegen Bridge and again my hopes were that I would soon be released by Allied forces. The Dutch prison officers were very kind and there was a great feeling of optimism among them and the local Dutch population. Regrettably it was premature. Two days later I was taken from the jail under armed escort for the journey to the German Luftwaffe interrogation centre at Oberursel near Frankfurt-am-Main. We joined a column of captured airborne forces from the Arnhem area. Amongst the British and American paratroopers and glider pilots were a few more RAF types and we were all herded into the infamous enclosed rail wagons. Lieutenant Colonel McCardie of the South Staffordshire Regiment was the senior British officer present and we helped him look after the walking wounded until they could be sent to a German hospital. Most of this group had survived ten days of intense fighting around Oosterbeek and I had the utmost admiration for their courage, tenacity and humour. [102]

Upon arrival at the Oberursel interrogation centre we were each allocated a sweat box. Originally designed for solitary confinement, the sweatbox was a small cell the temperature of which was controlled from outside and used to soften up prisoners prior to interrogation. There were however so many prisoners from Arnhem that these solitary cells were holding up to eight PoWs at a time.

The usual methods of interrogation were applied, but fortunately we had been forewarned of these German methods by our Squadron Intelligence Officer and were prepared. I think the German authorities were embarrassed by the number of prisoners at the centre and after seven days we were on the way to our permanent Kriegsgefangenlager (Prisoner of War Camp).

The following rail journey showed us just how much the Allied bombing campaign had affected the transport system throughout Germany. On our way north we passed through Rheydt/Mönchengladbach, a large rail communications centre which we had bombed a week before and there were still only a couple of lines intact taking any form of traffic.

Later the same day we were attacked by American fighter aircraft. The train suddenly stopped with a jerk and all the German guards jumped off the train and disappeared into the ditches that ran alongside the track. Fortunately the strafing attack was not too accurate as we were left locked inside the cattle trucks.

The camp was located near the town of Barth on the Baltic coast some thirty miles west of Stettin. From the camp we could see the test firing of V2 rockets from the area of Peenemünde. It was a typical PoW camp with its posten boxes, barbed and electrical wire, guards, dogs, machine gun posts and huts raised above the ground so that tunnels could be located more easily. The guard dogs, let loose in the compounds at night were often lured under the huts where they were dosed with a sprinkling of pepper in order to control their ability to pick up scents. Tunnels in the camp went up to 52 with no success. Over the last tunnel attempted in the camp a notice was erected by the German Kommandant with the following words:

R. I. P.
Roses are Red, Violets are blue.
This goddam tunnel makes fifty-two.

Routine for the day started with the emptying of the barrack blocks by the guards followed by the Appel (roll call). This was in the form of an outdoor parade inside the compound. Depending on how we felt, this could take up to two hours since there were many ways of putting doubt into the mind of the Oberfeldwebel (Regimental Sergeant Major) who was responsible for giving the number of prisoners present to the officer in charge of the parade.

Subject to availability, breakfast consisted of one or two slices of German ersatz black bread. This was a strange concoction. When mixed with water on the fire stove in the room it would cement bricks together!! Lunch and dinner was usually a helping of very watery soup supplied by the Germans from their cook-house, with one slice of bread. Sometimes sauerkraut, turnips and other vegetables were supplied by the Germans but these became very scarce towards the end. Apart from the soup collected from the German kitchen, all our cooking had to be done by ourselves on a coal fired field stove within the room.

If Red Cross parcels were available they supplemented the diet. The contents of a typical British Red Cross Parcel were as follows:

1 tin of Nestle's condensed milk
1 packet of prunes or apricots
½ lb of margarine
1 tin of bacon, salmon or pilchards
4 oz of cocoa (Terry's or Rowntree's)
12 oz tin of corned beef or Gallantine
1 cake of soap
4 oz slab of chocolate
1 slab of Tate and Lyle sugar
1 tin of cheese, ½lb of biscuits
1 lb tin of jam
Creamed rice or fruit pudding
2 oz of tea
1 tin of curried beef
50 cigarettes or 2 oz Tobacco
1 tin of Tate & Lyle syrup

These Red Cross parcels were excellent, but I cannot remember at any stage anyone receiving one parcel per person per week. It was always a shared ration and we received no parcels for three months in the Autumn/Winter of 1944 and none for the last two months of the war.

Life inside a Prisoner of War camp presents an ideal situation in which to study factors affecting morale. Factors such as the weather, quality and quantity of food, lack of home news and a continuous diet of censored news influenced our day to day outlook on life. However, by using various clandestine methods we did manage to receive the BBC news reports at least once a day. So by comparing the BBC broadcast with the German news service it was possible to keep track of the Allied army's progress during the last six months of the war.

Mail from home became almost non-existent. From my arrival in the camp, in late September 1944, I received no mail until two letters on 25th December and three more in February 1945, one letter in March and one in April. A letter posted in Dover on 28th December 1944 had a stamp on it saying 'This letter formed part of undelivered mail which fell into the hands of the Allied Forces in Germany. It is undeliverable as addressed and is therefore returned to you'. This was returned to its sender at the end of hostilities in Europe.

Home mail was naturally a great boost to morale, except in some cases where Dear John letters were received. Some letters were humorous and others very sad. A few excerpts are given below:

If you need any money let me know - to Lieutenant H.B. - from his mother.

I have been living with an army private since you were shot down, but please do not stop my allowance as he does not make as much money as you - to an RAF Sgt from his wife.

I knew I should have kept you here and joined the Air Corps myself. Even when you were a kid I knew you would end up in prison - to Lieutenant D.M. from his father.

When and if you return I'd like a divorce. I am living with a cadet and wish to marry him. He's wonderful and I know you'll like him - to Lieutenant V.R. from his wife.

Do you get to town often where you are? - to Lieutenant M.L. from his wife.

The German camp guards were kept busy all day with roll calls and searches for possible escape activity. To the prisoners these unfortunate guards were known as Goons (two pounds of shit in a one pound bag) and were baited constantly by the prisoners from the time they opened up the barrack blocks in the morning until the night shift left. They were also taunted with threats of being posted to the Russian front. One particularly successful time wasting raid was carried out by the prisoners on the German Administrative Block situated in the Vorlager. Many documents were stolen and destroyed. This resulted in our being locked outside our huts for about eight hours whilst the Goons carried out a massive search. Nothing was ever found. Occasionally the Germans complained to the British and American senior officers about the use of the word Goon by the prisoners. The following notice was displayed in the camp during July 1944.

Kriegsgefangenlager No. I,   Barth den 2.7.1944

de Luftwaffe.   Gruppe II

To	Senior American Officer	North Compound
	Senior American Officer	South Compound
	Senior British Officer	South Compound

Re   Use of the word GOON

The use of the word Goon was granted to prisoners of war by the Kommandant under the condition that this word would not have any dubious meaning.

It has, however, been reported to me that prisoners have been using the phrase rocking goon up, the meaning of which is beyond any doubt. Consequently, the use of the word Goon or Goon up is prohibited, severest punishment being inflicted in future disobedience against this order.

Shroder leiter   gez

V Gruppen.   Major

Fuel became very scarce during the winter months. Our bed bunks consisted of straw mattresses on top of wooden slats. These slats of wood provided excellent fuel and by the end of our time in the camp we were sleeping on an average of two slats per bunk.

During a lifetime one meets certain characters who are outstanding and their qualities remain in your memory. Such a character was Captain the Reverend H. A. M. Mitchell from Dunedin in New Zealand. He was our camp padre. For a time, before and after Christmas, food was very short and roll calls were eventually taken inside the barrack blocks as many of us were suffering with a degree of malnutrition and quite literally passing out during any form of exertion. It was well known that Captain the Reverend Mitchell had passed on his very meagre rations to those he thought were in greater need, until one Sunday morning during his sermon he became a victim of these privations and passed out!! The effect of his work, his cheery disposition and simple, very practical faith had a great influence on keeping up the morale of the camp. At Christmas 1944 he conducted the camp Carol Service. His meticulous organisation down to the printing of the service sheets with the facilities available within the camp had to be experienced to appreciate his untiring energy. The Remembrance Service in November, held on the parade area, was also an example of his indomitable spirit in difficult circumstances. After Christmas 1944 German rations became scarce and Red Cross parcels nonexistent and it was not until late March 1945 that there was a slight improvement. The end of the war was now in sight with the Allies as very obvious victors. Our typical menu for the first four months of 1945 based on German rations, no Red Cross parcels being available, was as follows:

Breakfast   2 slices of toast from German ersatz bread with turnip jam.
                      1 cup German ersatz coffee.
Lunch   1 slice toast with turnip jam.
                      2 slices toast with mashed turnips.
Dinner   Stew (?) consisting of German issue soup, potatoes and
                      turnips.

Note: by saving bread it was possible to make one cake with no fruit.

In April 1945 the Red Army opened up their offensive on Stettin. We became aware of this when the inevitable artillery barrage could be heard. On 29 April there was a discernible lack of discipline among the German guards. Eleven men were missing from our roll call to which the German Officer-in Charge of the parade just replied the equivalent of 'Oh, it doesn't matter a damn'. During the morning the Germans carried out the demolition of the apparatus at the Flak School that was situated adjacent to the Camp and throughout the day there was a noticeable panic in the Vorlager (German HQ). The goons even gave permission for us to dig slit trenches outside our huts with spades. There were rumours that the Germans were going to evacuate the camp at any time so we were placed on standby in case we were needed to take over the Postern Boxes from the German sentries. In the late afternoon an urgent meeting was arranged between the German camp Kommandant Colonel Warnstedt, the senior British officer Group Captain Weir and the senior American officer Colonel Zemke. The Kommandant stated that he had received orders to move the whole camp westward. Colonel Zemke stated that he was not prepared to move at all and asked what the German response would be to such a refusal. The Kommandant replied that he would not tolerate any bloodshed inside the camp. Furthermore, if we did not intend to move, he and his men would evacuate themselves and leave us in sole possession of the camp.

At approximately 01.30 hours on 30 April Major Steinhauer informed Group Captain Weir and Colonel Zemke that the Germans had evacuated the camp, leaving it in their charge. A few hours later the rest of camp woke up to find that the German guards had all discreetly disappeared and they were no longer under armed guard and comparatively free. As soon as it was light a scouting party consisting of Major Braithwaite and Sergeant Korson set out to try and make contact with the advancing Russians. This they did and at 22.25 hours Lieutenant Alec Nick Karmyzoff and his driver arrived in a lorry at the main gate.

After a back slapping welcome by Commanding Officers Weir and Zemke they went into the Kommandant's office and consumed a number of throat-burning Schnapps in toasts of 'Friendship between the Allies' and the total 'Destruction of Nazi Germany'.

The Russians arrived in full force on 2nd May and then quickly set about making the area secure and assessing the needs of the prisoners inside the camp. Adjacent to our camp was a Luftwaffe airfield and within its perimeter they found a fenced off accommodation block that housed several hundred forced labour workers. Four men, one Russian, one Hungarian and two Poles were found to be in a terrible state and immediately taken to our sick quarters for treatment. With permission from the Russian Commander, Stalag Luft 1 was thrown open and we were able to go outside the camp for the first time since the German guards left. My friend Jack Louden and I took the opportunity to stretch our legs and walked over to the far side of the Barth peninsula. Everywhere we went the Russian soldiers welcomed us with open arms and it was quite a reassuring sight to see the Red Army moving slowly through the town of Barth in an odd assortment of requisitioned vehicles. The joy of our newly obtained freedom was somewhat tainted when we came across five German dead bodies, including a baby in a pram.

The following day we were under full Russian Command and for our own safety martial law was introduced. On 4 May the Russian senior officer, Colonel Zchervynick, announced that Berlin was now in the hands of the Russian army and the long awaited link-up with the Western Allies had been achieved. As if in celebration two American Thunderbolts from Colonel Zemke's old 56th Fighter Group flew over in the late afternoon.

The following day the Russian field commander, Marshal Rokatofski, visited the camp and a parade was given in his honour. The first American front line troops arrived at around 16.00 hours and news quickly spread throughout the American and British compounds that they had brought detailed plans of a fast repatriation programme. During one of our walks outside the camp we visited the labour camp on the nearby airfield and found an unbelievable state of affairs. The inmates were living in filthy conditions and many of them had been without food and water for the last four days. Hospitalisation for the sick was underway and assessments were being carried out by Russian, British and French and Czech doctors. Lice and skin disease was widespread amongst the inmates and eighty-five of the poor devils were found to be suffering from tuberculosis, malnutrition and dysentery and almost beyond help.

On 6 May the Russians drove pigs and cattle into one of the compounds. Slaughter houses were quickly set up in the wood and fresh meat was assured at the camp for the rest of our stay. Some of the PoWs even supplemented their rations by catching fish in the nearby Baltic inlet. The following day we were told Nazi Germany had surrendered and all hostilities would end at midnight. To help us celebrate this marvellous news the Russian equivalent of an ENSA show arrived at the camp with three girl entertainers, a military band and Cossack dancers. Later a Russian news film of the Yalta Conference was screened and also a comedy short based on German's offensive in Russia. While we waited patiently for our turn to be repatriated, a daily news sheet was produced to keep us informed about what was going on. The same team of would be newspaper reporters set about publishing the one and only issue of a camp newsletter called the *BARTH HARD TIMES*. It was issued on 5th May 1945 and the headline read:

TENSE MOMENTS WHILE THE ALLIES TAKE CONTROL by War Correspondent Lowell Bennet.

'An air of tension hung over the camp for many days. The presence of the English and American armies on the Elbe and the Russian encirclement of Berlin made everyone feel that the end must be near. The commencement of a new Russian drive across the lower Oder towards the Baltic ports finally increased the tension to an almost unbearable pitch. Panic reigned in the Vorlager. No German had any more interest in guarding the prisoners, but only in saving his own life. Confidential reports were hurriedly burnt and even copies of Hitler's book Mein Kampf went to swell the flames.'

It was a great relief to everyone in the camp that the war was finally over and our Barb-Bound existence in Stalag Luft I was about to come to an end. For me and the rest of my long suffering comrades the end of the war meant we had survived and could at last go home to our families. The end of my eight month incarceration came in the last week of May thanks to the Russian army and the organisers of Operation 'Exodus'. This repatriation operation was quickly initiated at the end of hostilities to fly American, British and Commonwealth prisoners of war back to England. I returned aboard a Flying Fortress of the US 8th Air Force who had joined RAF Bomber Command in flying hundreds of shuttle sorties between the continent and the UK. All returning prisoners of war were first taken to a holding camp to be medically examined and assessed for further duty. After a thorough examination the doctors diagnosed, not surprisingly, that I was suffering from slight malnutrition and much to my surprise this condition enabled me to qualify for an expectant mothers ration card. The following few weeks were spent on leave with my family and sometimes I joined the queues of rather rotund ladies collecting extra milk, butter and eggs. [103]

Endnotes

102 Lieutenant Colonel W. Derek H. McCardie had served in the Territorial Army before the war and was given command of the 2nd South Staffords on 7 April 1943, shortly before the Battalion left for North Africa. Upon his release from captivity, Derek McCardie joined the Parachute Regiment and was given command of the 17th Parachute Battalion in Palestine. He died on 3 April 1977. See Air War Market-Garden by Martin W. Bowman (Pen & Sword 2013).

103 *Thundering Through The Clear Air; No.61 (Lincoln Imp) Squadron At War* by Derek Brammer (Toucann Books, 1997)

Chapter 22
Liberation

By the end of April 1945 Lancasters were largely redundant from their primary role - the destruction of the German war machine. They were assigned other tasks, such as the dropping of food supplies to the Dutch and giving ground personnel Cook's Tours of the damaged areas of what had been the Third Reich. A further task that many Lancaster squadrons were given and which also gave them great satisfaction, was the repatriation of former PoWs. As Europe was overrun, liberation came to dozens and then hundreds and finally thousands of prisoners of war and men in hiding. It came in many guises. Some knew of its approach long before the great day came. To others it came unexpectedly. Flight Sergeant John M. Farr RAAF was in a German Army hospital with nineteen other British prisoners, airborne men wounded in the Rhine crossing, when, unexpectedly, they were taken down to the air raid shelter and told that ambulances would be coming to take them away in an hour. The Germans had not long gone when they heard footsteps on the stairs

'Who's there?' they called out.

'Charlie,' came the reply.

'Charlie who?'

'It's the British Army here.'

And in came the British Army - one private with a Bren gun. Farr was so pleased to see him that he hugged him. Farr was mid-upper gunner in a Mitchell bomber which was raiding railway yards in the Ruhr just before the Rhine crossing when the aircraft was hit and caught fire and was burnt about the face and one hand before he bailed out.

Out of southern France, swiftly opened up by the Allied forces and the Maquis, came several strange stories of the German occupation. Among the escapees, evaders and prisoners liberated by the Allied advance were several Australians. One had posed for months as a deaf mute, living among German soldiers, eating at the same table with SS and Gestapo men and sheltering with them from Allied bombs. He was Warrant Officer G. K. E. Martin RAAF, pilot of a Typhoon which was hit and exploded after destroying a tank on a strafing mission near Lisieux on D-Day. A tree broke his parachute descent and he crashed into a small paddock with high hedges. German soldiers who had been firing at him came searching, but he lay still though they fired Tommy guns into the hedges and undergrowth. Presently they went away. Martin found he was badly burned on the arms and his right leg was broken and blistered by the flames. All that night he lay there and next day crawled to a canal. He could hear the Germans still searching for him, but he slipped into the water and floated along about 400 yards. The water stung his burns; with difficulty he hauled himself to the bank. Two French boys came to work in the fields. Martin called to them and they brought the village curé. The priest arranged for a horse and cart to pick Martin up and when it got dark he was moved some miles away to a tiny room in a barn where they locked him in with half a loaf and a quart of milk. For five days he lay on the floor with the priest's black cloak for bedding.

Delirious with pain, he remembered little about it afterwards, but he did recall that one day some German soldiers tried to get in, probably to loot. They tried to force the door and then peered through the little window. They looked straight at Martin, but they never saw him lying in the gloom covered by the priest's black cloak. After five days, the German troops seemed to have been moved and the priest came back. Martin was taken in the same cart to a farm a mile away in a village near which his Typhoon had crashed. He was put in a small room with a comfortable bed and it was decided that he was to act the part of a deaf mute refugee who had broken his leg in the Caen fighting. His friends produced a faked identity card, using a photograph Martin had with him when he crashed. They forged official signatures and stamped it with home-made rubber stamps copied from their own cards. The farmer and his wife looked after him. His burns and his broken leg were in bad condition by this time and none of his friends had any knowledge of medicine or surgery. All they could do was to bandage his leg and hand every day. For weeks Martin lived in the little room, inspected at intervals by German officers. Presently the fever died and although his broken leg was still painful he was able to get around on a pair of crutches the farmer made for him. He ate at the same table as the family and when there were German officers in the house ate with them as well. Gestapo officers were suspicious of him and one of them once fired a revolver behind him to see whether he really was a deaf mute. Martin did not move a muscle and he was accepted as what he purported to be. When British troops arrived in the area, Martin was taken away on a stretcher. A few weeks later he was notified of the award of a DFC.[104]

First news of Australian airmen liberated by the Soviet forces was of five aircrew and one ground staff man. They were Warrant Officer M. J. Muirhead, Warrant Officer P. P. Hardwick, Flight Sergeant W. F. Sutherland, Flight Sergeant C. A. F. Murray, Flight Sergeant M. J. O'Leary and AC1 J. Goodall. They were taken to the Middle East from Odessa.

Operation 'Exodus' was the name given to the repatriation by air of ex-PoWs, mainly from German and French airfields; Operation 'Dodge' concerned the repatriation of Eighth Army personnel and PoWs from the Italian theatre of operations.

In theory, the transporting of ex-PoWs (and returning soldiers of the Eighth Army) appeared a simple operation. In practice, it was nowhere near so simple. The airfields in France and Germany that were to be used for evacuating the men had earlier been frequent targets for Allied aircraft; they were often in a very poor state. Those airfields that Bomber Command and the US Eighth Air Force had not made inoperable were subjected to some very thorough demolitions by the retreating Germans. It was also found that even when runways were repaired, the surfaces quickly became worn out again with the traffic of heavy aircraft and there were a number of minor landing accidents. Servicing aircraft were despatched to deal with these, but there were not always adequate stocks of spare parts. As an illustration of the problem, at Juvincourt, one of the main bases used to fly ex-PoWs home, a desperate shortage of wheels led to an urgent call to the UK to supply 24 of them. Within a couple of hours of the arrival of the wheels, 20 had been used! A further problem was deciding how many men could safely be carried in each aircraft.

On 9 May (the day after VE-Day) Lancaster RF230 on 514 Squadron flown by Flight Lieutenant Donald Beaton DSO took off from Juvincourt with 25 passengers and a crew of six; it soon radioed that an emergency landing was necessary. It seems that the passengers were mainly positioned to the rear of the aircraft, which upset the flying trim and caused the pilot to lose control. In the crash that followed at Roye-Ami all aboard lost their lives. Subsequently a strict drill was evolved ensuring that no more than 24 passengers were carried, that they were positioned most carefully and that they remained in these allotted positions.

Well before VE-Day, thousands of prisoners of war were freed and brought from the Continent by air. No. 46 Group of Transport Command brought back to England more than 23,000 of them by the end of May 1945. They were from PoW camps in all parts of Germany and in most cases were carried as 'return loads' in Dakotas which had flown to the Continent laden with war supplies, key personnel and mail. Some came back as casualty cases in the daily flights of aircraft engaged on the air evacuation of the wounded. The RAAF sent five officers to Europe to assist liberated and repatriated prisoners of war. One of them, Squadron Leader G. V. Harris, had gone to Russia as early as February to help deal with Australians liberated in the Russian area. Later, Squadron Leader W. M. Melville, officer in charge of the prisoner of war administration at RAAF Overseas Headquarters in Kingsway, London, went with three other RAAF officers to the Continent on similar work.

Plans had already been drawn up for the evacuation of the RAAF prisoners, for their care on arrival in Britain and for their return home as quickly as possible. These five officers met the RAAF liberated prisoners and gave them all the assistance they could on the spot and during their evacuation. In England the men went to a reception centre in attractive surroundings where their rehabilitation, medical, educational and personal needs were attended.

After the 'Cease Fire' in Europe, the long stream of returning prisoners swelled to a flood. Some came back by sea, most by air. The Australian bomber squadrons were engaged in bringing them back, as well as dropping food in Holland. On VE-Day, 8 May they helped in the repatriation of more than 20,000 Allied troops. The aircraft went out exactly as though on a bombing attack, except that they were more widely spaced to avoid congestion at the emplaning airfield. Crossing to England, the liberated men looked out of the windows, talked in shouts above the roar of engines, or sent messages around. Australian flying-men carry poignant recollections of these journeys. Flying Officer J. A. Chalk, an Australian air bomber, glimpsed a slip of paper which was going the rounds on one trip. It said: 'Quarter-hour to Blighty.' Flying Officer A. C. Findlay RAAF remembers vividly how one Englishman's face 'lit up like a lamp' when Findlay pointed out the English coast. He had not seen England for more than five years. In the meantime the same job of air evacuation was being done in Italy, much of it by Liberators of

205 Group, in which a number of Australian aircrew had served on night strategic bombing in the Mediterranean from Alamein to the Alps.

Among the first RAAF prisoners of war to reach Britain after the capitulation of Germany were Flight Lieutenant Tony Burcher DFM, Flying Officer G. B. Hockey and Flight Sergeant T. A. Malcolm. They told their stories in London a few hours after their arrival. Burcher was the wireless operator on the Lancaster flown by Flight Lieutenant John Vere 'Hoppy' Hopgood DFC* on the famous attack on the Möhne and Eder dams on 16/17 May 1943. With the billowing white silk in his arms Burcher was blown out as the Lancaster exploded. He hit the top of the tail fin and broke his back. The next thing he knew he was being jerked in the air and seemed to hit the ground at the same time. Normally, a parachute jump landing is the equivalent of a twelve foot fall. He was told later by doctors that if he had had taken that impact of a twelve foot jump it would have snapped his spine completely. The jerk of the parachute and a combination of other things saved his life. After about three days hiding in a culvert in a field with delirium worsening a Hitler Youth pushing a bicycle spotted him and he was soon apprehended by a policeman and taken to the village police station. In hospital he was put in a concrete cast and after recuperation, was sent to Stalag Luft III.

Malcolm was the bomb aimer on Lancaster LM571on 463 Squadron RAAF when it was shot down on the operation on Prouville on 24/25 June 1944. He wandered about France for about month before he was picked up by the Gestapo, who took him to a civilian prison near Paris. When the Allies reached Paris, he was taken, with eight other Australians, to the notorious concentration camp at Buchenwald. There he saw the shrunken heads and the human skin lampshades which have been referred to in reports on the horror camp. After a few days, Malcolm was transferred to Stalag Luft III.

Hockey bailed out when the Lancaster on 115 Squadron that he was piloting on a bombing operation to Brunswick on the night of 12/13 August 1944 was hit by a fighter. He was the sole survivor of his crew. Wounded, he had to give himself up and was sent to Stalag Luft III, where he met Burcher. When the American Army approached the Stalag, the Germans gave the prisoners half an hour's notice to prepare for a force march north. On this march Malcolm joined Hockey and Burcher. They were ill-equipped for a long trek and with twenty-two degrees of frost on the ground it was a nightmare journey. They halted at a couple of places before they reached Lübeck, where they were eventually liberated by the 11th Armoured Division of the British 2nd Army and began their journey back to England.

Stories of two terrible marches, one of 600 miles and the other of 415 miles, were told by other RAAF prisoners of war when they reached England. Three who took part in the 600 mile march from Poland to Western Germany, where they were liberated, were Warrant Officers T. B. Gomins, pilot, J. S. Cameron, observer and J. S. Holder, pilot. In freezing cold and snow, they marched up to twenty-three miles a day, sleeping at night mainly in barns and often in sheds or disused factories. They had no blankets, no change of clothing and rations of four or five ounces of bread and a little meat and cheese-when they were lucky. They were supposed to be on German Army field rations and to receive soup and coffee. Coffee they hardly ever saw and soup was given to them on two days in thirteen.

At night, they burrowed into straw in barns and crowded close together. Once their column passed 500 Hungarian Jewesses who had been on the march for five months. They were ragged, dirty and weary. Most had lost their clothing. A blanket around the waist was a skirt and another around the shoulders was a shawl. Some wore old army boots, many wore clogs. Others had bound their feet with straw or pieces of blanket.

Two pilots, Warrant Officers A. K. Try and L. James and J. F. Wood, air gunner, took part in a 415 miles march from Gross Tsychow in East Pomerania to Fallingbostel in Western Germany. It took fifty-three days. Try flew with 452, the Australian Spitfire squadron, until he was shot down and captured in September 1941 when 'Paddy' Finucane was a flight commander and 'Bluey' Truscott a pilot officer on the squadron's strength. On the march their food was half a loaf every three days, four potatoes and a little margarine a day. Sometimes they had soup, twice they were given sausage. Try traded his watch, valued at £15, for four loaves of bread. He began the march with three shirts, but exchanged them for food on the way. They had been at Fallingbostel only a couple of weeks when the Germans, fearing the approach of the Allies, decided to march all the aircrew and airborne men east again. Cameron, Gomins, Holder, Try, James and Wood managed to stay on at the camp and were liberated.

A few days after being marched along a German country road under armed guard, an Australian ex-PoW, Warrant Officer C. H. Younger, himself became an armed guard for German prisoners marching back along the same road. Younger, navigator on Wellington Z1391 on 460 Squadron RAAF shot down near Dreux on the operation on Gennevilliers on 29/30 May 1942 was in Stalag 357, near Fallingbostel, when it was overrun by units of the 7th Armoured Division on 16 April. Two days later Younger and other ex-prisoners were out searching for eggs when they saw six German soldiers lying in a field. None of the prisoners was armed, but the Germans, though they had weapons, were not averse from being captured. The ex-prisoners took them out to the road-the same road they had marched along a few days before-and set them off in the direction of the camp. Some of the prisoners went off to tell the military, while the rest, with the Germans' weapons on their shoulders, marched them back to the camp.

One returning Australian prisoner, Flying Officer G. A. Clissold, told how he had been 'rocketed' by his own squadron while he was in German hands. He was a Typhoon pilot with the first RAF wing to operate from German territory and was on his fiftieth sortie from Germany when, three miles behind the enemy lines, he was shot down and taken prisoner. The Germans put him with other prisoners in cattle trucks, fifty to a truck and sent them along the Rhine-Münster railway line. This line had been the wing's favourite target and Clissold feared the worst as the train jolted on its way. The Australian's expectations were fulfilled when, while the train was halted at a station, Typhoons suddenly appeared and with rockets and cannon fire blew some of the trucks to pieces and set fire to the station. Two guards were killed and nine of the prisoners injured. The Germans got the prisoners out and made them march in a circle near the wrecked train while they themselves sought cover. Clissold escaped and got back to the British lines and thence to his squadron's airfield, when he learned that the attacking Typhoons had been from his own squadron.

Back from a prison camp too came Flight Lieutenant Keith Carmody, the Australian batsman who captained the Australian XI against England in 1943. He had been behind the wire ten months. Carmody was flying a Beaufighter on 455 Squadron when he was shot down off the Dutch coast in June, 1944. Taken first to Stalag III at Sagan, scene of the shooting of fifty escaping prisoners of war,[105] he took part in the mid-winter march to Luchenwald, near Berlin, where food was short and conditions poor until the camp was liberated by the Russians. With Carmody for a time was Flying Officer Peter Pearson, the Sydney left-hand bowler, whose wicket taking did much to win for Australia a 'Test' played in the PoW camp.

Back too came still more of the wounded. After D-Day 2nd TAF air ambulances carried many thousands of casualties from the front lines to base hospitals and took back thousands of pounds of blood. Wounded men were sometimes in the air half an hour after becoming a casualty. An Australian, Flying Officer F. C. Wilkinson, a pilot in a Dakota unit based near Brussels, for a time led the field for the honour of carrying most casualties. He carried more than 3,600 patients averaging two trips a day, often carrying eighteen stretcher cases and twelve 'sitters,' or thirty-five sitting cases on each trip.

The transporting aircraft were not all Lancasters - many Stirlings shared in the task. A most important part was played by the Dakotas of No. 46 Group, which also did intermediate ferrying of personnel as well as flights to the UK. An RAF observer who made several trips with No. 46 Group, reported: 'The enthusiasm for the task which aircrews displayed is understandable to anyone who has seen a crowd of ex-PoWs on a German airfield waiting for a plane to take them to England. They stand in patient groups, but inwardly they are sick with excitement. You realise, when you talk with them that in their hearts they have built up a picture of home that, as the months of separation have grown, has got more and more beautiful and noble and unreal. When the aircraft are sighted, the men throw off all pretence of patience. They pick up their kit, start to move forward - until the officer in charge tells them to 'take it easy'. But now their faces are wreathed in smiles and they grow voluble - but keeping one ear cocked for their name in the roll call of passengers.'

This same observer was to comment how his pilot was almost in tears when it was evident that 20 - 30 men were not going to be able to get on the last flight that night.

Other than those affecting safety, there were no hard and fast rules which might have delayed a PoW's return. Thousands were picked up on airfields to which they had hitchhiked and if there was an aircraft available they were flown directly home. These often arrived in England in the same sorry state in which they had left the PoW camp, but on arrival in England a well organised procedure was followed which provided for their immediate needs and which looked after them until they could go home.

Transit camps were set up near airfields where men could rest, feed and receive medical attention. They could get a bath, a shave and a haircut, get an issue of kit and clothing (including a Red Cross bag that had a safety razor, shaving brush, soap, toothbrush and bars of vitamin-enriched chocolate) and most likely have the welcome help of the WVS (Women's Volunteer Service) at sewing on badges on newly issued uniform. The repatriated serviceman was also given cigarettes (there were no health warnings then on the packets!), a railway warrant home and £5 cash (or a sum as an advance against pay).

Most of the RAF former PoWs went through No. 106 Personnel Receiving Centre at RAF Cosford. There were 9,374 from the European theatre of war who went through this process (3,371 were to follow from the Far East later). It was not uncommon to have a 1,000 a day arrive and 1,500 came on some peak days - this for a centre originally designed to deal with 250 arrivals per day!

The time between liberation and arrival at a UK reception centre in England varied between seven and ten days, but some made it in less than three! John Ivelaw-Chapman's book[106] about his father (who as an Air Commodore was the highest ranking RAF PoW) quotes from his father's notes:

'In April 1945 after having been a prisoner of war for close on a year, I was liberated by American Forces who overran the particular PoW Camp near Nuremburg where I had been for the past month. I got hold of a US Major and told him that I would like to get back to England pretty quickly. 'That's OK, Buddy,' he told me, 'I'll get you transportation to a repatriation unit and you'll be back home within ten days or a fortnight.' That was not my idea at all and I explained to him that despite the semi-civilian kit that I was wearing at the time, I was in fact an Air Commodore and I persuaded him to give me a Jeep to the nearest airstrip. Here I asked a US Colonel whether he had anything going to England that day. 'No,' he answered, 'but I've got a DC3 coming in this afternoon. It's not going straight to England. Would you mind going via Paris?' Would I mind a night in Paris after a year 'In the Bag', I ask you!'

The returning ex-PoW could have once more set foot on British soil at any one of a number of airfields, but the following were featured in Air Ministry Bulletins at the time; Dunsfold, Ford, Hixon, Knettishall, Manston, Methwold, Oakley, Odiham, Seighford, Tangmere, Tarrant Rushton, Westcott and Wing. Wherever it was they would be welcomed and although there would be opportunities to attend courses to bring them up to date on everything that had been happening while they were PoWs, although there were resettlement courses and advice on getting a job in civvy street, getting home and back with their loved ones was all that mattered to the vast majority. Fortunately, few needed lengthy hospitalisation - unlike many who were to return from Japanese camps. It should also be recorded that whereas 5% of British PoWs died while held by the Germans and the Italians, 25% of British PoWs died while held in Japanese hands and RAF prisoners in the Far East (most of who were not aircrew) suffered worst of all with 34% fatalities. For many who were to return home after years of confinement and deprivation, the road back to healthy normality would take a very long time.

Apart from the tragic Roye-Ami crash, on 13 October 1945 when a Liberator VI transport crashed on takeoff at Melsbroek in Belgium, about 74,000 ex-PoWs were brought safely back to Blighty by 28 May when the final evacuation was carried out. The Liberator VI, which was piloted by Flight Lieutenant Peter Green, carried a crew of five and 26 passengers; members of the RAMC including 223 Field Ambulance, a dentist and a member of the catering corps. (It was found that the aircraft had been incorrectly loaded). Everything was done that could be done under these circumstances for the comfort of the repatriated men. They were

232

provided with newspapers, magazines, Mae Wests, cushions, blankets and special rations to prevent air sickness. Bands played at the English airfields as aircraft landed and volunteer WAAFs served the men with tea and cakes. It was reported that at one airfield the men consumed 15,000 cups of tea and half a ton of cake!

Bomber Command and Transport Command were delighted to be able to airlift so many ex-prisoners and servicemen back to the UK. The standard of comfort, particularly in Bomber Command aircraft, doubtless fell far short of that in any airliner, but everybody who made the trip surely rated it the best flight of their lives.[107]

'Do not stand at my grave and weep;*
I am not there. I do not sleep.
I am a thousand winds that blow.
I am the diamond glints on snow.
I am the sunlight on ripened grain.
I am the gentle autumn rain.

'When you awaken in the morning's hush
I am the swift uplifting rush
Oh quiet birds in circled flight.
I am the soft stars that shine at night.
'Do not stand at my grave and civ;
I am not there. I did not die.

Endnotes

104 *RAAF Over Europe* edited by Frank Johnson (Eyre & Spottiswoode London 1946).

105 On the night of 24 March 1944 in what has since gone down in history as 'The Great Escape' no less than 76 Allied air force officers using a tunnel escaped before their flight was discovered. Only three of the escapers made 'home runs'. The rest were captured and Hitler ordered that fifty were to be shot in cold blood. *SS-Obergruppenführer* Dr. Ernst Kaltenbrunner, Himmler's deputy, issued the text of what became known as the 'Sagan Order'. He ordered that the *Kriminalpolitzei* hand over for interrogation to the Gestapo more than half of the recaptured officers and after interrogation they were to be taken in the direction of their original camp and shot en route. After the war many of the murderers were tried and convicted in War Crimes Trials in Nürnburg and Hamburg and sentenced to life imprisonment or death. Kaltenbrunner, along with other top Nazis, was hanged in October 1946.

106 *High Endeavour* published by Leo Cooper. On the night of 6/7 May 1944 when 52 Lancasters of 1 Group destroyed an ammunition dump at Aubigne, 25 miles south of Le Mans and about 120 miles inland of the Normandy coast a 576 Squadron Lancaster at Elsham Wolds was the only aircraft that was missing from this raid. Air Commodore Ronald 'Chaps' Ivelaw-Chapman, whose staff duties at Group included accessing details of the coming invasion, had gone along for the experience. At 0015 hours the World War One veteran pilot had taken off from Elsham Wolds in the Lancaster flown by Flight Lieutenant James Maxwell Shearer RNZAF. Now that the aircraft was missing the fear was that if 'Chaps' had survived the operation and was handed over to the Gestapo for 'questioning' then D-Day might be compromised. With help from the Resistance Ivelaw-Chapman and the bomb aimer, Sergeant J. A. Ford of the Royal Australian Air Force were able to evade capture for a month but finally 'Chaps' did fall into the hands of the Gestapo. Fortunately, they did not appreciate the importance of their prisoner and the man who became the most senior RAF officer to be captured flying on operations was sent to a PoW camp in the normal manner. See *The Bomber Command War Diaries: An Operational reference book 1939-1945.* Martin Middlebrook and Chris Everitt. (Midland 1985).

107 See *Exodus* in The Royal Air Force's Association VE-Day Commemorative Issue, May 1995.

Index